Truth vs. Falsehood

How to Tell The Difference

Also by David R. Hawkins.

I: Reality and Subjectivity
Eye of the I: From Which Nothing is Hidden
Power vs. Force: An Anatomy of Consciousness
Dialogues on Consciousness and Spirituality
*Qualitative and Quantitative Analysis and Calibration of the Levels
of Human Consciousness*
Orthomolecular Psychiatry (with Linus Pauling)

Truth vs. Falsehood
How to Tell The Difference

David R. Hawkins, M.D., Ph.D.

**Axial
Publishing
Company**

Toronto

Grateful acknowledgment is made for permission to reprint the following previously published material:

"10 Qualities That Define Us As Americans," by Mantoshe Singh Devji, which originally appeared in the *Arizona Republic*, 3 July 2004. Copyright © Mantoshe Singh Devji. Used by permission.

Axial Publishing Company
Canada Trust Tower
161 Bay Street-22nd Floor
Toronto, M5J 281, Ontario, Canada
www.axialbooks.com

Softbound ISBN: 0-9715007-2-X
Hardbound ISBN: 0-9715007-3-8
LCCN: 2004108362

Printed in the USA
Order Fulfillment: 800-247-6553

Enslavement by illusion is comfortable;
it is the liberation by Truth that people fear.

Straight and narrow is the path . . .
Waste no time.
Gloria in Excelsis Deo!

Table of Contents

Author's Statement   ix

Caveat: A Note to the Reader   xi

Foreword   xiii

Preface   xvii

Acknowledgments   xxii

Introduction   xxiii

Section I What is Truth?

Chapter	1	Historical Perspective	3
Chapter	2	The Science of Truth	11
Chapter	3	Truth as Enigma: The Challenge and the Struggle	17
Chapter	4	The Evolution of Consciousness	27
Chapter	5	The Essential Structure of Truth	43
Chapter	6	Manifestation versus Causality: Creation Versus Evolution	53
Chapter	7	The Physiology of Truth	61
Chapter	8	Fact versus Fiction: Reality and Illusion	73

Section II Practical Applications

Chapter	9	Social Structure and Functional Truth	83
Chapter	10	America	141
Chapter	11	The Downside of Society	181
Chapter	12	Problematic Issues	201

Section III Truth and the World

Chapter	13	Truth: The Pathway to Freedom	233
Chapter	14	Countries and Politics	261
Chapter	15	Truth and War	285

Section IV Higher Consciousness and Truth

Chapter 16	Religion and Truth	329
Chapter 17	Spiritual Truth	365
Chapter 18	Summary and Resolution	401

Appendices

Appendix A	Calibration of the Truth of the Chapters	410
Appendix B	Map of the Scale of Consciousness	412
Appendix C	How to Calibrate the Levels of Consciousness	413
Appendix D	Movies	419
Appendix E	Index of Calibration Tables and Illustrations	423
Appendix F	References	427

About the Author, Biographic and Autobiographic Notes — 483

Author's Statement

The work to be presented is the result of a lifetime dedicated to discovering the core and essence of Truth itself and how it can be recognized, expressed, and defined. As a consequence, a means of discerning truth from falsehood was discovered that was shocking in its implications, for it revealed not only the nature of the essence of truth but also that this technique was applicable, without limits, to anything and everything, anywhere in time or space.

Until now, humanity has been like a sailor at sea without a compass by which to discern truth from falsehood. The cost in terms of suffering has been enormous. Compassion for the human condition arises from the realization of the massive consequences of this inherent limitation of the human mind itself. The work herein presented is therefore devoted to overcoming this serious defect whereby falsity has been misidentified as truth.

Research indicated that truth is actually a variable relative to an absolute constant. Its degree of validity is identifiable on a calibratable scale that includes all of life in all its expressions throughout all of history. The accumulated data was overwhelming in its revelations and implications. Researchers using this new tool were like children with their first microscope, excitedly examining everything and anything in the human experience. The mass of accumulated data often revealed rather startling information. It became overwhelmingly apparent that appearance was not in accord with essence, and that the mind is basically naïve and easily deceived. Therefore, readers are forewarned that some of the material may be disturbing and confrontational to some cherished illusions.

The work has been progressively presented in a sequence of books, videocassettes, workshops, audiocassettes, and public lectures with audience participation. It has been translated and made available worldwide in fourteen languages. In addition, it has been presented to numerous ongoing study groups around the world and peer reviewed prior to publication.

The enormous mass of data has been organized and presented

in a sequence in order to facilitate comprehension across a wide spectrum of information. The subject matter is also contextualized to facilitate the awareness of intention. Seeming paradoxes dissolve with reflection, and much of the information is transformative in itself.

As with *Power vs. Force*, reading the material herein results in a progression of the reader's level of consciousness. Therefore, what at first exposure might seem confrontational, paradoxically, it resolves into greater awareness and an expanded capacity of discernment.

Note that because our current society is overly politicized on almost every aspect of life, it is important to know that the author places value and importance in agreement with clinically derived, calibratable levels of consciousness and their accord with subjectively experienced states of consciousness whose emergence has been described elsewhere (Hawkins, 1995, 2001, 2003).

The research techniques to be described were applied, as they were in previous books, to the manuscript of this volume. The calibrated levels of important statements are cited as they arise, and the level of truth of each chapter is documented (see Appendix A).

Caveat: A Note to the Reader

Emotional reactions are personally determined by one's inner positionalities and belief systems. They are not "caused" from without or by exposure to new information. As audiences to presentations of this material have discovered, an initial response dissolves, upon reflection, into a broader understanding and compassion for oneself and others.

The intention of this presentation is the alleviation of suffering by virtue of replacing falsehood with truth and sharing the knowledge of how to arrive at truth on one's own, for the pathway to its source resides within. For those who are aligned with truth, the path lights up; for those who refuse it, the path is darkened. All of us are free to choose.

On first reading, Section I may seem difficult or too academic. If so, skip to Section II, and after reading the rest of the book, Section I will be more quickly and easily grasped. People learn by different modalities—some process logically through the intellect before going to details, while others learn by familiarity and then are ready for explanations. Either way ends up at the goal of understanding and comprehension.

The reader will also note a seeming redundancy of certain key concepts. This is a purposeful pedagogical style that facilitates progressive comprehension of critical concepts that are new or unfamiliar at first reading but become obvious with subsequent representations.

Overall, the basic dictum to the information reported is that importance is not based on whether it is pleasing or not, but whether it is true or false and to what degree. The reported calibrations are the result of research and not the author's opinion. Thus, there is no point in writing querulous letters that usually follow the format of "how come you rated walruses higher than seals," etc. Like a calculator, the described methodology results in numbers, not subjective bias or opinion.

Extensive references are provided that give background information needed to better understand the reported research findings. The compilation of the manuscript itself took three years, including revisions, corrections, and incorporation of input from review committees and consultants, as well as feedback from a variety of experts. Thus, meticulous effort has been made to present the data with as much accuracy as possible.

The overall mission was guided by Socrates' dictum that all human error or wrongdoing is involuntary for man can only choose what he believes at the time to be a good that will bring happiness. His only error is that he cannot discern the real good from the illusory good. This work is devoted to clarifying what is the "real" and how it can be identified.

To preclude undue emotional upset, the publication of the book was delayed until information that had been discovered by prior research was revealed to the public. It was therefore decided to wait until after the 2004 elections, the Iraqi war, the United Nations scandal, Islamic terrorists' training in the United States, double agents in U. S. intelligence operations, clergy pedophilia, MS-13 gang infiltration, Iran's nuclear plans, etc., had occurred. All these events were identifiable back in 2003-2004, long before they became public news. Similarly, more could be said about events yet to surface.

Of greater importance is to describe the methodology and basic concepts that make such discoveries available to investigation, for this rather comprehensive study demonstrates that there are no longer any secrets, and truth can be instantly discovered by any integrous researcher.

Whether to reveal all that is discovered is problematic and requires reflection. The premise that occasioned the above decisions was that wisdom is the better part of valor.

Foreword

The ensuing presentation of material is unique in that it views the totality of the human experience and the evolution of life via a new and relatively recently discovered means of research. It includes new observations and understanding of not only the ordinary, supposedly objective world (nature), but also uniquely, for the first time in any research, simultaneously correlates the observations with the very means of observation itself (subjectivity). Thus, it bypasses and transcends the ages-old major source of error (duality) by means of the unity of nonduality, a rather transformational process in and of itself.

The calibrations of levels of truth were frequently startling, and, like the discovery of the x-ray, microscope, and telescope, they opened up staggeringly huge areas for investigation that had never before been accessible by any means. The dimensions of suitable subject matter expanded at an overwhelming rate, and eventually there was the realization that it could be applied to *everything*. While it could be assumed that a seminal discovery would be satisfying, in this instance, on the contrary, it was overwhelming and took years of reorientation and decision-making—could the understanding be explained? If so, how; and, finally, should it be?

The origination of the work was the consequence of cataclysmic, subjective changes of consciousness that occurred spontaneously, beginning in early life, and then, in 1965, revealed a whole new mode of knowingness that recontextualized the very core of experiencing. The shift was basically from content to context as the central focus of awareness from which all meaning then became transformed. (See "About the Author" at the end of the book.)

The research technique also revealed itself spontaneously in that witnessing and comprehension were now from the viewpoint of totality (field) instead of a personal or limited locus of "personal self." The basic instrument of experiential information processing, and even of experiencing itself, had shifted from the linear

xiii

particular and limited to the nonlinear, nonpersonal quality of autonomous awareness and consciousness.

The shift and its inferred possibilities necessitated leaving a huge psychiatric practice and spending twenty years of contemplation, out of which arose the basic research reported in "Qualitative and Quantitative Analysis and Calibration of the Levels of Human Consciousness," which was the forerunner to the publication of *Power vs. Force* in 1995. This subsequently set what could only be aptly described as a whole new culture of interest, investigation, and inspiration that led to the spontaneous emergence of numerous independent study groups worldwide.

The collection and mass of material became widespread in the public domain, where tens of thousands of people experimented with the new technique of calibrating the levels of consciousness of anything and everything. A widespread network of confirmation and feedback developed that was accelerated by dissemination of the information publicly by means of numerous formal lectures and workshops with public attendance and formal, recorded participant discussion and traditional question-and-answer sessions.

All the public presentations of the work have been recorded and videotaped throughout the United States as well as in the Orient (Korea) and Europe (Oxford Union). Thus, the information has been peer reviewed by many thousands of participant observers as well as by sophisticated, ongoing discussion groups.

While some of the raw data may not coincide with personal expectations, that is the anticipated response. The discovery of any new information of real significance has always provoked query and doubt and is to be expected. Data that are in conflict with personal belief are best handled by viewing such information as a "possible alternative" rather than as "make wrong," which automatically summons up ego protest or even indignation. Oddly, protest is often confirmation that a nail has been hit on the head.

Although the human mind likes to believe that it is "of course" dedicated to truth, in reality, what it really seeks is confirmation of what it already believes. The ego is innately prideful and does not welcome the revelation that much of its beliefs are merely perceptual illusions. By research analysis, actually only thirty-five percent of the public is really interested in truth for its own sake.

The discoveries and the work itself do not spring from a personal source but are a consequence of the advancement of human consciousness, i.e., the overall climate.

In general, the calibrated numbers are rounded off to the nearest integer of 5, e.g., 63 is reported as 65, 242 is reported as 240, etc. The real significance is to locate a level of consciousness relative to the overall Scale of Consciousness. More specific numbers are significant only when doing detailed research.

Some variation in numerical specifics is to be expected among different investigators and groups, but they are inherently consistent, and the variation is due to personal differences of technique (described in Appendix C). It is comparable to adjusting a barometer to different altitudes. The primary thrust of the overall approach is to know how to tell truth from falsehood, i.e., the absence of truth. Reliability depends primarily on the integrity of the questioner and the intention for asking the question. Dedication to truth itself is the rapid road to its discovery.

The first doubt block to be overcome is the startling discovery that the truth about anything whatsoever is readily available in a few seconds, just for the asking. The normal response to this discovery is disbelief, followed by paradigm shock, but then, curiosity prevails. The whole universe awaits discovery on a new level of understanding, out of which arise compassion and wisdom.

The purpose of the work is long term, and the information is best assimilated by reflection, which summons forth comprehension. The numerous doubts and questions that arise have already been extensively examined, sorted, discussed, and resolved by virtue of collective intention, because if mankind really did not want to know truth, the means to its discovery would not have arisen and revealed itself on the radar screen of human discovery.

Preface

An all-pervasive crisis of credibility and integrity is currently shredding the very fabric of all levels of society. The institutions and historic bulwarks of integrity and reliability upon which society has relied over great expanses of time are under political attack, and others have fallen into disgrace and scandal on an almost daily basis. These include not only governments and world leaders but also entire dominant political ideologies, monolithic religious institutions, government agencies, federal authorities, universities, school systems, corporate giants, banking institutions, major newspapers, news channels, and the media in general.

Even the court system has become a contentious political circus, and jurists legislate from the bench while juries award huge fortunes in order to "make a statement." Institutions that were founded to protect civil rights are now seen as their worst enemy and are seemingly intent upon destroying freedom as it has been known in the past.

In the criminal courts, carefully selected juries are purposely misled by fallacious argument and manipulated by histrionics and irrelevant fictions. Although distortions of truth historically have been part and parcel of the political arena, politics has degenerated from rational discussion and debate to personal vilification, overt fallacies, gross frauds, and prevarication. Avoid 'frum

Prior to our recent and current society, the fate of whole civilizations, as well as nations and cultures, was decided primarily by conquering enemies who relied solely on brute force. The same reliance on force was even adopted by religious institutions (as is currently the case in certain parts of the world), and often the conquered were given the choice of either becoming converts or being summarily executed. Force was then the predominant and ruling principle by which societies were dominated, and religions as theocracies perpetuated the reliance upon coercion and force, backed up by dire threats.

Because of current terrorism and zealously promoted threats to world peace, religion itself has surfaced as a focus of current public attention and discourse. The highly visible and volatile devotees of militant world religions have openly and formally declared war on the rest of the world and seek to exterminate all nonadherents to their restrictive belief systems. The egocentricity and megalomania of such extremist positions are now primary threats to the possibility of a peaceful world. The sophistry of such violent ideologies has even provoked the appearance in the Western world of naïve apologists and sympathizers who are unaware that they too are seen merely as infidels ("mushrikun"), fools, and "useful idiots" (Lenin's term) who equally deserve extermination as idolaters (Forsyth, 2004; Charon, 2003).

The bewilderment of current human society is evidenced by the lack of clarity or comprehension of the fundamental issues, which require identification and elucidation as well as validation of their credibility and authenticity. The primary defect now is, as it always has been, that the design of the human mind renders it intrinsically incapable of being able to tell truth from falsehood. This single, most crucial of all inherited defects lies at the root of all human distress and calamity.

Operationally, the mind is dualistic and thus sets up separatist mentations based on arbitrary, hypothetical positionalities that have no intrinsic reality. Thus, by design, the mind has the basic defect, as pointed out by Descartes, that it cannot differentiate *res cogitans* (also *cognitans*) from *res externa* (i.e., mentalizations about the seeming appearance of the world versus the world as it actually is). The mind thus confuses its own projections and mistakenly assumes that they have an external, independent existence, whereas, in reality, no such condition exists.

The design of the human mind is also comparable to that of a computer in which the brain is the hardware that is capable of playing any software programs fed into it. The hardware is, by design, incapable of protecting itself from false information, and, therefore, the mind will believe any software program with which society has programmed it, for it is innocently without any safeguard or protection. The same declaration has been made by all the greatest spiritual leaders of history who unanimously state that the basic defect of humanity is its relatively invincible ignorance, the recovery from which is operationally impossible without the help of a spiritual teacher.

The human mind, therefore, by virtue of its innate structure, is naïve, blind to its limitations, and innocently gullible. Everyone is the victim of the ignorance and limitation of the human ego. Not only is the majority of the content of the average mind fallacious (e.g., fifty percent of the information on the Worldwide Web tests as "false"), but it is also programmed to attack itself with self-hatred, depression, guilt, low self-esteem, envy, greed, conflict, and endless misery. These defects are then projected onto the world as hate, war, violence, and genocide. The ego defends its own limitations with prideful denial, thus becoming its own victim.

That the human mind, without help, is unable to tell truth from falsehood due to its own innate structure and design is so staggering a discovery that it is roughly comparable to the discovery by Copernicus that caused cultural shock in the sixteenth century. Because this single fact alone is confrontational to the average mind, it will probably not be welcomed or warmly greeted by those who profit from sophistry and its illusions.

In today's world, it is not just the seeker of spiritual truth who is focused as never before on discovering how to tell truth from falsehood. The general public is in a semi-paralysis state due to the quandary of doubt and futility of hoping for any kind of dependable authenticity in the current public discourse. Public interest is riveted on testimony before investigative panels. Mobs in Madrid chant, "We want the truth." Juries strain to sift through evidence, and protest groups vociferously challenge every aspect of society.

At this time, there is no common agreement on even the most basic, simple, and obvious questions: What to do? What to do when an avowed enemy slaughters thousands of innocent civilians? Should we "lock up" criminals or just see them as victims of society and let them run the streets as compulsive predators? Is it simple, common-sense police work to scrutinize obvious terrorist-group suspects, or is that to be forbidden by civil rights? It is not even clear who is the perpetrator and who is the victim. Who or what is to blame?

Over many centuries, the greatest minds of history have struggled with the problem of defining truth and the inability to decisively validate the credibility of its purported expressions.

The Great Books of the Western World collectively calibrate at the intellectual range of consciousness level 460.

Science itself (calibration level in the 400s), which has survived relatively intact and unscathed by the assaults on truth, has had its own internal dissentions of which the philosophic implications of the Heisenberg "uncertainty principle" have been the focus in the last few decades. This, in turn, has led to the awareness that no major advance in science can occur without a further understanding of the nature of consciousness itself.

As a result of the progressive evolution and advancement of the level of consciousness of mankind over the centuries, the decisive discovery was made during the late 1970s, and continued to develop on up to the present time, of how to actually tell truth from falsehood for the first time in the history of mankind. Although the fundamental physiological tool upon which it is based seems deceptively simplistic, like the advent of the telescope, it opened up a whole new universe of discovery. Because the test utilized the response of the universal energy fields of consciousness, the truth or falsehood of any statement about anything anywhere in time or space could be instantly discovered. In addition, it was revealed that there were calibratable levels of truth and that each, in turn, identified energy levels that dominated human consciousness.

Each identifiable, calibratable level of consciousness defines a range of options and possibilities as well as limitations. A new era of human knowledge has begun and has already brought about the discovery of an enormous amount of crucial and significant information of great importance to mankind. This has resulted in a recontextualization of the nature of the human experience in its manifold expressions. The implications, as will be seen, are profound.

The modern world is confronted with the complexities of integrating rapidly advancing technology, cultural and social ideological conflict, and the ambiguities of morality, ethics, religion, and spirituality, which have to be integrated with the demands of survival, war, and economic changes. Added to this has been amplification via the all-pervasive media, which are themselves a focus of debate.

The missing element throughout history, as well as in the modern world, is that humanity has had no means of truly and objectively discerning truth from falsehood. Thus, society itself is unsupported by verifiable validity in its multitudinous expressions. It is therefore of considerable interest and potential benefit that a means of discerning not only truth but also relative degrees of truth has developed.

This presentation of a new, clinical "Science of Truth" is therefore dedicated to the progress of humanity and the relief of suffering, which is the consequence of the advance in understanding the nature of consciousness in its pristine, pure expression as well as during ordinary life and its vicissitudes.

Acknowledgments

We are grateful for the input of the thousands of students, fellow researchers, members of study groups, and readers of the prior published works devoted to consciousness research, spirituality, and Truth. We are also grateful for the many organizations that have sponsored major lecture presentations and to the many audiences that have been most generous with their enthusiasm and support.

Special thanks go to Brock Hereford, J.D., for his assistance with research, which was also contributed to by the editor, Sonia Martin, M.A., who patiently went through a dozen revisions of the manuscript. Special thanks also go to Betty Bruckner, Nikko Hansen, Dr. and Mrs. Rudolph Kallenbach, and Gloria Grose for their contributions to the lectures and travel. Appreciation is also expressed for the patient efforts of the office staff in handling numerous requests and communications.

Sincere appreciation and gratitude are due the Peer Review Committee members for their feedback, suggestions, and timely responses: William Bartlett, Rev. Toni Boehm, Rev. Marj Britt, Brett Fontenot, Nikko Hansen, Rev. Dr. Robert H. Henderson, Sarah Humphrey, Ron Maehl, Paul Newton, Tom Whitney, Ralph Yager, Jarred Yaron, and Tom Zender.

It has also been my good fortune to have at my side a wonderful wife, co-worker, and helpmate, Susan, who has been a mainstay of research as well as associate at the many lecture presentations. She did over 7,000 calibrations for just this work alone, plus thousands of others devoted to intensive research projects around the clock, seven days a week, for years. Her own one-on-one teaching has been warmly received by the many hundreds who have experienced her warmth and personal interest.

All gratitude is due to the inspiration of the Presence of Divinity whose effulgence radiates forth to the world as the All Present Eternal Source of All that Exists, the formless out of which form is the actualized Infinite Potentiality of the ongoingness of Creation.

David R. Hawkins, M.D., Ph.D.

March 2005

INTRODUCTION

Interest in verifiable truth and its concordant reality is currently intense and constitutes the very core of discussions of current domestic and world events. This has caused a worldwide reassessment of basic ethical, spiritual, and religious values, with their implications for morality as well as survival on every level of current life. All discussions subtly or overtly imply a basic underlying standard of responsibility and accountability. Concomitantly, with the rise in ethical discussion, spiritual information itself is currently accelerating and expanding at an exponential rate due to the catalytic effect of recent advances in the overall level of human consciousness, as well as revelations emanating from research into the nature of consciousness.

Consciousness is the unlimited, omnipresent, universal energy field, carrier wave, and reservoir of all information available in the universe, and, more importantly, it is the very essence and substrate of the capacity to know or experience. Even more critically, consciousness is the irreducible, primary quality of all existence (calibration level 1,000).

In the 1990s, it was discovered that consciousness itself was not just an ineffable mystery or hypothetical postulate but was indeed an identifiable and concretely definable, calibratable reality that reflected a concordance of multiple levels of increasing truth, power, and influence. It was also discovered that humans were attuned to a specific level of consciousness by virtue of a combination of inherited propensity plus the consequence of choices made by the will over long periods of time.

Consciousness research revealed that these invisible, stratified energy levels dominate populations as well as individuals by the phenomenon of entrainment via "attractor fields" (Hawkins, 1995). The effect of each level of consciousness is identifiable by characteristics such as predominant emotional or psychological attitudes and capacities as well as brain physiology, world view, spiritual beliefs, philosophy, and creative potentialities. Each level also reflects a range of possibilities as well as limitations of choice or decision.

These levels can be demonstrated on a scale (logarithmic) of 1 to 1,000, where the number "1" indicates the lowest level of consciousness of life (bacteria) and "1,000" the highest level attainable by humans (the Great Avatars). The calibrated scale is readily applicable to the overall human experience as is demonstrated by the now relatively well-known Map of Consciousness (Hawkins, 1995, 2000, 2003), which is in use worldwide and spreading rapidly as a quick, easy method of discerning truth from falsehood about anything in a matter of seconds (see Appendix B).

The book, *Power vs. Force* (Hawkins, 1995) gives a complete, in-depth discussion of the various levels of consciousness denoted on the Map, which can be briefly summarized as follows:

All life emanates an invisible energy within the all-encompassing general field of consciousness itself, which is primordial to life. The field is permanent, infinite, and all-inclusive in dimension and exists independently, yet is inclusive of time, space, or location. The field records (imprints) all aspects of life in minute detail. This track is a permanent recording that is quickly and easily retrieved by the simple, few-second technique of testing changes in muscle strength in response to a stimulus, such as simply making a statement or envisioning a substance, object, person, or location. That which is "true" is recognized by the field of consciousness and thereby energizes the muscle to resist the challenge of an applied pressure. That which is "not true" is not recognized by the field of consciousness and thereby does not energize the muscle to resist the challenge of applied pressure. Consciousness instantly discerns truth from "falsehood" (i.e., the absence of truth), and even uncannily detects the degree of truth.

On the Map of Consciousness, energies that calibrate over 200 indicate "true" and those below 200 are "false" (i.e., "not true"). The scale represents a recapitulation of degrees of evolution, from the most primitive to the most evolved. The lowest are most animal-like and include the negative emotions. The positive emotions start out at calibration level 200 and move on up to reason and intellect in the 400s, and then to love at 500, and unconditional love at 540. The rare enlightened states start at 600 and over. Each level has definite, identifiable characteristics that are unmistakable and concordant with the totality of human experience universally.

The discovery that the truth can be known instantly about anything and everything, anywhere in time or space, resulted in the emergence and continuing development of numerous research study groups worldwide. Needless to say, the discovery of an instant technique that, in effect, "sees all and knows all" opens the door to endless investigation and exciting inquiry in a world in which frustration and impatience about the availability of verifiable truth is a predominant and overwhelming theme. All investigators find the basic concepts and simple technique exciting and a new adventure that leads to remarkable (often "astonishing") discoveries as well as the satisfaction of the subjective progression of the questioner's own level of consciousness. (See Appendix C.)

As will become quickly apparent, even a cursory inspection of the Map of Consciousness quickly recontextualizes the totality of all human experience and provides a common base of reference, with extensive implications as well as clarifications.

Map of The Scale of Consciousness

God-view	Self-view	Level	Log	Emotion	Process
Self	Is	Enlightenment	700-1,000	Ineffable	Pure Consciousness
All-being	Perfect	Peace	600	Bliss	Illumination
One	Complete	Joy	540	Serenity	Transfiguration
Loving	Benign	Love	500	Reverence	Revelation
Wise	Meaningful	Reason	400	Understanding	Abstraction
Merciful	Harmonious	Acceptance	350	Forgiveness	Transcendence
Inspiring	Hopeful	Willingness	310	Optimism	Intention
Enabling	Satisfactory	Neutrality	250	Trust	Release
Permitting	Feasible	Courage	200	Affirmation	Empowerment
Indifferent	Demanding	Pride	175	Scorn	Inflation
Vengeful	Antagonistic	Anger	150	Hate	Aggression
Denying	Disappointing	Desire	125	Craving	Enslavement
Punitive	Frightening	Fear	100	Anxiety	Withdrawal
Uncaring	Tragic	Grief	75	Regret	Despondency
Condemning	Hopeless	Apathy, hatred	50	Despair	Abdication
Vindictive	Evil	Guilt	30	Blame	Destruction
Despising	Hateful	Shame	20	Humiliation	Elimination

Above 200: Levels of Truth
Below 200: Levels of Falsehood

The fields of consciousness denote levels of the evolution of consciousness and represent calibratable power or force in a manner comparable or analogous to the physical world and the electromagnetic spectrum of a progressive range of frequencies. The higher levels of calibrated consciousness showed a rapid increase in frequencies that required the construction of a logarithmic rather than an arithmetic scale to facilitate their mathematical range and denotations.

As in the physical domain, each identifiable level has its own inherent qualities, with both limits and constraints intrinsic to the field. This progression of levels of observation and their concordant appearance are in general agreement with advances in the other fields of scientific discovery. The densest levels were measured and described by Newtonian physics. Scientific discovery then progressed beyond differential calculus to the more advanced understanding of quantum mechanics, subparticle physics, nonlinear dynamics, the currently evolving "M-theory," and other basic energy theories.

The elucidation of the Heisenberg uncertainty principle was pivotal in its discovery that consciousness itself has a profound effect on the submicroscopic substratum of the observable, measurable universe. Intention itself became recognized as instrumental to the appearance of events.

Rupert Sheldrake (Sheldrake, 1981) formulated the principle that form occurs first within the field of consciousness, so that "morphogenic" patterns plus intention are essential to activating potentiality into actuality. Current string theory postulates that the ultimate substratum of all that exists in the universe consists of a universal energy, so all that can be said to exist arises out of a common substrate. The possibility of the transformation from potentiality to actuality is provided by the infinite power of the primordial substrate of all existence, which alone has the power to transform the unmanifest into the realm of the manifest (cal. level 1,000).

The universe is now defined as an interactive wholeness of myriad energy fields of infinite, potentially differing frequencies merely awaiting the influence of the introduction of intention plus form. Thus, we now have a means by which to describe and understand the easily identifiable principle that Creation and Evolution are actually one and the same process (cal. level 1,000), which will be elucidated later.

While at first glance, all these discoveries may seem to be irrelevant to everyday life, in practice, major advances in the understanding of the essential nature of the universe and the evolution of consciousness profoundly facilitate secular as well as spiritual awareness and the comprehension of physical and spiritual evolution. It is no longer necessary to forsake reason, intelligence, and rationality to grasp the reality of nonlinear, invisible influences that advance one's own understanding and final realization of the ultimate reality underlying that characteristic of consciousness termed "subjectivity."

Consciousness research is of great pragmatic value not only to the scientist but also to all of society in its myriad expressions, from the arts to business, commerce, politics, international relations, diplomacy, and the prevention of war. Additionally, this new arena of discovery has wide applications in every area of research, including methodology and theory.

To the intellectual, the discoveries are exciting and fascinating, and their philosophic implications are profound. Definitive resolutions to ages-old impasses and enigmas of humankind are now clearly apparent.

Numerous social puzzles and seeming dilemmas are resolved simply as a result of finding the missing pieces by which resolution is the automatic consequence of recontextualization. That process is the very basis for the "aha!" experiences. The data and information that follow are transformative and accelerate the evolution of consciousness and awareness.

Familiarity with the basic concepts to be presented is of benefit in that it results in automatically seeing things differently, with a consequent resolution of conflict and ensuing peace of mind. As will be discovered, the world is not what it appears to be, nor are its residents the "who" that they presume themselves to be.

SECTION I
WHAT IS TRUTH?

CHAPTER 1
Historical Perspective

From earliest times to the present day, mankind has pondered and struggled with the enigma of its origin, purpose, and destiny: Who are we? Where did we come from? Where do we go after death of the body, if anywhere?

Over the millennia, a myriad of plausible postulations have sought to offer a satisfying resolution. There arose a number of myths, systems, and philosophical discussions, as well as a plethora of imaginative and creative cosmologies, each of which, however, became the starting point for a whole additional set of questions, doubts, and conflicts.

It was postulated that mankind came from the heavens or that the earth was the primordial mother. Pantheism suggested that animal spirits and nature were the origin of human life that evolved into polytheism and pantheons of god-like, divine figures, each with personalities and limited, but specified, domains.

In various parts of the world, however, truth via spiritual inspiration and information emerged through the fabled sages and then in the form of the great avatars who founded the great religions that brought some resolution in regional sections of the world's population, but again, neither peace nor certainty arose. In fact, the followers of each leader often fragmented themselves into competitive factions that utilized religious belief systems as the justification and basis for persecution, hatred, and genocide. Paradoxically, in practice, some misinterpretations of the major religions became the blatantly diametrical opposite of the core of their own teachings.

These deviations from the truth of their own teachings created skepticism about the authority and integrity of not only

3

the institution but also of its theology. In addition to the loss of credibility, there was a negative impact on public opinion. Theocracies appeared to be not only dogmatic but also oppressive, and often, adherence to their tenets was from fear rather than respect for an intuitive recognition of truth. In many parts of the world, the reputation of religion progressively deteriorated. At the present time, for example, Western Europe and large parts of North America have shown a progressive secularization that is now accelerated by the negative impact of the current militant Islamics and the scandals of some Christian churches.

Religious and spiritual skepticism was also a by-product of the fall of authoritarianism as a sufficiency upon which to place confidence. In the last few centuries, the emergence of the dominance of science and the scientific paradigm of reality further diminished the credibility of religious dogma, particularly ecclesiastic authority. Religious conflict was progressively replaced by political ideologies that, paradoxically, were as oppressive as the dogmas they were purported to replace.

A new period of inquisition arrived, such as that to which the peoples of Tibet, China, Russia, Eastern Europe, Southeast Asia, North Africa, the Arabic countries, and Cuba have been subjected in recent times. Then, unfortunately for the world, there was a merging of political extremism with religious zealotry, as exemplified by Islamic radicalism that threatens the world with its violence and fanaticism, in contrast to which secularization seems a welcome relief.

Unlike power, which has no opposite, force always precipitates counterforce, whether the opposing forces are political, religious, or both. Truth, however, has no opposite because falsehood is not the opposite of truth but merely its absence, just as darkness is not the opposite of light but merely represents the lack of it.

At approximately the time of the Harmonic Convergence in the late 1980s, the consciousness level of mankind suddenly jumped from the limited level of 190, which had dominated mankind for centuries, to 205, which is above the critical level of truth and integrity at 200. In more advanced cultures of the world, this rise in the consciousness level resulted in replacing gain with integrity as the yardstick of success. Then ensued a period of time in which nonintegrous companies and their CEOs were at the center of scandal, while at the same time, the company that had the highest level of integrity of the giant corporations worldwide became the largest and most successful company in the world.

Of critical importance is that in November 2003, at the time of (but not "caused by") the Harmonic Concordance, the consciousness level of mankind, after being stable for nearly two decades, rose again to the present level of 207.

During the same time period, consciousness research advanced as a consequence of the discovery of a means to differentiate truth from falsehood. It was found that truth was not a simple "yes" or "no" but that it was expressible over a calibrated, logarithmic scale from 1 to 1,000. Because consciousness is present everywhere and beyond the limitations of time or space, there is a whole new science of consciousness that, because it has no limits, also enables research into spiritual concepts, spiritual teachings, and the verification of spiritual realities as well as every aspect of society. A new definition of truth emerged that is defined not as a consequence of just content, as in Newtonian physics, but as the consequence of content within a specific field. It was discovered that without reference to the field, there was no possible, reliable statement of truth.

Because consciousness research has no limitations as to subject matter, it allows investigation into areas previously thought to be accessible only by advanced science, the mystic, or great spiritual geniuses over time. Thus, by the use of the same investigative method, it was possible to identify and calibrate the levels of truth of spiritual concepts, teachers and teachings, as well as religions and ecclesiastic doctrines. Upon investigation, it was found that the highest levels of truth in history were realized by the great mystics whose energy fields still impact all mankind to this day, whether acknowledged or not.

Even when spiritual reality is denied, such as by the atheist or skeptic, an overall context of ethics and morality still remains that rules all mankind in all ages, even though recognition of its origination is denied. At the present time, intellectual as well as ethical and spiritual endeavor are facilitated by these advances of consciousness overall as well as by the rapid development of information about the quality of consciousness itself.

The most recent advances in scientific theory postulate that there is a common submatrix to all physical existence, consisting of high-frequency fields of energy (this statement calibrates at 1,000). The difficulty with integrating spiritual truth, consciousness research, and advanced theoretical physics is that the mind thinks dualistically. Thus, to observation and description, perceived "reality" seems to be separated into different categories of domains or realms, such as the physical versus the nonphysical, or the experiential versus the observable, as demarcated by the following list of comparisons:

Physical vs. nonphysical	Philosophy vs. materiality
Experiential vs. observable	Microscopic vs. macroscopic
Subjective vs. objective	Measurable vs. nonmeasurable
Linear vs. nonlinear	Predictable vs. nonpredictable
Secular vs. spiritual	Matter vs. spirit
Intellectual vs. emotional	Definable vs. ineffable
Scientific vs. nonscientific	Truth vs. falsehood
Spiritual vs. egoistic	Abstract vs. concrete
Known vs. unknown	Limited vs. unlimited
Science vs. religion	Phenomenal vs. actual

From the above, it becomes clear that what was thought to be distinct categories of existence, reality, or experience are primarily just different categories of perception and mentation, i.e., Descartes' *res cogitans*. In reality, as in Reality, there are no separations or distinct realms of independent existence (*res externa*). Operationally, however, descriptions seem to apply specifically only to seemingly separate realms, and intellectually, there seems to be no common ground to these perceived disparate realms.

The sought-for commonality to all realms of subjective experience and investigation turns out to be the omnipresent energy field traditionally denoted as "consciousness," the very substrate and core of all existence and of intelligence itself. Consciousness alone has all the qualities by which to compare and unite these

seemingly disparate realms into a comprehensive unity with stratified expressions. Consciousness itself is the key to the sought-for
"unified field theory of everything" (statement calibrates at 1,000).
Beyond the field of consciousness, nothing exists because it is
universal and independent of time or location. Curiously, at the
same time, it is knowable, able to be experienced, and its levels
are discernable and identifiable.

We can start from the beginning and then address the following questions:

1. What is common, necessary, and intrinsic to all possibilities
    of existence, experience, or expressions thereof?

2. What is the irreducible substrate of the visible and the invis-
    ible, the subjective and the objective, form and formless, and
    identifiable anywhere in time or space, i.e., the Absolute?

3. Is the presence of such universality identifiable, to what
    degree, and under what circumstances?

The field of consciousness alone fulfills all the requirements.
Its presence can be discovered only via the exercise of its own
innate quality, i.e., the sole tool by which consciousness can be
identified, studied, and examined is by utilization of the qualities
of that consciousness itself. Comparably, it is only life itself that
can study and experience life because it is the core and substrate
of awareness. For a comparable reason, the irreducible substrate
of epistemology is subjectivity, of which gnosis is an experiential
potentiality that becomes actualized at its highest level of expression in the enlightened state of the sages of all time.

As will become apparent from further examination and discussion, the understanding of consciousness reveals that all that
exists, with no exception, both subjective and objective, physical
and nonphysical, with or without form, irrespective of state or
qualities, has its existence along an identifiable and describable
continuum. There is no discontinuity, for in reality, there is only
energy that is expressed in the characteristics of its different frequency ranges. The physical universe is a vibrational frequency
spectrum, beyond which the physical dissolves into the invisible
but increasingly powerful ranges of energy that go on up through

extremely high ranges and their ultra-high harmonics to the very source of existence itself. At the most primordial level, the manifest is an actualization of the unmanifest, by which the potential becomes the actual (i.e., Creation).

Is a single "theory of everything" a verifiable reality? Is it a practical tool or an abstract hypothesis? Through study, it will become obvious that such a theory is of the utmost practicality and equally applicable to every aspect of the human experience as well as the universe. Its utilitarian value is immeasurable in that it differentiates the possible from the impossible, the actual from the potential, and the unreal from the real (cal. level 1,000).

That a verifiable truth about everything and anything anywhere in the universe is accessible for the mere asking is so astonishing that it challenges every basic human assumption. Upon investigation, it becomes starkly obvious that all existence throughout all time, beyond all duration and location, including the human experience thereof in all of its possibilities, is an expression of one single, all-encompassing energy field of infinite potential, and that a quality of the field itself is its capacity to actualize potential from the formless into actual, identifiable form.

Whether one chooses to label the omniscient, omnipresent, omnipotent, universal, all-encompassing, all-present, beyond-all-time-and-space field as divine or not is a personal choice. Historically, because the word "God" has been so maligned, abused, and misrepresented over the course of time, the Buddha recommended that the term not be used at all because it is misleading and prejudicial. Any serious students of Truth (who themselves are integrous and whose questions are integrous) can verify the above statements for themselves. Factually and verifiably beyond measurable time, duration, or location, there is an omnipotent, omnipresent, all-powerful universal field of infinite potentiality that can become manifest experientially or in form, e.g., atomic energy.

Throughout time, spiritually inspired individuals who have been devoted to the inner search for the core truth itself have reported that beyond ordinary mind, there is a potential experiential capacity that enables the realization of the presence of the field itself as the source of all existence. Its innate qualities illuminate and reveal all that has ever been described as reality or Reality. The phenomenon traditionally called Enlightenment reportedly has been extremely rare because few are the persons able, karmically endowed, or willing to surrender their favorite illusions, identifications, or their personalities. This rarity exists because a clear, precise, and verifiable definition of truth was lacking. Advanced research into the nature of consciousness now demonstrates conclusively that there is no division between science and spirituality. In fact, they merely represent different frequency ranges of their common substrate.

In the gross physical world, the seemingly "different" energies are labeled gravity (weight), weak force, strong force, horsepower, chemical bond, heat, light, electricity, radiation, short wave, long wave, photons, electrons, neutrons, protons, sound, lightning, music, earthquake, alpha wave, beta wave, magnetic fields, aurora borealis, steam, vapor, flood, atomic energy, fission, fusion, vegetative and animal life, emotion, physiology, EEG waves, movement, EKG waves, television, transmitters and receivers, volcanoes, cosmic radiation, subliminal elephant thumps, thinking, feelings, vision, intuition, concepts, forms, colors, vibrations, and fire, as well as the galaxies and black holes where gravity is so intense that even light cannot escape.

Are all of the above "separate," unique, and different "realities"? We already know the laws of conservation of energy and matter and that $E=mc^2$. From the above, it is not difficult to conclude as well as intuit that there is only a single omnipresent source of energy whose qualities primarily reflect a difference of frequency, location, prevalence, style, and locus of observations and their interpretations.

Beyond the physical level, the vibrational frequency of energy increases even farther past the Newtonian paradigm to its nonphysical experiences as the matrix of thought itself, of which the brain is its physical corollary. Beyond the limitation of the protoplasmic brain are the energy ("etheric") brain and the field of awareness/consciousness, which are the light of the manifest energy from the unmanifest, the primordial source of existence out of which creation arises.

Mankind has intuited all the above throughout all time because awareness was not constricted by the limitation of the paradigm of Newtonian science or the limitation of logic. Descartes' *res cogitans (interna)* and *res externa* are not separate but alternate loci of observation of form and represent different levels of a spectrum from "thing" to "ideation about the thing."

Within all form, there is the universal presence of the formless by which all is encompassed and unified. That reality allows for a "Unified Field Theory of Everything." The reason that this is both obvious and plausible is because all that exists arises from a single, common source. The universe, both subjectively human as well as physical, is thus an expression of the infinite potentialities of energy itself, i.e., the unmanifest becomes manifest as formless, primordial energy that then becomes the field of nonlinear consciousness, which itself is beyond form, time, or locality. It then serves as the matrix for differentiation into the spectrum of levels of subjective and linear form, which represents the actualization of potentiality. Thus, evolution represents and expresses creation and not causality. All that exists has a source but no "cause," which is merely a very limited concept, i.e., *res cogitans* (calibrates as "true").

The simple and rather obvious truth is that evolution *is* Creation. Therefore, Creation is continuous, ongoing, and witnessed sequentially as evolution. Evolution and Creation are one and the same reality.

CHAPTER 2
The Science of Truth

Classically, the essential requirements of science consist of an organized body of confirmable information that is comprehensible, logical, and replicable. In practice, therefore, science is composed of theory plus testable hypotheses capable of experimental (experiential) confirmation.

Although "truth" has been the focus of erudite intellectual discourse and attention for thousands of years, no totally universal agreement has ever been reached that would conclude the open-ended, ongoing discussion (e.g., see *The Great Books of the Western World*). Within stated contexts, however, workable definitions of heuristic value have, for periods of time, served a practical purpose. Each definition, however, has been limited by the lack of description of context or parameters. Therefore, as will be elucidated, no testable statements of any presentation of ostensible truth have any real validity because validity depends on context, content, and the specificity of their delineation.

In addition to the above difficulty, all definitions and terms include presumptions about semantics as well as the dialectics of logic, epistemological premises, and perceptions, all of which end up at the impasse of the conundrum: How do we know, or how do we even know that we know? The conundrum then continues on into discussions of theology, metaphysics, and, eventually, the epistemological dilemma of differentiation between the subjective and the supposedly objective categories of argument and experience. This core dilemma of investigation attempts to differentiate Descartes' *res cogitans* from *res externa* (i.e., the mind cannot know the world itself but only its selective, abstract mentalization about it, just as a photo is not the object photographed). It becomes the ultimate of all intellectual argument and irresolvable because of the dualistic nature of mentation itself, which artificially separates subject and object and thus becomes the very source of the intrinsic error that it seeks to resolve via circuitous tautologies.

The end point of intellectual investigation arrives at the obvious conclusion that the mind and the intellect are each inherently defective and therefore incapable of arriving at absolute truth. The principle of causality itself calibrates at only 460, i.e., dualistic and therefore limited by virtue of its contextual paradigm and the limitation intrinsic to the structure of its dialectic.

All mental approaches to a definition of truth are eventually confronted by the necessity of making a paradigm jump from the abstract to the experiential, and from the supposedly objective to the radically subjective. Thus, the statement "Only the objective is real" is a purely subjective premise. The mechanistic reductionist, therefore, actually lives in an intrapsychic, subjective reality, the same as everyone else. The resolution of the dilemma of a description and knowingness of absolute truth requires the leap into the field of research of consciousness itself, which makes it clear that the only actual, verifiable reality of knowingness is by the virtue of "being" (i.e., all intellectualizations are "about" something), which requires that the observer be extraneous in order to be the witness of the thing to be examined. For example, a human observation can "know about" a cat, but only a cat really knows what it is to be a cat by virtue of the quality of *being* a cat.

In essence, the above observation is the explanation of the diversity of opinion about spiritual reality and theological discussions concerning divinity that cannot reach any great degree of truth without arriving at the purely subjective knowingness of self-realization, the state of enlightenment in which the essence of subjectivity is self-revealing as the very substrate of the core of truth and reality.

As will be described later, consciousness research reveals that the capacity of the human mind to comprehend and understand the levels of truth depends on an individual's level of consciousness, which itself is in a state of continuous evolutionary development. This process has been continuous not only over preceding eons of evolutionary time, but also continues on in present time and during maturation. (See Chapter 7.)

It is important to know that at the time of birth, every individual human being already has a calibratable level of consciousness. These levels vary quite markedly and, in fact, to extreme degrees. The calibratable level denotes a capacity to resonate to an identifiable range of frequencies similar to a radio or television antenna. In addition, the brain does not reach full maturity until approximately age twenty-five to even thirty-five, and the significantly most human part of the brain, the prefrontal cortex, does not fully mature until the very last, a fact that is now being taken into consideration in court determinations of the sentencing of juveniles.

From an overall view, it is apparent that comprehending truth is innately challenging and seemingly complex. The problem of defining and understanding truth results in many different conclusions, depending on a great multiplicity of factors in which even the overall level of consciousness of mankind at the time is a significant factor. Each level of consciousness results in a definition of truth that is concordant to that specified level, together with its own languaging and qualifications that fit its culture and time. Discord arises from definitions that are appropriate to other levels of consciousness, even of the same era. Even if there is agreement about the facts or definition of truth, there remains disagreement as to what it "means" or signifies (i.e., hermeneutics).

The progressive development of a pragmatic yet theoretically elegant (a term that is used in scientific dialog to denote a germinal context) science of consciousness has already been presented in some detail (Hawkins, 1995-2004), including extensive demonstration and confirmation (Hawkins' video lecture series, 2002, 2003, 2004).

Summary of the Essential Principles
of the Science of Consciousness

1. Consciousness is the formless, invisible field of energy of infinite dimension and potentiality, the substrate of all existence, independent of time, space, or location, of which it is independent yet all inclusive and all present.

2. Because the field of consciousness encompasses all existence beyond all limitation, dimension, or time, it registers all events, no matter how seemingly miniscule, such as even a fleeting thought.

3. Because the registration of all events occurs outside of time and place, they are timelessly accessible due to the unique qualities inherent to the energy field of consciousness itself.

4. Consciousness is the irreducible substrate of the human capacity to know or experience, to perceive or witness, and it is the essence of the capacity for awareness itself.

5. The field of consciousness exists independently of mankind yet is included within it. It is the irreducible substrate, the Absolute, in comparison to which all that exists is relative.

6. Consciousness represents a field of infinite power and potential, out of which the manifest universe as Creation arises as a continuous, ongoing process.

7. The entire universe, both known and unknown, exists independently of human description and is essentially one unified, total field within which are variable levels of vibrational frequencies that appear as the observable universe. As in the physical domain, the higher the frequency of the vibrational energy, the greater the power.

8. The universal, all-encompassing vibrational field of energy is descriptively omnipresent and is therefore omniscient and all-powerful (omnipotent). The presence of the field of consciousness is known by all sentient beings as the subjective awareness of existence itself. Thus, the awareness of the

presence of consciousness as the substrate of existence is the primordial subjective reality underlying all possible human experience.

9. The levels of consciousness are identifiable by use of a simple quality of consciousness itself, and the omniscience of consciousness recognizes and responds to that which has existence and is true by virtue of the fact of that existence. Thus, consciousness, like a mirror, impersonally reflects actuality, which is unchanged and unaffected by that process. Consciousness, therefore, does not "do" anything, but, similar to gravity, it provides the context out of which potentiality actualizes from formless to form, from nonexperienced to experienced.

10. Comparable to the laws of the conservation of energy or conservation of matter, the law of the conservation of life prevails. Life itself is not capable of being destroyed but can only change form by shifting to a different frequency range (in human experience, the "etheric," the "spiritual," and other energy realms described throughout time).

11. Because all that exists represents a level of energy vibration, a scale of consciousness can be constructed that is internally consistent and of pragmatic value. A logarithmic scale of consciousness from 1 to 1,000, which starts at number "1" as the existence of life itself and continues to 1,000 (the highest level of consciousness ever reached by mankind), is sufficient to include all possible frequency ranges of human consciousness. Such a scale can be demonstrated to be highly informative and of great practical as well as theoretical value in understanding mankind, the question of divinity, and the universe.

12. Consciousness research is the only science available to mankind at the present time that enables investigation of the relative energy levels of both linear and nonlinear paradigms, their domains, and the realities that are beyond time, location, or dimension and that exist as both identifiably objective as well as subjective.

The above statements calibrate at consciousness level 1,000, which is the highest level of truth and knowability of the current human condition.

As in a doctoral dissertation, the above statements will be treated as though they are hypotheses to be clarified, amplified, demonstrated, and documented by presenting data that is sufficient to justify the fulfillment of the null hypothesis.

CHAPTER 3
Truth as Enigma:
The Challenge and the Struggle

The requisite foundation and essential basis for the development of a pristine, verifiable science of truth is the understanding of the nature of consciousness itself. Without such a foundation, clarification of its essential nature has floundered between the mechanistic reductionism of brain chemistry (calibration level 410) and the abstract intellectualizations of philosophy (cal. level 460). This results in circuitous tautologies that eventually lead to metaphysics (cal. level 450), theology (cal. level 450), and, finally, epistemology (cal. level 460), i.e., how do we know, and how do we know that we know, and is there even a primordial bedrock upon which faith and credibility can be placed?

Within the Newtonian paradigm (cal. level 460), science (cal. level 460) has been both informative and reliably, pragmatically productive. The domain of traditional science has been secured by its innate limitations and discipline of structure and form. The linear is predictable and has an innate reliability that resulted in a shift of society's faith from the unseen, such as traditional religion, to the demonstrable reliability and benefits of science.

To the modern mind, science is "real" and "objective," whereas the nonphysical phenomena and experiences of a mental or a subjective nature are considered unsubstantial, of questionable authenticity, and subject to doubt and argument (Arehart-Treichel, 2004). The appearance of quantum mechanics (cal. level 460) and the Heisenberg uncertainty principle (cal. level 460) spell the end of the dominance of the Newtonian paradigm of reality and the beginning of the emergence of a more sophisticated and advanced evolution of science that leads from the predictable linear to the unpredictable nonlinear (cal. level 500 on up to infinity).

Throughout the ages, the human mind and its intellect have been both the tool as well as the subject of investigation of the enormous complexity of reason and rationality. The sheer volume of man's investigations filled vast libraries and grew to enormous proportions. Inquiry led to a bewildering proliferation of information rather than a conclusive resolution or simplification. As a consequence, in the 1950s an erudite group of educators and scholars, chaired by Mortimer Adler, sought to give organizational recognition to the intellectual efforts of the great thinkers over the centuries. This resulted in the production of *The Great Books of the Western World* (1952), which included the works of the most excellent of the excellent scholars and thinkers in their best efforts in the attempt to arrive at and define truth. This study of man's intellectual history is continuous and widespread, and its value is currently supported by the National Association of Scholars (Fields, 2000), which recommends that one schedule a serious study of *The Great Books* over a ten-year period. Its contents include the major contributions of the following great thinkers of all history.

Calibrations of *The Great Books of the Western World*

Aeschylus 425	Darwin 450	Goethe 465
Appollonius 420	Descartes 490	Harvey 470
Aquinas, Thomas 460	Dostoevsky 465	Hegel 470
Archimedes 455	Engels 200	Herodotus 440
Aristophanes 445	Epictetus 430	Hippocrates 485
Aristotle 498	Euclid 440	Hobbes 435
Augustine 503	Euripides 470	Homer 455
Aurelius, Marcus 445	Faraday 415	Hume 445
Bacon, Francis 485	Fielding 440Fourier 405	Huygens 465
Berkeley 470	Freud 499	James, William 490
Boswell 460	Galen 450	Kant 460
Cervantes 430	Galileo 485	Kepler 470
Chaucer 480	Gibbon 445	Lavoisier 425
Copernicus 455	Gilbert 450	Locke 470
Dante 505		Lucretius 420

Machiavelli 440	Pascal 465	Sophocles 465
Marx 130	Plato 485	Spinoza 480
Melville 460	Plotinus 503	Sterne 430
Mill, J. S. 465	Plutarch 460	Swift 445
Milton 470	Ptolemy 435	Tacitus 420
Montaigne 440	Rabelais 435	Thucydides 420
Montesquieu 435	Rousseau 465	Tolstoy 420
Newton 499	Shakespeare 465	Virgil 445
Nicomachus 435	Smith, Adam 455	

Collectively, *The Great Books* calibrate at 450, but with the elimination of Karl Marx, they calibrate at 465. Thus, philosophies that calibrate below 200 (the critical level that discerns truth from falsehood) have a seriously negative impact, as history and current research well demonstrate. (In contrast, Socrates, not an author himself, calibrates at 540.)

The crucial importance of discovering the essential nature of truth can be deduced from the sheer size and intensity of effort of the world's greatest thinkers and scholars. These authors represent only the Western world. Similar efforts and a comparable list of great thinkers can be derived from other cultures and intellectual traditions of both Asia and the Middle East. Unfortunately, records of man's earliest works were lost in the fire at the Great Library at Alexandria in the year 48 B.C.

Subsequent to the many centuries of scholastic and intellectual inquiry, a new system of inquiry began in which the scientific method, which had been so successful in the physical domain, was applied to the study of the human mind and its physiology. It is notable that the final volume in *The Great Books of the Western World* is devoted to Freud, whose most seminal discovery was that of the importance of the unconscious mind and its primary role in all aspects of mental and emotional life. The great contribution of psychoanalysis was that it demonstrated the decisive role of subjectivity as the *a priori* substrate of experience and its interpretation and intrapsychic dynamics.

After Freud, a proliferation of psychologies ensued, of which the discoveries of Carl Jung were the most significant in that he included the human spirit as a powerful, significant element in human consciousness, both individually and collectively. To further clarify the unconscious, Jung elucidated the inherent patterns as the great archetypes. Whereas the work of Freud calibrates at 499, that of Jung calibrates at 520, which signals an important, critical advancement of paradigm.

Experimental academic psychology confined itself to more mechanistic issues and learning theory. During approximately the same time period, semanticists studied linguistics and the basic structure of language itself. Hayakawa (1971) and Ayer (1966) explained the essential point, which had been made earlier by Descartes (*res cogitans* versus *res externa*), that "the map is not the territory," in which the importance of this defect of human mentation was emphasized. Consciousness itself became a focus of scientific inquiry as a consequence of the crucial discovery and inference of the Heisenberg uncertainty principle. Although Einstein (whose work calibrates at 499) rejected the philosophical implications of the Heisenberg principle, they were understood by David Bohm, who described and delineated the implicit/explicit and enfolded/unfolded paradigms of reality. (The consciousness level of Bohm's work is 505.) This more advanced contextualization of the universe recognized the reality of both the unmanifest substrate of existence and its unfoldment from potentiality to actuality.

The conceptual and philosophical implications of quantum mechanics and the emerging science of nonlinear dynamics led to a series of annual academic meetings on the subject of "science and consciousness" at the University of Arizona (Hemeroff, et al., 1996), and elsewhere. This was followed by the publication of the *Journal of Consciousness Studies* (1996). The consciousness level of these conferences and journals was at approximately 410 to 450, which indicates that they were primarily efforts of the intellect, advantaged by advanced scientific theory and the associated mathematics.

During approximately the same time period, psychiatry as a field of study had deserted psychoanalysis and the whole realm of subjective reality by which man experiences and interprets his existence as a continuum, not only from event to event but also as an evolutionary unity. Psychiatry also succumbed to the mechanistic reductionism of brain chemistry and, paradoxically, became increasingly dehumanized, with a progressive loss of empathy for the uniquely personal human experience (Kendler, 2001). The everyday practice of psychiatry became dominated by the development of effective psychopharmacology as well as by the business model introduced by the insurance industry. The upside of these developments, however, was the benefit and pragmatic value of a widespread reduction in the suffering from painful subjective symptoms, such as psychosis, depression, and anxiety. These benefits became readily available and accessible to large numbers of patients, whereas, prior to the development of the pharmaceutical industry, few patients could afford the time or an actual investment in intensive psychotherapy, such as psychoanalysis.

To help fill the vacuum of human need, nonmedical psychotherapists fulfilled the role of the empathic healer whose main modality was the inculcation of psychological insight and emotional education, which again reemphasized the critical importance of subjectivity and the value and meaning of personal experience.

A very significant aspect of the development of the psychotherapies was the reaffirmation of the importance of the spiritual aspects of the human psyche and their contribution to happiness and fulfillment in both physical and mental health. Ministerial counseling had a centuries-old foundation in which the idea of healing as a whole concept was central. Research also revealed that people whose lives included spirituality or religious values had better health, lived longer, and experienced less disease, less crime, and less poverty as well as lower divorce rates. They were happier, better adjusted, and had better functioning children (Robb, 2004). This is currently being studied in a four-year research project on attitudes and self-images of adolescents by the Lilly Endowment-funded National Study of Youth and Religion. Major psychological associations, such as the Association for Transpersonal Psychology, emphasized the importance of the recognition of spiritual realities and their contribution to physical and emotional health. The *Journal of Spiritual Health* is devoted exclusively to the subject.

A major development that affected the lives and recoveries of millions of people around the earth was the appearance of the Twelve-Step recovery program that arose out of Alcoholics Anonymous (cal. level 540). It evolved into the more generalized and widespread acceptance of "recovery" as an effective and transformative solution to multiple personal and social problems and behaviors. Great multitudes of people recovered from grave and incurable illnesses, and these recoveries were witnessed by millions more of relatives, families, employers, friends, and grateful spouses.

Faith-based therapy groups in prison populations reduced the recidivism rate by thirty-five percent (per consciousness research). Despite the widespread proliferation and application of the twelve-step principles to a great diversity of ostensibly hopeless human problems, the core of the twelve-step recovery model and discipline remained pristine and unsullied. It resisted commercialization or exploitation and did not fall prey to worldly commercialization or the temptation of control over others. By the internal discipline of the spiritual truths upon which it was structured, the twelve-step movement had "no opinions on outside issues" and rejected wealth, prestige, and political influence (Wilson, "Bill W.," 1939, 1953). Its power was based solely on its consciousness level of unconditional love and selfless honesty, which calibrate at level 540.

The populace of today's world is naïve in that it presumes that the prevalence of available knowledge of society has always been the human condition, whereas the opposite has been true. Historically, information of great value was guarded by the privileged few and unavailable to the masses. The printing press had not yet been invented, and the educated were very few in number. Even the most favored and erudite scholars had no instrument or means by which to discern truth from falsehood. Therefore, the inclusion of error was inevitable, e.g., the severe drop in the level of consciousness of Christianity that occurred after the Council of Nicaea. The exclusive province of access to knowledge then became a temptation by which to control others, and claim to exclusivity became the very fuel that fired intolerance and strife.

In addition, the disputative mind clings to exaggeration of the irrelevant details that divide people rather than emphasis of the central point of truth, which would thereby unite them.

Despite the above, major religions developed ecclesiastic authority that was intended to prevent disruptive disagreement by the specification of agreed-upon scripture, the authenticity of which was then authorized by the process of "canonization." This, however, led to further abuse and the utilization of dire threats to enforce adherence to orthodoxy.

In contrast, by means of consciousness research, the truth of the world's foremost teachings indicates that high levels of truth have always been available and continue to be, just as the great spiritual classics that have stood the test of time. Additional verification of these truths has been provided by the documented, independent rediscoveries of the same basic truths repeatedly throughout diverse cultures and in widely separated time periods. Every verifiably genuine mystic or person with advanced consciousness declares essentially the same historic truths, independent of cultural setting or personality. The calibratable levels of consciousness confirm an intrinsic reality that has been reaffirmed repeatedly over great periods of time (see Chapter 18).

The maximum calibrated level of consciousness possible in the human domain historically has been at 1,000, which is that of the world's acknowledged great avatars (saviors of mankind) and divinely realized, enlightened sages of antiquity. In contrast, the top limits of the intellect, the mind, reason, and logic calibrate at 499, which represents the mastery of the linear domain. Consciousness level 500, however, reflects the emergence of a new, more advanced paradigm of reality that unfolds by inclusion of the subjective and experiential substrate of consciousness itself, knowable only by virtue of its irreducible, experiential reality. While the ego is narcissistic by design and primarily self-oriented, at level 500, consideration and the loving of others become dominant, and that unique quality called "love" gives life its meaning and value. Statistically, level 500 is reached by 4 percent of the world's population, unconditional love at level 540 by 0.4 percent, and over level 600 by only a few.

Very advanced states of consciousness are extremely rare. At the present time, there are six sages (anonymous) on the planet who calibrate at 600 or over. Of these, three are between 600-700, one between 700-800, one between 800-900, and one between 900-1,000. Together with the populace that calibrates over 200, they counterbalance and offset the massive negativity of the majority of the world's population that calibrates at less than 200. The net consequence is that the overall consciousness level of mankind is currently at 207.

As love appears on the calibrated Scale of Consciousness, its first appearance is emotional and dualistic (i.e., between a "me" and a "you," or "myself" and "it"). With further evolution, it is progressively nondualistic and becomes a way of living and not just an emotion; instead, it signifies what one has become. The power of love is transformative and recontextualizes experience that is progressively focused on the nonlinear prevalence of the field instead of the limited linear content of the field as form. The emphasis then moves from getting to giving, and it is discovered that happiness is the intrinsic, automatic consequence of contributing to the happiness of others, thereby fulfilling one's own potentiality as well as autonomy.

Clinically, it can be observed that all healing ministries, faith systems, and recovery modalities trust the importance of letting go of or surrendering negative belief systems and emotions and adopting a more merciful and forgiving attitude towards self and others. When one relinquishes emergency emotions, resentments, and judgmentalism, the guilt and self-hatred that were previously projected onto others diminish, and instead, the positive (welfare) healthy emotions replace the negative ones (Rado, Tiebout, 1949-53; Rado, 1933), with the resultant change in the dominant physiological pathways in the brain itself. As will be described later in Chapter 7, information in the spiritually-oriented person is actually processed differently by the brain, producing positive psychological and physiological benefits.

Paradoxically, benefit is derived by the self-interest of the ego when it begins to realize that there is a great advantage to unselfishness. When it learns of the benefit of letting go of egocentric goals, the ego itself then becomes the springboard to spiritual inquiry and the means to its own transcendence, realizing that humility is strength, not weakness, and that it is wisdom and not ignorance. The willingness to "forgive and forget" calibrates at 450. The willingness to "forgive and surrender to God" calibrates at 550.

CHAPTER 4
The Evolution of Consciousness

I t has been generally assumed throughout intellectual history that the mind, with its capacity for reason and symbolic thinking, is the irreducible, fundamental hallmark of humanness. It is often quoted that it is the capacity to think that differentiates man from the animal. Upon examination, however, we shall discover that the mind is actually not a fundamental but an epiphenomenon of consciousness, with a circumscribed range of usefulness and reliability.

Intellectualization calibrates at 410, indicating that the belief that the intellect is the ultimate capacity of man is in itself a limitation. In examining mental functions, it is useful to realize that an almost automatic accompaniment to the mind is its innate, unstated, but ever-present naïve presumptiveness. This becomes the basis for lack of insight into the mind's limitations by the mechanisms of denial and pride, i.e., "I think, therefore I am" (cal. level 400), rather than its corollary, "I am, therefore I think" (cal. level 480).

Everyone secretly believes that their view of the world is correct and any other is wrong. Thereby opinion becomes promoted to ostensible "fact" and pseudovalidity.

Inasmuch as the mind is readily observed to be a product of consciousness rather than its substrate (calibrates as "true"), then it is essential to understand in detail the nature of consciousness and its origins, development, and potential. Consciousness is an expression or quality of the essence of life itself (calibrates as "true"). A fundamental, verifiable statement about life is that it is neither subject to nor vulnerable to death but can only be made to change form. Like the laws of conservation of the energy

27

of matter, the law of conservation of life is almost identical. It cannot be destroyed but can only change form (cal. at 1,000). It is astonishing that mankind has not been aware of this crucial understanding. A probable reason is that although all the great sages, avatars, and spiritually advanced teachers throughout history have made statements that life is eternal, this great truth was compartmentalized by the ordinary mind, which assumed that the statement was limited to teachings of spirituality or religion rather than being a general truth. It was therefore inferred to be a matter of faith rather than fact.

Another obvious explanation for this unawareness is that the average human identifies life with a body, and death is therefore viewed as primarily a physical, and therefore a terminal, phenomenon. Despite this seemingly plausible belief, the majority of mankind has also generally surmised and believed that after physical death, the life of the spirit continues on with relatively well-understood implications as to its destiny.

In spite of the massive accumulation of knowledge that man has acquired over the centuries, uncertainty still dominates all philosophical and intellectual discussions, and spiritual teachings are considered to be belief systems rather than provable facts. Therefore, a thorough investigation of the matter is of general interest to a mankind that still asks the basic questions: "Who are we? Where do we come from? And where do we go?" Despite the purported erudition of the great intellects and philosophers of the past, the questions still remain unanswered because the questions asked cannot be answered by the mind at all. They can only be discovered by delving into its source—consciousness—without which the mind could not exist and without which man would not even know that he has a mind. The nature of consciousness itself—how it arose, what it is, and how it functions—becomes apparent from the study of its evolution.

Planet Earth apparently arose as a spin-off of condensed energy of galactic origin, the mechanics of which are still under study by advanced theoretical physics as well as astronomy. The irreducible substrate of all physicality is that of the primordial energy of consciousness itself, with its innate potentiality of infinite possibilities and expressions discernible as form. Out of energy arose visible mass as well as unseen "dark" energy and matter that constitute the greater part of the detectible universe.

Only four percent of the universe is visible matter, twenty-three percent is invisible "dark" matter, and seventy-three percent is invisible "dark" energy (Howe, 2004). Thus, the invisible domain is analogous to potentiality, and the visible represents manifestation of confirmable actuality. The details of the exact relationships between energy, mass, gravity, space, matter, and antimatter constitute the focus of study of the leading edge of the possibilities of the intellect. Although quantum mechanics provides a means of understanding the transition between the linear and the nonlinear domains, to do so requires a paradigm jump that begins at the calibrated consciousness level of 500 (i.e., beyond the limitation of the concept of causality).

As can be discerned by consciousness research at this time, the infinite potentiality of the unmanifest became manifest as the energetic submatrix of the potential physical universe. The energy of consciousness in its contact with matter actualized the potential of biological life. Consciousness as life is one and the same basic reality (calibrates as "true"). In spiritual terminology, consciousness is the radiance of Divinity ("the light of God" of Genesis). Because the terms "God" or "Divinity" are problematic, in their place one can refer to Deity as "the ultimate omnipotent reality," the absolute, irreducible source of all existence.

When the surface of the molten mass of earth cooled sufficiently, consciousness plus matter evolved first as primitive, simple life forms, such as algae or lichens. Eons later, the intelligence of animal life first appeared as the DNA of viruses, and later, of bacteria. The first conscious organisms were bacteria, and on the Scale of Consciousness, they calibrate at "1." Although viruses reproduce their own DNA and are a product of the intelligence of consciousness, they themselves are not innately conscious, i.e., they lack subjectivity. A significant observation is that the exact locus of the process of evolution, including form and function, is specifically within the field of consciousness itself, where the *anlage* of form is a pattern potentiality that was termed a *morpho-*

genetic field by Rupert Sheldrake (calibrates as true).

Potentiality resides as patterns (the information of intelligence) in the field of consciousness and transforms into actuality as an appearance in the phenomenal world when conditions are favorable and actualized by intention. This is facilitated by the capacity of the unmanifest to become manifest by virtue of its omnipresence, omnipotence, and the quality classically termed "omniscience," meaning that the all-inclusive primordial Reality incorporates all the known and the knowable because it is the source, substrate, and context of the Allness of Existence. Intelligence is the quality of omniscience by which information (i.e., form) becomes known and thereby transmissible.

For life to survive and later evolve, the prime requisite is that it be designed with survival as its primary goal or consequence. Self-propagation, self-interest, and self-servingness were *a priori* requirements for any primitive life form to survive or to succeed. In turn, the survival of life in form depends on the accumulation, organization, utilization, and integration of pure energy itself. Energy is a necessity of life that had to be acquired. On the vegetative level, photosynthesis became the primary mechanism by which chemical molecules could be integrated and utilized. Microorganisms developed integrated systems that incorporated molecular components of the environment. The survival of life depended on the acquisition of needed energy sources of whatever forms were available.

The fulfillment of this basic necessity was accomplished by the development of survival systems of extraordinary complexity and ingenuity. These were developments of the quality of intelligence innate to the field of consciousness itself before they appeared in the physical world as living forms. Learning occurred specifically within the nonphysical domain of the energy field of consciousness. This was the level designated by Rupert Sheldrake as "formative causation" (Sheldrake, 1981).

Digital or
Electric
devices of

Signals to
corresponds to
physical change

Imprinted information in the form of recorded energy frequen-cies and patterns is common in the modern world as both analog and digital program sources, including radio, television, CDs, DVDs, etc. Form itself is encoded information transferable into instruction, such as the genetic code. Analogous processes occur in the imprinting of images in digital cameras, and chemistry and physics use the electromagnetic spectrum frequencies to identify the presence of specific chemical properties by electrospectrom-etry. Thus, the modern mind accepts that invisible energy pat-terns, which include not only information but also even specific instructions, precede and are the source of their appearance and unfolding as programs or structures within the observable New-tonian dimension of physicality and form.

A characteristic of the energy field of consciousness is its in-nate propensity to evolve to higher and higher levels in order to give expression to the highest potentialities. At some point along the progression of the field of consciousness, the capacity for awareness occurs, which provides the *a priori* substrate of subjectivity and the capacity for experiencing, thinking, feeling, and understanding that generally have been considered to be primary animal as well as human capabilities.

The demonstration of the above propositions reveals that when we calibrate the level of consciousness of the animal kingdom, we see a very definite progression of consciousness over great eons of temporal time.

Animal Kingdom

Bacteria	1	Wolves	190
Protozoa	2	Hippopotamus	190
Crustaceans	3	Javalina	195
Insects	6	*Grazers:*	
Arachnids	7	Zebra, gazelle, giraffe	200
Amphibians	17	Deer	205
Fish	20	Bison	205
Octopus	20	Domestic pig	205
Sharks	24	Elk	210
Vipers	35	Dairy cow	210
Komodo dragon	40	Sheep	210
Reptiles	40	Range cattle	210
Predatory Mammals:		Elephants	210
Hyena, lion, tiger	40	Monkeys	210
Snakes	45	Farm horse	240
Alligators	45	Cats	240
Dinosaurs	60	Parrot, African Gray	240
Whales	85	Family Cat	245
Dolphins	95	Race horse	245
Migratory birds	105	Dogs	245
Birds of prey	105	Family pig	250
Rodents	105	Black Crow	250
Rhinoceros	105	Gorilla	275
Baboons	105	Chimpanzees	305
Song birds	125	*Exceptions:*	
Doves	145	Alex, trained African	
Polar bear	160	Grey parrot	401
Grizzly bear	160	Koko (trained gorilla)	405
Water buffalo	175	Song bird's song	500
Black bear	180	Cat's purr	500
Jackal, foxes	185	Dog's wagging tail	500

From the map of consciousness of the animal kingdom, we can make several interesting and very significant observations. Up to level 200, animal life survives by predation and, therefore, the very life of the predator is solely dependent upon consumption of the prey. From the viewpoint of human values, animal life up to that level is totally "egocentric," "selfish," and "self-centered," as well as voracious. Survival at that level is not dependant upon choice but upon necessity. The predator sees the prey not as something to kill but strictly as a meal. If we ask, through consciousness research, whether the predator intends the killing of its seeming victim, we get the answer "no." Its intention is not to kill but to eat (i.e., it is dependent upon predation to acquire the energy necessary to sustain its life). Inasmuch as life itself cannot be killed (calibrates as "true") but can only change form, the animal spirit lives on to inhabit another physical body. In the case of the human, the spirit does not enter the fetus until the third month of gestation (calibrates as "true"). In the lower animals, it occurs earlier but still awaits a viable fetus to energize.

With consciousness research, it can also be discovered that the "prey" does not actually value physical life in the way humans do and, in fact, does not even notice the transition from physicality to its etheric continuation and subsequent periodic return to other physical bodies. If a fly or a moth is swatted, it goes right on flying along in its etheric body, unaware of the change, and soon returns in another physical body (calibrates as "true"). According to the ancient *Rig Veda* (cal. 705), each level of organic life "sacrifices" its life to the higher and thus karmically sanctifies its life and earns its own evolution to higher forms (life serves higher life).

Humans who have had either near-death or out-of-body experiences or have experienced past-life regression can appreciate these statements. In all of these, the sense of self-identity is unchanged. It is always the same "me." Similarly, in dreams, the dreamer's sense of self remains unimpaired. This is also true in hypnotically induced past-life recall where the subject relives a very clear-cut lifetime experience and situation. It is always the same sense of self-identity, no matter what type of body form may prevail. Insects, therefore, don't even notice the transition, and animals consider their dream worlds to have the same degree of reality and validity as their everyday physicality. To the cat or dog, the dream chase has the same authenticity as a waking chase (calibrates as "true").

The calibrated levels of the animal kingdom represent averages of the total population within which there is individual variation, and there is also variation in calibrated levels of behavior. Thus, "play" calibrates about ten points higher than the average level of function, which is significant. Once a human family adopts an animal, the animal's level of consciousness advances by five or ten points. Another area of major interest is that certain birds and animals that have experienced prolonged interaction with humans actually calibrate at 400. This calibration level indicates the capacity for thinking and reason; thus, the calibration level helps to resolve the argument among experimental scientists about whether or not certain animal behaviors actually reflect the capacity for reason.

A unique discovery is that a cat's purr, a song bird's song, and a dog's wagging tail all calibrate extremely high—in fact, higher than a large portion of the human population. That pet animals have the capacity to interact and emanate love indicates an area for further research to discover why these beloved animals are capable of love, i.e., they exhibit an advanced development of the "heart chakra" and have a therapeutic healing effect on people with a variety of illnesses (Banda and Lightmark, 2004).

In the evolution of animal consciousness, we know that at level 200, there is a major change in the quality of life that marks the appearance of the benign herbivores that do not need to eat others in order to survive. The grazer returns nitrogen-rich fertilizer to the soil and thereby sustains life. In addition, it spreads seeds in its manure, thus supporting the propagation of vegetation.

The prelude to what will later emerge as love and the progression of consciousness overall first appears in the animal kingdom in its primitive form as protection of the eggs and the young. This evolves in the higher animals into the maternal instinct. Thus, the critical level of consciousness at 200 demonstrates a major change of quality of consciousness from solely self-servingness at the cost of the lives of others to the more benign levels of caring for others and the emergence of family bonding.

With the emergence of bonding, group loyalty and social tribal behaviors appear, which, in themselves, secondarily subserve survival. However, group loyalty and pack formation also signal social conflict, with struggles for dominance, mating rites, and territorial domination, all of which are common to the human species as well.

From a developmental analysis utilizing consciousness research techniques, it then appears that the human ego itself is primarily the product and continuation of the presence of the survival core of animal evolution. This eventually is represented in the basic structure and physiology of the human brain.

Comparable to the evolution of consciousness in the animal kingdom, in the human domain, consciousness level 200 again demarcates a major critical change of quality. The levels below 200 indicate varying degrees of emotionalized egocentricity in which the rights of others are ignored, and above 200 there is the emergence of benign civility and concern for the lives and rights of others. At the present period of human evolution, seventy-eight percent of the total human population on the planet calibrates below consciousness level 200, so the lack of concern for the rights of others is demonstrated on a daily basis, as reported by the news media (Public Agenda Poll 2002) and reflected in international savageries. (Currently in America, forty-nine percent of the overall population calibrates below 200.)

When we view the evolution of consciousness and the origins of the ego in the animal domain, we can understand that the ego is primarily the continuation of the animal level of consciousness within the human psyche. When viewed from an evolutionary perspective, an understanding arises that allows for compassion for that which has been traditionally demonized and condemned and has been the source of much conflict, guilt, and suffering. The ego is not overcome by condemnation, hatred, and guilt; rather, one deenergizes it by viewing it objectively for what it truly is, i.e., a vestigial remnant of man's evolutionary origins.

Paradoxically, the ego is reinforced by condemnation, labeling it as "sin," sackcloth and ashes, and wallowing in guilt, which is merely utilizing the ego to attack the ego, thereby reinforcing it. The vilification of the ego creates so much guilt that the most common way that human consciousness handles the conflict is through denial, secularism, and by projecting blame onto others. This is represented in our current society, which is obsessed with the model of perpetrator versus victim, leading to world conflict and the litigious and contentious qualities of society.

As Freud discovered, out of guilt the animal nature of man becomes repressed and then projected onto others or a deity that purportedly has the same character defects as man. Historically, man paradoxically fears his own projections and confuses divinity with the repressed dark side of his own nature. The ego is dissolved not by denunciation or self-hatred, which are expressions of the ego, but by benign and nonmoralistic acceptance and compassion that arise out of understanding its intrinsic nature and origin.

Although guilt and repentance may have a certain pragmatic usefulness for brief periods in one's spiritual evolution, it is to be noted from examining the Map of Consciousness that guilt, self-hatred, remorse, regret, despondency, and all such negative positionalities are at the bottom of the list, whereas forgiveness, love, acceptance, and joy are at the top of the list, leading to enlightenment. The ego's cleverness and innate self-dedication to survival can be appreciated in that large segments of mankind, often aided and abetted by dark interpretations of religion, have led the masses to seek at the bottom of the Map of Consciousness, which are the avenues to negativity, rather than at the top of the Map, which leads to the realizations of advanced spiritual awareness, the knowledge of Divinity, and the nonjudgmental reality that underlies all existence and Creation.

The evolution of consciousness is also demonstrated by its progression in the evolution of hominids. Neanderthal Man calibrated at consciousness level 75; then Java man, Homo erectus, emerged at 80; Heidelberg man at 80-85; and then, six hundred thousand years ago, Homo sapiens idelta (cal. 80) appeared in Ethiopia as a possible forerunner of modern man.

Of very recent discovery is the hominid *Homo floresiensis*, a diminutive evolutionary ancestor who lived on the Indonesian island of Flores until approximately thirteen thousand years ago. They compensated for their small brain size by having increased neuronal complexity and calibrate at 85.

The evolution of consciousness of humankind overall has been seemingly slow. It did not reach level 90 until the time of the birth of the Buddha at approximately 563 B.C. The rate of evolution then appears to have accelerated, so that by the time of the birth of Jesus Christ, the consciousness level of the totality of mankind had reached 100. During each time period, the percentage of the population that calibrated over 200 was quite small. Nevertheless, the *Vedas* out of ancient India's Aryan culture calibrated in the high 900s, with Krishna at 1,000, which was the same level demonstrated by Jesus Christ and the Buddha. It took approximately two thousand years, however, for the overall consciousness level of mankind to move from 100 to the level of 205 in the late 1980s, and then again move another two points in November 2003, at the time of the Harmonic Concordance, to its current level of 207.

In addition to tracking the calibrated levels of consciousness of life in both animal and human forms over great periods of time, a significant inference is derived from calibrating the levels of consciousness of all life on planet Earth through the great archeological eons of prehistory.

Consciousness Levels of Archeological Eras

TIME PERIODS ROCK SYSTEMS	APPROX DURATION MILLION YEARS	LIFE FORMS	CALIBRATED LEVEL OF LIFE
Quaternary	1	Rise and dominance of man	212
Upper Tertiary		Modern animals and plants	212
Lower Tertiary	60	Rapid development of modern mammals insects and plants	112
Upper Cretaceous	60	Primitive mammals; last dinosaurs	84
Lower Cretaceous		Rise of flowering plants	
Jurassic	35	First birds, first mammals. Diversification of reptiles; coniferous trees.	68
Triassic	35	Rise of dinosaurs; cycad-like plants; bony fishes	62
Permian	25	Rise of reptiles. Modern insects. Last of many plant and animal groups	45
Pennsylvanian (Carboniferous)	85	First reptiles, amphibians, primitive insects; seed ferns; primitive conifers	35
Mississippian (Carboniferous)		Climax of shell-crushing sharks.	33
Devonian	50	First amphibians, first land snails. Primitive land plants. Climax of brachiopods	27
Silurian	40	First traces of land life. Scorpions, First lungfishes Widespread coral reefs.	17
Ordovician	90	First fish. Climax of trilobites. First appearance of many marine invertebrates.	12
Cambrian	70	First marine invertebrates	8
Proterozic Archeozoic (Precambrian)	Over 1300	Protozoa	2
		Algae, Lichens, Bacteria	1
Age of oldest dated rocks is about 1,850,000,000 years			

Source: Adapted from Britannica World Language Dictionary. New York: Funk & Wagnalls Co.

From the above, we derive further evidence to support the demonstration that consciousness has been progressively and unrelentingly evolving and that this advancement of consciousness is a quality innate to consciousness itself.

Evolution of Human Consciousness

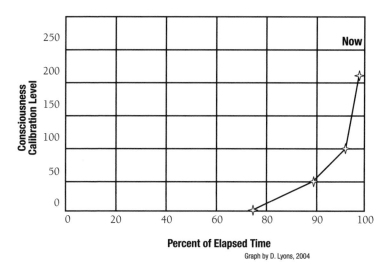

Graph by D. Lyons, 2004

A seemingly reasonable probability could be derived from all the above that consciousness will continue to evolve because that is its nature, and the future of mankind can be realistically viewed as optimistic. This progression also implies that consciousness seeks to return to the awareness of its own source (calibrates as "true"). Spiritually advanced members of the human race have repeatedly reported throughout history that consciousness can and does successfully return to the awareness of its own essence and source (see Chapter 8). The ultimate levels of the progression of consciousness can be studied in the fully recognized sages, saints, and great enlightened beings that represent the most advanced levels of the evolution of consciousness in the human domain.

The Map of Consciousness primarily delineates consciousness levels up to 600 because, in so doing, the Map includes over ninety-nine percent of mankind. Although few in number, the extremely advanced levels of consciousness reported by the great sages of history reaffirm the evolutionary quality of consciousness and its ultimate progression on the human level.

As will be described later, the evolution of consciousness over level 200 results in a change in the brain's physiology as well as the development of an "etheric" brain that is nonphysical and composed solely of energy patterns. The higher frequencies of more advanced consciousness transcend the response capabilities of the physicality of the Newtonian paradigm and a protoplasmic brain. They instead require a purely energy body ("spiritual," "etheric," "soul") capable of response to very high frequency vibrational energy fields (analogous to the capacity and capability of a computer chip versus a vacuum tube). Therefore, research devoted solely to brain physiology and chemistry, as interpreted by advanced theoretical physics and mathematics, is limited, and all such academic conferences dealing with the subject calibrate in the low to mid-400s.

The processing of spiritual information requires a nonphysical vehicle, and the brain is then understood as being a receiving set for information, as described by Sir John Eccles (1986, 1989). A description of the changes in brain physiology and its mode of processing will be presented in Chapter 7. However, it is interesting that the Buddha categorized thinkingness as a sensory modality and the brain as a sense organ, indicating that mentalization was a modality akin to sensation, touch, hearing, seeing, and taste. Thus, the Buddha listed man as having six senses rather than the traditional Western view of only five.

In summary of the above survey of the evolution of consciousness and its evolution as man, it is of critical importance to note that the capacity to think, reason, and thus mentalize did not *replace* the mental processes of the animal, but instead was merely *added on* to it. The animal consciousness is interested only in its own survival (including family and pack) and is not interested in providing for, nor does it recognize, the needs, the wants, or much less, the value of others. The downside of the consequence of the capacity for cognition when added to animal instincts is comparable to that of giving a child or a mentally impaired person a gun.

To the ego, the intellect and reason were just additional tools and modalities of survival so that the intrinsic narcissistic core of the ego utilized mentalization to attack others. The mind could then subserve predatory purposes and pursue primarily narcissistic goals, which it still does in seventy-eight percent of the world's population. Thus, the spiritually unevolved ego merely utilizes the advances and technical discoveries of civilization for its own ends. Tribal war becomes nuclear war, teeth and claws become mine fields, and guns become the tools for robbery and murder. Instead of sticks, stones, and arrows, ballistic missiles subserve the pack mentality, territorial aggression, and the competitive dominance of the alpha males. Thus, humanity has been the victim of the unbridled oppression of egocentricity in its expression as megalomania (fueled by testosterone), which has killed more people than any other factor in history. ("Malignant messianic narcissism" calibrates at 30.)

The unbridled ego is insatiable, does not care about the rights of others or even the lives of others, and thus views Divinity as the ultimate opposition to its drive for absolute sovereignty. Cleverly, however, it solves this impasse by claiming to have God's authorization for barbarism done "in the name of God," "Allah," for the "good of the faith," "for Christ," for the Sun God Quatzelcoetal (cal. level 85), or the God of Attila the Hun. (Even Hitler claimed God's approval.) To the animal nature of the ego, religion is merely another tool in its arsenal by which to control others, thereby revealing the paradoxical truth that its inherent weakness is its dependence on others for survival, whereas true power is independent, self-sufficient, and devoid of neediness.

The power of love is demonstrated by the act of giving, and the weakness of the ego is shown by its neediness and insufficiency. Because the continuance of the ego is dependent on fulfilling its basic needs, it lives in fear (all megalomaniacs are paranoid), whereas, love is fearless.

A unique incident that demonstrates the transformational quality of love was reported in the Toronto newspapers (Dube, 2004).

A disturbed man, and potential mass murderer, had six thousand rounds of ammunition and multiple weapons. He intended to kill as many people as possible and then commit suicide. He could not be dissuaded; however, he was interrupted by a dog with a Frisbee who begged him to play. The would-be killer suddenly had a "change of heart," dropped the weapons, surrendered, and then sought help for his state of mind. The lovingness of the dog (named Elvis), which calibrates at 500, effortlessly accomplished the miraculous, which neither reason nor entreaty could do.

From the viewpoint of evolutionary development, *Homo sapiens* is unique in that it shows such a wide spectrum of calibrated levels of consciousness within the same species. It is only very recently, in the late 1980s, that the overall consciousness level rose from 190, where it had been for centuries, to 205, and now to 207 (i.e., it moved collectively from self-saving predation to concern for others).

Despite progression of the statistical average, seventy-eight percent of the world's population is still below consciousness level 200, which denotes truth, integrity, and concern for others. It is from this vast reservoir of negativity that the world's problems arise. World conflict would seem to be inevitable because of the great disparity between highly evolved segments and the vast proportion that lags behind and is thereby limited.

CHAPTER 5
The Essential Structure of Truth

The human mind has been unable to resolve the enigma of truth for several crucial reasons:

1. The lack of knowledge of the evolution of consciousness and its levels.
2. The lack of understanding the nature and structure of the ego and its origin.
3. The inherent defects and limitations of the ego.
4. The failure to realize the importance of the relationship between context and content.
5. The significance of a paradigm shift as a consequence of contextualization.

In the perceived, supposedly discreet, domain of the Newtonian linear paradigm, statements ("facts") are assumed to exist independently of the field or the context. The presumption, therefore, is that "things," including ideas, exist in some purportedly "objective," independent, self-sufficient, identifiable "reality." As such, it is inferred that objective data exist independently of any knower of the alleged facts. Because these isolated facts meet the requirements of their own definition, they are therefore considered provable, and the hypothesis of a requirement for proof appears to be rational and capable of fulfillment. Upon examination, however, it will be discovered that proofs are primarily circuitous reifications of definition by which intention already determines the result by the process of selection of acceptable data, i.e., category blindness.

To each is their Truth — not another's Truth — but our own

With sophistication and maturity, however, it becomes progressively clear that the criteria for truth change, or are even completely offset by a change in the overall field. A statement is only true within a specific context, and the same exact statement can become blatantly false in a different context (situational ethics, impaired responsibility, mitigating circumstances, different time period or setting, different culture or historical period, etc.). These circumstances alter perceived truth and responsibility. It becomes clear that a reliable understanding of truth requires definition and description of not only the content but also the context, the overall field, and the intention of the observer.

Verifiable truth is thus a product of (1) content, (2) the point of observation, plus (3) the influence of intention, and (4) context, which again reflects (5) a paradigm (meaning). Academic science is struggling with the realization that the evolution of science is itself a product of consciousness, and that it has therefore moved on from the limitations of the linear Newtonian/mathematical model of reality to nonlinear dynamics and quantum mechanics, in which the Heisenberg principle marks the transition from a purportedly objective reality to the more advanced comprehension that no knowing of anything is possible from within the self-contained Newtonian paradigm itself. Nothing is describable or comprehensible except by the consciousness of the observer. Beyond those advances in awareness is the more recent discovery that by calibrating the levels of consciousness, there appear to be different domains of possibility and therefore actuality, as well as a critical differentiation between the qualities of force and power.

Content always exists within context as well as within a field of observation. The primary defect of the Newtonian paradigm is, however, the adherence to the intellectual construct of the principle of causality (cal. 450), which has only a limited pragmatic application. A simple diagram can clarify the situation:

CONTENT, FIELD, AND CONTEXT

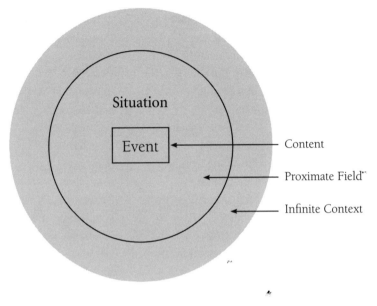

Event: Perceived, linear, content

Situation: Time, place, circumstances, influences, contributory factors, both known and unknown. Linear and nonlinear. Proximate field

Infinite Context: Nonlinear, infinite, omnipresent, timeless. Records all events and circumstances forever.

CONTENT, FIELD, AND CONTEXT

Content	Proximate Field	Context
Ego	Spiritual ego	Consciousness
Linear	Semi-linear	Nonlinear
Limited	Semi-limited	Unlimited
Definable	Describable	Experiential
Predictable	Random	Self-existent
Newtonian	Nonlinear Dynamics	Spiritual
Measurable	Identifiable	Observable
Objective	Prevailing Conditions	Subjective
Measurable	Describable	Knowable
Circumscribed	Diffuse	General
Force	Influence	Potentiation (Power)
Time	Calculable	Timeless
Specific Location	Generalized/Intertangled	Nonlocal
Provable	Estimated	Knowable
Selected	Variable	Absolute

In the above illustrations, content is any describable object, statement, fact, idea, or supposedly self-existent "thing," (i.e., form). The "field" is the time, place, and circumstances that prevail. Because the components are knowable, the field can be viewed as proximate or as having a probable effect on the content. The field is thus like the weather or location and therefore may vary and also include intangible factors, such as public opinion, influential prior events, or belief systems, both conscious and unconscious.

Beyond the form of content and the proximate field or conditions, however, is the absolute, overall formless context that is unlimited by even time or dimension, but within which human consciousness operates and functions as a frame of reference from which one can select points of observation. The overall context is the infinite field of consciousness itself, which is unlimited, beyond form, yet capable of registering form as minute as a passing thought. Without the base of consciousness, the mind is incapable of awareness; as a result, no statement of any kind can be made. Therefore, any definition of truth has to include content, a knowable field, and an awareness of ultimate context.

There is a progression of comprehension and the capacity or capability to know truth as one moves from content to field to context. The capacity to know is further dependent on the observer's brain physiology, intention, maturity, and calibrated level of consciousness (described in Chapter 7).

Upon examination, the discernment of truth turns out to be a relatively complex process that operationally, with familiarity, becomes relatively simple and obvious. An understanding of its nature is also intuitive and readily grasped without undue deliberation.

In everyday practice, context is unstated but content is, of course, always stated. The important and most frequent defect is to fail to state or to falsely imply the nature of the proximate field. For example, a current common error is to take a specific social behavior, project it into a different time frame, and then become judgmental about it.

If we examine the concept of causation (cal. level 450), it will be discovered that "cause" is a concept that has no actual existence in reality. It is a superimposition of rationalization to explain and is a supposition. For example, to explain the whereabouts of a speck of dust in a room requires the inclusion of the effects of climate, air movement, humidity, temperature, barometric pressure, location, the house, the lot, the neighborhood, the country, the planet, and onward to include the evolution of the galaxy and the universe itself. Thus, upon examination, the number of contributory, observable "causal" factors is infinite in every instance.

To explain a so-called "event" is even more complex because there are no actual events as such except by arbitrary selection of the "when" an event supposedly starts and the "when" it supposedly ends. Thus, one finds that there are actually no such things as an "event" or a "happening," and that these are arbitrary selections of observation for the sake of convenience that exist in the mind of the observer and not in some external reality. A similar tautology is represented by the term "relationship," which is strictly an arbitrary mentation, a concept (*res interna*) projected onto arbitrarily selected points of observation, which may or may not be stated as being included in the referenced field.

As can be seen, the meaning of content requires inclusion of both the proximate field and the context. Therefore, truth is a product of observation of all three, plus an awareness of the capacity and the qualities of the observer.

An unobserved "event" is devoid of meaning, which is a super-imposed mentation; therefore, the consciousness of the observer becomes a variable because it is subject to the limitations of each calibratable level of consciousness. Perception is edited observation in contrast to the terms "vision," "realization," and "aware-ness," which refer to meaning and comprehension and therefore to a greater expanse of observation that includes not only the field but also the context. Context is inclusive rather than exclusive, and "proximate field" places the observed presumed event or lin-ear designation within a time frame. (An example is both the time-independent and time-dependent equations of the Schrödinger equations in quantum mechanics). Eventually, supposed "events" or "things" are seen as transitory, evolutionary epiphenomena of observation without any independent existence.

Often statements are made that include unstated presumptions or conditions, such as implied intentionality (i.e., teleological reasoning). Because a statement of all contributing factors is operationally impossible (there are always more that could be added), the mind transcends the linear and pragmatically ab-stracts essence. Thus, effective communication includes aware-ness of the integrity, consciousness level, and subjectivity of the observer as well as that of the listener (Aristotle's *logos, ethos,* and *pathos*). All seeming knowledge is therefore tentative at best and operationally pragmatic or plausible rather than provable. As the level of consciousness advances, the awareness of the observer rapidly ascertains essence and intention as well as the proximate field and simultaneously places it in the overall context.

The consciousness level of our own society is progressively increasing as evidenced by the recent frequent inclusion of the term "perceived," which indicates an awareness of the possible bias of the observer. Thus, the news declares that the "perceived attacker" was such-and-such, or the "perceived event" was seen by the witness in the following way. (In legal proceedings, witnesses misidentify suspects and misinterpret events up to forty-nine percent of the time. Many such errors have been revealed by DNA testing.)

Truth is not only a product of content and context, but it is also critically related to a specific level of consciousness to the degree that what is true at one level of consciousness is seen as untrue at another. This is starkly obvious in the relationship to social mores, international diplomacy, religious conflicts, and contentious political positionalities.

Content by itself is already a product of an infinite number of variables as is the proximate field, which is a product of a great number of factors. For an "event" to be reported, an observer has already edited and made a selection that is the result of intention-alities and unstated positionalities in that there is the unstated intention of a specific effect on the listener. Few observers are capable of clarity or a purity of intention, much less dedication to truth. The intention can often be intuited from the tone and timing of the presentation in which the passions of the messenger completely outweigh or even overturn the message. Thus, the emotionality of the observer as well as the proximate climate require careful consideration. Purity of intention or devotion to truth is not expected of public figures, who routinely distort facts and truth in order to win and persuade. For the seeker of truth, however, the surrendering of attachments to positionalities is a necessary requirement and therefore a primary challenge.

The progress of consciousness is facilitated by an awareness of the evolutionary nature of the ego and its structure. The most common error that deters the development of both individuals and society is to create a positionality that demonizes the ego, and then compound the error by trying to dissolve the ego by attacking it with guilt, shame, and negative self-judgments. The ego is already tenacious, and moralistically attacking it merely gives it more energy. More importantly, one can see that by understanding the evolution of the ego over a great expanse of time, it is relatively intrinsically innocent and merely programmed to be what it is, based on the necessities of animal survival.

It is also well to remember that the human psyche is like the hardware of a computer, which innocently accepts any software with which it has been programmed. This was stated by Socrates as "all wrong-doing is involuntary for man always chooses what he believes to be for his good." He is merely mistaken in what is really the source of goodness and happiness and thus mistakenly chooses externals (illusions) instead of Truth. Instead of vilifying the ego and indulging in guilt, shame, and self-hatred, it is far more productive to accept it for what it is, appreciate its historic value, and adopt it as one would a naïve pet.

We can accept that the ego is, "of course," desirous of gain, advantage, greed, etc. By simply expecting it to be as it is, its nature can be accepted and then transcended. The ego just does what it has been trained to do over the millennia, and it still thinks that its survival depends on adherence to and the practice of its programs that, because of evolution, have now become the antithesis of the intentions of the ethical person of today or of the serious spiritual seeker.

In approaching the ego, it is well to remember that it feeds off of and is seduced by the energy of the negativity of pain, suffering, hate, and guilt to which it gets attached (addicted). It secretly nurtures the "juice" it gets from being the martyr or the victim, and it loves hatred, being "right," and revenge. The consciousness level of the ego is based on the utilization of the qualities of force, whether they are emotional, intellectual, or physical. The undoing of the ego, consequently, is not by the utilization of moralistic or emotional counterforce but by use of the power of truth itself.

Force, by its nature, triggers counterforce, and every ego position has its opposite. Thus, the use of even a single spiritual concept, such as the willingness to be forgiving, can undo even long-standing egoistic positions. We see this in the example of the veterans on both sides of World War II having long ago forgiven their former enemies, despite the widespread death and destruction they witnessed. This demonstrates that even the most severe circumstances and experiences can be healed. The mechanism that allows this healing to operate is the willingness to surrender judgmentalism for peace, and hatred for love.

While the mind secretly believes that its survival is due to the ego, on the contrary, the person's survival is due to the spirit that energizes the ego to accomplish important tasks. It is because of the intention of the spirit that the lower self or ego even remembers to take its vitamins. In truth, we exist and survive, not because of the ego, but in spite of it.

Consciousness research reveals some other decisive factors that can contribute to peace of mind. There is already a calibratable level of consciousness at the time of one's birth, and at the same time of birth, the exact time of bodily death is already preset. Although the time of bodily death is already set at birth, the means is not predetermined. (The above has repeatedly calibrated as true during lecture demonstrations.) The other good news is that due to the relationship of content to context, it is impossible to experience one's own physical death because the very means of experiencing instantly leaves the body, which is no longer viewed as "me" but as an "it" (calibrates as "true"). This actuality is confirmed by the experience of those who have had out-of-body or near-death experiences in which the spirit, the sense of "I" or one's identity, departs the physicality. The sense of self-identity, of "me," or of "I" transcends physicality, temporality, and all conditions. This is because the real "I" is context and not content. People who have investigated past lifetimes through hypnotic regression report that no matter what story they find themselves in, it is always the same identical sense of "I" that prevails under all conditions.

Persons who transcend consciousness level 600 in their spiritual evolution, where there is no longer identification with either the mind or the body as one's identity, recall past lifetimes with clarity. Again, no matter what kind of body or circumstance prevailed at the time, the identical sense of "me" or "I" was present as it is now. In each past-life recall, there seems to be the purpose of a significant spiritual lesson, and the different conditions merely specify a role most suitable for that learning objective. This discovery would be in line with the premise that consciousness evolves over great expanses of time, and that evolution is an innate quality of consciousness itself.

CHAPTER 6
Manifestation Versus Causality:
Creation Versus Evolution

The consciousness level of humans relatively rarely reaches calibrated level 500 (only 4% of the population), much less the level of Unconditional Love at level 540 (0.4% of the population). Many of history's greatest scientific geniuses (Newton, Freud, and Einstein), rather peculiarly, calibrated at exactly 499. Thus, the 400s (America currently calibrates at 421) represent the great productivity and benefits of science, technology, engineering, and medicine. To the spiritual seeker, the 400s represent the level of spiritual education, but subsequently, the mind, reason, and intellect become the roadblocks to transcending the ego in order to reach the important paradigm shift that occurs at calibrated level 500. The difficulty with the consciousness levels of the 400s is that they are the levels at which the mind is dualistic, and its innate structure thus prevents it from moving from perception and mentation to their replacement by the vision and critical recontextualizing subjectivity of the 500s.

The core of the dualistic mind and its intellect is the essential notion of the Newtonian paradigm of causality (cal. 450). While that notion is serviceable within that paradigm and its traditional Newtonian science, it obscures the comprehension of reality that is only possible from a nondualistic viewpoint. The understanding of the relationship of content to context provides the basis for a more advanced, nondualistic comprehension by which to explain observations, human behaviors, and perceived occurrences. The dualistic proclivity of the mind prevents the realization of the Oneness of Reality or the occurrence of Self-realization because the dualistic belief system as represented in language presumes a

53

"this" causing a "that." It therefore simultaneously and automatically also views the self as being a separate (and moralistically judged) "doer of deeds." This dualistic system of mentation reinforces the ego's positionalities that, in turn, produce the perceptual "illusion of the opposites" that stands at the gateway to enlightenment.

As was described in *Power vs. Force* (Hawkins, 1995), perception sees sequence and imputes a hypothetical principle to explain the perceived epiphenomenon based on the principles of form. It takes a leap of consciousness to realize that causality is strictly a mentalization and a concept that is a product of thinkingness, but which is neither innate nor has existence in nature. Sequence itself is a mental concept that refers to the perception of selective observation. Like time, sequence is a property of the observer and not the observed; thus, sequence is not "cause." This is recognized by the classical fallacy of "post hoc ergo propter hoc," i.e., because an event is observed to follow another, it was therefore "caused" by the earlier event. The dualistic mind sees what appears to be an "event," a happening, or a "thing" and hypothesizes another concept, that of "change." The mind seeks explanations and is naïve as to its own structure, motivations, and limitations. In language, it is said that the "I" or an "it" caused a "that," much like that which is intrinsic to sentence structure in which a subject acts on an object via a verb.

The self then presumes that there is an inner primary causal agent, e.g., the "doer" of deeds, the "thinker" of thoughts, the "decider" of decisions, etc. Without such a dualistic explanation, the linear mind is at a loss to explain the appearance of phenomena.

The downside of seeing one's self (ego) as primary to action is that, although it seems to earn credit for success, it is then to blame for failure and thus is prone to anger, guilt, jealousy, hate, revenge, etc. The dualistic ego is competitive and also fearful, and by virtue of imagination, fears multiply and create a constant, subtle, continuous background of anxiety ("existential angst") and proneness to paranoid misinterpretation.

If presumed "events" are not the consequences of causality, then how do they come about and what explanation could possibly surpass the attractive simplicity of the premise of causality? In Reality, from a nondualistic viewpoint, it can be both observed and experienced that everything is actually occurring spontaneously as the field effect of the automatic consequence of the manifesting of potentiality into actuality. Unseen is the underlying power of the infinite context of Consciousness/Reality/Divinity and its effect on content. The nonlinear, infinite field of power is equally present within, without, and beyond. Potentiality becomes actuality when conditions permit or are favorable. The process is empowered by intention as well as by the innate impersonal quality of consciousness itself.

All that exists does so within an infinite field of infinite power that alone has the capacity to bring forth the potential into the domain of the actual, called "existence" (calibrates at 1,000). When conditions are favorable, including intentionality, the potential within the seed emerges as the flower, but nothing is forcing or causing it to do so. Manifestation is the consequence of the power of the infinite field of consciousness. It is not innate to the content of the field. By virtue of the quality and power of the infinite context, traditionally called Reality, manifestation occurs, which is knowable directly by observation and subjectively as the very matrix and substrate of subjectivity and the capacity of awareness and experiencing. Even the sense of a personal agent or self as "I" or "me" is also a product of the overall field. It is not separate from the field but merely part of it.

The infinite contextual field of power could be likened operationally to a giant electromagnetic field through which all content within that field becomes automatically aligned, comparable to iron filings in a magnetic field. Movement or position within the field is not "caused" by the iron filings or "caused" by the power of the field. All occurs spontaneously within the field as a consequence of their own innate, intrinsic properties and not by virtue of some external condition. Potentiality becomes actuality by virtue of the power of the infinite overall field when conditions permit, but conditions of the proximate field are not "cause" (the most common error).

This same principle applies to the content of mind in which examination reveals that thinkingness itself, including even the intention to be "deliberate," occurs spontaneously. Each thought actually arises out of nothingness, or the blank field of silent mind, and is not, as presumed, caused by a preceding thought. It is presumed that there is a purpose or intention that would be a supposed cause. However, such intention or implied purpose arises spontaneously as does each desire, emotion, or impulse. The truth of this observation can be verified by anyone in focused meditation. In the observable world, there is also no permanency as such because everything is in the process of an ongoing, continuous, evolutionary creation.

Consciousness research also confirms that approximately ninety-nine percent of the "mind" is silent and only one percent is actually processing images. The observer self is actually hypnotized by that one percent of activity and identifies with it as "me." It is oblivious to the silent ninety-nine percent of the field because it is invisibly formless. (This is reminiscent of the fact that ninety-six percent of the universe is also invisible as so-called "dark" [unseen] matter and energy.)

"Events" emerge as a consequence of the inner qualities of content and field, and the explanatory principle of one-to-one linear causation that dominates our current society is an insufficient explanation for events. As an example, the accident involving the insulation of the space shuttle led initially to a search for a singular cause or a responsible individual, but none was found. Then, with a brilliant jump of consciousness, the researchers deduced that the event was the impersonal consequence of the "climate" of NASA at the time (*The International Herald Tribune* headline, August 27, 2003). Similar insights have emerged in the world of business in which success is understood to be a product of a culture and its values (Davis, 2003). A similar awareness has emerged from the investigation of the failures of government intelligence operations prior to the catastrophe of 9/11, which was the consequence of the policies and climate that ensued from the collective effect of the Church/Pike Committee hearings, subsequent administration policies, the implementation of the Torricelli principle (all of which calibrate below 200), withdrawal of funding for the intelligence agencies, prioritization, etc. (Intelligence operations are determined solely by Congress, not by the President.)

Any seeming "event" is a selected observation that arbitrarily encompasses an artificial partialization of the whole, and the selection may be based on time, place, or even just newsworthiness. Seeming occurrences, happenings, or events are merely selective, transitory appearances to observation that come about spontaneously as a consequence of the nature of the overall field (context) and its consequences to content. An illustration that is easy to see is that of the appearance of a cloud in the sky, which represents a condensation of an accumulation when specific circumstances, such as humidity, temperature, barometric pressure, or wind speed reach a critical point. The cloud seems to appear out of nothing. It is not caused or forced into an appearance but instead represents the condensation of the totality of the field and its content, which has no predetermined form.

If we study the Darwinian Theory of Evolution (cal. level 450), we come upon the same comprehension. The actual process of evolution itself does not occur within or as a consequence of the physical domain, but instead is merely expressed there as a physicality. The evolutionary process occurs invisibly in the infinite field of consciousness itself. Each branch of the evolutionary tree springs forth full-blown. Each branch, as exemplified on the level of the hominids, displays the consequence of a progression of consciousness. Within the physical domain, however, the so-called "missing links" of archeology or zoology are not found to exist. For example, Neanderthal man did not evolve into Homo erectus but instead was completely supplanted by that higher species. That branch, too, was completed at the time of its appearance. Homo erectus did not evolve into Homo sapiens; instead, Homo sapiens came forth already evolved as its own branch. No transitional "missing links" are to be found within the hominids or within the whole animal kingdom. Transitional forms exist only as patterns within consciousness itself, the so-called *morphogenetic fields*, as described by Sheldrake.

The field of consciousness records all events, all history, and all evolutionary patterns. Its "intelligence" accumulates all information, no matter how minute or seemingly singularly individualistic. It is on this level that the collective experience of all life in all its forms accumulates because, within the physical domain, when an individual physically dies, its genetic material dies with it, i.e., what it has "learned" cannot be physically transmitted.

The science of nonlinear dynamics exhibits that, in seemingly random information data, there are hidden organizational energy patterns called "attractors." There are attractor fields within each level of consciousness, including that of the animal kingdom. It is factual that these patterns can be correctly labeled as "animal spirits," which is a long-held awareness of mankind from primitive times and calibrates as true by consciousness research. Thus, each group of animals has its own collective memory, unspoken understandings, and behavior patterns. It is on this level of information that they are integrated. These energy patterns are subject to the influence of even higher energy patterns because each one sequentially becomes the content of a higher context. Thus, within the evolution of the species, there are an innate intelligence, creativity, and an impressive aesthetic quality.

Millions of years ago, primitive marine life "learned" how to produce electricity. Other supposedly nonintelligent life forms learned how to manipulate aerodynamics as well as hydraulics and to maximize the inherent properties of air, land, and sea. A study of biology and the multitudinous life forms of nature reveals an innate ingenuity, the complexity of which would tax a human of very considerable intelligence.

Evolution is thus descriptively the appearance of the unfolding of sequential observations to perception. Creation itself is a continuous, ongoing process with neither a beginning nor an end. With contemplation, it becomes stunningly apparent that evolution and creation are one and the same process. Its source is the infinite power of the unmanifest's becoming manifest as potentiality, with its inherent invisible patterning emerging in the visible physical domain as existence. Throughout the ages, this ultimate source has been universally intuited as well as subjectively experienced as Divinity, which alone has the power to transform the potential into the actual, the Unmanifest (i.e., the Godhead) into the manifest, and nonexistence into existence (e.g., Bohm's enfolded and unfolded universes).

That which manifests and is then said to exist is knowable by virtue of awareness alone, which is that quality of consciousness that allows the knowledge, experience, and awareness that one "exists" or that one "is." To "be" is one thing, but to "know that you are" is another.

If human existence, as well as that of other living things, is not explicable by the limited formula of causality, then, as has been described, mankind did spring forth from the unmanifest to the manifest as an expression. It is an expression, therefore, of the actualization of potential that, of necessity, has a source. The argument of cause, by definition, separates cause from consequence. If mankind were the result of cause, it would not be able to know its own source, which would, by definition, be external, neither innate nor within, and therefore not truly knowable. To know is to be, in contrast to knowing about, which is merely the acquisition of information. Because mankind is an actualization of a potential by its source, that source is ever present and directly knowable as the subjective essence of the Self. The experience of the Presence as Self is transformative and is also identical throughout history, as reported by the sages of widely divergent cultures. The gift of Divinity is the potentiality within man's own consciousness to return via that consciousness to the very source of his existence. With the realization of the Self (the infinite context), the field and the content merge into the reality of the Oneness of the Source itself.

In contrast, in the common field of ordinary mentation, consequent to the belief in duality and its principle of causality, all things are believed to have both a beginning and an end. This conclusion is the automatic byproduct of selective observation and a hypothetical rather than a confirmable reality. The limited mind cannot really comprehend infinity at all except as a definition and a concept. The ultimate source of existence has no cause nor does it have a beginning or an end. The closest appropriate description is conveyed by the terms "foreverness" or "alwaysness." This unique quality is forever present and available as a major subjective quality of the Reality of Enlightenment.

The Reality of the source of existence is outside time and space, which, in itself, is a limiting intellectual concept. All "starts" and "stops" or "beginnings" and endings" impute the condition of temporality. By whatever name it is called, the Infinite Source of All Existence is inclusive of existence but not subject to it. It is not subject to limitation as implied by the concepts of beginning or ending. While these same conclusions can be reached through the study of epistemology and then ontology (the science of being), the actual subjective experience and knowingness of the reality of foreverness is reported equally by sages as well as by people who have had near-death experiences.

As the state of Enlightenment unfolds upon the dissolution of the ego, the timelessness of the Presence as the Allness of Existence is a stunning revelation that initially precipitates awe in the last remnants of the dissolving ego. The Infinite field of the Source of All Existence is a radiant effulgence that shines forth, and its consequences as Creation are forever unified. Creator and Creation are one. It also becomes clear that all such terms as "existence" or "nonexistence" are, in and of themselves, merely intellectual constructs and attempts to convey the ultimate Truth, which is only knowable by the oneness of the identity of the merging of self into the Self. The best the mind can do is "know about," and upon its dissolution, "knowing" is replaced by the identity of being at one with the Source of Existence itself, the radiance of which is revealed in the exclamation "Gloria in Excelsis Deo!"

CHAPTER 7
The Physiology of Truth

The capacity to recognize and comprehend truth is concordant with the levels of consciousness as reflected not only in the evolution of brain anatomy but, more importantly, also by changes in the physiology of the human brain and its prevalent patterns of processing information. These, in turn, depend on underlying, unseen energy fields. In humans, critical and profound changes occur in the brain's physiology and patterns of processing information at consciousness level 200. These can be summarized as follows:

Below Consciousness Level 200

The left brain (in right-handed people) is dominant in information processing (the right brain in left-handed people). Input is directly processed via the relay centers (thalamus) to the emotional/instinctual centers (the amygdale) via a fast track, and only belatedly from the precentral area of the forebrain via a slower track. Thus, emotional response occurs before intelligence and cognition have a chance to modify the response.

Memory of an event is stored in the hippocampus region of the brain as learning and for recall. This left-brain process is akin in function to the animal brain in that it is directed towards personal survival, and thus, in the human, it subserves the ego. From this orientation, "others," including family or tribal (pack) members, are seen primarily as objects or means to personal survival. Also of great importance is that the information supplied by the delayed input of intelligence from the prefrontal cortex is not only slower to reach the response center, but when it does, it has already become subordinated to the previously elicited emotional response (Genova, 2003). Thus, the intellect becomes primarily a tool of animal drives and self-serving goals. Subsequent responses are therefore primitive, survival oriented, and routinely through the fight-or-flight patterns with their neurohormonal consequences, such as the release of cortisone or adrenalin, which, in turn, stress the physiology of the acupuncture and immune systems.

This left-brain, self-centered response system is accompanied by the transitory weakening of the body's musculature and a negative or weak kinesiologic response. The body's energy system, however, quickly recovers and restores the acupuncture balance so that the overall energy system is again poised for the next stimulus response cycle. The stress-reaction patterns were described by Hans Selye (1956, 1974) as follows:

1. Alarm reaction.

2 Stage of resistance.

3. Stage of exhaustion and physiological impairment (catabolic).

Left-brain dominance is also reflected by limited or even nonexistent spiritual awareness since it is programmed for animal survival. The memories of this sequence of events are stored in the brain's region of the hippocampus; thus, later recall will reawaken memory of the sequence as it was contextualized by the ego's primitive survival goals and techniques. Memories are therefore negatively emotionalized and stored, along with fear, anxiety, anger, resentment, or pleasure of gain.

Above Consciousness Level 200

The right brain in right-handed people (the left brain in left-handed people) becomes dominant above consciousness level 200. Input is fast-tracked via the relay center to the prefrontal cortex and hence to the emotional center. (As we shall see later, this occurs even more rapidly through the prefrontal region of the etheric brain.) Perception is therefore modified by intelligence, and the overall meaning of the event is contextualized according to the prevailing level of consciousness. Generally, recall is that of a more benign event than would have been recorded by a strictly left-brain response. With right-brain spiritualized brain processing and physiology, the neurohormonal response is anabolic, which releases endorphins and balances the acupuncture system. There is also the release of oxytocin and vesopressin to the amygdale (emotional center), which relates to maternal instincts, paternal behavior, pair bonding, and social capacity via the "social brain" (Moran, 2004) of mammals.

At the same time, the kinesiologic test response is strong and positive. The propensity to process information via the healthier pathways is influenced by early life training and exposure to classical music, aesthetics, and religious affiliation, all of which affect neuronal patterning and connections (see Chapter 9).

Similar findings have been reported by Professor Roy Mathews of Duke University. In his book, *True Path*, brain research shows that the nondominant brain hemisphere is stimulated by art, nature, music, spirituality, and aesthetics, resulting in increased altruism, inner calm, and higher levels of consciousness. Further research on Tibetan Buddhist monks demonstrated the brain's "neuroplasticity" and changes of physiology as a result of meditation (Begley, 2004).

These major and significant differences can be summarized in chart form as follows:

BRAIN FUNCTION AND PHYSIOLOGY

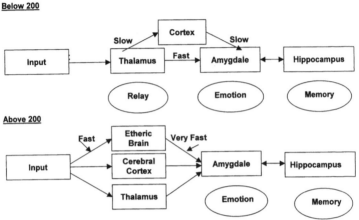

Below 200

Above 200

Below 200	**Above 200**
Left-brain dominance	Right-brain dominance
Linear Non-linear	
Stress – Adrenaline	Peace – Endorphins
Fight or flight	Positive emotion
Alarm – Resistance – Exhaustion	Support thymus
(Selye – Cannon: Fight/Flight)	
↓ Killer cells and immunity	↑ Killer cells
Thymus stress	↑ Immunity
Disrupt acupuncture meridian	Healing
Disease	Balanced acupuncture system
Negative kinesiological response	Positive kinesiological response
↓ Neurotransmitters – Serotonin	
Track to emotions twice as fast as through prefrontal cortex to emotions	Track to emotion slower than from prefrontal and etheric cortexes

Importance:

Spiritual endeavor and intention change the brain function and
the body's physiology and establish a specific area for spiritual
information in the right-brain prefrontal cortex and its concordant
etheric (energy) brain.

While these basic differences in brain physiology that occur above and below the important consciousness level of 200 are decisive, even more significant change occurs at that level because above level 200, a unique energy field emerges for the first time in evolution. It is concordant operationally with the physical right brain but is specific to spiritual awareness and consciousness. For want of better terminology, this specific energy field has been labeled the "etheric brain" to denote that it is purely energetic and not protoplasmic or anatomical in nature. This etheric brain, or spiritual energy body, registers higher energy frequencies to which protoplasm is unable to respond. This is similar to the physical world, where more delicate instruments are required to discern higher-frequency energy fields beyond the capacities of the senses (e.g., the ear cannot hear radio waves themselves nor can the eye see actual television transmission signals, and the computer chip exceeds the response capacity of the old radio vacuum tube).

The reality of an energy body that exists independently of the physical brain has been recognized in all cultures throughout history. Although designated by different terminology, the intuited existence of such a basic reality has been consistent. All cultures have known that the physicality of animals, as well as humans, is energized by a more basic primary energy source that takes over the body at or just prior to birth and then leaves it at the time of physical death (e.g., the "Soul," the "Ka" of ancient Egypt, etc.). This energy body is a product of the evolution of consciousness and not of physical origin. In the animal kingdom, each species has an attractor-field-dominated group energy field—a group consciousness—in which the group memory is stored and is the locus of the process of evolution (i.e., "animal spirits").

In contrast, in the human, the spiritual or etheric body is individual and is again the specific site of the patterns and vibrational field of the evolving levels of consciousness. Below consciousness level 200, the attractor fields of consciousness are primarily of an animal-group nature. Above level 200, the etheric brain emerges as a differentiated area of energy that supersedes the life of the physical body. It is more specialized than is the more general basic form of physical life energy itself.

The etheric brain thus becomes the nonphysical vehicle of an individualized spiritual content (i.e., karma). Below consciousness level 200, the individual is dominated by the collective field of consciousness of that level from which a uniquely personal, spiritualized etheric brain has yet to evolve and only does so by the exercise of free choice, which can take the individual consciousness level above the critical point of 200. To break loose from the dominance of the collective field of consciousness may even require heroic efforts that often entail seemingly drastic decisions of will, such as are occasioned by precipitating circumstances and events. What appears to naïve perception as a cataclysmic event is the very opportunity utilizable by the will to transcend prior barriers because transcendence requires subordination of the goals of the animal ego-self and surrender to a higher principle, e.g., to risk one's life to help others, to choose humility rather than pride, to forgive rather than hate, to accept surrender to a divinity by a decision of the personal will, or to surrender falsehood for truth or gain for selfless service.

The extremes to which circumstances seem to have to go to precipitate such a major change are often rather astonishing. The ego can be fiercely tenacious and drive one even to death's door before it is willing to "let go" (the classic "hitting bottom"), which is widely recognized as a crucial phenomenon. The recognition of the importance of this critical spiritual step has been one of the major contributions of the collective experience of members of recovery groups, such as Alcoholics Anonymous, over the years. The recognition of this phenomenon first appeared in the medical psychiatric literature in its exposition by the psychiatrist Harry Tiebout in his classic papers on "Surrender" (Tiebout, 1949, 1951).

While the surrender of one's will to God is a well-known premise of all true spiritual traditions and teachings, its application outside the fields of religion or spirituality has only recently been recognized in our society as crucial to the resolution of other individual or collective human problems.

The "higher Self" of the spirit has traditionally "taken advantage of" circumstances that seemed catastrophic to the ego. To the spirit, great opportunities present themselves in seeming calamities, such as war, extremes of jeopardy, earthquakes, floods, fire, major family disruptions, or serious health conditions. In these momentous instances, choice has to be made in a split second to follow a spiritual principle or to follow the habitual dictates of the ego. This choice has even been facilitated by certain cultural traditions and ceremonies, such as occur in the military, the act of hari-kari, acts of heroism and unselfishness, sacrifice of one's life for the safety of others, acts of kindness or forgiveness, pardon, admissions of responsibility instead of denial, and breakthroughs of honesty and self-sacrifice for love.

Over time, the form of this evolutionary step has been exhibited by women through the act of childbirth, which had a very high mortality rate. The woman was willing to sacrifice her life and face possible death in the interest of the furtherance of new life. If she survived that ordeal, she traditionally became self-sacrificial for the sake of children, family, or spouse. The pathway of subservience to authority in whatever form was traditional in a given culture became an established pathway to God. The church utilized the same mechanism in its requirement for subordination of the personal will to a higher principle.

In the military tradition, acts of heroism or bravery ultimately resulted in leaps of consciousness as a consequence of the spiritual choice of risking or surrendering one's life to a higher cause, such as duty, obligation to comrades, and the service to one's country. The same principle applied to other seemingly high-risk-taking behaviors, such as dueling or meeting fearsome challenges head on. In today's world we see the same phenomenon, with young men rising to the challenge to sacrifice their lives for their country or a spiritual belief system. Volunteers do not need to be sought for suicidal missions. The eager volunteers of today's world are comparable to the kamikaze pilots of World War II, in which the number of volunteers greatly exceeded the necessary requirement.

The critical transcendence of consciousness level 200 does not, of course, always entail or require such dramatic actions. It more commonly takes place quietly in such forms as the decision to forgive, the acceptance of moral responsibility instead of denial, and a more general surrender of one's will to the will of God, to Love, or to Truth itself.

Another example of this critical transition is demonstrated by so-called conversion experiences that become critical turning points of life. Commonly, medical or other personal crises are the precipitating factors, and many survivors of heart attacks have recounted a similar major change in their overall view of life (Siegel, 1986). In recovery from addictions, the sudden shift from denial and resistance to a "sweetly reasonable" attitude denotes the beginning of successful recovery (Bill W., founder of AA). With the ending of defiance and pride, recovery from many human calamities ensues. This "turnaround" can be sudden or slowly incremental, and the resulting changes can be quite profound and exactly calibratable by consciousness research techniques.

When this critical level of consciousness has been crossed, the energy of life in the brain demonstrates a remarkable change, subsequent to which this spiritualized energy has been given specific recognition because of its unique qualities and properties. Although it has not been recognized specifically in the Western world, in older cultures (e.g., Chinese, Hindu), it has been traditionally termed "kundalini" energy (Krishna, 1971). It is this unique energy that brings about the specific changes in the brain physiology and potentiates the emergence and development of the etheric (energy) brain itself. One profound consequence of the emergence of an etheric brain is its survival of a physical death and the accumulation of karmic patterns. While karmic evolutionary patterns develop below consciousness level 200, they do so in the collective field of consciousness that dominates the levels below 200. They actually do not become individualized as such until the consciousness level reaches 200 (calibrates as "true").

Thus, we observe that at the time of birth, each individual already possesses a calibratable level of consciousness. While the form and functions of the body are presumed to be genetically determined by genes, chromosomes, and DNA, these are just the mechanisms of karmic inheritance. On the spiritual level, the karmic inheritances of the etheric brain are not subject to the linear laws of physicality because they exist in a different domain.

Concordant with the appearance of this spiritual energy is the beginning of a transformation of the sense of self. Spiritual values become more dominant in behavior and decision-making as well as in interpretations of the world and other people. These evolutionary phenomena have long been reported by mankind, and the change of paradigm may be slow and subtle, or fast and quite dramatic. "I see things differently now" is a common saying in all recovery groups. Even sensory experience undergoes subtle changes, and beauty itself becomes more apparent and appreciated. The changes of attitudes and emotions become progressively more benign and compassionate towards all life.

This spiritual energy, or kundalini, as it is often called (Sannella, 1992), eventually is more strongly dominant with the progression of consciousness until, finally, its presence becomes detectable by sensation. By the time consciousness levels reach the 500s, and especially in the high 500s, this energy tends to flow in a generalized way and influences not only subjectivity but perceived experience as well. Life experiences become progressively more benign and fortuitous. What is held in mind tends to present itself almost effortlessly as though by the miraculous. The subjective sensation of this energy field is exquisite and sweetly pleasurable. Characteristically, it is experienced as flowing up the back and the spine into the brain where it can be made to flow into any specific area of the brain by merely focusing attention. At times, the energy flows of its own accord out the front of the body from the heart region by virtue of its own intrinsic nature. The energy flow potentiates healings or transformations in self and others. It is the influential energy field that potentiates the "miraculous" (calibrates as "true"). (Hawkins, 2001).

Another accompaniment to the dominance of this energy field may be the appearance of the so-called *siddhis*, or seemingly extraordinary "paranormal" capabilities or capacities that various cultures have described over the centuries. For example, the phenomenon of psychometry appears with its capacity to discern prior ownership or the history of previous owners of touched objects. The capacity for astral projection, bilocation (e.g., Father Pio), distance viewing, clairvoyance, clairaudience, and telepathic communication may also appear. These phenomena occur spontaneously and automatically and are not the result of, nor are they controllable by personal intention. Information reveals itself effortlessly, full-blown, and finalized, rather than as the result of mentalization. The timing of progressive revelations could also be described as miraculous in their meticulous precision.

The overall appearance of the ongoingness of life changes so that it does not seem to be sequential or caused by anything external. Instead, the world and all events are seen as interconnected, and the unfolding of events is related to potentiality's becoming actuality by virtue of the overall field and not as a consequence of sequential "causes." The witnessing of potentiality's becoming actuality by virtue of the field is not limited to just the physical but also includes the appearance of thoughts and the process of mentation (Hawkins, 2003).

The spiritual energy brings about spontaneous healings of bodily ailments that may well have been chronic and intractable. This phenomenon also occurs to various persons who come within the province of the field in an unpredictable fashion. There appears to be a karmic ripeness associated with these healing phenomena that again occur spontaneously and independently of any volition. The unfolding of life no longer is explicable or comprehensible by mere logic or reason, which are knowably inapplicable and irrelevant to the unfolding of phenomena. With constant surrendering, for instance, even the impaired eyesight of childhood corrects itself, and the previously indistinct, fuzzy world becomes distinct and clear within a sudden, unexpected split second. With the exclusion of bilocation, all the above phenomena were experienced in this lifetime. The abilities last for years, and their content is very accurate. For instance, in an unfamiliar area, one "knows" and "sees" the direction and accurately drives right to it, including even a specific parking space (Hawkins, Video Series 2002).

Concurrent with the spontaneous occurrence of these reported phenomena is the spontaneous unfolding of spiritual understandings. What had previously been obscure and beyond the comprehension of the intellect now becomes obvious as a consequence of its own self-revealing luminescence. As this occurs, wants and desires simultaneously fade away and nothing seems to be lacking or necessary, including even the desire for the continuation of bodily existence itself. The body moves about spontaneously as a consequence of the overall field rather than as a result of some centralized agent or focus of intention formally invested with the identification of "me" or "I."

The period of time during which these phenomena occur is variable but may continue for many years and then slowly disappear or become quiescent. Each progressive period of unfolding seems to reveal a new dimension that has to be surrendered, and the capacity for functioning has to be relearned in order to permit functioning in the world to resume. However, the resumption of functioning may not occur, it may occur very briefly, or it may occur only after periods of years that allow only the possibilities for meditation or contemplation, during which there is no subjective agent, "person," "doer," or "decider" of such actions. The states are self-existent and nonvolitional.

While the experience of the progressive levels of consciousness is profoundly subjective and transformative, it is verifiable, trackable, and identifiable by means of consciousness calibration research techniques (as described elsewhere). For example, interestingly, the physical remains ("relics" or bone fragments) of past enlightened beings still calibrate extremely high. This was verified when a spiritual research group visited a display of the relics of the Buddha that were part of an exhibit traveling around the world. It was sponsored by a Buddhist organization that has been and still is responsible for their preservation. The relics are those of not only the Buddha but also of subsequent great spiritual masters and patriarchs. After all these years, the relics surprisingly still calibrate in the range of the 900s. This phenomenon is also true of the bones of St. Peter, buried under the altar in the Basilica of St. Peter in the Vatican. They also calibrate in the 900s, even after 2,000 years. Thus, the high spiritual energy is a permanent quality and apparently not subject to physical degradation over even great expanses of time.

Throughout history and in all cultures, spiritual phenomena have been consistently reported that are almost identical, despite the fact that the cultures at the time had no communication with each other or even knew of each other's existence. The possibility that suggestion or expectation could be a factor in deriving these results is also disqualified as an argument by the simple demonstration that blind experiments give the same results. This is easily shown by having the tester hold an image or thought in mind without the test subject's being aware of it at all. The same response occurs even if the test subject has no knowledge whatsoever of the content of the statement to be calibrated (Hawkins, video, 1995). The investigative diagnostic system and its techniques are internally consistent, verifiable, and hold true over the entire discernible spectrum of levels of consciousness, from their evolution throughout the animal kingdom to their evolution in human consciousness, from the earliest primitive levels on up through the levels of advanced spiritual awareness.

This display of range and practical confirmation, together with a vast amount of research data, confirms that, on at least the pragmatic level, a science of truth is available, with potentially profound implications as well as benefits for human life and society. Seemingly unrelated data begin to reveal hidden significances and meanings when recontextualized within an overall, all-inclusive nonlinear field that includes not only the observable or objective but also the subjective in order to transcend the limitations of paradigm. By such contextualization, meanings and significances appear that are not possible when data are viewed from a more limited context. The "real" becomes illuminated when recontextualized within the omnipresent field of consciousness. Truth reveals itself by virtue of the omniscience of the field of consciousness, in which omniscience recognizes the reality of Truth and does not give recognition to falsity, which is properly defined not as the opposite of truth but as its absence.

It now becomes obvious why the use of the kinesiologic test is limited to people whose consciousness levels are over 200 and in whom the statement to be verified is integrous rather than subservient to personal or vested interest. That requirement in itself necessitates surrender of the ego to the higher goal of surrendering personal goals to the "highest good" of verifiable spiritual truth.

CHAPTER 8
Fact Versus Fiction:
Reality and Illusion

The comfortably dependable form and function of the world of science and its Newtonian paradigm of reality are the safe haven of modern man. It is reliable and relatively free of conflict, and its unresolved issues are primarily peripheral rather than central (environmental, etc.). Technology is the focus of the society and is engaging as a topic as well as entertaining and tangibly beneficial. However, technology is only the concrete content of thingness and doingness and thus has no intrinsic meaning as such. The human psyche is far too complex and demanding to be completely satisfied with just the products of ingenuity and clever engineering. Therefore, social as well as personal argument, conflict, and discussion engage the populace.

Although the successful resolutions of many ages-old dangers and diseases are very impressive accomplishments, they are not sufficient or significant enough to calm the unrest and disquietude that prevail in current society. It seems that the resolution of human conflict, both social and personal, is only fleeting and soon replaced by yet another conflict. An unresolved central issue pervades all discourse and nags at the edges of society's ongoing dialog. There is a prevailing uncertainty that pervades human life, no matter how seemingly successful it may appear to be. Even that historically much-lauded goal of "success" itself is now seen as the very locus of some possible disaster, conflict, or controversy. In today's society, success brings envy, malice, vilification, attack, or even the bombing of the innocent (Flynn, 2002; Sowell, 2003). So where is that longed-for security and truly safe haven where one can feel secure?

At the bottom, one can see that underneath all the controversy and unease, there is basically one primordial issue, that of the enigma of trust. Who and what is verifiably, reliably, and unreservedly able to be trusted? The great institutions that have historically represented the very foundations of trust have themselves fallen into disrepute. Essentially, everyone senses that the matter rests solely on the discovery and elucidation of Truth itself, without which trust is not only potentially and painfully disillusioning but also actually dangerous and a threat to happiness and survival. Without verifiable truth or trust, peace is merely a fantasy and becomes primarily a political slogan rather than an achievable reality. Peace comes from within. Safety is a social issue that is basically external. One can, in fact, face certain death with equanimity but suffer from severe anxiety, even when one is actually physically safe.

Certainty is the consequence and the fulfillment of the requirements of subjectivity. The quality of "realness" is itself a purely subjective condition. Therein, however, lies the trap of illusion. The central problem of illusion is not that it is unreal or fallacious, but that it seems real, as noted by Socrates twenty-five hundred years ago. Thus, even certainty is a primary illusion that is often clung to out of fear, doubt, or uncertainty (Arehart-Treichal, 2004). On the other hand, with maturity, doubt can be accepted and reconceptualized as being necessary to progress and therefore a useful tool for investigation and growth.

The closed mind is seemingly comfortable because it often only represents a state of maturational arrest. Denial, on the other hand, is only a temporary fix because it is based on a vulnerable premise. The difficulty with a closed mind is that it is innately prideful. Maturity entails the capacity to live with the unanswered and uncertainty and take pleasure from the fact that it is a stimulus to learning and further growth and leads to progressive discovery.

The mature mind knows that it is evolving and that growth and development are satisfying and pleasurable in and of themselves. Maturity implies that one has learned how to be comfortable with uncertainty and has included it as a legitimate ingredient. Uncertainty leads to discovery, whereas skepticism is stultifying.

Operationally, moment-to-moment human life is lived pragmatically, despite unresolved issues whose resolution often depends upon and entails transcendence of paradigm or content. Therefore, performance and satisfaction often depend more on the presumption of internal definition than on impersonal or objective verification.

Discomfort may be internal or intrapsychic, or it may be reactive to the more generalized conflicts of a society that is inclined to be confrontational and in turmoil. Because of identifications, the sense of personalized self very often tends to include some aspects of the social discord in the definitions of self and others, thus mistakenly including societal elements that are extraneous. In severe cases, people internalize social issues and become emotionally imbalanced over external events to the point of extreme behaviors or self-destruction. The seduction of "causes" and victimhood are the pitfall of the unbalanced personality. To be "passionate for a principle" is a sought-for and prideful label to which many become addicted. As can be observed from history, today's cause can become tomorrow's catastrophe, despite the noble labels applied to such endeavors. Externals are attractive because they represent projections of the internal. These lead to the discovery that unbalanced positionalities tend to trigger reactive counterforce, resulting in unforeseen consequences. The differentiation between revolution and evolution is a matter of wisdom rather than a seemingly conflicting duality.

Like social evolution, internal growth and development may be disquieting and tumultuous. The differentiation between fact and fallacy is challenging and requires both integrity and courage. The most important quality necessary for true growth and evolution is the practice and principle of humility. It is far less painful to voluntarily adopt a fundamental attitude of humility than to have it thrust upon oneself as the painful consequence of ineptitude. Humility, despite its negative public and social image in some quarters of society, is indicative of expertise, wisdom, and maturity. Because truth is the very bedrock and ultimate reality upon which humility is based, it is not a vulnerability in and of itself. Humility reveals that the mind can only "know about," and that it cannot differentiate between appearance and essence.

It will be discovered that the only final and completely fulfilling resolution of doubt is the illumination of its very source. Underlying all fear, doubt, and uncertainty is the seeming uncertainty of existence itself. Only the realization of Self as the Reality out of which even existence arises has the power to extinguish all doubt forever.

Faith is a roadway but not a destination, for the term implies an as yet unresolved premise that exists only in the future. In contrast, only the present is truly knowable, and so what is sought by faith in the future exists only in the current moment and in every instant. Without faith and belief, life would not be livable or tolerable; however, on the absolute level, they eventually have to be replaced by the certainty of their final resolution as realization itself. The ultimate resolution is not in time but in the timeless. Truth and Reality are identical and eternally present, merely awaiting discovery.

Spiritual endeavor is the process by which the source of uncertainty is progressively relinquished. In the process of spiritual evolution, safety is provided for periods of time by the guidelines of verifiably reliable pathways. Providing these is the responsibility of the teacher of a body of verifiable truths. Just as the successful mountain climber relies on basic tools, plus a map, a guide, and the experience of others, the seeker of Truth relies on the accumulated wisdom and verifiable reality, which is knowable by the actual process of Realization itself. It is this specific condition of Realization that is the true teacher and the Source of the teachings of the sage.

There is only one identical question underlying all human problems, conflicts, and anxiety, and that is the resolution of what truth is and by what means it is knowable. All roads, however, eventually lead to the same path in which trust, truth, faith, and humility recur as the central themes. Of these qualities, humility is the "open sesame" that, in parallel with fearlessness, accomplishes the seemingly impossible.

Humility is a critical quality because it is based on the recognition and incorporation of the basic truth that, unaided, the human mind is intrinsically incapable of discovering truth. Upon examination, it is readily seen that the mind lacks that capability, primarily because of its own structure and engineering. This discovery may be disappointing at first, but its recognition, along with humility and courage, is a requisite for successful progress. Paradoxically, humility is empowering in that it is relieved of the guilt that accompanies doubt and denial. The pretext of the ego/mind that it is capable of knowing Reality results in an innate pride and defensiveness as well as unconscious guilt. One can witness that the ego tends to go into storms of outrage about being "right" and therefore vilifies disagreement. The ramparts of ignorance are guarded by egocentricity in which the ego reinforces its claim to sovereignty by often vociferous extremes, such as literally slaughtering, killing, or executing one hundred million people (in just recent times). The ego sees Truth as its ultimate enemy. It is the epitome of threat, and therefore, the ego disguisedly hates and despises truth and does all it can to undermine it and discredit its true expressions. This is exemplified in current society by the contentious socio-political positions that represent expressions of consciousness levels 180-190.

In contrast to the innate arrogance of the ego, true intelligence is a quality of consciousness/awareness and is not subject to attack because its essence is nonlinear. It is, however, utilized by the ego in its expression as mind, which then becomes and subserves the ego's drive for survival. Thus, the ego really uses the mind as camouflage and becomes hidden in its clever constructions. This recognition clarifies why its masquerade as religion and the undermining of spiritual truths have been central to its domination of large cultures for extended periods of time (see Chapter 17).

If humility is the admission of limitation, how can it be the very instrument by which truth can be reached? Also, what would replace its sense of self-confidence, as fallacious as it may be, that ensues from the illusion of supposedly "knowing" itself? Humility relies on no externals but is secure within itself by virtue of its own innate truth. It has no content but instead is an attitude and a position of inquiry. It results in one's becoming a scholar and a student of truth who has no pedestals from which to fall, except for the paradox of pride in one's humility, which can in itself become an ego-reinforcing pose (like pretentious piety or pseudohumility).

Experientially, truth reveals itself progressively as the veils fall away. This process may at times result in a temporary feeling or fear of being lost, but then one remembers that being lost does not preclude the possibility of being found (e.g., the promise of the Sermon on the Mount).

Uncertainty is tolerable when accompanied by faith and humility. Each step along the way becomes the subject or a state to be surrendered. The search for Truth is not for the faint-hearted, and it presents recurring challenges along the way.

Although the Heisenberg uncertainty principle presents an open door to the discovery of subjectivity as the royal road to truth, the academic world resists the principle because it adheres to the respectability of "provability," which is limited to the academic Newtonian paradigm. Only facts can be proven. Truth is not subject to proof, as it exists in another paradigm.

In academic science, even after many years, the Heisenberg uncertainty principle is still either ignored or the core of seemingly endless discussions that tend to circle around in the territory of tautologies and disregard the innate structure of mental mechanisms and their innate limitations of paradigm. This results in what science considers the "hard problem" of physics, which is only resolvable by comprehending the nature of consciousness itself.

In the 1990s, this awareness led to international conferences, such as the Conferences on Science and Consciousness in Albuquerque, New Mexico (cal. 410), and at the University of Arizona (cal. 440). There is also a *Journal of Consciousness Studies* (cal. 440), as well as publications addressing science and theology, e.g., *Zygon,* (cal. 415), and *Science and Theology* (cal. 420).

These intellectual approaches calibrate in the mid-400s, thus indicating the restriction of the range of usefulness in that they represent the limitation of the very paradigm that requires transcendence for resolution. These endeavors push the intellect to its limits. One can almost hear it groan under the pressure. The focus of the effort is like looking for lost keys under the lamp-post because the light is better there. The resolution lies in the seeming paradox that the problem can only be resolved by going outside itself to a larger, more inclusive paradigm, which starts at calibration level 500.

Upon examination, it becomes obvious that the secrets of life are revealed not within the linear domain of content but only in the subjective, nonlinear experiential domain. It is one thing to write about the chemical constituents of chocolate, but it is something else altogether to eat chocolate. They are different paradigms. Theology calibrates in the 400s, and although it leads to the study of epistemology and gnosis, they also lead to the same closed door. It takes courage to leave the intellect and its illusory security of certainty. Experiential is describable but not provable or explicable. Einstein, whose work calibrates at 499, represents the very peak of the capacity of the intellect. He turned his back on the Heisenberg principle and reportedly stated that he preferred to believe that there is an objective, self-existent universe (reality) "out there" that is independent of (human) observation. He was, however, seriously religious, as have been the majority of the great geniuses of scientific history.

In contrast to the erudition of academic science and research, the arm of an innocent child has the capability to reveal the truths underneath mankind's greatest enigmas (cal. level 600+). The arm of the child goes strong in the presence of truth and weak in its absence, i.e., falsehood (Hawkins, et al., demonstration video, 1995). That the arm of a naïve child can reveal truths that have defied the greatest thinkers of history is a confrontation to the ego inherent in mind and is a test of humility. It seems, upon superficial observation, to be a challenge to rationality, which itself has become a faith-based religion of science and modern man. Until some better means are discovered, consciousness research techniques have revealed the first concordant, verifiable science of truth that represents and is a product of the evolution of human consciousness.

SECTION II
PRACTICAL APPLICATIONS

CHAPTER 9
Social Structure and Functional Truth

Due to the comprehensive diversity of this chapter, an index of topics is provided:

Introduction	85
Distribution of Levels of Consciousness of Mankind	
Overall World Population 2004	89
Distribution of World Levels of Consciousness (charts)	89-91
Distribution of Levels of Consciousness – Regional Samples	91
Calibrations of Places of Interest	92
Daily Life	94
Energy of Music – Modern	97
Music – Classical	98
Music – Spiritual	98
Classical Music – Performers	98
Classical Music Eras	99
Artists – Creative Works	104
Authentication Process	104
Sports and Hobbies	106
Movies	107
Television	110
The Social Impact of Famous Persons	110
Entertainers/Humorists	111
News Broadcast Media	113
Politics and the Election 2004	115
Diagnostic Scale—Politics and The Election 2004	116
News Commentators and the Political Spectrum	120
News Print Media	121
Others	122

"100 Most Influential People in the World"   122
Literary Works of Authors   124
Industries (United States)   126
Television Commercials   128
Energy Fields of Famous Industrialists   129
Philanthropic Foundations   130
Corporations   131
Unions   133
Law Enforcement   134
Science – Theory   134
    Clinical   137
    Scientists   139
Major Universities and Schools   140

Introduction

In the evolution of human consciousness, limitation presents challenge and the desire for light. The intrinsic creativity of consciousness is expressed in endless, ever-amazing discoveries by which mankind compensates for the restrictions inherent to the design of the human body, the mind, and the environment.

Human society, in its multitudinous expressions, represents the interaction of the physicality of the world and the human body as interpreted by mind and emotion, which in turn reflects the collective expression of the evolution of consciousness.

The capacity to discern truth constitutes the very base and core of the quality of life. The capacity for the awareness and recognition of truth as reality is the irreducible fundamental upon which any society is built, yet society is, experientially and conceptually, a baffling house of mirrors.

In evaluating the progress made by various cultures, we could use several different yardsticks:

1. Calibrate the overall levels of consciousness of various cultures, past and present.

2. Assess visible qualities and products of various cultures (i.e., "by their fruits ye shall know them").

3. Correlate the consciousness level with identifiable core principles of each culture or society and thereby discern which are constructive and which are not.

4. Identify sources of beneficial information versus the sources of fallacy and failure.

5. Differentiate appearance from essence in social expression.

The state of a society is discernible primarily via the operational success of the collective information, which is the product of its collective interpretation of experience. In our present culture, the sheer volume of data is overwhelming. Without very sophisticated processing, its significance, essential meaning, and importance are easily obscured by the absence of, or failure to appreciate, even one very simple piece of evidence. Because of the consequences of seemingly minor error (i.e., the "sensitive dependence on initial conditions" of the science of nonlinear dynamics), the search for verifiable truth often becomes quite intense, as reflected by the focus of the media.

The progress of society seems to hang in a state of perpetual anticipation of the next discovery or elucidation of some previously obscure fact of vital data. Thus, the enticement of the news keeps the world sitting on the edge of the seat of expectancy and witnessing the unfolding of creation as evolution.

From the already presented perspectives of the evolution of consciousness and the physiology of brain function, some appreciation for inherent difficulties that present obstacles to the recognition and elucidation of truth is already apparent. Superimposed on these basic general conditions are the contributing factors that either enable or preclude the capacity for the derivation or recognition of "meaning." Vocabulary itself demonstrates the collective effort to create pragmatic structure and form for information and to organize raw linear data in order to have significant importance and value as well as specificity.

The ongoing progressive evolution of the Worldwide Web and its massive accumulation of information and data is a spectacular recapitulation of the development of the human mind in that it incorporates not only information already accumulated but also continuously develops intricate correlations and the emergence of new definitions and implications of meaning. In so doing, it also reflects silent, unspoken philosophical assumptions and positionalities, as well as schools of semantic and artistic development.

A brilliant insight into the significance of how the mind and society approach and categorize information was presented in an article in *Time* magazine about the development of the Worldwide Web (Grossman, 2003). It described the search engine as a "lens through which we see or fail to see information" and indicated the importance of the fact that "how we search affects what we find" and how and what we know. That result is the consequence of intention is a very interesting recognition and description of the practice of the Heisenberg principle. This in turn affects not only who we are but also what we think we are and, therefore, what we are to become. The critical importance of intention is explored in Wayne Dyer's *The Power of Intention* (Dyer, 2004).

Meaning, language, and society are interactively unified experientially and are further subjected to personalized processing by both the individual and the collective consciousnesses that, by circularity, influence language, description, and meaning as an ongoing developmental process.

In line with this collective intention, consciousness research and a pragmatic calibration system for discerning specific levels of consciousness are not only useful but have the unique benefit of freedom of application. Prior barriers to knowledge can now be transcended, and areas formerly obscured by darkness can be illuminated.

To this end, the technique was applied as a study to broad areas of the human experience, which provided a two-fold benefit. First, it researched the efficacy and capability of consciousness research itself for pragmatic as well as theoretical reasons. Second, it revealed areas of limitation that, when properly recontextualized, can be converted to avenues of progress. Society's seemingly unsolvable enigmas are obstinate because they are merely the surface expression of undiagnosed underlying factors; therefore, use of the technique as a research tool opens the doors to discovery and resolution, and to greater understanding and compassion.

Calibrated figures are solely the result of more than two hundred fifty thousand that have been done since the mid-1970s as research projects by experienced experts. *They are impersonal and do not reflect personal opinion.* The commentary following each section of tables is kept separate from the raw data.

Because the panorama of study is encyclopedic, due to space restrictions, examples are limited for pragmatic reasons. They are primarily illustrative and reveal previously unknown information.

Some data will undoubtedly be at variance with personal or social opinions, which confirms that not only are appearance and essence not identical but also sometimes disturbingly extremely divergent to the point that common human beliefs are often the exact opposite of the underlying truth. Many of the seeming disparities resolve upon reflection and, like a Zen *koan*, turn out to be extremely beneficial and informative. The best attitude is one of devotion to truth rather than being contentious towards falsehood. Open-minded curiosity leads to progressive discovery of information never before available, which may therefore seem confrontational upon first exposure.

It is well to repeat that falsehood is not the opposite of truth but its absence, and that to prefer chocolate, one does not have to hate and vilify vanilla. *Specific calibrations are subject to change with shifts of conditions and people's intentions.* The calibrations presented in the charts were taken from a database of 9,000 calibrations done in late 2003 and throughout 2004. To repeat: *The calibrations represent research data and not personal opinion.*

Derivation of Calibrations

All that exists now or did so in the past gives off multiple energy radiations, a fact utilized by Max Planck in his famous Black Box Radiation experiment from which he derived the famous "Planck constant" of Quantum physics ($h = 6.62606826 \times 10^{-34}$ $J \cdot s$). Deep-sea rays (fish) and sharks detect prey through their muscle-produced electrical fields.

These energy emissions are trackable and calibratable along a whole electromagnetic spectrum, from ions and photons to infrared, ultraviolet, heat, sound, absorptive and reflective capacities of various energies, as well as electrical and other radiation phenomena. In addition to light vibration and absorption (e.g., ordinary photography), or infrared photography, a great many variables can be detected and measured or calibrated at a distance along an arbitrary continuum. The biological energy of life itself is likewise radiated continuously and registers permanently in the nonlinear field of consciousness, which is an invariable context (the Absolute).

All that exists or has ever existed, including even passing thoughts, is automatically imprinted in a readable, timeless dimension. Thus, there are no "secrets" in the universe, and all of life in all its expressions is accountable to the universe. That "every hair on one's head is counted" is an impersonal and scientifically verifiable fact. Access to consciousness calibration is limited by the requirements as denoted in Appendix C. Like temperature or barometric pressure readings, the reported calibration levels are impersonal and merely represent research data devoid of personal opinion.

Distribution of Levels of Consciousness of Mankind

Overall World Population 2004

As noted elsewhere, the overall average consciousness level of mankind evolved very slowly over vast periods of time and was at 90 at the time of the Buddha, 100 at the time of the birth of Jesus Christ, and then evolved slowly to 190, where it stayed over the last millennium until the late 1980s, when it jumped to 205. In November 2003, it moved up to the current level of 207. The distribution in the world shows that approximately seventy-eight percent of the world's population calibrates below 200. (The comparative figure for the United States, however, is forty-nine percent). The innate distribution is displayed as a progression curve, as follows:

Distribution of World Level of Consciousness

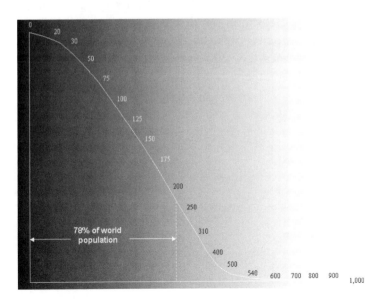

This information can be displayed in the form of a pyramid, which gives a better sense of the mass of humanity.

Distribution of the Levels of Consciousness of Mankind

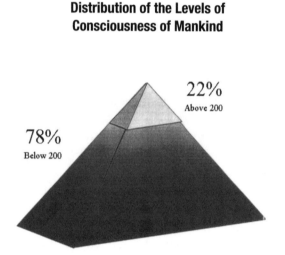

The calibratable levels of consciousness also denote power, which explains why the sheer mass of humanity that calibrates below 200 does not simply self-destruct by its pervasive negativity. In effect, the power of the twenty-two percent that calibrates above consciousness level 200 counterbalances the seventy-eight percent, as seen on the next diagram.

Distribution of the Levels of Consciousness of Mankind

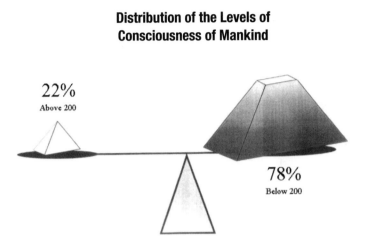

22%
Above 200

78%
Below 200

The levels of consciousness delineate subpopulations that tend to stratify in society, as do corks in the sea where position is a consequence of innate buoyancy, i.e., a field phenomenon rather than due to cause and effect. Movement within the field is a result of intrinsic factors such as choice, the range of which is also innate to the field. Society also represents a stratified range of expectations.

Distribution of Levels of Consciousness – Regional Samples

United States		States		Cities	
Presidency	460	Alabama	350	Chicago	445
Government	440	California	280	Lake Shore Dr	450
People	420	Florida	425	South Side	200
Regions		Iowa	405		
East Coast	360	Massachusetts	305	New York City	385
West Coast	290	No. Dakota	380	Upper E. Side	430
Midwest	440	Ohio	410	West Side	245
Canada		Texas	385	Inner City	135
Banff	410	Wisconsin	415		
Montreal	380	Wyoming	440	Phoenix	425
Ottawa	400	**Mexico**		Washington,	
Toronto	425	Mexico City	305	DC	450
Quebec	380			Hollywood	190

Calibrations of Places of Interest

Airplane	300	Louvre, Modernistic	
Airports	205	Additions to	180
Ambulance	300	Louvre, The (Paris)	500
Autobahn (Germany)	315	Methamphetamine	
Automobile	205	Laboratory	40
Burma Shave Signs	240	Metropolitan Museum of	
Bus, Taxi	205	Art (NYC)	505
Channel (English		Mines	105
and French)	380	Motels	220
Circus	305	Nursing Home	201
Clinton Library	450	Olympics	340
Coffee Shops	250	Operating Rooms	395
College Dormitory	250	Orient Express (train)	315
Community Church	402	Parks	350
Cruise Ships	320	Parthenon	305
Department Stores	250	Playgrounds	345
Edinburgh Castle		Plaza Hotel (New York City)	420
(Scotland)	445	Police Stations	265
Eiffel Tower	485	Psychiatric Hospital	355
Empire State Building	425	Psychiatrist's Office	420-506
European Union		Public Library	400
Parliament	345	Rijks Museum (Amsterdam)	535
Factories	195	Rodeo Drive (Beverly Hills)	220
Factory Assembly Line	200	Roman Coliseum	305
Farm, Commercial	210	San Simeon (Calif.)	425
Farm, Family	380	Sidewalk Café in Paris	400
Fast Food Outlets	200	Smithsonian Museum of	
Federal Buildings	200	Native Americans	460
Fort Knox	275	Staten Island Ferry	385
Funeral Home	215	Statue of Liberty	500
Gas Stations	202	Subway (London)	225
Golf Courses	315	Subway (Mexico City)	195
Great Wall of China, The	305	Subway (Moscow)	375
Hermitage, The		Subway (with graffiti)	195
(Russian museum)	505	Subway (Paris)	215
Historic Route 66	225	Supermarkets	220
Hospitals	180	Times Square (New York City)	270
Inner-city		Titanic, The (ship)	310
Neighborhoods	65-80	Trailer Park	205
Interstate Highway	215	Trinity College (Dublin)	455
Limousine	400	Twin Towers (NYC), pre-9/11	205
Lincoln Center (New York		Vatican Library	500
City)	355	Yosemite National Park	435
Lockheed Martin "Skunk Works"	395	Zoo (Bronx, New York)	350

From observation, the low 200s signify dependable, integrous performance, e.g., the bus station, automobiles, and taxis, and reliables such as the post office and the airport. These venues often have the appearance of stripped-down functionality in which the color gray is predominant, along with "no nonsense" gray metal furniture. With the addition of some human intention and personality, calibrations rise with the folksy innovations of historic "Old Route 66" and its Burma Shave signs. As human participation, creativity, and intention increase, the calibrated numbers rise to those of the high 200s, as represented by the police station and Times Square.

With the addition of human expertise and intention, the calibrated numbers rise into the 300s, which are exemplified by the airplane, ambulance, operating room, cruise ship, park, playground, circus, family farm, psychiatric hospital, and even the Olympics. The German autobahn includes stricter as well as more advanced engineering and construction, and despite its lack of a speed limit (traffic routinely moves at 110 miles per hour), the accident rate is lower than that on U. S. federal highways. The difference is also explicable by the fact that German drivers tend to be more skilled, have to be older to get a driver's license, and are better trained. The autobahns have no intersections, low inclines, and deeper roadbeds. They are also better policed, with poor drivers quickly pulled off the road.

The 400s represent the introduction of creativity, aesthetics, and active intellectual pursuit, e.g., the library, the Paris café, Yosemite National Park, the community church, San Simeon (California), and even the Empire State Building, whose construction from start to finish took only one year and was facilitated by the courage and skill of Native American workers (primarily the Mohawks) who had no fear of heights and could successfully walk a steel beam six inches high, six inches wide, and seventy-five stories above the streets of New York City.

The 500s reflect devotion to beauty and reverence for the great artistic creations of mankind. (Rembrandt calibrates at an amazing 700.) For centuries, millions of admirers have waited in line with awe for even a glimpse of such fabled greatness. The calibration levels are beyond those of the Newtonian paradigm with its gray steel desks and predictability, rising to the subjectivity of love, devotion, reverence, and intuiting the source of perfection.

A visit to the Louvre in Paris is treasured by almost everyone. Visitors are surprised that they are allowed to freely take photographs of all the greatest of the world's art treasures. In contrast, in the middle of the former courtyard stands a modernistic structure (cal. 180) that results in an unanticipated aesthetic shock. The design of the anomalous but very functional entrance structure represents the architecture (by E. M. Pei) of modernism. It became the subject of worldwide aesthetic debate, as would be expected from the disparity of a stark structure that calibrates at 180 being located in the courtyard of one of the world's most historic buildings, which calibrates at 500+.

Daily Life

Abortion Pill (RU 486)	200	Food, Blessed Homemade	215
Alta Vista	208	Food, Blessed Machine-	
Animal Body	200	made	207
Arm & Hammer Baking		Food, Commercial Cat	192-202
Soda (product)	320	Food, Commercial	207
Aunt Jemima's Flour (product)	350	Food, Commercial	
Barbie Doll	205	Machine-made	188-200
Biofeedback	202	Food, Homemade	209+
Body Piercing	180	Fortune Cookie Messages	345
Campbell's Soup (product)	325	Google.com	209
Cloning (Animal)	200	Hatha Yoga	260
Cloning (Human)	180	High Fashion	295
Coca-Cola (beverage)	305	Hope Diamond, The	205
Contraception	205	Human Body	205
Cookies Made for Family	520	Internet System (not content)	205
Cryonics	200	Little Red Hen (story)	295
Donald Duck (cartoon)	205	Mad Cow Disease	50
Earth (planet)	200	Medical Marijuana	235
Emergency Medical Technicians	290	Mickey Mouse	205
Environmentalism	260	Money	205
Euthanasia	200	Mother Making Christmas	
Feminism	320	Fudge and Cookies	520
Food	200	Multilateralism	200

Murphy's Law	280	Sidewalk Vendors	205
Paparazzi	180	Street Beggar	160
Pepsi (beverage)	305	Street Performer Group	480
Peter Principle, The	260	Thanksgiving Day	515
Political Cartoonists	190	Tea, Green	300
Polygamy	145	Uncle Ben's Rice (product)	315
Position of Children in the U.S.	405	Vegetarianism	205
Position of Men in U.S.	425	Vick's (product)	345
Position of Women in		Willow Trees	245
the U.S.	405	Window Washers (high)	290
Quaker Oats	305	Worldwide Web Content	50-445
Quilting	345	Yahoo.com	206
Roadside Farm Stands	355	Yard Work	250
Rodeo	255	Yogi Bear	205
Santa Claus	390	Zero-temperature weather	205
Sex	250		

Notable is that the Internet system calibrates at a reliable 205-208, including its major search engines. In contrast, the content of the material that appears on the Internet reflects the whole range of human consciousness, calibrating from 50 to 445. It is therefore currently the greatest source of disinformation. Thus, the naïve belief that there "must be some truth for it to appear on the Internet" is apparently quite fallacious and often damaging in its consequences. Calibration reveals that approximately fifty percent of the information provided on the Internet is at less than 200, which, interestingly, is almost exactly the same figure represented by the consciousness calibration of the current American population (forty-nine percent below 200 and fifty-one percent above 200).

The privacy and anonymity of the Internet provide a means of expression for those people rejected by society as being imbalanced and having special personal problems, e.g., political extremism and socially rejected sexual proclivities, as well as irrationality and elaborate paranoid delusional systems. The Internet is the great playground for the "me" generation, as reflected by website names themselves, e.g., "Bill's Turn," "My Place," etc. These often reflect the dictum that an opinion is a routine idea inflated by the ego in order to sound profound and important.

Sixty-seven percent of "blogger" websites calibrate below 200 and primarily represent outlets for expression of negative emotions, resentments, and frustrated personality problems

The supposed satire of political cartoonists is actually a sly form of vilification as indicated by its calibration level of 190. Some even seem deliberately malicious, with obvious intention to hurt or damage a hated target.

Money calibrates as neutral, and sex is at 250. Both apparently are intrinsically neutral but the intentions to which they are put make the difference. It is interesting that animal cloning is at 200, whereas human cloning is at 180.

A rather significant finding is the calibrated difference between blessed and unblessed food. Machine-made bread from a local supermarket calibrates at 188, but when blessed, it goes up over 200. Bread from the same supermarket but from the bakery department calibrates initially at 203, and again shows a rise if it is blessed. If food is homemade, it arises from its original 200 to 209, and if blessed, it rises up to 215. This is a unique demonstration analogous to the Heisenberg principle in that the introduction of human spiritual consciousness and intention alter the field. It also gives evidence that prayer itself is more than just wishful thinking.

Some brand names reflect affection (e.g., Jell-O, Route 66, Campbell's Soup) and become imbued with cultural American mystique. They represent trust in the intention of a whole industry, which is expressed as brand loyalty.

Of interest are the calibrations of the fortunes enclosed in fortune cookies that, at 345, are frankly above the principles upon which large sections of the populace base their lives. For example, "One kindly word can change your whole life" contains really profound wisdom. (A fortune-cookie life is a good life.)

The positions of women and children in the United States, at level 405, are in stark contrast to their positions in repressive countries (such as Islamic and others), where they calibrate at 140, indicating a rather severe cultural lag in which the populace and their governmental leaders also calibrate quite low. Although the gap is closing from what it was in the 1930s, there is still a 20-point disparity in the United States between the level of men and that of women and children. Social change takes time, and apparently the "glass ceiling" is now quickly disappearing as revealed by the fact that corporations led by female CEOs in 2003 exceeded the earnings of corporations led by male CEOs (*Fortune*, January 2004).

Historically, in a primitive or agrarian culture, the physical strength of men is necessary as is testosterone-led aggressiveness, and thus males tend to dominate. As civilization progresses, however, and valued skills become less physical and more mental or creative, the social ranks of the sexes approach equality. The word "primitive" implies predominance of persistent animal patterns of behavior where "biology is fate." In the modern world, the evolution of consciousness plus education and the intellect are the decisive factors.

Energy of Music – Modern
Music (not personality) of:

Anderson, Marian	510	Gangster Rap, Punk Rock,	
Armstrong, Louis	590	Heavy Metal, Gothic,	
Beatles, The	460	Violent-Antisocial	
Beach Boys, The	400	Groups	35-95
Bee Gees	510	Garland, Judy	405
Berlin, Irving	415	Gass, Robert ("Kyrie")	705
Bocelli, Andrea	550	Harrison, George	540
Caruso, Enrico	560	Hip Hop	270
Cash, Johnny	504	Iglesias, Julio	400
Charles, Ray	485	Jones, Spike	350
Cole, Nat King	470	Joplin, Janis	495
Country Western	255	Lane, Christy	500
Crosby, Bing	485	Liberace	365
Disco	235	Mamas and the Papas, The	495
Dorsey, Tommy	450	Manilow, Barry	505
Dylan, Bob	500	Pop Rock	205
Ellington, Duke	450	Presley, Elvis	420
Elliott, Cass	505	Riverdance	500
Fitzgerald, Ella	465	Rolling Stones	340
		Santana	515
		Welk, Lawrence	475

Music – Classical

Bach, J. S.	530	Kabalefsky, D.	480
Bagpipes (Black Watch)	505	Leoncavello, R.	475
Barber, S.	480	Lizst, F.	490
Bartók, B.	475	Mendelssohn, F.	480
Beethoven, L	510	Mozart, A.	540
Berlioz, H.	480	Mussorgsky, M.	485
Bizet, G.	425	Offenbach, J.	480
Brahms, J.	495	Pachebel, J. ("Canon")	690
Cherubini, M.	485	Paganini, N.	515
Christmas Carols	550	Puccini, G.	550
Chopin, F.	500	Rachmaninoff, S.	490
Classical Ballet	525	Ravel, M.	475
Copeland, A.	465	Rossini, G.	490
Debussy, C.	485	Schubert, F.	460
Dvorák, A.	490	Shostakovich, D.	480
Glinka, M.	480	Sibelius, J.	485
Gluck, C.	475	Smetana, B.	470
Gounod, C.	420	Stravinsky, I.	465
Grand Opera	525	Strauss, R.	475
Grieg, E.	490	Tschaikowski, P.	550
Handel, G.	510	Vangelis	485
Hayden, F.	490	Weber, C. M. von	485
Humperdinck, E.	490	Wagner, R.	500

Spiritual Music

Ave Maria	575	Amazing Grace	575
Silent Night	575	U. S. Navy Hymn	575
Joy to The World	575		

Classical Music – Performers

Callas, Maria	485	Metropolitan Opera House	465
Caruso, Enrico	500	Pinza, E.	480
Chaliapin, F.	485	San Francisco Opera House	465
Cliburn, V.	480	Tagliavini, F.	485
Heifitz, J	490	Tebaldi, R.	485
La Scala Opera House		Tibbett, L.	490
(Milan)	465	Toscanini, A.	490
Menuhin, Y.	485	Paganini, N.	495

Classical Music Eras
(Starting from most recent [LaFave, 2004])

Eclecticism	460	Romanticism	465
Minimalism	450	Classicism	460
Serialism	450	Rococo	460
Dodecaphony (12-tone)	400	Baroque	470
Neoclassicism	440	Renaissance	470
Impressionism (Debussy)	440	Medieval	470

We see that the effects of compassion, love, and the energy of the heart result in extremely high calibrations, which signify devotion to beauty, both aesthetic and affective. This is also a physiological phenomenon, as demonstrated by the "goose bumps" feeling of an appreciative audience that also frequently weeps with tears of joy. Audiences unabashedly weep at performances of the blind Andrea Bocelli, as they once did at those of Enrico Caruso. The music of George Harrison was openly devotional. Bagpipes, at 505, signify valor rather than just courage and therefore instill consternation in a would-be enemy.

Of interest is the sound of the "keening" of Celtic ballads, such as those heard in the videotape of "Riverdance." The high-soprano solos have a hauntingly beautiful energy that calibrates at 640-650. The Irish bagpipes convey the same "other worldliness." The effect is entrancing and best described as ethereal. The total effect is similar to the state of consciousness that prevails past consciousness level 600. There is sound but it is enshrouded in infinite stillness and timelessness. The sound also awakens a sense of ancient familiarity and a longing to return to a pristine existence of purity, clarity, peace, and beauty.

Military music is in a class by itself and importantly reveals the disparity between appearance and essence. The Edinburgh Castle Military Tattoo (cal. 505) is an annual event that draws many thousands of spectators from all over the world. More than one thousand performers from the world's major countries represent their cultures' most skilled and highly trained military bands and precision drill teams. Their performances are breathtaking, and the huge crowd of spectators becomes silent with respect for the high degree of excellence displayed (e.g., the Swiss drum teams). Then to their surprise, the spectators begin to cry from the upsurge of a deeply stirring emotion (cal. 520) that is the energy of honor, valor, and love for one's human heritage and its representation as family, culture, and fellow man. The male bonding in war is at calibration level 510 (World War II). At the end of the Tattoo, one hundred bagpipes play "Queen of My Heart," which calibrates at 525 and leaves the audience in a state of awed silence at the surprising and unexpected upsurge of deep, profound emotion. It is this hidden human trend that is then exploited by rulers who know how to manipulate this underlying, deep reservoir of intrinsically integrous, dormant energy for political purposes.

The loyalty of the populace to their country and culture is unsophisticated and arises from early childhood, where faith and trust in one's parents are total and as yet unblemished by intellection or external influences. It is the trusting heart of the inner child that is captured by the wily political manipulations of fallacy. This trusting, uncritical naïveté is even more vulnerable to seduction by persuasive political leaders who have religious power or authority. The lambs are led to slaughter by virtue of their innocence, which is simultaneously their weakness and their strength.

This is an inner awareness among former military men who openly weep at reunions, including those with former enemies. Notably, it is always the military themselves who are the first to quickly forgive their former enemies at war's end (Brooke, 2004). This phenomenon, surprisingly, is experienced almost immediately after the last gunshot has been fired. Many men cover up the deep emotion by joining the jubilant celebration, but deep within is an inner knowingness of the depths out of which love and integrity arise, the core meaning of what *Valhalla* really signifies. It is not about war at all, but it took war to bring it to the surface. The mutual respect for honorable valor is demonstrated by the military career of the famous "Red Baron" of World War I, Manfred von Richthofen (cal. 385). As the leading "ace of aces" pilot for the Luftwaffe, he won eighty air combats and shot down fifty-two British planes but was finally killed in combat. He was so respected that the Allies (Australia Flying Corps) gave him a full military funeral. The greatness of the "Great Generation" of World War II was of the heart, not just the result of winning, for the winning was just the consequence of the power of the inner heart itself.

The naïveté of the heart is exploited by propaganda that appeals to serve the "Fatherland" or the "Motherland." Trustingly, the followers give allegiance to "the Great Leader" and fall into childlike obedience. Like lemmings, they follow the megalomaniac Pied Piper over the cliff. Thus, naïveté can and does lead to devastation. The only possible protection is to know the real truth via calibrated levels of consciousness/truth of leaders or teachers. False spiritual leaders and "gurus" present the same pitfalls to ensnare the unwary.

The energy of classical music has a very positive impact on later behaviors and learning capacity, and increases the level of consciousness. It results in more advanced development of neuronal connections and patterning. Interestingly, it also results in higher mathematical capability and the transitioning from lower to higher mind (see Chapter 14). The exposure to classical music in childhood and early life results in attraction to peace, truth, and beauty, and aversion to violence, falsity, and gross vulgarity. The sensitivity to aesthetics provides a natural crossover network that also facilitates the emergence of spiritual awareness and non-ego awareness.

Clinically, the benefits of early life exposure to the classical arts are confirmed by a seventy-five-percent lower rate of crime. If that is also combined with a religious upbringing, the later-life incidences of crime drop by ninety percent. (If playing chess is added, the rate drops another one percent.)

Rock-and-roll, hip-hop, and disco, as well as country-western music, have a broad appeal in which the rhythm itself carries an unseen energy in response to which people feel glad to be alive, and the dancing is a collective celebration. It is interesting to look at the difference in the consciousness level of the Beatles' music and that of the Rolling Stones, "the greatest rock-and-roll band that ever lived." In the performance of the Beatles, we see dedication to music as a creative art. Eventually, the group disbanded due to the individuality of its members, each following their own muse. In contrast, the Rolling Stones group has continued to perform for more than thirty years, held together by a group commitment similar to that of a team. While the creativity of the Beatles was primarily guided by the expression of inner musical inspiration, the Stones are highly participatory and interact intuitively with the emotionality of the audience, which is pulled into the performance rather than just remaining as spectators.

At lower calibration levels, music becomes predominately sensationalistic and celebrates the lowest elements of humanity by glamorizing rape, criminality, violence, death by hollow-point bullets, and other extremes and excesses of brutality. As was described in *Power vs. Force*, it is the energy of the music itself, even without the lyrics, that negatively affects the body's acupuncture system and makes it go weak. This was originally discovered by Dr. John Diamond, who published the information in the late 1970s (Diamond, 1979).

The lower calibration levels show that violence and sexuality are heavily exploited ("sex sells"), and an allure is cast over unrestricted hedonism. This message goes out via the media to impact impressionable adolescents who are easily captivated by the energy of "glamour" itself. This unique energy was first described in one of Alice Bailey's books (*Glamour*, 1950). It is an energy that is projected externally and imbues its object with exaggerated desirability that quickly fades because it is not a quality of the admired object but an ego projection from the observer. The public does the same thing with the images of the megalomaniacal dictators who, when stripped of their trappings, appear pathetic and forlorn and ultimately choose suicide to prevent exposure of the illusion.

The behavioral consequences of such low-energy programming in adolescents desensitizes and blunts sensitivity, resulting in behaviors for which the parents are blamed, whereas the source of the negative influence actually stems from the media and the culture of peer groups. The seriousness of this deleterious effect was brought to public attention by CORE (Congress of Racial Equality), which created the "five worst" list (group calibration 80) of negative "gangster rap" entertainers (CNN News, 3/8/04). In defense, the rappers state that they are climbing out of poverty and demonstrating the benefits of free enterprise, i.e., they are a stepping stone out of squalor, hopelessness, and poverty, after which they become entrepreneurs and hopefully merge into more integrous business enterprises.

Adolescents respond primarily to the pressures of peers and the media and give lip service to parents. This disrespect for parents is aided and abetted by current social, educational, and political forces that derive a sense of power from disclaiming the authenticity of all authority. The error is based on the misperception of integrous, true authority as nonauthentic authoritarianism, i.e., the "postmodern" rejection of logic, intelligence, rationality, and ethics.

Thus, today's adolescent is barraged with nonintegrous programming and seduction by the media and peers (Guthrie, 2004). At the same time, the protections of traditional standards of ethics and morality are under vociferous attack. The difficulty is that free speech, in and of itself, is actually neutral and, like money, it is the use to which it is put that ascertains whether it is beneficial or harmful. The downside is somewhat analogous to giving guns to children who have had no training in safety, much less morality or ethics.

A society that rejects morality becomes dominated by sensationalism, glamour, and expediency. It finds that the downside of its youth is difficult to salvage because it lacks the strength of the convictions of ethical certainty in times of decisional crises. The consciousness field of this subculture is like an engine without a governor or a flywheel. Interestingly, shopping malls have discovered that playing classical music in the parking lot repels adolescents, who then quit "hanging out" in them.

Artists – Creative Works

Cézanne	510	Parrish	495
Dali, Salvador	455	Picasso	365
Degas	540	*Pieta,* The	590
de Kooning	465	Political Protest Art	180
Da Vinci, Leonardo	565	Pollock	425
Graffiti	140	Pornography	105
Holbein	465	Rembrandt	700
Lautrec, Toulouse	450	Rockwell	500
Matisse	525	Ruberg	510
Michelangelo	590	Surrealism	385
Miro	490	Van Gogh	480
Mona Lisa, The	499	Vermeer	515
Munch, Edvard	495	Warhol	200

For lack of space, the list is limited, and there are many more in the database. Art, like any other form of communication, reflects the intention as well as the vision or genius of its creator, some of whom become celebrated.

Of great value to artwork is the discovery that consciousness research techniques can instantly detect forgery. This was demonstrated in the 1995 videotape where a fake Picasso made the test subject's arm go weak (Hawkins, Videotape #1). This is important to art gallery owners as well as art collectors who are the target of forgers.

Authentication Process (Cal. 600)

The testing technique to verify authenticity of art, antiques, relics, historical documents, archeological specimens, or any other objects is simply to make a series of statements and utilize the simple arm-strength response. The item does not have to be actually present but merely silently held in mind or visualized by the tester, e.g., "The painting I am holding in mind is authentic." Then quickly press down with two fingers on the test subject's wrist. To validate, additional questions can follow, e.g., "The painting is an original Vermeer." (Yes or not-yes response.) "It is over 100 years old." (Yes or not yes.) "It calibrates over 400." (Yes.) "Over 450." (Yes.) "Over 500." (Yes.) "Over 505." (Yes.) "Over 510." (Yes.) "At 515." (Yes.) "Over 515." (No.)

This can be followed by statements about the details, history, location, etc., to trace the item's pedigree, age of the canvas, age of the paint, integrity of the artist, and other facts. These statements can be made verbally, silently, or imaged. Inasmuch as great works of art sell for millions of dollars, and even experts are sometimes puzzled or disagree about their authenticity, the verification process is obviously of great value and easily detects forgeries in less than a minute.

While an explanation of the verification technique appears detailed or even laborious or time consuming, in practice, it is very simple and actually only takes a matter of seconds to perform. It is also obvious that the same technique instantly detects whether a witness or public figure is telling the truth, or whether a product advertised on television will do what is claimed. It will be discovered that often the statements of a public figure are actually one-hundred-percent lies.

When the above process is applied to the daily news, the results are quite astonishing and can be initially somewhat dismaying regarding famous crimes, trials, and worldly affairs where deception prevails. In contrast, it can be gratifying to discover that accusations are frequently false, and justice often does prevail.

For accurate results, it is necessary that both persons doing the test procedure are integrous, and the intention of the questions is devoted to the discernment of truth for its own sake and not biased in trying to prove a point or obtain supportive evidence of a personal viewpoint. In practice, "checking out the truth" of various aspects of life and truth leads to progressive wisdom and compassion. A sense of humor also helps.

Sports and Hobbies

Aikido	260	National Basketball Assn.	
Auto Racing	200	Finals	455
Baseball	330	Olympics	390
Basketball	345	Pasadena Rose Bowl Parade	410
Bicycling	350	Play	375
Body-Building Fixation	185	Poaching Elephant Ivory	130
Bowling	295	Prairie Dog Hunting	30
Boxing	180	Recreation	395
Bridge	410	Riots	105
Bull Fighting	35	Rose Bowl	405
Calisthenics	290	Running (aerobic)	350
Chess Game	415	Sexual Misconduct	160
Dancing, Ballroom	475	Skeet and Trap	400
Dog or Cock Fights	35	Soccer	450
Dove/Squirrel Hunting	65	Spelunking	205
Exercise Gym	320	Sports Stars	340-400
Extreme Sports	110	Steroids	160
Feldenkrais Exercises	410	Super Bowl	480
"Fixing" a game	90	Swimming	310
Football, American	330	Tai Chi	305
Foul Play	120	Tennis	350
Gambling	180	Tennis (Wimbledon)	440
Golf	400	Trophy Big-Game Hunting	190
Massage	250	World Cup	490
Mountain Climbing	205		

Sports can be roughly divided into competitive and recreational, both of which calibrate quite highly and thus represent enthusiasm, the pleasures of games, and the spontaneity and fun redolent of youth and its physical vigor. With age, chess, bridge, and golf provide the benefits of recreation, which calibrates at a very positive level.

Physiologically and psychologically, the effect of rest is anabolic. Physicians as early as Hippocrates often prescribed it for grave illnesses. He recommended the therapeutic benefits of massage, exercise, rest, and beauty, such as are afforded by today's health resorts.

Sports and hobbies calibrating below 200 derive the energy from more innate primitive animal levels of rivalrous battle, accompanied by the cheers and admiration of the crowds. At the very bottom of the so-called sports is the no-contest killing for the sake of killing itself, a very primitive level of consciousness. (The Roman gladiator arena calibrates at 80.)

The lure of gambling is vigorously glamorized, and the bait is not only money but also the thrill of "winning," which, as society has learned, can become addictive (due to dopamine released in the brain [Volkow, 2004]). Gambling has always been of questionable morality. In the traditional mid-twentieth century, parental ethics determined whether or not the game of marbles was allowed to be played "for keeps." In the same era, slot machines were confined to not-for-profit charities and fraternal and benevolent tax-exempt organizations. Bingo was a church-oriented source of revenue, but gambling itself was illegal, and police raids were looked upon with approval.

Gambling, at consciousness level 180, continues to be a moral enigma, the politics of which are another form of game playing. Society has found a compromise by having the profits regulated by law as to their distribution, which, as the media has revealed, are often bypassed by foreign nationals at great cost to the Native Americans.

Movies
(See Appendix for Calibrated List of Over 200 Movies)

2001, A Space Odyssey	440	Casablanca	385
A Beautiful Mind	375	Cat in the Hat	130
About Schmidt	435	Celsius 41.11	320
A Clockwork Orange	70	Color Purple, The	475
African Queen, The	395	Doctor Zhivago	415
Aliens	145	Easy Rider	195
Amadeus	455	Empire of the Sun	490
American Beauty	380	Fahrenheit 9/11	180
Big Blue	700	FahrenHYPE 9/11	290
Big One, The	180	Gandhi	455
Birth of A Nation, The	140	Harry Potter	215
Bonnie and Clyde	105	In Cold Blood	80
Bowling for Columbine	185	It's A Wonderful Life	450
Canadian Bacon	180	Jaws	140

Lord of the Rings	350	Santa Claus 2	190
M*A*S*H*	360	Silence of the Lambs	45
Matrix	165	Sound of Music	425
My Fair Lady	405	SpongeBob SquarePants	385
One Flew Over the		Star Wars	250
Cuckoo's Nest	160	Supersize Me	180
Passion of Christ, The		There's Something About	
(edited)	395	Mary	105
Passion of Christ, The		Titanic, The	405
(unedited)	190	TV Nation	180
Pretty Woman	375	Twin Towers, The	350
Psycho	80	What the #$*! Do We	
Ray (Charles)	475	Know?	455
Return of the King	350	Winged Migration	495
Roger and Me	180	Wizard of Oz, The	450

This decidedly American product escalated to become a worldwide industry, of which Hollywood is the symbol. As an art form, it is unexcelled in that it includes acting, dance, music, cinematography, and drama, plus creative engineering and technology that utilize the best of available talents. (Above calibrations denote consciousness level of the presented material, not the quality of the movie itself, e.g., horror films are meant to be that level and therefore artistically successful as denoted by calibrations less than 100.)

Of note is that a rather unique movie, *Big Blue*, which was noted in *Power vs. Force*, calibrated at an amazing 700. Beneath the story line was the contextualization of the Oneness of all life and the option open to human choice of selecting the eternal or the physical life. *The Passion of Christ* is very integrous of intention (cal. 490) but the prolonged torture/violence scenes bring down the overall calibration. If those ten minutes of gross detail were eliminated, the resultant movie would calibrate at 395.

What the #$! Do We Know?* is a non-Hollywood film that humorously demonstrates the greater reality behind appearances—science and spirituality; nonlinear dynamics; quantum reality; the effect of thought on changing reality; responsibility rests on human consciousness and what that implies about freedom. The film has been acclaimed as unique and has continually expanding showings.

The accusations that America is an immoral society are belied by the extent to which the importance of the morality of the media is a focus of much debate. Exploitation of the freedom of expression pushes the envelope of nihilistic hedonism until moral outrage counters with the setting of limits. The entertainment media proclaim their innocence, i.e., "We don't create public opinion, we just reflect it," which, however, is circuitous in that the public opinion to which they refer is, to a considerable extent, a consequence of the media output in the first place.

The artist has to choose which aspects of life to emphasize through artistic endeavor, and so the media are a major influence on social mores and belief systems. This is reflected in the overall calibration of the Hollywood film industry (cal. 180). Also notable is the recent spate of anti-Christmas spirit movies (Waxman, 2004), which collectively calibrate at 170. Movie economics, however, reflects the public's real areas of interest. Fortune magazine (January 2005) reports that although only three percent of Hollywood films are rated "G," they produce more income than the sixty-nine percent of films that are rated "R." Also interesting is that the movie industry of India (which features the generally acclaimed "most beautiful women in the world") is more sexually restrained and subtle, but worldwide, it has triple the sales of Hollywood. Its overall output also calibrates ten points higher, at 210, than Hollywood at 200.

A new genre of movies has recently emerged with the production of *Fahrenheit 9/11,* which received much publicity prior to the November 2004 presidential election. Its calibration at 180 reflects the political position it represents. After the election, corrective counter-information was presented by *FahrenHYPE 9/11* (cal. 290), as well as *Celsius 41.11* (cal. 390), which humorously represents the temperature at which brain death occurs. The emergence of political propaganda movies aimed at the voters may further deter integrous leaders from seeking public office.

Television

"700 Club"	400	*I Love Lucy*	395
Action Movies	180	Infomercials	180
All in the Family	255	*Kukla, Fran, and Ollie*	405
American Idol	180	*Married with Children*	190
America's Most Wanted	345	MTV	130
Animal/Nature	405	*Muppets, The*	310
Bill Cosby Show	385	*National Geographic*	450
Biography Channel	405	*Oprah Winfrey Show*	510
Broadcast Programming (overall)	275	PBS	405
Cable Programming (overall)	300	"Reality" Show Contests	125
		"Reality" Shows	130
Cheers	250	Sitcoms (Situation Comedies)	180
Children's Cartoons	180	Sports	375
Children's Programs	355	Sullivan, Ed	435
Crime Programs	180	"Terry Jones Medieval History"	410
History, Discovery, Science Channels	405	Weather	405
Homemaking, Decorating, Woodshop	345	Web M. D.	200

The above calibrations are relatively self-explanatory.

The Social Impact of Famous Persons

Astronauts	460	Duncan, Isodora	460
Baker, Josephine	445	Earhart, Amelia	395
Balanchine, George	430	Eisenhower, Dwight D.	480
Bell, Alexander Graham	450	F. D. R. Fireside Chats	500
Booth, John Wilkes	135	Franklin, Benjamin	480
Bryant, William Jennings	450	Geronimo	445
Carnegie, Andrew	490	Gorbachev, Mikhail	500
Carnegie, Dale	425	Graham, Martha	420
Carson, Rachel	485	Henry, Patrick	445
Carver, George Washington	435	Hoover, J. Edgar	255
Chisolm, Shirley	400	Jones, Bobby	485
Churchill, Winston	510	Keller, Helen	520
Columbus, Christopher	375	Kübler-Ross, Elisabeth	485
Comstock, Anthony	250	LaGuardia, Fiorello	460
Darrow, Clarence	455	Lee, Bruce	480
de Mille, Agnes	425	Lewis and Clark	440
DiMaggio, Joe	480	Lindberg, Charles	395

Mandela, Nelson	505	Rockne, Knute	455
Markova, Alicia	475	Rogers, Fred ("Mister	
Marrick, Joseph, the		Rogers")	500
Elephant Man	590	Roosevelt, Eleanor	495
Najinski	530	Ruby, Jack	180
Nation, Carrie	235	Shriver, Sargent	460
Nightingale, Florence	465	Sitting Bull	420
Oswald, Lee Harvey	180	Tubman, Harriet	350
Peale, Norman Vincent	435	Washington, Booker T.	460
Reagan, Ronald (President)	502	Washington, George	455
Rockwell, Norman	500	Wright Brothers	455
Ruth, Babe	440	Zanuck, Daryl	425

The potential list of famous persons is so long that only a few illustrative examples can be chosen. Of note is the extremely high calibration of the so-called "Elephant Man," who, because of a bone disease, became extremely disfigured. Despite taunting, ridicule, and social rejection, his attitude and demeanor were described as truly saintly. He was gentle, forgiving, nonreactive, and compassionate, even to man's most base ignorance. His uniqueness is singular and implies that his life symbolized spiritual possibility under even extreme conditions. Notably, he ignored the temptations of self-pity, victimhood, resentment, and hatred of his tormentors, as well as social rejection and ridicule. At calibration level 590, he stood at the doorway of Enlightenment and was at peace with himself and the world.

Entertainers/Humorists
(Programs, Not Persons)

Ball, Lucille	440	Hope, Bob	465
Benny, Jack	485	Mobley, Moms	465
Burnett, Carol	460	Skelton, Red	480
Burns, George	485	Tomlin, Lilly	460
Carson, Johnny	480	Tucker, Sophie	440
Diller, Phyllis	440		

Humor results from juxtaposition of alternative contexts. The play on words or meaning expands the context so that expectation is replaced by a contrast that sheds new light and meaning. Parody allows us to laugh at human nature and therefore ourselves. It also confronts us with absurdities and contradictions. Humor is life supporting and associated with increased life span, overall health, and satisfaction with life. It decreases anxiety and, interestingly, increases the overall level of consciousness because it results in a more benign view of life. A sense of humor is characteristic of very successful people (e.g., President Reagan) as it subserves social amenity and interpersonal and diplomatic skills. Like music composers and orchestra leaders (Diamond, 1979), humorists are long-lived (e.g. George Burns lived to be 100 years old).

Humor decreases conflict because it reduces negative feelings and resolves conflict by expanding context from "either/or" to "both" by a simple twist of meaning. Sometimes it does so by integrating appearances with essence, thereby replacing fallacy with a higher degree of truth.

Humor is important to the maturation process whereby we learn how to not take ourselves so seriously and learn to laugh at ourselves, thus decreasing narcissistic defensiveness. To be prone to "hurt feelings" is egocentric and a form of social paranoia. When we admit our downside and learn to laugh at it, we are no longer vulnerable to slights and insults. It is beneficial to list all of one's human foibles and limitations and make peace with them in order to be at peace with oneself. Humorists play off their own downside regularly and are beloved for their humility. The block to self-acceptance is pride, which is a vulnerability that actually attracts negative social responses. To laugh "about" a subject deflects being laughed "at" it. That is the benefit of good-natured "kidding," which is a form of acceptance rather than rejection (e.g., "Kiss me, I'm Polish" bumper stickers, etc.) True ethnic humor decreases prejudice while racist jokes are demeaning and increase prejudice.

News Broadcast Media
Programs (not individuals)

ABC News Broadcasts	205	*Huntley/Brinkley Show*	460
Air America	200	*Larry King Live*	295
al-Jazeera	195	Lehrer, Jim	460
BBC News Broadcasts	210	Murrow, Edward R.	465
Brokaw, Tom	455	National Public	
CBS News Broadcasts:		Radio News	200
prior to 9/15/04	255	NBC News Broadcasts	255
after 9/15/04	200	*O'Reilly Factor, The*	460
CNN News Broadcasts	260	Rather, Dan (CBS News)	205
Cronkite, Walter	460	Reuters News Service	305
Fox News	380	Rivera, Geraldo	455
Hannity and Colmes	460	Walters, Barbara	455

In traditional America, news media exercised discretion and received respect. They reflected an innate moral responsibility and were generally considered to be integrous. Editorializing was limited to the editorial pages of the major newspapers. In modern times, however, the implied objectivity of news reporting has come under suspicion, which was escalated by the Iraqi war. The argument is primarily between so-called liberals and conservatives, with accusations of distortion and partiality. Because the argument is relatively two-sided, each side, of course, sees bias on the part of the other. Therefore, the calibrated levels are informative in trying to ascertain the facts.

Upon examination and from the research data reported thus far, it is unlikely that anyone in our society is free from bias in their observations and derived opinions. This is merely a consequence of the structure of the ego and its associated brain physiology. Thus, integrity can be maintained if the reporting venue states its sympathies or alignments. The mere act of selection is already an editing function, and emphasis can be given to one side or the other of a debate merely by an extra second of exposure to a chosen scene, e.g., "perpetrator" or "victim," depending on one's point of observation.

A more serious and misleading distortion is the consequence of naïve attempts to appear "fair" in that undue exposure is given to deviant and extremist viewpoints, which are given disproportionate importance or significance and thus gain publicity primarily as a consequence of their contentious nature rather than their intrinsic merit. The repetitious phrase "but critics say" is usually spurious and the supposed "critics" are "anonymous" (or probably imaginary). This misleads the public to think that "critics" represent a significant segment of society, whereas, in actuality, they represent only a very small percentage, i.e., a skewed, rather than an imbalanced, presentation. This can mislead world opinion and result in serious miscalculations.

Broadcast network news programs declined overall in audience size and also as a result of bias scandals. The public turned to other sources of news (the Internet, etc.) but cable news showed a major increase, notably Fox News, and especially Bill O'Reilly's *The O'Reilly Factor* program, which developed a huge following (they get 14,000 emails per week). O'Reilly is like a bellwether of integrity. He has an uncanny knack for spotting nonintegrity, and the rule of thumb is that if O'Reilly dislikes a public figure or a "cause," it calibrates below 200 (handy for those who cannot do the calibration technique). Alternately, those that he views favorably almost always calibrate over 200, even if he disagrees with them. (In contrast, subjects favored by the Far Left commentators calibrate below 200, and those that are disliked or opposed calibrate above 200.)

Politics and The Election 2004

Consciousness calibration analysis is beneficial in that it clarifies ambiguities and allows greater understanding of complex social interactions. The overall consciousness level of the American populace is at 420 (America overall calibrates at 421 if government and the presidency are included). According to E. J. Dionne (Washington Post Writers Group 2004), the electorate is positioned as follows: Conservatives, thirty-four percent; Moderates, forty-five percent; and Liberals, twenty-one percent.

By calibration, the overall average consciousness level of all actual voters was at 410 (sixty percent of the electorate). The forty percent who did not vote calibrated collectively at 190.

The actual voters calibrated as follows:

Conservatives	415	Liberal	255
Democrats	325	Moderates	375
Far Left	185	Republicans	405

For reference, the Goldwater Institute calibrates at level 355, Progressives at 330-360 (Lyndon Johnson), "Freethinkers" at 335, and the "Golden Rule" at 405. Free speech calibrates at 235, the Patriot Act at 375, "Hollywood Far Left elitists" at 180, emotional political diatribes at 125-165, statesmen at 430, "politician" at 180, the moral majority at 245, and acrimony at 160.

President Bush's 2005 Inaugural Address calibrates at 480, and the Inaugural protesters as a group calibrate at 180.

Diagnostic Scale—Politics and The Election 2004

"Them" Electorate   "Us" Political Party

Level	Log		Log	
Love	500		500	
			415	Conservatives
Electorate	410			
			405	Republicans
Reason	400		400	
	375		375	Moderates
Acceptance	350		350	
	325		325	Democrats
Willingness	310		310	
	255		255	Liberals
Neutrality	250		250	
Courage	200		200	
	185		185	Ultra Liberal, Far Left
Pride	175		175	
Anger and Hate	150		150	
	135		135	Far Left diatribes
Desire	125		125	
Fear	100		100	Anarchists
	90		90	Non-voters
Grief	75		75	
Apathy	50		50	
Guilt	30		30	
Shame	20		20	

The levels below 200 indicate defective reasoning, narcissism, and progressive inability to differentiate *res interna* from *res externa*. In contrast, above 200, emotions and partiality are replaced by reliance on reason, fact, and the balance that results from inclusion of context. As could be predicted from the above chart, all of the Far Left's predictions proved false in subsequent world events (OPEC, not Bush, controls Middle East oil, business is booming, etc.)

The Great Books of The Western World calibrate at approximately 450-460. People who calibrate in the 400s are called conservatives, and below 200, the Far Left. Moderates fall into the range of 310-390, which is reasonable, responsible, and balanced but not necessarily intellectual per se.

From a calibrated overall view, it can be seen that the electorate is attracted by sincerity, integrity, and humanitarianism that is both moral and rational, and that extremism and negative propaganda have a harmful effect. A well-designed political platform would thus target its prospective audience and align its agenda to coincide. Chapter 13 outlines in detail winner and loser attitudes and approaches examples of which were quite overtly displayed in the election process and its aftermath.

Political analysts, such as John Leo (2004), were in considerable agreement that the Democratic Party had strayed too far to the Left into questionable "entitlements" (cal. 180), "rights," and minority issues that were antagonistic to the views of the majority, such as contempt for religious and moral values. Extremism then triggered a backlash and reaffirmation of spiritual/ethical mores and public standards. There is little popular support to eliminate Santa Claus (cal. 385), the Macy's annual parade, or the lighting of Christmas trees in Rockefeller Plaza and the Nation's Capital in Washington, D.C. Note also that Christmas holiday shopping amounts to forty percent of annual retail sales. The elimination of references to God is not even a tenable legal position as protagonist Newdow discovered after going all the way to the Supreme Court, which kept "under God" in the Pledge of Allegiance (USA Today, June 2004).

Commentators asked, "If the Far-Left Grinches succeeded, to whom would we give thanks on Thanksgiving Day? The idea that a more generic term like 'holiday' be substituted will not work either for it denotes the specialness of a holy ('holi') day. Also, the calendars will have to eliminate dates, especially 'A.D.' and 'B.C.,' and dates will have to be removed from all history books and the world's literature, but that still leaves a numbered year, e.g., '2005'." What does "2005" indicate? The years in the entire Western world mean one and the same thing, whether it is subterfuge or not—two thousand and five years since the birth of Jesus Christ. What else could it possibly mean? Will secularists invent a new numbering scheme? (Remember the 1980s' brief enthusiasm for speedometers and road signs reading in kilometers.) Even New Year's Day will have to be renamed. "New Year" means "New year of the birth of the Lord, Anno Domini." With the elimination of all holy days, will new union contracts be needed?

The secular Grinch does not like Kris Kringle, Christmas stockings, Easter Eggs, or Thanksgiving turkeys. Also, the Far Left hates America so the 4th of July can no longer be a celebration, and the National Anthem will have to be eliminated. Good-bye "American Pie," flags, or parades for veterans and their families. "Amazing Grace" will have to be eliminated at funerals. The United States would also have to eliminate diplomatic recognition of the Vatican and its ambassador.

Future presidents could not be sworn in with their hand on the Bible, nor could courts begin with "to tell the truth and nothing but the truth, so help me God." Goodbye to Christianity, Bar Mitzvahs, Yom Kipper, and Passover. Yamakas would be forbidden, as would public wearing of Islamic headdresses.

De-religionizing and de-spiritualizing society represents the emergence of another form of repression and relativistic fallacy of rule of the majority by the minority (ninety percent of Americans are theistic).

Consciousness research indicates that a successful political campaign evolves from ascertaining the average consciousness level of the targeted population and presenting a platform and candidates that are in accord and therefore appealing to that segment. In the 2004 election, the Republican platform calibrated at 395, and the Democratic platform was at level 295.

Middle America calibrates collectively at 355 and could be described as moderate in that it includes conservative liberals and liberal conservatives, as well as the really nonpolitical, average, "common sense" person who is simultaneously humanitarian but also practical and not given to extremes, feverish shrill ranting, or theatrical poses. Elections are more than just an exercise in dramatics.

In particular, the majority of voters is repelled by overt hatred, viciousness, and childish emotional displays (cal 135). They expect the leader of the country to be calm, rational, thoughtful, and emotionally stable, and to be perceived as a respectable authority figure. Thus, Bill Clinton was, and still is, widely popular and survived all the hatreds that were unwisely unleashed by Republican extremists. His political position was at calibration level 390 (i.e., popular). Disapproval at calibration level 240 is quite far from hatred at cal. 80. (To choose chocolate, one does not have to hate vanilla.)

Of interest and confirmative of the above analysis is the significant observation of unrecognized importance to politicians that the major trends of society are reflected by significant book sales, e.g., the major book of the current era is Rick Warren's *The Purpose Driven Life* (2004), which has sold more than 17 million copies (e.g., more than John Grisham, Stephen King, or even J. K. Rowling). According to *Publishers Weekly* (November 2004), sales represent that people are looking for meaning, direction, and how to improve relationships. The thrust is toward integrity, purposeful self-fulfillment, and spiritual significance. The book calibrates at 345 and is therefore in accord with the rapidly growing "cultural creatives" movement. A successful political campaign has to have greater awareness of moderate stability that is also interested in the individual minorities, but not at the expense of the majority. In this regard, centrist coalition as suggested by Senator Lieberman calibrates at 365. In contrast, collectively, the people threatening to or leaving the country because of the election calibrate at 175.

When we ask, as critics allege, if the "far left" is out to destroy the country, we get the answer "no." Their intention is simply self-indulgence. The ego inflation of "entitlement" (cal. 180) is to give self-indulgence legal respectability.

News Commentators and the Political Spectrum

The media reflect the consciousness levels of the various strata of society and subcultures and therefore represent the political/social spectrum of the public and various positionalities and viewpoints that, by consciousness calibration research, are distributed as follows:

Radical Left	135	Moderate	260-350
Far Left	135-145	Conservative	350-455
Leftist	170-190	High Integrity/Conservative	460
Liberal	180-200	Ultraconservative	300
Neutral	200-260	Radical Conservative	175

The calibrations are indicative of the balance between the conservative moderation of reason, with its constraints of logic, validity, proof, and rationality, in contrast with emotionality, sentiment, popularity, and aversion to the constraints of rationality and intellectual discipline.

The level of consciousness of America at 421 indicates that extremism is disliked and unpopular with the majority of the population, and that while emotionality has an attraction, it is not where the majority of the populace is willing to place their survival. Far Left or Right is therefore viewed as titillating or entertaining, but reasonable people would not want an automobile, or a house, or a doctor, or an investment that calibrates below 200 (witness the exuberant high-tech stock market collapse). On the other hand, the populace looks to politics for drama, and its living-theater productions provide excitement to offset the mundane responsibilities of ordinary daily life.

Whether a political position is perceived to be liberal or conservative often reflects the observer's own point of view, as the human proclivity is to seek agreement and reinforcement of a positionality rather than truth itself.

It will be noted that there is some disparity between the calibration of political writers and the calibrations of the political parties in Chapter 10. This is due to the writers' personal editorializing and "playing to the choir" of the readership. Thus, differences may be overemphasized to more clearly make a point.

News Print Media

Boston Globe Editorial Section	200	New York Times Editorial Section (2004)	190-195
Chicago Tribune	350		
Christian Science Monitor	425		
Economist, The	445	New York Times Editorial on President G. Bush (June 2004)	175
Financial Times	410		
Los Angeles Times	300		
Los Angeles Times Editorial Section	200	Rolling Stone	205
New Orleans Times-Picayune	345	Time Magazine	375
		USA Today	350
Newsweek	385	U.S. News & World Report	390
New York Times (2000)	250	Wall Street Journal	440
New York Times (2004)	195	Washington Post	340
New York Times (2005)	200	Weekly Standard	440

Business Week (June 14, 2004) reported a scientific study, "A Measure of Media Bias," by the Universities of Chicago and California at Los Angeles at a conference at Stanford University. The study shows that by objectively scored ratings, the media (television news and major newspapers) are skewed substantially to the left of the members of Congress. By calibration technique, the editorial sections of major U. S. newspapers reflect a similar bias, and they calibrate lower than the papers' strictly news sections. Other independent studies reach the same conclusion, e.g., Bob Kohn's *Journalistic Fraud* (2004).

The media's editorial viewpoints reflect the spectrum of prevailing levels of segments of society for which they are meaningful and of interest. Each columnist has their own following, as people want to see their own viewpoints expressed. This is common to all social expression, from architecture to music, movies, and news reporting.

Therefore, a true liberal supports the rights of conservatives to express their own views, even though they differ. Likewise, a true conservative defends the freedom of the liberal press. Integrous commentators of either persuasion protest extremes of slander, defamation, and gross prevarication, although, as noted by Newt Gingrich, "there are no rules anymore" (Gingrich, 2004).

Collectively, society represents a continuum of viewpoints and lifestyles that reflects predominance of values. One segment emphasizes excitement, novelty, rebel causes, "hot" issues, glamour, emotionality, and refutation of tradition as ethics, morality, or reason. In contrast is the population that emphasizes civility, logic, stewardship, familiarity, security, and preservation. These values can be expressed to varying degrees, from mild to extreme, as represented by the political spectrum of editorial presentations, which range from calm to frenetic and reflect the balance between evolution and revolution.

The publications that calibrate in the mid- to high 400s apparently have achieved an integrous balance without compromising reporting itself. For others, unstated positionalities lower the calibrations, although they are still above 200. The public is uncritical if it is presented with honesty. It may disagree with a viewpoint but not feel inclined to attack it as it does when it feels it has been surreptitiously misled.

Others

Barron's Magazine	340	Webster's Dictionary	465
Encyclopedia Britannica	465	Who's Who in America	460
Fortune Magazine	405	Who's Who in The World	460
Playboy Magazine	310		

Time magazine's "100 Most Influential People in the World" (2004; 2005 approx. the same)

Categories	Calibration
"Leaders and Revolutionaries"	190
"Leaders and Revolutionaries" (minus Bush, Rice, Gates, and the Clintons)	170
"Builders and Titans"	245
"Artists and Entertainers"	180
"Scientists and Thinkers"	240
"Heroes and Icons"	200
"Heroes and Icons" (minus M. Gibson, A. Schwarzenegger O. Winfrey, and T. Woods)	175

This selection is important in that it reflects the judgment of the staff of a major print medium that itself currently calibrates at an integrous 375 and is written to be of interest to the general reading public. If their judgment is correct, then the overall calibration of the list at 198 is cautionary, and the "Leaders and Revolutionaries" group at 190 even more so, because when just four integrous leaders are arbitrarily selected and removed, the calibration level of "leaders" drops to a very nonintegrous 170. When coupled with the fact that the current United Nations calibrates at 195, it is rather ominous.

With the arbitrary removal of just four integrous people (there could be more), the "Heroes and Icons" list drops to calibration level 175. This deleterious signal gives added importance to the low calibration of only 180 for the selected list of artists and entertainers. These collectively reflect the focus of the media whereby their influence is unduly magnified, e.g. various celebrities made headlines by personally vilifying the President as being like Stalin (cal. 90), Hitler (cal. 45), Hussein (cal. 65), etc. Their comments calibrate at level 130, and their gross fallacy is demonstrated by the fact that the President's position calibrates at 460.

The vilification of integrity to such extremes reflects the serious pathology due to infection of the virus of malignant "memes" (the spread or persistence of ideas via a key term, concept, or word) that appeal to media celebrities who themselves are the victims of media-induced inflated narcissism and thereby the loss of reality testing. In contrast, honest dissent calibrates from 210-330.

Comparatively, the positive elements of "Scientists and Thinkers" receive little media attention, and the "Builders and Titans" are frequently the focus of criticism, although they calibrate collectively at 245.

It is interesting to compare the media's viewpoint of important people with the massive collections of biographies in *Who's Who* in both America and the world, both of which calibrate at 460, which would confirm that figure (460 indicates real-life excellence). It is the same calibration as in other areas as well (science, music, spirituality, etc.)

Literary Works of Authors
(Not Their Personal Calibration)

Austin, Jane	440	Longfellow, Henry	
Baldwin, Charles	420	Wadsworth	465
Baum, L. Frank		Macabre Novels	150
(The Oz Books)	220	Mailer, Norman	400
Browning, Elizabeth	460	Mann, Thomas	445
Browning, Robert	450	Maugham, Somerset	395
Bryson, Bill	420	Michener, James	420
Buck, Pearl	445	Miller, Arthur	350
Capote, Truman	200	Mitchell, Margaret	400
Chekhov, Anton	460	Orwell, George	410
Clancy, Tom	405	Owens, Ronn	405
"Darkside" Pop Novels	170	Poe, Edgar Allen	450
Dawkins, Richard	450	Sagan, Carl	420
Dickens, Charles	540	Shakespeare	500
Dickenson, Emily	435	Shaw, George Bernard	400
Dostoevsky, Fyodor	465	Shelley, Mary	360
Doyle, Arthur Conan	385	Sontag, Susan	200
Emerson, Ralph Waldo	475	Steinbeck, John	400
Fielding, Harry	430	Tolkein, John R. R.	390
Frost, Robert	440	Tolstoy, Leo	455
Grisham, John	405	Twain, Mark	465
Hemingway, John	400	Voltaire	340
Hugo, Victor	455	Walker, Alice	440
Huxley, Aldous	425	Warren, Robert Penn	435
Joyce, James	440	Wharton, Edith	405
Kerouak, Jack	420	Wilde, Oscar	440
Lewis, C. S.	455	Whitman, Walt	460
Lewis, Sinclair	400	Woolf, Virginia	415
London, Jack	420	Wordsworth, William	430

Only a relatively few writers have been represented on the chart above, which is primarily for illustrative purposes. As would be expected, the subject matter of books and their integrity is similar to that currently observable on the Internet. These range from instruction manuals on how to commit successful murder and bomb buildings to the search for spirituality and enlightenment.

In some countries, such as Japan, more than ten thousand new titles are published annually, and an author is grateful if he is fortunate to sell even one thousand books. Amazon.com lists three million titles. Via web sites, anyone can publish a new book that is printed on request by a purchaser. True freedom of the press, however, is not a worldwide reality, and censorship is still very active in repressive regimes, such as in secular Socialist, Communist, and Islamic countries. In the United States, freedom of the press is cherished as a First Amendment legal right.

In recent times, anxious parents were relieved to discover that, like the last generation's Oz books, the Harry Potter books calibrate above 200, as do the works of Tolkein and others that focus on the theme of the search for truth and integrity. As the above writers reflect, life can be seen as a morality play, a comedy, a tragedy, or a fantasy, depending on one's point of observation and intention.

The totality of man's creative output over the entire evolution of history can be compared to the observations that ensue from viewing the different points of a hologram. In the past, the impact of great writing was limited to the elite few. Hieroglyphics, picture drawings, and pictographs that were inscribed on papyrus were very labor intensive; therefore, the destruction by fire of the great library of Alexandria, which contained the collective wisdom of the ancient world, brought grief and loss of not only the wisdom but also the enormous collective human effort that had gone into its composition. The calibrated level of that great library is 200-500. Thus, we can conclude that besides the wisdom and discoveries that were lost, history's awareness of itself as an evolutionary and cultural phenomenon was destroyed because the 200s reflect the warp and woof out of which society is constructed.

Dramas of human error are of value because they serve as learning examples. Maturity often evolves through painful errors and mistakes and is therefore accompanied by rueful irony and satire, as well as comedy.

Literature includes the presumed subjectivity and participation of the reader. Innate to all writings, including the current Harry Potter books, is the theme of implied or overtly stated ethics and morality, which is, in fact, the very core and key upon which the tension of the drama is dependent. This is subserved by nuance, subtlety, and selection of words in which meaningful shades of expression evidence uniqueness of style and elicit loyal reader response. The calibrations of literary output reflect the audience for which they are intended and are indicative of the level of interest of a writer's readership.

Writers were not listed whose works are not really literary but merely extremes of political polemics, both far left and far right. They all calibrate far below 200, and some, although supposedly humorous or satirical, are even below calibration level 100. Their content is not only fallacious but also motivated by overt hatred and represents major excesses of narcissism.

Industries (United States)

Advertising	195	Insurance	205
Aeronautics	215	Internet Music Piracy	195
Airline	204	Liquor	165
Amtrak	205	Manufacturing	202
Automobile	215	Petroleum	190
Banking	208	Pharmaceutical	205
Breweries	200	Publishing, General	204
Coal	205	Publishing, Newspaper	200
Commercial Tobacco	160	Railroad	202
Communications	210	Shipping	202
Fishing	190	Telemarketing	185
Gambling Casinos	160	Telephone	200
Gun	202	Television, Cable	205
Health	210	Television, Network	200
HMOs	170	Trucking	206
Hollywood Film	180	Utilities	205
House Construction	205	Vintners	300

In the world of business, profit is an obvious primary goal, and compromises are deemed necessary to subserve survival. Giant industries, such as petroleum, are international and have to deal with and survive in foreign cultures that operate according to different rules. Most businesses and their CEOs are under intense pressure to show a profit; thus, shortcuts are rationalized as "just human nature" in order to survive.

The gun industry calibration at 204 was repeatedly confirmed since the popular view would expect it to be lower. However, guns calibrate as neutral at 200, and therefore it is the use to which they are put that gives different calibrations, e.g., similar to a tool such as a knife (cal. 200).

Of concern are the HMOs that please neither the medical profession nor the patients overall. The practice of medicine itself calibrates at 440, but its control by commercialization for profit preempts the tradition of humanitarian ethics. The role of the physician has been reduced to the business model of a "vendor" or "provider of services," surrounded by a plethora of rules, regulations, requirements, dire legal threats, and malpractice insurance rates. The risks are so high that physicians, especially obstetrician/gynecologists, have gone out of practice or are unavailable in twenty-three states, and the number is increasing yearly (Arizona Medical News, 2004). Medicine has become a high-risk profession and is practiced defensively.

Medical school applications submitted by native-born Americans have fallen sharply while those from foreign countries have risen progressively. What was once a highly motivated and rewarding profession has become contentious. Doctors now view patients as potential litigants, and HMOs are primarily profit motivated. The newspapers report that the officers of the HMOs have multimillion-dollar salaries yet refuse to pay for needed services. Provision for mental health services has collapsed to nearly zero. A severely suicidal patient is lucky to be admitted to a hospital even for just overnight, and the required paperwork and red tape are overwhelming, discouraging even consulting about a high-risk patient. The professional jeopardy of treating the mentally ill is so high that they are just abandoned to wander the streets. The jails have now replaced the mental hospitals that were fallaciously demonized in past decades by relativistic politicalization.

Television Commercials (not products)

Alka-Seltzer	245	Lending Tree	385
Apple Computer	410	Listerine	355
Bayer Aspirin	350	McDonalds	200
Cruise Lines	245	Off-road Vehicles	190
Diet Pills	120	Orkin	305
"Dumb," "Boring,"		Pedigree Dog Food	435
"Confused"	135-140	Planter's Mr. Peanut	380
eBay	410	Puffs	400
Enzyte	455	St. Joseph Aspirin	250
Exercise Machines	150	Webex	365
Geico	345	Whiskers Cat Food	325
Hair-restore Products	200	Viagra	215
Imodium A-D	370		
Kibbles 'n Bits HomeStyle			
Dog Food	385		

The calibration of the advertising industry may reflect disparity between presentation and the reality of the product (Preston, 1996). Huge amounts of money are spent on advertisements and commercials that make people feel bad and go weak, thus creating an unconscious aversion to the product. There are also portions of ads that have a negative effect, whereas the rest of it may be neutral. Similarly, there are background sound tracks that produce negative psychological and physiological responses. Sixty-five percent of parents would also appreciate that certain advertisements be discretely aired later in the evening, after family viewing time, rather than having to go into sexual details about side effects that warn, "after four hours, call a doctor."

The calibration levels of television ads at the time of this writing currently range from a high of 455 (e.g., "Bob" of Enzyte, and other companies) to as low as 100. A series of ads by one of America's largest and most prestigious corporations calibrates at 145 and ran continuously with irritatingly frequent repetition. The overall cost must be in the multimillions of dollars. Other than a three-letter designation of the company's logo, it is not even clear just what the company is trying to sell. In contrast, ads that have a "heart," especially with animals or comic scenes of animal behavior, calibrate high, as do commercials that are humorous (e.g., e-Bay). Interestingly, broadcast-band commercials overall calibrate thirty points higher than cable television advertisements.

Another very major discovery is that everyone *unconsciously* knows when they are being lied to. Thus, substituting actors and actresses for testimonials cancels fifty percent of the benefit of that expensive advertising. A real-life sufferer who found true benefit from using the actual product itself has *twice* the convincing effect on the viewer as that of an actress or actor. The application of consciousness research techniques to advertising could increase the return on investment by 250 percent.

Energy Fields of Famous Industrialists
(Not Personal Calibrations)

Bell, Alexander Graham	495	Ford, Henry	380
Carnegie, Andrew	490	Morgan, J. P	420
Edison, Thomas	430	Nobel, Alfred	410
Forbes "Top Ten" List (2004)	460	Westinghouse, George	455
Forbes "Top 400" List	440		

American society ambivalently encourages and lauds success, and, at the same time, it can turn on a dime to attack and vilify it. As a consequence, the "really rich" often live in safe enclaves and are quite aware that they are the hated targets of envy. They therefore usually shun celebrities and the spotlight and communicate by inner subcultural subtleties of expression by which they recognize and acknowledge each other.

Industrial barons, however, reflect other creative strengths, such as inventive enterprise, fixity of purpose, and pursuit of goals with underlying effort. Almost all major industrialists tend to calibrate in the high 300s and 400s and therefore have well-developed intellects as well as intrinsic overall integrity. Because of this, the collapse of the Howard Hughes enterprise (initial calibration, 490; later, 180) was a shock to the public and viewed as a tragedy.

Philanthropic Foundations

Gates, Ford, Mellon, Carnegie	400
Kellogg, Pew, Duke, Wal-Mart	400
Lilly, Rockefeller, F. W. Johnson	400
Templeton	500
Wheelchair Foundation (K. Behring)	520
Others	400

Not only did the inspired genius of industrialists and inventors create entire industries and multimillions of jobs worldwide but also products that accelerated America's economic and financial ascendancy. In addition to these gifts to society, they established non-profit foundations into which are poured billions of dollars, and from which many billions of dollars more continue to pour forth, often with unheralded benefits to society in the form of libraries, humanities, education, health, and scientific research. Their overall output to society is prolific and continues for decades after the deaths of their founders.

From this we see that wealth, in and of itself, is not a morally suspect, superficial self-indulgence, but, on the contrary, for their producers and their subsequent stewards, wealth is a heavy burden and a moral responsibility. The holders of great wealth are acutely aware of social responsibility, ethics, and the most judicious use of monetary capital for the greatest good (e.g., the Gates Foundation alone has twenty-six billion dollars in assets). To this end, they employ the world's best talents and academics to act as expert guides. Interestingly, the major philanthropic foundations and trusts all calibrate at 400, with the exception of the Templeton Foundation, which funds programs and research based on love, spirituality, and their positive therapeutic effects.

Corporations

American Spirit Tobacco Co.	285	IBM	250
American Spirit Tobacco		IKEA	210
(product)	205	Kellogg Co.	355
Bayer (pharmaceuticals)	350	K-Mart	225
Ben & Jerry's	340	Lowe's	300
Bean, L. L.	330	Macy's Department Store	270
Bloomingdale's Department		McDonald's	205
Store	255	Microsoft Corp.	345
Boeing Corp.	320	Nordstrom's Department	
Campbell's (soup)	280	Store	260
Coca Cola	211	Pepsi	209
Costco	310	Pfizer	205
Dillard's Department Store	350	Sears, Roebuck (catalog era)	350
Dow Chemical	325	Singapore Airlines	275
Fed-Ex	340	Smuckers	340
Ford Motor Co.	205	Southwest Airlines	345
General Electric	205	Starbucks	245
General Motors	205	Viacom	240
Gulf, Exxon	205	Union Carbide Corp.	235
Harley Davidson	300	UPS	216
Heinz Co., H. J.	280	Wal-Mart	365
Homco	305	Wendy's	245
Home Depot	305		

Prior to the scandalous collapse of WorldCom, Enron, and others, there were a number of major corporations that calibrated below 200. However, many are not included in the current list because they are all in a period of transition and reconstruction. Of major interest is that over ninety percent of the Fortune "500" companies calibrate at or above 200, with the majority between 202 and 210. This implies reliability, dependability, and integrity of function. Some, such as Fed-Ex, Smuckers, Harley-Davidson, and Southwest Airlines, indicate above-average excellence. Envious critics of corporate wealth and power often fail to appreciate that many great corporations have been in business for more than a century.

In a class by itself, Wal-Mart is the pace-setting product of the integrity of Sam Walton, as was noted in *Power vs. Force* back in 1995. Despite critics, Wal-Mart is the biggest and most successful corporation the world has ever seen, and, more importantly, it serves as the prime example that integrity shows up on the bottom line. Sam Walton's founding business principles calibrate at 385, and even now, the company is at a high 365. Wal-Mart is responsive to criticism and is self-correcting. It represents commerce and not sainthood. It has expanded into philanthropic community service and established a philanthropic foundation. In addition, it provides over one million jobs and wide opportunity at the entry level. Critics abound but they themselves shop at Wal-Mart. It is the buying public that made Wal-Mart so huge. This ambivalence was well-stated in the newspaper editorial, "We trash Wal-Mart but beat a path to it." (*Arizona Republic*, 9/18/04.)

Wal-Mart is the biggest retailer in the United States and China is the largest exporter, so the effect is to decrease inflation and consumer costs in the U. S. and increase the standard of living in China. This brought China into an alliance with the U. S. (Talton, 2004), which precludes China from being a nuclear threat, as had been feared in the prior decade. Notable is that Wal-Mart's operation is so efficient that it operates on only a three-percent profit margin. (In Germany, Wal-Mart hosts "singles" events on Friday nights in ninety-one stores, and many couples that meet there are later married [Zimmerman/Schoenfeld, 2004].)

Business and industry are caught up in worldwide economic and technical changes, such as the Internet itself, which mandate outsourcing for survival by cities, local governments, and even radiologists (Tanner, 2004). Most big corporations are multi-national and driven by changes in foreign economies, banking, export laws, rates of currency exchange, etc. Therefore, "blaming" an individual company or industry reflects a personal bias rather than a bonifide complaint. The whole world is the context to "blame" for shifting economic factors beyond the control of individual companies. The "mom and pop" era is over, as is the era that preferred men in higher executive positions. In that older culture, men were career oriented, whereas women were family oriented and less committed to business. Wal-Mart, like other retailers, is in a highly competitive business, and pricing and promotion strategies are now available through price-optimization software (Larson, 2004).

Unions

Airlines	205	Steelworkers	202
Others (general)	200-208	Teamsters (current)	205

While many unions calibrate in the 200s, indicating integrity of purpose and function, seventy-eight percent fall below 200 for reasons unclear, except perhaps their compromising for the sake of self-interest, e.g., featherbedding at 190. On the other hand, they actively pursue what society and its members presume they are supposed to do, and thus, self-interest and leverage for gain are considered to be part and parcel of the game. In general, the public tends to take errors in union functioning with a grain of salt unless it results in the defrauding of union members.

Classically, union politics was a rough-and-tumble game that was played on its own turf. However, that rough-and-tumble nature resulted in congressional hearings and improved regulations. Paradoxically, unions themselves have now become almost identical to big corporations, with boards of directors and huge accumulations of capital that require corporate structures similar to those of corporate America. Many unions pioneered safety for workers, such as the IBEW did for the electrical linemen whose jobs entail high risk such as handling very high voltage. Some, such as the Teachers Union, are prominently the target of criticism and controversy. Overall, union membership has been steadily declining and now represents only thirteen percent of the workforce. If we ask why some unions calibrate low, the answer that calibrates as true is that the leaders are exploiting the workers for profit, power, and personal gain. In fact, union demands historically have driven some industries nearly out of business. However, the Federal General Accounting Office reports that outsourcing has not affected the overall U. S. job market (Geewax, 2004).

The unions' press for improved employee benefits and working conditions paradoxically resulted in overall job loss because the employer is then less competitive in a world market. The escalating cost of employee benefits is a major factor that makes outsourcing a necessity for many businesses (Portes, 2004). The "union era" is rapidly declining and being replaced by labor laws and employee benefit plans.

Law Enforcement

United States		International	
Federal	205	Interpol	205
State	250	Scotland Yard	210
Local	305		

The reasons for the above disparities remain an interesting subject for future research. A primary impairment in the U. S. is failure to enforce the law (calibrates as "true").

Science – Theory

Attractor Fields (Nonlinear Dynamics)	460	(Divinity as Source of Universe	Infinite)
"Big Bang" Source-of-Universe Theory	False	Drake Equation	350
Biofield	460	Earth's magnetic field weakening	True
Black Hole Theory rev. 2004 (Hawking)	455	Earth slowly reversing magnetic poles	460
Bootstrap Theory	455	Earth warming due to pollution	False
Chaos Theory	455	Earth warming due to solar magnetic surface cycles	455
Collective Unconscious (Jung)	455		
Consciousness as Consequence of Neuronal Activity	140	$E=mc^2$	455
		Entanglement (Quantum Theory)	False
Consciousness Calibration	605		
Darwinian Theory of Evolution	450	Frame Dragging	460
		"God" gene	False
Dinosaur Extinction Theory	200	"Greenhouse" gas earth-warming theory	False
Dirac Equations	455		
Discovery of Double Helix of DNA	460	HeartMath	460
		Heisenberg Uncertainty Principle	460
"Distant Healing"	False		

Hormesis	180	"Parallel Universe"	
"Holographic Universe"	395	Theory	False
Inflation Theory		Quantum Coherence	460
(post-Big Bang)	450	Quantum Gravity	460
Intelligent Design	480	Quantum Mechanics	460
Microbe Organisms on		Schrödinger Equations	455
Mars	True	Singularities	455
Mind Fields Entangled		S-Matrix Theory	455
with Divinity	True	Spiritual Experience as	
Mind Fields Entangled		the Consequence	
with Others	False	of Neuronal Activity	125
Morphic Resonance	460	"Steady State" Theory	
Morphogenetic Fields		of ongoing expansion	
(Sheldrake)	460	of the universe	405
M-Theory (formerly		Stem Cell Research	245
String Theory)	460	Subparticle Physics	455
Multiple Universes	True	Telekinesis	True
Newtonian Causality		Teleportation of	
Principle	460	Quantum States	
Nonlinear Dynamics	460	(electrons in ions)	400
Prayer Increases Healing	True	United States Space	
Nuclear Fission Reaction		Program	400
(actuality)	200	von Neumann Process	450
Nuclear Fission Theory	455	Water on Mars	True
Organisms on Mars	True		

Interestingly, we see that all major scientific theories, which are predominantly mathematical in nature, calibrate in the range of 450 to 460, including quantum mechanics. Calibrating the levels is pragmatically useful because a number below 200 indicates that further pursuit is a waste of time, energy, and money (e.g., the parallel universe theory). There is some limitation indicated by the current dinosaur extinction theories, which are primarily based on the supposition of major global changes rather than looking into evolutionary changes and the nature of life itself that occurred at that time. "Hormesis" is the theory that small doses of toxins can have a beneficial effect (Celebrese, 2004).

The Drake equation is complex in that it combines multiple levels of science and mathematics, including nonlinear dynamics, to predict the likelihood of other intelligent civilizations in the universe. At present, it predicts approximately ten thousand such probabilities in just the Milky Way alone.

It is interesting that nuclear fission calibrates at 200 (as do guns), and thus it is the purpose for which it is used, e.g., dynamite and gunpowder have multiple uses such as a fireworks display or bombs and bullets. Intention is the decisive factor. (The intention in dropping the atomic bomb that ended World War II calibrates at 455.)

Surprising was the negative answer to the quantum theory of "entanglement." It is an incorrect conceptualization; the phenomenon to which it has been applied can be explained differently: The coherence of "A" and "B" is not due to "A" influencing "B", but instead, both are influenced by "C." This can be observed in the flight pattern of birds and fish that wheel about in geometric patterns. Each fish or bird is *not* influenced by the pattern of the others; instead, each is individually attuned to an overall attractor energy pattern, much as the dancing couples in a ballroom are not attuned to each other but simultaneously to the same music.

HeartMath is a discovery that the heart literally has a mind of its own (intuitive), and its electromagnetic field is dominant over cerebral rhythm. The heart field thus affects brain physiology, as illustrated in Chapter 7.

Similarly, "distant healing" (i.e., from "A" to "B") is negative, but prayer influences healing because of the commonality of "C" in that all minds are intertangled with the infinite energy field of Divinity (calibrates as "true").

When a series of calibrations falls within a close range, it indicates a limitation of paradigm and implies that further investigation will just reveal more of the same caliber. The obvious conclusion is that if science is to make progress, it has to move to a paradigm that calibrates on a higher level; otherwise, it is dealing in circuitous refinement rather than discovery.

A notable value of consciousness calibration is its application to any kind of research, including industrial, marketing, and product development. The application of obvious benefit is to scientific research itself where the value of a project can be elucidated before expending valuable time, money, and resources. As an example, the research of years ago that discovered the double helix structure of DNA calibrates at 460. The current research project with the California Institute of Technology to discover a strictly neurobiological basis for consciousness calibrates at 140. The research may therefore reflect an initial bias in that in a recent interview, the lead researcher stated that "educated people will believe in due time that there is no soul independent of the body and hence, no life after death." (Crick, *New York Times* interview by M. Westheimer, as reported April 1, 2004). The statement calibrates as false, and the research design calibrates at 140.

The discovery of electricity calibrates at 445; the creation of the "Tucker" automobile at 175; the Ford automobile at 445, etc. Diversely, the research technique can be usefully applied to any area of science, such as archeology or paleontology (e.g., Piltdown man was a hoax? "True"). Thus, a tool is now available to save vast amounts of time, money, and energy in diverse fields of application, including pharmaceuticals and the numerous branches of biologic research. It is interesting that science projects funded by the federal government calibrate collectively at 150 points lower than those relying on other sources.

Science – Clinical

Acupuncture	405	Internal Medicine	440
America's Best Hospitals	450	Medicine, General	440
Clinical Kinesiology	600	Medicine, Holistic	440
Clinical Psychology	380	Oriental Medicine	395
Consciousness Levels		Pharmacology	450
Calibration	605	Psychiatry	440
DBT Psychology	385	Psychoanalysis (Freud)	460
Energy Medicine	460	Psychoanalysis (Jung)	460
Homeopathy	200	Surgery	440

All of the major therapeutic modalities in current use calibrate well, and we see that psychoanalysis is of a high level of excellence for those who have the time, motivation, and financial resources for it. Its emphasis is on subjectivity and the evolution of personal growth and awareness.

As a diagnostic tool, kinesiology at 600 indicates a major shift of paradigm because it is at the interface of the linear and the nonlinear domains. Its major value is that there is no other instrument or technique available at such a level, which indicates a shift from just that of the observed ("objective"), but also includes the observer as well as the impersonal field of consciousness itself. Thus, kinesiology could be a tool *par excellence* for the advancement of science and knowledge.

When public health issues are addressed by various health agencies (Centers for Disease Control (CDC), U. S. Public Health Service, Center for Science in the Public Interest, etc.), manipulation of data is rather frequent and reflects politicized issues and the negative influence of preconceived policies. Grant money is often dependent on whether the proposed project will support a politically correct notion. Thus, anti-smoking and anti-obesity projects proliferated and the public reports were frequently fear-inducing exaggerations. The grossest examples had to do with "second-hand smoke," which was rather transparently designed to demonize it and thus gain public support for the anti-smoking lobby. Fudging on statistics is rationalized because it is "good for you," (meaning good for the reporting agency). (Charen, 2004)

Clinical fallacies are rationalized as permissible because they support what is perceived to be "good for you." Second-hand smoke supposedly caused an endless variety of ill effects, from sudden infant crib death to psoriasis, etc. Most of the studies also made the error of assuming that statistical correlation is therefore "cause" (i.e., correlation of "A" and "B" does not prove that "A" causes "B," and both are actually a consequence of "C", to which both "A" and "B" are independently related). As an example, seventy-five percent of people who develop tuberculosis wear brown shoes. Sixty-five percent of second-hand smoke studies were fallacious. The findings of the Environmental Protection Agency (EPA) were invalidated by a judicial investigation (U. S. District Court Judge William Osteen, 1998), which proved the EPA had "cherry picked" data and completely ignored the primary conclusions and data that showed no statistically significant health risk from secondhand smoke (Singer, 2004). The EPA defended itself from the Congressional rebuke by saying the EPA action was "for a worthy cause."

The same trends continue currently with obesity studies, which the CDC admitted were erroneous due to a "math error" (Yee, 2004). Also fallacious were reports that smoking and obesity deaths were the cause of increased costs to the public. Actually, the medical costs at life's end are approximately the same by whatever illness is fatal (all human life is ultimately fatal in the end). Death at age 70 instead of age 90 actually saves twenty years of Social Security payout (at least $250,000), plus twenty years of other Medicare expenses. Now that people are living longer, it is not illness but improved health and greater longevity that are escalating federal program costs (Pear, 2005). Social security would recoup quickly if retirement age were increased from age 65 to 67.

Science – Scientists

Bohm, David	505	Halley, Edmond	460
Bohr, Niels	450	Harvey, William	475
Boole, George	460	Heisenberg, Werner	485
Burbank, Luther	450	Hippocrates	485
Copernicus, Nicolaus	455	Jung, Carl	520
Curie, Madam Marie	505	Kepler, Johannes	460
Darwin, Charles	450	Mendel, Gregor	460
Edison, Thomas	470	Maxwell, James	445
Einstein, Albert	499	Newton, Isaac	499
Faraday, Michael	440	Pasteur, Louis	485
Fermi, Enrico	455	Pauling, Linus	450
Freud, Sigmund	499	Planck, Max	475
Fuller, Buckminster	445	Rutherford, Ernest	450
Galen, Claudius	475	Salk, Jonas	455
Galileo (Galilei)	455	Steinmetz, Charles	455
Gödel, Kurt	455	Tesla, Nicola	460

The significance of these findings has been mentioned elsewhere. Einstein, Newton, and Freud pushed the limits of the intellect to the edge, just short of the significant level of 500 where there is the shift of paradigm that includes the subjective and the reality of the spiritual, which was transcended by both Bohm and Jung and the inspiration of Madam Curie. These calibrations also illustrate the enormous, beneficial impact that their collective work has had on society and the advancement of civilization.

Major Universities and Schools

Acadèmie Française	415	Heidelberg, University of	445
Arizona, University of		Ivy League Colleges	455
(Tucson)	405	Jones, Bob, University	400
Baylor University	430	Marquette University	440
Big-10 Universities	460	Medical College of	
Bryn Mawr University	455	Wisconsin	440
California, Univ. of,		Meherry Medical College	420
Berkeley	385	Morehouse School	
California, Univ. of,		of Medicine	410
Los Angeles	385	Motorola University	400
Cambridge University	455	Oxford Union	495
Chicago, University of	425	Oxford University	435
Duke University	430	Sandhurst Military	
Duke University Medical		Academy (U.K.)	465
School	435	Sorbonne, The (Paris)	415
Edinburgh, University of,		So. Florida University	305
Scotland	425	Stanford University	400
Exeter Academy	465	Tuskegee University	400
Fordham University	440	Wellesley	440
Harvard Divinity School	455	West Point Military	
Harvard Medical School	445	Academy	425

The levels of these institutions reflect the caliber of the faculty, which would be expected to be at least 400 (reason and intellect) at the minimum. Those below 400 reflect the substitution of philosophic relativism and socio-political positionalities. Naïve parents send their children to college to become educated and are dismayed when they discover that they have instead become indoctrinated with problematic philosophies (Shapiro, 2004). Radicalization of students calibrates at 180. As will be discussed later, the presidents of six major universities calibrate below 200, as do numerous academic professors and their departments, some of which are actually lower in calibration than that of their student bodies.

CHAPTER 10
America

Introduction

A survey of the evolution of consciousness throughout human history reveals a relentless drive to discover truth in all areas of human activity. There is a persistent intention to translate potentiality into actuality. Intuitively, humanity has sensed that within its core is the innate capacity to evolve to greater levels of perfection. Curiosity leads to discovery and the desire to know more about reality, such as the exploration of outer space, advancing scientific knowledge, the discovery of cures for diseases, and the constant attempt to perfect political and governmental ideologies. The search for truth is the central theme of the greatest intellects of history, as demonstrated by *The Great Books of the Western World*, and currently, by the incredibly rapid expansion of information on the Internet, the content of which is surpassing the world's greatest libraries. Mankind has great faith that life will get better and that the royal road to that success is through the accumulation of knowledge, education, learning, and research.

In current worldwide events, the focus is incessantly on the necessity of learning the truth behind events, many of which have international consequences and are of grave concern. Ethics is very much a part of national and international dialogs. One senses that in its frustration, society is about ready to dump sophistry, political rhetoric, and pretense in exchange for a verifiable reality in the interest of survival. There is a pressing need for closure of many major events of recent history that still leave nagging uncertainties and doubts. When facts cannot be ascertained, conspiracy theories (cal. 165) proliferate for decades.

It is significant that society's need for truth expresses as concern about morality, along with a need to feel certain that justice is being served, sometimes to an obsessive degree. International courts of justice and tribunals frequently take years (e.g., Milosevic) in searching the minute evidence, which in itself is indicative that mankind is indeed quite preoccupied with truth, ethics, and spiritual responsibility. When society is frustrated in its search for the truth, it sometimes resorts to desperate measures, such as threats of intimidation, execution, war, and, in the case of war prisoners, torture.

As would be expected, science has been called upon to try to solve the problem. The lie detector has been a rudimentary attempt in that direction, but it is fallible as well as unreliable and, in some situations, useless for persons with delusions or for criminals who lack a conscience. The efforts of science are now focused in the direction of brain physiology, including the use of MRI and other scans to detect subtle areas of change in the brain physiology when a person intends to lie or deceive.

As we have already seen from consciousness research, the truth and falsehood of a response can be instantly detected by a third-party investigative team skilled in the use of kinesiology, which stems from a biological science rather than a traditional science based on mathematics and mechanical principles. More advanced techniques require an explanation based on a higher and more inclusive paradigm, which necessitates an understanding of the nature of consciousness itself. It is not possible to arrive at truth and ignore consciousness because truth is the very product of consciousness. Basic to this awareness is the fact already described, that truth is a consequence of both content and field, and the calibratable level of consciousness expressed indicates its level of verifiability.

Levels of Truth and Social Institutions

Everything that exists in the physical (e.g., buildings, parks, and animals), mental (e.g., beliefs, thoughts, and motives), emotional (e.g., hate, fear, and desire), or spiritual domains (e.g., love, trust, or compassion) is calibratable. Each calibratable level reflects the essence of the degree of truth that is being expressed on a spectrum that is of great pragmatic value. Consciousness instantly discerns not only falsehood from truth, but also the level of the degree of truth and, therefore, its verifiability.

By trial and error, the practicality and range of usefulness of a new instrument can be derived from experimentation. In the process, new information arises that reveals not only specifics but also implications, nuances, and a new dimension of perspective. This was the path that was followed after the invention of the microscope, the telescope, the X-ray, and the silicone chip. Historically, this has been a fruitful approach that stems from the application of a new research technique to a wide variety of topics, followed by the study and correlation of the results. When that data shows a confirmable, internal consistency, pragmatic benefits ensue and result in a progression of further discovery as an ongoing process.

The following calibrations were part of eighty-five hundred that were done as a research study in 2003 and 2004 by an expert team. Other investigative teams sometimes get slightly different results, but they are also internally consistent due to variations in details of the technique. The results are the same whether the statement is made verbally or held silently in mind—the so-called "blind" technique. Thus, a blind technique with a naïve test subject, such as a small child, gives about the same results. For accuracy, the focus has to be on the integrity of intention, and both investigators have to calibrate over 200. The details of the technique were described briefly in *Power vs. Force* (Hawkins, 1995; also see Appendix C), and more extensively by Dr. John Diamond (Diamond, 1979).

The science of calibration of levels of truth is based on a relatively simple phenomenon: All life radiates an invisible field of energy, and the intensity increases with the level of consciousness or truth. The effect is similar to a light bulb where brightness varies with the voltage. This radiant energy can be read at a distance because of the nonlocality of the infinite nonlinear dimension.

There is a major change of radiance at calibration level 200, so that just as light increases from level 200 on up, it decreases quickly from level 200 down. Thus, the simple kinesiologic test merely indicates when the "light" is "on" (truth) or "off" (falsehood) because the basic energy field of consciousness is nonlocal (i.e., everywhere present).

The radiant energy of each living being is not only in the public domain but leaves a permanent, identifiable track undiminished by temporal time or duration to which the infinite field of consciousness is not subject or restricted. Even objects, buildings, and localities reflect the input of collective human intention and therefore imprint the effects of love, devotion, aesthetics, and integrity, as well as concepts, thoughts, and feelings.

America – U. S. Government

United States Constitution	710	United States Flag	510
Declaration of		United States Supreme	
Independence	705	Court	480
Bill of Rights	640	Office of the Presidency	460
Signers of the U. S.		Congress/House of	
Constitution	515	Representatives	455
Gettysburg Address	550	Great Seal of the U. S.:	
Patriotism	520	"E Pluribus Unum"	
Pledge of Allegiance	510	(out of many, one)	605
National Anthem	510		

The United States Constitution and government calibrate higher than that of any country on earth or of any other country in history, which helps to explain why America is such a successful and powerful nation. It is also a fact to be respected and taken into consideration by factions that wish to tamper with this outstanding, integrous foundation from which has arisen such a cornucopia of benefits.

The above-cited documents can be analyzed sentence by sentence, and the core of the power becomes revealed as the spiritual truth upon which the documents were based, i.e., the equality of all men arises by virtue of the divinity of their Creator and thus specifies that the rights of Americans do not stem from political ideologies or arbitrary government fiat; they do not depend on secular authority; and they are inalienable by virtue of their origin and basis.

The statement that the source of the government is spiritual rather than religious results in freedom *of* religion as well as freedom *from* religion. This is a crucial differentiation. The word "God" is actually a generic term for Divinity and is not innately religious as such. The word "God" is a noun like any other noun, and the concepts of God are the subject of academic study in theology, comparative religion, history, and philosophy. Paradoxically, God is also the core subject of atheism and the target of secularism.

As a consequence of the Constitution, the word "God" appears on court buildings, including the Supreme Court, and on currency and is thereby a reminder of the seat, the basis, and the fundamental origin of individual freedom; consequently, it is irrefutable and permanent. This is reflected in the research data that indicate that secular governments of other countries (see Chapter 14) calibrate only in the 300s.

There is a crucial difference between patriotism and nationalism. Patriotism includes and reflects love of one's country and is therefore inclusive of respect, appreciation, value, meaning, and good will towards one's fellowman. It also includes a self-esteem that is based on a commonality of reverence for all that the Constitution and the Bill of Rights specify—the equality of all men by virtue of the Divinity of their Creator.

This explains why patriotism (hand over heart) calibrates in the 500s, while secular nationalism (arm salute) calibrates at 305. Patriotism is of the heart, whereas nationalism, in contrast, stems from the mind and is therefore merely a political position. From the preceding calibration, one can see the error made by those who reject patriotism because they confuse it with nationalism. They are not the same thing at all. This comprehension was crystallized by Sir Walter Scott in *The Lay of the Last Minstrel*, the famous poem known by every school child:

> Breathes there a man, with soul so dead,
> Who never to himself hath said,
> This is my own, my native land!

It is interesting that the political position that seeks to remove all reference to God in the public arena calibrates at only 190, the egoistic level of pride and arrogance that seeks to replace the reality and the power of truth by weak, narcissistic intellectualism.

As has been described, a "meme" is a germinal idea or phrase that is catchy and tends to be repeated until, by sheer repetition, it becomes commonly accepted as if it were fact. An example is the meme "separation of Church and State," which is accepted uncritically at face value as representing the law of the land. This phrase is utilized to leverage secular agendas. If examined, it will be found that there is no such statement in the U. S. Constitution, the Declaration of Independence, or the Bill of Rights. In fact, none of these three words appears at all—no "separation," no "Church," and no "State." Instead it says, "Let Congress not establish any religion nor prohibit the free practice thereof" (cal. 640). Obviously, to abolish even the word "God" from society violates the actual freedom "to practice," as actually stated, as well as the First Amendment right to free speech. The intention of the actual wording is obvious: to avoid theocracy, yet guarantee religious freedom.

Paradoxically, if the secularist movement were to make any reference to God illegal in governmental or public life, it would invalidate the Constitution of the United States as well as the Declaration of Independence, Lincoln's Gettysburg Address, official pronouncements of U. S. presidents throughout history, etc. If the equality of man stems from his creator, then abolishing "the Creator" would abolish the basis of equality also, because, from the ordinary viewpoint, people are decidedly very unequal in hundreds of ways, right from the moment of birth.

Oddly, on the very day the above was written, synchronistically, the nightly news reported that a school principal in California forbade the teaching of the Declaration of Independence because of its references to God (cal. 180). From the same extremist viewpoint then, the U. S. government is illegal and, therefore, so are the judiciary, the Congress, the Bill of Rights, etc. The American populace will have to decide whether to side with wisdom or sophomoric absurdity and fulfill Socrates' dire prediction that democracies eventually fall due to giving equal voice and votes to the nonintegrous and ignorant segment of the population (cal. 465). Historians point out that the average duration of a democracy is thus usually only two-to-three hundred years before the self-centered voters deplete the country of its resources and political erudition. This weakness of democracy is why Socrates recommended the oligarchic form of government. (The United Nations is probably the most glaring example of Socrates' prediction.)

The calibrations of the offices of the Presidency and the Supreme Court indicate a high level of integrity, reason, and objective-based high intelligence, and exclude emotionality. The High Court is charged with the analysis of intricate logic, reason, and language out of which law is constructed.

The majority of the presidents of the United States have calibrated in the mid-400s, with many in the high 400s or at just 500. Their function is dedication to the task of defending the country against attackers, against enemies, and to uphold the Constitution. To this end, the President takes an oath with his hand on the Bible, which is witnessed by a representative of the Supreme Court. The President is expected to sublimate political partisanship and move from politician to statesman for the good of the country. Thus, the President's attitude is expected to be "the best possible course of action" rather than "anti" the opposition. Additionally, the President is expected to be inspirational and sincere, to unite the country by transcending factionalism and not responding in kind to vicious attack, slander, vociferous provocation, or being blamed for every social problem.

The demands on the President of the most powerful nation on earth are quite extreme, and the presidency is under constant public exposure by the media and subject to critical attack consequent to being in the spotlight. At times, it is of a brutally invasive media that magnifies the slightest trivia, such as stumbling on a step or losing one's balance. One can see that the lack of respect inherent in today's media reflects that same quality of a society in which disrespect pervades even childhood so that it has brought down the calibration of the ordinary classroom from 400 in traditional America to today's classroom at 190.

To this day, there is a compassionate respect for the agonizing decision that was forced on President Truman regarding the necessity of a triage benefit of dropping the atomic bomb. He had to weigh the morality of killing 180,000 civilians in order to prevent the estimated death of six or seven million people, had conventional warfare continued, which was therefore a problem of the situational ethics of triage. His decision calibrates at 475. The whole nation regretfully mourned the obvious decision that had to be made, along with the moral dilemma. It is, however, notable that the bombs that had to be dropped to end World War II were the last atomic bombs that have ever been dropped, which indicates that the world understood the underlying lesson and that the sacrifice apparently was not in vain.

President Roosevelt's frequent "Fireside Chats" (cal. 500) made the populace feel cared about and therefore more homogenous in attitude and supportive of the presidency itself, which is often between a rock and a hard place and is forced to choose the lesser of two evils.

When evaluating the spiritual aspects of the event, it is of interest to refer to the teachings of the ancient *Rig Veda* (cal. 705), which say that each level of life sacrifices itself to support life on a higher level, out of which there is accrued karmic merit as well as the undoing of past negative karma. This phenomenon underlies the concept of group karma and implies an answer to such questions as "What is the group karma of the vast hordes who, for centuries, massacred whole populations of innocent civilians, and why are millions of innocent populations periodically wiped out by genocide?"

U. S. Politics

Anarchy	105	Green Party	180
Abortion		Far Left Liberal	185
Anti-	250	Far Right Conservative	135-145
Pro-	235	Liberal	180-200
Church/Pike Committee		Libertarian Party	295
Hearings	185	McCarthy Hearings	185
Conservative Party	310	Moderates	200-390
Cultural Creatives	335	Republican Party	315
Democratic Party	310	Secularism	180
Domestic Partnership Law	335	Socialist Party	265
Evangelical Right		Torricelli Principle	160
(Moral Majority)	245-255	"Section 527"	
Gay Marriage Law		Organizations	200
(Massachusetts)	265		

Political parties operate at the interface between the populace and the government. Out of necessity, however, they have their own agendas and motives in order to survive, which are influenced by public opinion, personal viewpoints, philosophic agendas, and the need to serve vested interests, such as party contributors. Thus, there is the necessity for compromise, and the calibrations of the political parties reflect degrees of partialities, positionalities, and subserving the need to win. The various strategies employed are often similar to those of sports gamesmanship, and pollsters play an influential role. Calibrated levels tend to change as various positions and personalities fluctuate and reflect shifts of opinion.

Because emotional appeal and personal charisma are deemed as necessary to win, they frequently tend to override rationality and truth or spiritual principles. These factors bring down the overall calibrated levels of political parties from the lofty 500s of love or the 400s of reason to the practical "get it done" attitude of the high 200s and 300s, which is characterized by willingness, service, and productivity. Although politics may cite moral or even religious issues, it sometimes does so primarily for secular reasons, e.g., to win votes.

As would be suspected, extremists calibrate below 200, the level of truth and integrity. The Far Right tends to become fascist

(fascist ideology calibrates at 125), and the Far Left moves into the sophistry of thinly disguised Marxism (Marx calibrates at 130, communism at 160) and its distortion of reality (i.e., perpetrator/victim model).

U. S. Government Departments and Agencies (12/17/04)

Agriculture, Department of	200	Federal Bureau of	
Bureau of Indian Affairs,		Investigation	210
Dept. of the Interior,		Federal Drug	
Immigration and		Administration	200
Naturalization Service,		Homeland Security Agency	310
War on Drugs (group)	180-185	Internal Revenue Service	202
Center for Disease Control	210	National Security Council	250
Central Intelligence Agency	210	Nuclear Policy	460
CMS (Medicare/Medicaid)	206	Pentagon, The	210
Diplomatic Security Service	210	Public Health Service	212
Drug Enforcement Agency	202	Social Security	206
Federal Aviation			
Administration	205		

U. S. Policies and Agencies (12/17/04)

Border Protection	200	Security Intelligence	
Federal Anti-Terrorism Bill	405	Agencies	195
Immigration Policy		Terrorism Protection	
(Security/Function)	180	Overall	199

Interestingly, most government departments calibrate at about the same level as the giant international corporations and therefore reflect a business-like orientation. Implementation of government policies and regulations requires legalization plus vast government bureaucracies and agencies to carry out the complicated and practical requirements of those policies. This requires uniformity, dutiful job performance, and strict adherence to details. Their implementation requires vast amounts of paperwork, regulations, data accumulation, and giant electronic information networks. Efficiency is required at the interface of the budget vis-à-vis a demanding or even critical public as well as the judiciary and adversarial attacks by special interest groups. A bureaucratic official is thus saddled with enormous responsibility, along with the functional, practical, as well as political, resolutions of an incredibly complex mass of details and specifics. For example, Medicare regulations run over 10,000 pages, the U.S. Tax Code stacks to the ceiling, and there are forty-seven million files on science/research.

In addition to the requirements for complicated functioning, fairness of application is also a legal requisite, and, therefore, the heavily laden bureaucracies have to display equitable application to all segments of the population, which in itself can become quite contentious and litigious.

In addition to all the above-mentioned stresses, employees' on-the-job performances are constantly monitored, graded, and documented. In response to this, the overall stress of the bureaucratic world tends to result in their becoming fearful, defensive, cautious, and highly regimented. Therefore, documentation of compliance is seen to be highly important. In the health field, the inflexible rule is "If it isn't documented, it never happened" (and therefore will not be reimbursed).

It is understandable that, as a consequence of multiple complexities and pressures, the functions of some governmental departments have fallen below calibration level 200. As the public well knows, some departments have "lost" billions of dollars that are not even traceable due to the complexities of the system. Impairments of the government are the focus of both research and criticism (Stossel, 2004). Some departments are impaired because the top figures are political appointees rather than experts in their field (e.g., having a military general run the war on drugs), or the politicians have imposed restrictions such as those by the Church/Pike Committee of the 1970s (cal. 180), or the Torricelli Principle (cal. 160), which helped cripple the CIA and FBI, as did the Reno/Gorelick "wall" policy (cal. 190) that preceded the events of 9/11, which then triggered the Iraqi War. Paradoxically, the same elements that impaired government operations then attacked the later administration for the debacle of which they were primary designers.

Calibrations indicate that United States intelligence (but not the Pentagon) is compromised by undetected double agents that consist of a mix of (1) Far-Left ideologists, (2) Islamic converts, and (3) compartmentalized dual personalities (discussed in Chapter 11; also see Sperry, 2005).

Government operations became impaired by politicized obstructionism based on purposeful misrepresentation of issues and contradictory directions. An example is the Mexican immigration issue, which is obscured by irrelevancies. The actual problem is merely whether legality should be required or not, which is really not even an issue since the law is clear and comparable to the requirement for drivers' licenses. Whether the immigrants are Mexican or needed as workers by the economy has nothing to do with a legal registration requirement.

The country is under immanent threat by terrorists dedicated to destroying the country and who seek entry by all possible means. The front door to the United States through major airports and Customs border stations is apparently now reasonably functional (after fifteen obvious terrorists got through prior to 9/11), but now the back door is a wide-open invitation. European countries with lax immigration policies have come to regret them, and some countries are now actually held hostage by militant group threats (i.e., Sweden and France).

To clarify the issue, it is interesting to note that illegal immigration calibrates at 180 (therefore, technically a crime), while legal immigration calibrates at 210. Of importance is that Cuba's Castro is a leading coordinator of terrorists worldwide and is therefore hospitable to anti-U. S. operatives who simply go through South and Central America (where there is already a connection between the Mara Salvatrucha "MS-13" criminal gang and al-Qaeda) into Mexico and then into the United States through the wide-open Mexican border, where a million foreign nationals cross over yearly. That is equivalent to giving terrorists *carte blanche*, an opportunity that is equally enjoyed by drug smugglers and criminal escapees from foreign countries.

Another obstructionist issue to border control enforcement is the factor of operational costs and budget constraints that stand in contrast to the enormous annual expenditures for endless pork-barrel projects that are noncontributory to the national security, which would be assumed to have current priority, inasmuch as militant extremists are presently planning and pursuing strategies for additional terrorist attacks on vulnerable targets (calibrates as "true"). The nature and extent of such plans, as well as their details, are easily diagnosed by consciousness calibration technology, which also readily tracks the location of key figures, such as bin Ladin. As emphasized in earlier chapters, there are no secrets anymore—all is readily transparent. It does not take a $50-million reward to locate a wanted fugitive. The information is freely available in a matter of less than a minute (no budget requirements).

The tax-paying public might get greater satisfaction if they were supportive, friendly, and helpful to government agencies instead of subjecting them to an endless barrage of criticism and manipulative, politically-based lawsuits, such as the continuous assault by environmental activists (cal. 195). The budgets of forestry and parks departments are nearly wiped out by these disruptive partisan actions that seek to serve their own interests at a cost to the public (e.g., the Forestry Department currently has over five thousand pending lawsuits, so the money does not go to preserving the forests but instead is sidetracked to legal costs). As an observer remarked, "We can't save the trees because of the legal fees."

Judicial System

U. S. Supreme Court	480	Municipal Courts	305
Federal Judiciary	460	"Activist" Judges (collectively)	195
State Court System	405	U. S. Ninth Circuit Court	
Courts of Appeal	350	of Appeals	195

Judicial activism evolved over the course of decades, starting with Oliver Wendell Holmes who instituted the concept that the common law should conform to the feelings and demands of the community, "whether right or wrong," which resulted in politics' influencing what had previously been the "rule of law" (logic).

Displeasure with the degree to which politics have influenced the judiciary ("legislating from the bench") was expressed by the move in the U. S. House of Representatives to divide the U. S. Ninth Circuit Court of Appeals in San Francisco into three courts because the Ninth Circuit represents nine states with rapidly growing populations and has had a burgeoning caseload. The move would create fifty-eight new judgeships (Sherman, 2004). Criticism of the Ninth Circuit Court of Appeals results from its rulings that are often unconstitutional and constantly overturn rulings of the U. S. Supreme Court. If that is the record, one wonders why breaking up the Court with such a record would be opposed (Fox News, 12/2/04).

Public Service Organizations and Programs

4-H Clubs	370	Knights of Pythias	360
AARP	210	More, Thomas, Law	
American Legion	300	Center	455
American Medical		Red Cross, American	380
Association	300	Rotary	375
Big Brother-Big Sister	320	Salvation Army	375
Congress of Racial		Southern Poverty Law	
Equality (CORE)	345	Center	310
Doctors without Borders	500	United Way	360
Elks	375	USO	385
Girl Scouts/Boy Scouts	450	Veterans of Foreign Wars	270
Humane Society	285	Wounded Warrior Project	485
Innocence Project	475	YMCA/YWCA	380
Knights of Columbus	360		

Calibrations in the 200s indicate integrous service, function, and purpose. In the 300s, helpfulness, cordiality, and good will become prominent. These organizations collectively have public respect and support. Although each organization has its own requirements, such requirements stem from their stated intentions, adherence to principles, and the right of assembly and self-determination. Overall, they are humane and benevolent by intention, and membership or participation is restricted by the underlying tenets upon which each organization was formed. Membership is voluntary, and funding is by public support rather than by taxation, which allows them more autonomy than a government agency. Thus, they are simultaneously both private and public, subject to the pressures of political and cultural change. Faith-based institutions often have separate public service programs that are nondenominational and publicly funded, such as Catholic Charities, Jewish Family Services, and several Protestant social agencies. The taxpayer monies do not go to the organizations themselves but solely to their public service functions (a distinction often overlooked by critics).

Several prominent organizations that a decade ago calibrated as integrous have subsequently fallen greatly, and instead of being truly of public service in their policies and functioning, they have now become dedicated to political activism (Flynn, 2004.)

A Survey of America: The Country

The reason why critics fail to accurately describe the truth about America is that, until very recently, it was not possible to accurately identify exactly what truth really is. Unless one suspects that appearance is not essence, social evaluations reflect positionalities, which result from duality. The biases of the ego automatically determine what it perceives. Analogously, prior to the discoveries of X-rays, MRIs, or blood counts, clinicians were often incorrect in their diagnoses for lack of those tools and the availability of modern technology.

America is a very impressive subject to study, and consciousness research is a whole new method of viewing and analyzing, which, like an X-ray, reveals the hidden underpinnings of both weakness and strength. The study can start with some indisputable and statistically verifiable facts with which to pursue the investigation.

America is a democratic meritocracy, a constitutional republic, and currently the world's most powerful nation. It has high per-capita income, high overall level of health, long life span, low infant mortality rate, high hourly-worker productivity, and high economic output, all of which occur in a free economy, with personal liberty as well as safety nets below the lowest economic level. Its benevolence, both as a country (fifty-nine billion dollars in foreign aid annually) and individually, exceeds that of any other nation and is unequaled in history. (It provides forty percent of the world's philanthropy.). U.S. government aid is supplemented by huge contributions from the personal sector as well as almost all major corporations, such as Pfizer, Coca Cola, Exxon, Citigroup, the Gates Foundation Abbott Laboratories, Johnson & Johnson, Nike, General Electric, First Data, PepsiCo, Marriott, Starbucks, and numerous others (Regan, 12/31/04). America is a country that forgives its former enemies and then voluntarily rebuilds their country as the United States citizens sacrifice their work through taxes. America allows for freedom *for* religion and, simultaneously, freedom *from* religion. Every person has an equal vote, and the literary world and the media are free of government censorship.

In addition, there is freedom of speech to an unprecedented degree. The wealth of the average American is beyond even the wildest imagination of other cultures (sixty-eight percent of families own their own homes). There are nations that still labor long days for less than a dollar a day. Sixty-seven percent of the world's population lives on the equivalent of two U. S dollars or less per day. Education is omnipresent, available to everyone, and the taxed citizens support the education of children who are not even their own.

America also has a very high literacy rate, and public education is integrous, free, and widely available, with no requirements. Great libraries, museums, and art galleries abound, as do endless recreational areas, parks, playgrounds, pools, aquariums, and planetariums. Even the poorest citizen has access to the conse-quences of wealth that were unavailable to even the greatest of previous monarchs.

Technical healthcare is of such an advanced quality that citizens from other countries, including even their rulers, flock to this country for its advanced medical expertise. However, approximately one-third of Americans below age 64 do not have health insurance (82 million as of June 2004), but neither does the same percentage have life insurance, nor do they have legal wills. Because of the rising cost, medical benefits are being dropped by employers who are now in worldwide competition with countries where labor costs are much lower because of not only lower wages but also the absence of employee benefits that inflate costs (the "Catch 22" of current unionization). Medical insurance is usually a financial, not a health decision, and it is notable that even illegal immigrants have access to medical care, as do the poor through a variety of publicly funded programs. The pharmaceuticals developed in the United States spread across a world that is not required to share in the multimillion-dollar cost of developing a new drug (currently $7 million). The foreign countries, sheltered by national borders, then copy the results of this research and undersell the U. S. market.

The cost of medical care in the United States is the highest in the world and has risen because of the rapid inflation of layers of administrative, bureaucratic, and legal regulatory require- ments. Healthcare regulations cost the U. S. $256 billion per year with a cost/benefit ratio of 2 to 1 and price at least seven million Americans out of the healthcare system. The Food and Drug Administration's regulations cost $49 billion annually but provide only $7 billion in benefits.

The medical liability system costs $114 billion but provides only $33 billion in benefits. Mandated coverage rules cost $15 billion to provide $13 billion in benefits (Arizona Medical Jour- nal, 2004). Malpractice insurance has also escalated the charges for medical services while actual physicians' fees have primarily merely kept up with inflation and are only ten percent of the actual cost. It is not the actual cost of medical malpractice insur- ance itself that escalates medical care expenditure but instead, it is the overall litigious climate in which tort law has resulted in *The*

Lawsuit Lottery (Lodmell and Lodmell, 2004), which encourages litigation in a society that is progressively "entitled" and operates progressively in accord with the victim/perpetrator model. This creates the unreal expectancy for only optimal outcomes, and if anybody dies of a fatal illness, it must be somebody's fault, etc. This results in the practice of defensive medicine, which includes the ordering of endless expensive tests and duplication of procedures (e.g., a $3,000 MRI instead of a $100 X-ray, etc.)

Consciousness research indicates that only about four percent of the people at the bottom of society calibrate over 200, and that the majority calibrate extremely low—actually well below 100 (i.e., apathy). The really "down and out" are afflicted with drugs, jail, prison, criminality, poverty, brutality, and lack of concern for others. They rely very heavily on blame, excuses, and other self-weakening ego mechanisms.

Approximately three to four percent of the overall population is in jail, prison, or on probation, and in this subcultural subgroup, the average level of consciousness is 40 to 50. This recidivist population is characterized by widespread addiction, criminality, and personality disorders, including a sizeable proportion of psychopathic personalities with demonstrable, impaired development of the prefrontal cortex as a genetic factor. Some important characteristics of the problem populations are the inability to control impulses or to delay gratification, the failure to learn from experience, disrespect for authority and the rights of others, and the failure to anticipate consequences. The lack of motivation and the resistance to treatment or re-motivation are due to an intractable core of overinflated, self-centered narcissism.

From previous discussions and data presented, it becomes obvious that social failure of individuals or groups is not "caused" by anything external, such as race, American politics, or society (i.e., the limited Newtonian paradigm), but instead is a consequence of the field effect. The content of the field is the consequence of the quality of the field itself (e.g., the "broken window" principle). Just as the cook's pot attracts salt and pepper, carrots, potatoes, tomatoes, pieces of beef, and leftover chicken, so a low energy field equally attracts drugs, violence, sickness, malnutrition, poverty, violence, prison, drugs, alcohol, and squalor. The "cooking pot" of a negative energy field attracts the ingredients. The carrots do not "cause" the potatoes, nor do the salt and pepper "cause" the scraps of chicken or result in boiling water. The source of the phenomenon is endogenous, intrinsic and innate, and not exogenous as the consequence of externals. Nobody "causes" someone to throw their trash on the street, which is, in and of itself, a very significant, diagnostic telltale sign.

Correlation of Levels of Consciousness and Societal Problems

Level of Consciousness	Rate of Unemployment	Rate of Poverty	Happiness Rate "Life is OK"	Rate of Criminality
600+	0%	0.0%	100%	0.0%
500-600	0%	0.0%	98%	0.5%
400-500	2%	0.5%	79%	2.0%
300-400	7%	1.0%	70%	5.0%
200-300	8%	1.5%	60%	9.0%
100-200	50%	22.0%	15%	50.0%
50-100	75%	40.0%	2%	91.0%
<50	97%	65.0%	0%	98.0%

We can see that the downside is not "caused" by the overall American culture, economy, or nation but is the automatic consequence of the human population itself representing the whole spectrum of the evolution of human consciousness in *all* countries. Whether it seems "fair" or not (see end of this chapter), each element just "is that which it is" as an expression of its own potential in a given context and time.

According to the U. S. Census Bureau (August 2004), poverty is the condition of approximately 12.5%, or 35.9 million Americans (out of a total population of 300 million). The reported poverty level is the consequence of its bureaucratic definition. The percentage increases if the poverty level income is raised and decreases as the poverty level income is defined as occurring at a lower figure. What is designated as "poverty level" in the U. S. would exceed the income of ninety percent of the population of poorer countries.

The median household income for the U. S. is $43,318. The poor in America have the availability of cars or public transportation, refrigeration, radios, plumbing, pure water, electricity, medical assistance, welfare, emergency and police services, etc., all of which are unavailable to the poverty stricken of other cultures. The underlying problems reflect the negative energy inputs that collectively influence the impact of the overall field. Of major sociological importance is the very dramatic major change that takes place below consciousness level 200. Unemployment jumps from just 8 percent to 50 percent; poverty escalates from 1.5 to 22 percent; happiness decreases from 60 to only 15 percent, and criminality skyrockets from 9 to 50 percent.

Similar correlation charts can be constructed that show the almost identical pattern for the percentage of each consciousness level with incidence of physical illness, mental disorders, victims of crime, automobile accidents, health insurance coverage, rates of AIDS and STDs, arrest rate, domestic violence, child abuse, incarceration, birth rate, gang membership, exposure to violent media, drugs, and the time children spend watching television. A typical child watches twenty-eight or more hours of low-level television programming per week, seeing more than eight thousand murders while just in elementary school (Winik, 2004). In seventy-five percent of murder stories, the killer goes free and gets away, unremorseful, and often with an inflated hero image, complete with brutality, profanity, obscenity, and strong sexual imagery.

While public attention is focused primarily on the socio-economic problems of inner-city neighborhoods, the same impairments are visible in semi-rural areas as well. Small-town newspaper reports reflect the same types of problems that prevail in the big cities. The *Court Report* (July 2004) for a typical town of a few thousand people lists (for one week) twenty-seven arrests for disorderly conduct, trespass, intoxication, driving without a license or on a suspended license, domestic violence, driving under the influence or without insurance, etc. Collectively, the law violators calibrate at 185 and represent recidivism and lack of personal responsibility.

The rate of true poverty is far higher in non-free-enterprise systems. The price of freedom entails some degree of risk, which, in turn, spurs greater effort and enterprise. In contrast, welfare societies are more complacent and less innovative because the government assumes responsibility for their survival.

The Strength of America

Both the pessimist and the optimist ruefully observe that earthly human life is not universally beatific nor is it exactly a celestial realm, and the thinking person concludes that it seems to be a proving ground, a staging area, or a school of opportunity that offers an almost infinite potential for individual and spiritual growth. To help understand the seeming inequality of human life, it is important to remember that at the moment of birth, every individual already has a calibratable level of consciousness, and the overall course of the ship already appears on the compass.

Despite its limitations, America's society calibrates at 421, higher than that of any country in the world. The very foundation and structure of the government arise from the loftiest of ideals. Democracy (actually a constitutional republic) calibrates higher than any other prevalent form of government (at 410); however, it does not guarantee perfection but only a relatively high level of integrity, intention, and accountability. The power of government is by free consent of the governed, which in itself differs dramatically from governments based solely on force and within which there is no free consent. A positive view of America is not optimistic but simply factual.

The unique greatness of America was the thrust of de Toc- queville's *Democracy in America* (1835; cal. 455) and has been corroborated continuously by numerous thinkers and statesmen ever since. Hillary Clinton stated, "America is the greatest country the world has ever seen" (TV News, New York, June 21, 2004). This theme continued in *Defining America,* the subject of a special issue of *U. S. News & World Report* (June, 2004).

Calibrating levels of truth and consciousness is very pragmatic. It saves time and laborious efforts to understand phenomena by cutting through rhetoric and appearance and getting quickly to the core of an issue. A calibration is like a fast snapshot that captures the essence of an issue. The calibrated level reveals in capsule form what it is really all about.

The United States Economy

This is the "great giant" that Admiral Yamamoto ruefully regretted having awakened at the time of the attack on Pearl Harbor. It also turned out to be the formidable nemesis because American industrial might proved to be unbeatable. This economy, the product of free enterprise and financial capital, turned out to be the great bulwark and fortress of freedom that the free world enjoys to this day. Inasmuch as a vast economy cannot arise without capital, the nature of capital itself deserves examination.

The common conception is that capital means wealth or money in the bank. It fails to recognize that the true source of capital is the creativity of the mind from which the accumulation of money is the inevitable consequence or the automatic result of creativity, genius, inspiration, dedication, hard work, integrous and often grueling self-sacrifice and effort, as well as discipline and resourcefulness. One single brilliant idea (e.g., Edison-electricity) can, does, and has spawned more wealth than the total product of the economies of whole nations. The enormous accomplishments of America are well-documented in the book, *They Made America* (Evans, 2004).

Why America is Successful

The field of consciousness innate to America supports creativity, invention, education, and innovation, and it rewards self-initiated efforts with acclaim and excitement. The discovery of electricity, direct and alternating current, and the light bulb resulted in lighting up the entire world as well as providing a ubiquitous, ready source of power for industry and productivity on all levels, from giant machinery to the kitchen toaster.

Out of America's inventiveness, as if electricity were not enough, arose the telephone, the telegraph, radio, television, the airplane, the computer chip, the Dictaphone, the computer, the whole electronics industry, the Internet, computer hardware and software, and the list goes on. The entire worldwide airline industry arose from the flight at Kittyhawk. A worldwide entertainment industry arose from the invention of the movies. Add to these the seminal discoveries in medicine, pharmaceuticals, materials research, and a cornucopia of scientific inventions that pours forth and benefits the entire world.

In addition to this enormous productivity are added carefully crafted merchandising and supply-and-delivery retail systems, such that Wal-Mart is the largest corporation in the world, with over one million employees. Corporate America is catching up on sexual equality, which is not just an American phenomenon but is a worldwide social shift in other countries as well, such as Denmark, Canada, etc. (ATF, 2004).

The calibrated level of most of the big corporations in the world (Ford, General Motors, etc.) is at approximately the same level as the U. S. government agencies, which reflects responsible, accountable performance and pragmatic integrity. (Jack Welch, former president of GE, at one time was proclaimed by *Fortune* magazine as the foremost CEO in America, a reputation hard to obtain in the field of very competitive, high-performance CEOs.)

Add to America's discoveries those of refrigeration, air conditioning, the microwave oven plus hundreds of appliances, the steamboat of Robert Fulton, the Watt/Evans steam engine, Howe's sewing machine, the Winchester rifle, the Smith & Wesson revolver, multistage evaporation and distillation (sugar refining), radiology, clipper ships, the Otis elevator, escalators, robotics, cybernetics, the razor blade, the cotton gin, skyscrapers, FM radio, the super heterodyne circuit, Polaroid imaging, copy machines, digital computers, transistors, software, hardware, medical devices (MRI and CAT scan), plastics, and, last but not least, atomic energy. Henry Ford perfected the assembly line and introduced time/motion studies out of which eventually evolved safety devices and the science of ergonomics.

The life of Ben Franklin exemplifies the essentials of the American tradition. He was inventive (Franklin stove, bifocals, electricity, the lightning rod), self-educated, dedicated to self-improvement (*Poor Richard's Almanac*), and of virtuous generosity (he founded the University of Pennsylvania). He demonstrated entrepreneurship (owner of a printing business), personal freedom, and broke through the social class (from poverty to wealth, from daily worker to international diplomat and social icon). He supported all religions and taught that the worship of God was best served by doing good for self and others. He also demonstrated continuous self-improvement as a lifestyle. He was a writer and publisher, accomplished politician, and statesman who assisted in construction of the United States Constitution. All in all, he personified the potential and realization of what became the American dream of opportunity.

Similar creativity and ingenuity are exemplified by the legendary life of Andrew Carnegie (cal. 490), who arrived from Scotland with twenty-five cents in his pocket. He built the steel industry and then established the tradition of philanthropy. He even tried to stop World War I by offering the Kaiser a huge fortune to not go to war but was sadly unsuccessful. Both Franklin and Carnegie demonstrated the potentiality of the essence of America.

It is this immense creativity that is the "capital" out of which monetary wealth automatically evolves, along with millions of jobs and a rise in prosperity in which, like a rise in sea level, everyone is lifted because it eventuates into the public arena rather than just private ownership. It manifests as the enormous infrastructure, including public holdings, the transportation industry, and the enormous commerce that supports all governmental operations. Capital thus becomes the enormous uplifting energy of the entire field of a society that recognizes and supports the value of individual and private ownership. That was the very thing lacking in Mao's China, which calibrated at 150 and saw the greatest starvation (30 million people) the world has ever seen, indicating the total failure of Marxism, collectivism, and the philosophy upon which they are based (i.e., Karl Marx, level 130). All governments are operationally capitalistic for they all depend for survival and operations on capital, whether its acquisition is by conquest, confiscation, or taxation.

A free-enterprise society rewards individual invention and creativity. (Twelve million people in the United States are self-employed.) Everyone is free to create a new idea, obtain a patent, and then solicit venture capital and investors, e.g., Microsoft. An unrecognized, enormous benefit that arises from capitalism is the emergence of another typically American institution, that of the great philanthropists who then return to the populace the immeasurable benefits of the great museums, parks, art galleries, colleges, universities, planetariums, research laboratories, and music halls. Carnegie's legacy was the establishment of great libraries all over the country, where every citizen has free access to the world's information that is now being transferred to the Worldwide Web. The great philanthropic foundations are legendary (Rockefeller, Gates, Carnegie, Ford, Mellon, et al.) and pour billions of dollars back into society.

The capitalistic culture produces tens of millions of jobs and self-employment opportunities, of which there have been no actual serious shortage since the end of the Great Depression. The official unemployment rate is a misleading statistic in that it reports applicants for unemployment claims. In this lifetime, there has never been unavailability of self-employment opportunities or even of "jobs," only unavailability of "jobs" that people want. While the front pages of newspapers report a current unemployment rate, in the back of the newspapers are page after page of advertised, unfilled jobs and opportunities, and there are "Help Wanted" signs in most store windows for jobs that may not fulfill ambitions but would provide money if that were the most important lack. Paradoxically, people go back to work when their unemployment insurance runs out. The truly unemployable rely on the infrastructure safety net that provides numerous supportive and educational programs. The unemployment rate in the United States averages forty to fifty percent lower than that of socialist countries. The huge economic engine of a free capitalistic enterprise system produces an economic base of staggering proportions ($1.5 trillion per year) that allows America to be the biggest philanthropic nation on earth.

A quick glance at the total capital worth of the federal government reveals that the hypothetical "national debt" is a misnomer and a misleading statistic. The wealth of the government is currently (by calibration) $9 quadrillion inasmuch as it owns multimillions of acres of extremely valuable land, including oil potential, timber, mining, etc. In addition, its capital assets, if one considers all the ownerships—the property of the military, all the government buildings, highways, warehouses, and rights-of-way—are prodigious. The concept of a national debt is comparable to a multimillionaire who uses a small portion of his wealth to buy a new company with a fifty-percent down payment, with the balance to be paid on a scheduled basis. He now reports that he is "in debt" because he has payments to make on the balance of his loan. Such a millionaire cannot really be said to be "in debt" at all but arbitrarily behind in payments, which he could easily pay off completely by selling assets.

Spending money faster than it is coming in, e.g., "budget deficit" (Greenspan, 2004) is not the same as being in debt. In real debt, a person owes more than their assets are worth and therefore has a negative net worth, which could hardly be said of the federal government. There are states, especially in the western U. S., where the federal government actually owns eighty-five percent of the land, together with the water, timber, and mining rights. It can hardly be said to be "in debt" when its real problem is budgeting for a vast array of programs, many of which are of dubious merit and represent political ideologies rather than actual public need.

When a society becomes industrialized and moves from an agrarian to a commercial culture, there is a time lag. This transition occurred not only in America but also in every other developing country. During this period, children and women labor at low-pay factory jobs. Emerging industries initially depend on low wages, long working hours, nonexistent employee benefits, and stressful working conditions. However, twenty years later, in a basically integrous society, the whole picture changes and the accumulated capital is now distributed through better working conditions and higher wages, which are the byproducts of economic development.

Henry Ford dazzled the world of workers in 1914 when he paid five dollars a day, which eventually became five dollars an hour and attracted workers from all over the country. In those days, the average pay for unskilled labor was thirty-five cents an hour. On the other hand, Ford forbade humor or laughing in the work place, and bathroom visits were by permission of the foreman only and were time monitored.

Cultural Changes

Prior to World War II, the American economy was fifty-percent agrarian. Half of America lived on farms where work was equally divided between men and women, and domestically, women were held in high esteem. Out of respect, men desisted from vulgarity, stood up when women entered the room, and opened doors for them. Overall, the woman, especially the mother, was honored and revered and had authority over the domestic aspects of life while the men tended to the crops, livestock, and equipment. The wife was not a job seeker in the commercial work force unless she happened to be a teacher or a nurse. It was the social responsibility of the man to support the woman. For a wife to "have to go to work" was a disgrace, and a man would "die of shame" at such public evidence of his inadequacy as a provider. People felt sorry for a wife who "had to go to work."

Areas of interest were relatively genderized overall. Women exhibited little interest in business or politics. Men went into another room after dinner to discuss such subjects. Women did not noticeably enter the employment world until World War II, when "Rosie, the Riveter" was celebrated as saving the day.

With cultural change, women entered the workforce in greater numbers, and the prejudice they had to overcome was based primarily on habitual stereotypes, not on economic competition or prejudice as such. Frankly, nobody had ever met a lady plumber, and no women were CEOs of giant corporations because they were absent from that culture rather than being prohibited from it (i.e., a field effect).

The benefit to the overall economy and its capitalistic base escalated when women became progressively more involved. They have now evolved to become CEOs of very major U. S. corporations and to hold high offices in the government as well. In other areas, women have become legendary billionaires solely out of their own potential initiative. They also have brought a major new energy into the media, that of caring and love. The most admired personality on television today is a woman who runs the most successful television show, which has the highest calibration of any such program in the media, currently over 500. She and other prominent women CEOs now appear with regularity on the front cover of *Fortune* magazine, which had formerly been a solely male institution. In 2003, corporations led by women CEOs outperformed those led by men.

All the above is cited to demonstrate that America is not only a land of opportunity but, even more importantly, it is also a flexible, self-correcting society based on a sense of balance and fairness in which the injustices of inequities call forth corrective and sympathetic responses. There is practically no cause that lacks supporters. Thus, the social reality is inherently integrous, which is the consequence of the overall proximate field, the level of which was already set by a Constitution that calibrates over 700. Thus, a field of high integrity has an invisible influence in that it reveals itself in injustice and nonintegrity, much like a clean shirt reveals a spot.

Curiosity arises as to why America represents such an enormous confluence of so many remarkable qualities—material, psychological, and inspirational. Creative genius birthed the majority of the great industries and inventions that support the economy today. The most productive society in history emerged and spawned a free, self-correcting society on top of a governmental foundation of the highest possible calibration. All of this emerged within a land that itself is of enormous space and endless breathtaking beauty and contains freestanding and endless riches—gold, silver, copper, platinum, rare metals, timber, wild-life, and, most importantly, iron, the basic ingredient of steel.

Again, seemingly fortuitously, the engineering and structural use of steel was facilitated by another ready asset, the availability of Native American workers who had no fear of heights. Thus arose the great structures and bridges, and out of creative inspiration came the symbolic Empire State Building. This was the fruit of the coalition of creative genius, skill, and the power of an economy with the availability of working capital made up of the earnings and savings of the workforce of America, without which there could be no railroads, airlines, sidewalks, stores, automobiles, life-saving drugs, federal budget, Medicare, welfare, or telephone system—in fact, not even a public restroom.

From the foregoing overall analysis and historical review, as well as calibrations of the levels of integrity of its elements, it can be readily observed that in all critical and important areas of human life, America represents prodigious accomplishment and overall integrity worthy of respect. Whereas citizens in a free country, as part of the ongoing political process and social evolution, are free or even encouraged to criticize the country (honest dissent calibrates from 210-330), in contrast, political extremists calibrate at 160. (Note that America, typically alone, is pouring millions of dollars and medicine toward conquering AIDS in far-away Africa.) An example of negative distortion is provided by the denunciation of outsourcing as due to "greed" or "the President" (calibrates as "false"), whereas it is actually a consequence of the Internet and international economics (calibrates as "true"). Outsourcing is currently done by most countries, cities, states, localities, and corporations for economic survival. Even Mexico has been outsourcing to China (Brezosky, 2005; Kniazkov, 2005).

In contrast to native-born denouncers of their own native land, America embraces immigrants who are appreciative of the true land of opportunity. Impressive for its open-eyed honesty and integrity is this description of America by a fluent, talented immigrant. It appeared in brief form in an editorial (Devji, 2004) but with permission from the author, her "Ten Noble Traits of Americans" (cal. 470) is abridged here:

I am an American. I love being American! All that is beautiful, righteous, and joyous in me is enhanced and affirmed by being American. Ten traits mark who we are as a people:

1. **GODLY**: Almost all of us acknowledge that a power beyond us guides the swirling destinies of men; the Native Americans pray to a 'Great Spirit' and with a reverent heart tie it to the sacred earth and skies of America.

2. **TOLERANT**: European Christians settled this land and wrote its constitution. They then opened their arms wide and welcomed people from the rest of the world. Now mosques, synagogues, and temples pepper the landscape along with churches. Muslims can worship more freely here than in most Moslem countries. Sikhs wear their turbans and Jews their yamakas.

3. **VISIONARY**: While we are an earthbound nation enjoying our material success, we are also an extraordinarily vision-ary people. We dare dream impossible dreams. We soar the skies searching the stars. We have landed on planets that lie shrouded in billions of years of silence. On earth, our vision in the healing arts will literally make the lame walk and the blind see.

4. **PROSPEROUS**: The capacity of Americans to work hard joy-ously is the stuff of which the wealth of this country is made. Our work ethic is unmatched. We are the richest country in the world, but our children start baby-sitting, bagging groceries, and cutting lawns when they are still in school.

5. **GENEROUS**: There is possibly no country on earth that has been untouched by the generosity of Americans. We respond to earthquakes, floods, and famines with compassionate hearts. We send money, medicines, clothes, and prayers to victims of every color and creed, and even to our "enemies." We know that we are custodians of wealth, not its owners.

6. **RESILIENT**: Americans have an uncanny capacity to bounce back from adversity—accidents, bankruptcies, and divorces.

They rebuild their bodies, businesses, and lives. They do not sit in dark corners; they fight back

7. **COURAGEOUS**: A four-year-old in my neighborhood comes around the corner wearing a helmet, riding a scooter, and my aunts in India still hold on to their 14-year-olds protectively! Americans seem to be born with an extra streak of courage. It seems to be seared into our soul. We teach the world the meaning of the word with our daring spirits and our exploits.

8. **HUMOROUS**: We love laughter and life. You can tell an American abroad because he is generally the one who has the biggest smile, sometimes the loudest voice and laughter, and is the most approachable. An American will fill a room with his infectious goodwill and just will not treat anyone as a stranger.

9. **SELF-INTROSPECTION**: Occupying the unique position that we do in the world, we could be really arrogant and indifferent to people's opinions. But we are childlike in our need for approval. We are a self-introspective people, we dissect our actions and thoughts, we form committees, and we discuss them in newspapers, television, and town hall meetings.

10. **SWEETNESS**: Countries, like people, become dry and arid if the quality of sweetness is absent from the souls of their citizens. Americans have been blessed with a rare quality of sweetness of the soul.

Because of its positive qualities, America attracts millions of immigrants from all over the world, as it has for centuries. Although Devji's description of America is specific to the United States, her capacity to see the positives reflects what could also be apparent to visitors or immigrants to other countries that also represent freedom and opportunity. Her statements (cal. 470) are included to serve as a contrast to the current "hate America" views, which all calibrate below 200. While other countries, such as Canada, calibrate high, they are not under an orchestrated vilification from both within and without. Critics attack policies but not their own country, which represents the malice of personality problems and not politics. (To "bite the hand that feeds you" calibrates at 160, indicating a loss of reality testing.)

Apropos of Canada, the following are the results of a Gallup Organization Survey reported in the Business section of Toronto's *Globe and Mail* newspaper on October 18, 2004:

		United States	Canada	Great Britain
1.	Completely satisfied with opportunities for promotion	40%	29%	25%
2.	Completely satisfied with their boss	60%	47%	42%
3.	Completely satisfied with recognition of work accomplishments	48%	37%	37%
4.	Belief in God	90%	71%	52%
5.	Belief in the Devil	70%	37%	29%
6.	Belief in Angels	78%	56%	36%
7.	Average hours worked per week	42%	41%	39%
8.	Work more than 45 hours per week	45%	30%	28%

The evolution of consciousness, the development of mankind, and spiritual evolution follow along roughly parallel lines as outlined by the Map of Consciousness (see Appendix B). The bottom represents self-interest. Its intention is survival, and when it lacks energy, it ends as apathy and death. Once this energy is sufficient, life survives. It moves up to mastery, assertiveness, doingness, the capacity to perform, competition, acquisition or accumulation, and pride. Only then does the person become more interested in the rights and welfare of others. The emergence of the intellect then subserves survival and social expansion. The predominant life energy eventually moves to the heart, and the capacity for love, from an evolutionary viewpoint, could be viewed as a luxury not available when life is still clinging by its fingernails to a precipice.

From an evolutionary viewpoint, love first appears as the maternal instinct, and the male does not participate in that energy field until relatively quite late in evolution. In fact, romantic love is a very recent phenomenon of human culture. From the heart, through evolution, the spiritual energy results in creativity, spiritual discernment, and finally, advanced spiritual awareness.

Throughout America's development and history, one sees a society that has been bulwarked and reinforced by the ethics of an intrinsic religiosity. The great majority of citizens (approximately ninety-two percent) believes in God and thus holds itself to be ultimately answerable to a higher authority. It was this intrinsic core of integrity that called forth the necessity of transcending slavery and then eventually racism itself. Intimidation by the Ku Klux Klan in the South came to an end. The historic Civil War ended slavery at the cost of thousands of lives of volunteer soldiers on both sides of the conflict. Men die for their beliefs, and that is why calibrating the levels of belief systems is so important. The Civil War pitted human rights against states' rights and the vested interests of the plantation owners. In the end, as would be expected from a country such as America, justice and equality prevailed, emerging victoriously over the principles of self-interest. Although there is a conflict of force within a linearly defined area for a time, eventually the power of the contextual field corrects the imbalance and guarantees the final result.

From a spiritual or humanistic/moral viewpoint, the 1800s were America's darkest period. Sweatshops and the abuse of workers were prevalent, and an orchestrated genocide of the Native American Plains Indians was horrific and savage, as was the purposeful killing of fifty million buffalo. The nobility of the great Plains Indian leaders, such as Black Kettle, White Antelope, Sitting Bull, and Crazy Horse was unrecognized, as they were perceived as "heathen," despite the fact that White Antelope had been awarded the Peace Medal by President Lincoln. Racial prejudice was rampant, and the end of the Civil War triggered the rise of the Ku Klux Klan.

It took another whole century before civil rights were established and even longer for them to be actually socially implemented. The downside of the whole era was the consequence of the dominance of the survival emotions of hate and fear coming from the old animal brain of the evolutionary ego.

The social emancipation of blacks in America took almost a century and finally emerged victorious under President Lyndon Johnson in the 1960s, energized by Martin Luther King's peaceful demonstrations. From there, equality in the workplace evolved, and now blacks are at the top of government, academic, and military posts, and in an advisory capacity to the President. The Oprah Winfrey Show is the most popular in America, as was the Bill Cosby Show. It would appear that reverse discrimination and racial quota systems have been supplanted by the public recognition of integrity and performance, irrespective of race. (The "racial card" play calibrates at 185.)

Some moral restitution due to the Native Americans has emerged at last in the Smithsonian Institution's Museum of the American Indian in Washington, DC, which, at calibration level 460, is an integrous recognition of their great culture. The five-story building covers ten thousand years of history. At one time of Western expansion, there were approximately six to nine million natives whose number diminished to 250,000 by the year 1900. The population has since risen to 2.5 million (*Arizona Republic*, 9/19/04).

The unfolding of the evolutionary process to observation appears to be sequential and due to local causes. Actually, it is the spontaneous, impersonal field effect in which everyone is potentiated to play a role. Evolution appears as change, which is merely the emergence of evolution because creation and evolution are one and the same thing.

Appearance is not essence, perception is not reality, and the cover is not the book. Error is quite often convincing, which is an unpleasant fact to consider and accept. Everyone secretly believes that their own personal view of the world is "real," factual and true.

Anti- ("Hate") America (cal. 90-190)

This phenomenon demonstrates the negative effect of memes that calibrate below 200 (135-185). In this case, the contagious spread of the meme/virus of disinformation stemmed from several origins simultaneously:

1. Envy of power and success—endemic in France after their poor showing in World War II; fueled by the pomposity of Gen. Charles de Gaulle.

2. Islamic Fundamentalism—Wahhabism, al-Qaeda, etc.

3. Duplicitous members of the United Nations ("food for oil," etc.)

4. Rivalry of European Union nations.

5. Anti-American propaganda of the U. S. Far Left.

6. Dissemination of the French-published book *9/11: The Big Lie*, by Thierry Meyssan (2002).

7. Anti-Israel political positions and anti-Semitism of Protestant church organizations.

8. Pro-Palestine, revolutionary, and terrorist organizations.

9. Islamic fundamentalist recruits, terrorists, and sympathizers (mosques in the U. S. and Europe funded from Iran, Saudi Arabia, et al.)

10. Academic leftists—Chomsky, et al.

11. Leftist columnists and media in the United States.

12. al-Jazeera television in Arab countries.

13. Anti-United States memes (e.g., "America is evil") in Canada and secular countries (40% of Canadian schoolchildren).

14. Hollywood and celebrity "cultural elite" and moviemakers.

15. Ultra-rich benefactors of Far Left organizations and propaganda.

16. Secular, "anti-God," and "anti-Christian" Circuit Court activist judicial rulings by legislation from the bench.

17. Narcissistic personality disorders ("bite the hand that feeds you," cal. 160).

18. The "vilify the leader" syndrome (discussed elsewhere). The Anti-America syndrome has been well-covered in the literature by writers Coulter, Timmerman, Frum, Gartz, Goldberg, Ravel, Gibson, et al., and was the subject of a four-part series (*Hating America*) on the Fox News Channel (November 23-26, 2004). It was discussed by many television guests.

19. Naïveté and the lack of development of consciousness of seventy-eight percent of the world's population (forty-nine percent in the U. S.) who are prone to "hating the rich uncle on the hill."

20. Fear of the world's most powerful nation arising from international rivalry and power politics.

21. Rivalry of political leaders and political systems, e.g., democracy vs. socialism, imperialism, theocracies, dictatorships, and feudal/tribal underdeveloped nations and societies.

22. Greed for and envy of power and success.

23. Unresolved psychological problems in poorly parented people with repressed hostility, envy, and hatred of all authority figures, which are viewed as authoritarian, repressive, and tyrannical rather than as integrous, protective, and supportive.

25. Shame and guilt of lesser-developed cultures that are confronted by the more advanced culture and overall level of consciousness of the United States.

26. Persistence of instinctual animal behaviors in populations below consciousness level 200 (as described in Section I), such as wolf-pack rivalry for Alpha-male position to be the reigning "beachmaster."

27. Lack of dominance of positive motives in the less evolved world population, e.g., altruism, loyalty, integrity, truth, compassionate humanitarianism, etc.

28. Readiness of naïve intellects to be programmed by propaganda or memes, especially when propagated via the media—a lack of intellectual critical function.

29. Class rivalry.

30. The inner excitement of the spectator and participant (politics as a spectator sport).

31. Outlet for personal narcissistic frustrations and projected blame.

32. Satisfaction from perverse contrariness and faultfinding.

33. Intolerance of any defect in idealized father figures.

34. The persistence of Marxist ideology in disguised form (perpetrator/victim).

35. Overt religious hatred and bigotry.

36. The overall preponderance of ignorance and naïveté in the human population.

37. The pattern exhibited by the anti-Semitic impact of the infamous *Protocol of the Elders of Zion* (cal. 90) on spreading anti-Semitic hatred that fueled Nazi Germany and World War II, the concentration camps, and genocide of six million people. The infectious falsity even affected Henry Ford and thereby numerous Americans. The seeds that were dormant are again being fertilized.

38. Freud's "Thanatos"—the deeply repressed death instinct that triggers self-destruction, suicide, and the seduction of the thrill of danger and mayhem, especially if there is mass participation and its implied approval.

39. Denial of the obvious (an elephant is in the living room) because it would elicit fear.

40. Conspiracy theories (cal. 165).

41. The preponderance of the collective ignorance of mankind, which only very recently moved collectively from consciousness level 190 to the current 207.

42. Envy of praise starts from the illusion that criticalness indicates intelligence and from the fear that recognition of the excellence of others diminishes one's own stature.

Conflicting observations are resolved by an understanding of a quote from *The Rubaiyat of Omar Khayyam* (cal. 700) that says:

> I sent my soul into the afterlife,
> Some glimpse of the truth to tell,
> and my soul returned to me and said,
> 'I myself am heaven and hell.'

It is difficult for integrous people to feel compassion or forgiveness for the dark forces in the world and for their obvious seeming destructiveness. This becomes possible if that which is negative is recontextualized and thereby seen differently as useful. Proven from worldwide experience of millions of people is this quote paraphrased from the famous Chapter 5 of the book *Alcoholics Anonymous* (cal. 540), as follows:

> Rarely have we seen persons fail except people who are constitutionally incapable of being honest with themselves. There are such unfortunates, and they are not at fault, for they seem to have been born that way. They are naturally incapable of vigorous honesty. Some, too, suffer from grave emotional and mental disorders, but even some of them do recover if they still have the capacity to be honest.

Use of the consciousness calibration technique helps to clarify the nature and purposes of this seemingly puzzling earthly life. Research reveals the astonishing fact (which calibrates at consciousness level 998) that the circumstances of our birth and life are precisely karmically perfect. All that we face and endure—the obstacles, the challenges—serves the evolution of consciousness in which we simultaneously undo the negative consequences of the past and derive advancement for spiritually positive choices.

This discovery—that we are all passengers on an evolutionary train—recontextualizes life in that all that we suffer, endure, and ultimately transcend serves our individual and collective ultimate goal. This understanding brings gratitude and peace to our life. The realization allows us to transcend self-pity and resentment and to dedicate our life to love and to God, thus sanctifying it. In so doing, we coalesce the ultimate goals of all religions. The spiritual love with which this commitment is made coalesces the commitments of life. We are then ready for the pathway of devotional nonduality in which the teachings of the world's greatest avatars merge—Jesus, the Christ; Buddha, the Enlightened; Krishna, the Supreme; Allah, the All Merciful; Brahma; and all the other nominal denotations of Divinity. Thus, we, the living, plus all those who have ever lived, are equally part of Creation, and in knowing this, we derive the peace of coexistence that arises out of compassion.

CHAPTER 11
The Downside of Society

Introduction

Although the consciousness level of America is currently at 421, approximately forty-nine percent of the population calibrates below 200. The fifty-one percent above 200 represents the solution, and the forty-nine percent 200 represents the problem. To facilitate a discussion of the downside, calibrations have been roughly grouped as antisocial/behavioral, criminal, and espionage, although it is obvious that there is considerable overlap among all three.

Antisocial

Anti-Semitism	155	Motorcycle Outlaw Gangs	140
Corporate Fraud	160	Perpetrators of Internet	
Drug Traffickers (street)	55	Worms and Viruses	85
Homeless Street People	95	Petty Thievery	145
Inner-city Street Gangs	125	Pickpocket	175
Internet Hackers	145	Prostitution	140
Internet Porn (Adult)	75	Racist Hate Groups	150
Internet Porn (Child)	60	Slavery	20
Laser Beam Blinding of Pilots	80	Vandalism	175

Many in this group derive a sense of importance through deviant behaviors. However, their cost to society is enormous, as in the case of Internet hackers and those who plant destructive Internet viruses that cost the economy millions of dollars as a consequence of their self-indulgence.

The subcultures of street and motorcycle outlaw gangs are well-studied sociologically and represent a subculture in which status is derived from being perceived as being "bad." They achieve additional status from media depictions of them as glamorized folk symbols, e.g., "the wild and free," devil-may-care stereotype. This follows the macho image that courage means the capacity to flirt with danger and thus demonstrate courage.

Racist hate groups, including anti-Semitic, anti-Black, and white supremacist groups have a long history in the United States, of which the Ku Klux Klan is the most flagrant example. They demonstrate a dualistic split in the psyche and the projection of self-hatred onto subgroups. This is also based on inner inferiority. People with adequate self-esteem have no need to hate others.

Slavery can be understood only in its historical context. For thousands of years, it was an accepted worldwide lifestyle, and in the days of ancient Rome, slaves outnumbered free men by ten to one. Slaves from that culture entered all levels of society. The caste system in India prevailed for thousands of years and was an established way of life there as well as in North Africa (Arabic Sudan until the present time [Deng, 2004]).

Historically, the west coast of Africa lacked any marketable commodity or basis upon which to build an economy. The tribal chieftains raided other tribes, and the captured people were then marketed at seaports for an already active slave trade. Paradoxically, this was an evolutionary improvement because, prior to that, they were simply slaughtered. All the barbarian groups that invaded Europe for centuries, such as the Vikings, made the same discovery and also sold off some of the captured instead of massacring them. Consequently, slavery was worldwide and constitutes part of the cultural background of all ethnic groups alive today. It slowly lost impetus and died out with the end of colonialization, and in America, it came to a dramatic end with the Civil War. Only very recently, in 1962, did the very last country make slavery illegal (at the urging of President John F. Kennedy).

Although seen as an injustice in today's world, over the course of cultural and social evolution, it was merely a transitory phase. Thus, slavery is not intrinsically an ethnic issue although it always has had ethnic expressions. An unseen benefit of slavery in America's history was that the lifespan of American slaves was twice that of the native Africans who remained in their original communities and were subject to tribal warfare.

Homeless street people are a conglomerate of the impaired from various strata and are well-studied sociologically. Their numbers greatly increased as a result of the closing of the state hospital system, which had provided a safe haven for many of the mentally disabled in a protective environment where they were accepted, understood, and provided with a home, sustenance, medical and dental care, as well as appropriate psychiatric services, psychologists, group therapists, social workers, and case workers. The old state hospital was an established subculture that calibrates as integrous at level 215. Its demise was considerably the consequence of the movies, *One Flew Over the Cuckoo's Nest* (cal. 180) and *The Snake Pit* (cal. 150), which represent distortions that have had a major downside that was accelerated by the spurious notion that mental illness is a "myth" (cal. at 110 [Szasz, 1974]).

Behavioral

Child Abuse	140	Stalker	60
Wife Beater	95	Sexual Sadist	35
Pedophilia	65	Sadist Child Pornographer	5

These disorders result from a variety of psychiatric, genetic, neurological, and psychological pathologies. These people tend to be obsessive and are characterized by chronic resistance to insight or the need for treatment. They are therefore psychopathic in quality. In treatment, people with these disorders are seen as recalcitrant, unmotivated, and adept at deception and "dissembling" (pretending normalcy). Although addressed by the criminal court system and incarceration, these disorders usually recur upon discharge from prison, e.g., the famous, grotesque Singleton case. There appears to be little motivation for recovery, except in those who choose faith-based 12-step programs and stay involved with them after discharge. Note that faith-based treatment programs are under political attack by the same group that supports the "rights" of pedophiliacs. Interestingly, if the boys who are seduced and raped were girls, the predators would be guilty of statutory rape. (Who pays for the boys' surgical repairs and AIDS treatment?)

Pedophilia is a form of obsessive-compulsive disorder, accompanied by psychopathic trends. Those who are arrested for a supposedly single incident typically have previously molested hundreds of children and continue to do so after their release from prison. The adequate treatment of this condition is an area of civil rights discussion, which can be summarized as the difficulty of balancing the civil rights of the innocent victims against the perceived civil rights of the perpetrator. Similar discussions arose in past decades about persons who had active-infection tuberculosis and refused to respect the rights of others. The arguments involve the basic concepts of triage, which also come up in the military when the survival of one soldier is weighed against the life of an entire regiment, or whether a ship and its crew should be sacrificed to save one seaman who has fallen overboard.

Overt Violence

Anti-abortion Violence	90	Public Beheading of Captives	20
Arson	10	Public Riots	80
Ecoterrorism	160	Serial Child Killers	5
Infanticide	60	Shoe Bomber	120
"Just Snapped"	140	Teenage Classmate Killers	35
Political-Protest and		Terrorism	10-35
Public-Building Bomber	35-60	Islamic Terrorists	35-70

The killer instinct is in the most repressed, hidden recesses of the ego (Freud's "Id"), which is the level of killing for the love of violence for its own sake, i.e., without psychological premises, as the act itself is its own source and fulfillment. Historically, it is seen in the "berserk" activity of the Viking conquerors who slaughtered people needlessly; in the Japanese in the 1930s; and in the concentration camps of World War II. It is simultaneously the extreme of megalomania/egocentricity (malignant narcissism) unleashed by brainwashing, inflammatory political rhetoric, or religious zealotry (cal. at 80).

Arson has been included with behavioral disorders because it is also compulsive and repetitive. Whereas teenage classmate killers can be triggered by having been abused or bullied, the basic psychopathology is actually intrapsychic (Brooks, 2004) and not "caused" by external factors. The intrinsic factor is narcissistic grandiosity and contempt for "inferiors." The same psychopathology is seen in gangster rappers to whom normal people are "scumbags" or "whores." In addition, there is another personal element contributed by violent video games that, by Pavlovian conditioning (i.e., kill—reward), results in desensitization and a trance-like automaticity in which the behavioral conditioning translates into acting out behaviors to "see what it's like."

It is significant that sixty-five percent of the population suffers from various degrees of PTSD (Post-Traumatic Stress Disorder) as a consequence of television and movie violence. A memorable example was the post-*Psycho*-movie (cal. 80) syndrome. Multitudes of people were afraid to take showers alone in the home for years afterward, and everybody locked their bathroom doors. (PTSD is characterized by fearful flashbacks.)

Drugs and Alcohol

Alcohol Addiction	90	Drunken Driving	55
Cocaine	7	Heroin	6
Drug Addiction	95	Methamphetamines	6

In the past, these were completely hopeless and untreatable conditions because they are not only psychological and behavioral, but physiological as well. From a medical viewpoint, true addiction is denoted by withdrawal symptoms. Psychological addiction, such as dependence on marijuana, lacks physical withdrawal symptoms. Opiates are addictive even to brain cell neurons that are raised in a laboratory culture medium. When the addictive substance is removed from the culture medium, the neuron shrivels and dies.

Psychologically, the addictions fall into two somewhat different classes—those of the sedatives, such as alcohol, heroin, barbiturates, and tranquilizers—and those that are excitatory, such as amphetamines and cocaine. The sedative disorders have only been recoverable since the advent of Alcoholic Anonymous, which is the offshoot of the transformative spiritual experience of its founder, Bill Wilson. The movement is now spread out across the world. (AA calibrates at 540.) The addictions are so severe that reason, which calibrates in the 400s, has insufficient power and is only offset by the energy field that calibrates at 540. Upon analysis, the addiction is to the artificial consciousness level that characterizes the "high" that is experienced due to the drug's effect of blocking out the lower levels of conscious experience. By following the 12-step program, people progressively relinquish the ego, which is replaced by spiritual energy that is maintained by following a spiritual program of proven value.

Severe Behavioral/Psychiatric Disorders

| Borderline Personality | 65-150 | "Possessed"/Psychotic | |
| Psychopath | 45-60 | Murderers | 5-11 |

These involve psychotic levels of mental impairment, with transitory periods of quasi-normal behavior. In the borderline personality disorder, the hold on reality is tenuous, and psychological conflict triggers regression to more extreme and severe states of emotionality under even very slight provocation.

"Possessed" murderers are a class unto themselves. Many of them hear voices or God telling them to kill themselves or others and involve paranoid psychosis. The psychopathic disorder is relatively well-known as a lack of conscience that typifies the classic "con" man and the sociopath of criminal subcultures. In psychiatry, these are technically classified as character disorders, or "dysocial," if they are primarily a response to cultural conditions (e.g., street gangs).

Personality Disorders

According to the most recent National Institutes of Health survey, approximately fifteen percent of U. S. adults (31 million) have diagnosable personality disorders as follows:

Obsessive-Compulsive Disorder	7.9%	Schizoid Disorder	3.1%
		Histrionic Disorder	1.8%
Paranoid Disorder	4.4%	Dependent Personality	
Antisocial Disorder	3.6%	Disorder	0.5%
Avoidance Disorder	4.9%		

All of these psychological diagnoses are associated with considerable emotional, social, and occupational impairment and interpersonal conflicts, as well as deviant attitudes and belief systems (2002 National Epidemiological Study, NESARC Report, 2004).

Criminality
Present Inmate Population – Average Group Calibrations

Federal	60
State	65
County	65
Death Row	20

Criminals

Bonnie and Clyde	22	Jack the Ripper	6
John Dillinger	160	Serial Killers	6-15
Al Capone	35	"Starkweather"-type	
"Baby Face" Nelson	60	Killers	6
"Machine Gun" Kelly	55	Organized Crime	40
Bruno Hauptmann	50	Blackmail	35
Nathan Leopold/Richard		Pimp	14
Loeb	25	Carlos the Jackal	35
Mafia	65	Major Serial	
Drug Traffickers		Murderers	5
(organized crime)	60	Jack Ruby	170
Bank Robbers	55	Lee Harvey Oswald	170
Ma Barker	40		

The extremely low calibration levels indicate primitiveness and the predominance of animal instincts, thus representing a maturational arrest of the evolution of consciousness. Some become perceived in a pseudofolk-hero kind of distortion. In reality, they are, as the calibrated levels indicate, deadly killers, whether they are stylized as Machine Gun Kelley, Scarface, the Godfather, Babyface Nelson, "Liberators," etc. In more ethical conservative cultures, the media would not glamorize such criminals nor would entertainers gain social status by associating with them. Media hype contributes to the attraction of the criminal lifestyle for impressionable "wannabe" adolescents and gives a stamp of approval to serious deviancy.

Research on the assassination of President John F. Kennedy reveals three shots fired, two shots hit, one by Lee Harvey Oswald, and the other by an accomplice from the "grassy knoll."

The psychopath lacks a conscience and thus is capable of fooling even a so-called lie detector that triggers the anxiety that would arise from deception in a normal person. With no conscience, there is no sense of guilt as moral, ethical, and spiritual values are absent. A century ago, the formal psychiatric diagnosis was "Moral Imbecility" (cal. 90).

The Nature of Criminality

It is unlikely that a cure can be found for any human ailment without accurate diagnosis and elucidation of the underlying pathology. Nowhere is this more apparent than in the world's failure to comprehend the essential nature of criminality and its expression on the international level as war. The application of consciousness research elucidates basic elements that are not otherwise observable, including essential characteristics to which society habitually turns a blind eye.

Clarification first requires a differentiation of violations of the law from crime and criminality. A violation of the law is a legal and moral issue and includes a high proportion of relatively "normal" citizens of any country. These violations are transitory and often due to immaturity, opportunity, carelessness, neglect, ignorance, lack of attention, lack of acculturation, transitory illness, physical and mental impairments, age, and distraction by other affairs or temporary conditions, such as marital strife, loss of a job, or simply the lack of education.

On a more serious level is the subject of true crime, which may be temporary or isolated and due to emotional pressure, intoxication, provocation, personality defect, lack of inhibition, instability, financial pressures, lapses of conscience, or something as simple as thrill seeking or "falling in with bad company." In the case of "violations of the law" and "isolated crimes," it is presumed that the perpetrator is of normal mental and emotional capacity and that fines and jail time will bring these violations or crimes to a halt.

Criminality, however, is of a different nature altogether and akin to a disease. Essentially, it is a chronic, serious mental disorder that has emotional, behavioral, and psychological characteristics. In addition, there is often a genetic impairment of adequate development of the frontal cortex of the brain (Arahart-Treichel, 2002). Criminality has a childhood onset characterized by the inability to delay gratification, the lack of capacity to foresee or fear consequences, the lack of concern for others, and a narcissistic core of egocentricity. Psychological research reveals that it is often diagnosable by age three.

Rather than the erroneously hypothesized low self-esteem, on the contrary, criminals have an exaggerated, inflated, grandiose, and egoistic sense of self-importance. There is a denial of personal responsibility, along with impulsivity and lack of conscience, guilt, or remorse. It is a pervasive lifestyle characterized by a narcissistic lack of concern for the rights of others or the incorporation of society's values, such as morality or ethics. In Freudian terminology, there is a lack of superego development and a failure to introject and identify with an adequate authority figure.

In addition to the above, there is often a verbal faculty characterized as glibness as well as impulsiveness, the inability to learn from experience, emotional instability, and a proclivity and attraction to crime, drugs, and sensationalism. The lack of incorporation of social values and the respect for authority are expressed as defiance, impulsiveness, and narcissistic egocentricity. Psychiatrically, they are often diagnosed early in life as having Oppositional Defiant Disorder or Conduct Disorder, with psychopathic or sociopathic trends.

The early childhood symptoms of some forms of this chronic mental disorder are often characterized as the triad of fire setting, cruelty to animals, and enuresis (persistent bedwetting past the expected age of control). There is a proclivity to prevarication and being a "pathological liar," with an impaired sense of reality and capacity for comprehension. Some become convincing fabricators and invent believable stories by which they often accuse innocent people whose lives are thereby destroyed. This is one situation in which the calibration of truth can be crucial, as the false accusers are quite often convincing to authorities. Because of the commonness of false accusations, male personnel in adolescent treatment centers are fearful of being alone with any female patient for even brief moments. The residents know only too well the disastrous impact of accusations that are often due to malicious spite resulting from perceived slights to the inflated narcissism.

Recidivism is associated with the inner grandiosity and attraction to thrills, danger, excitement, and a denial of reality, which are seen as obstructive to the inner infantile omnipotence. These characteristics lead to chaotic marital and family situations, and chronic school and behavioral problems. These individuals frequently become dropouts and join gangs and antisocial countercultures. Most true criminals have a long "rap sheet" that goes back to childhood. Seventy-five percent of discharged felons are back in prison within three years.

Youth violence, as reported by a current, ongoing study by the National Institutes of Health (Kaplan, 2004), is characterized in early childhood by low I. Q., delayed speech development, lower resting heart rate, genetic factors, negative emotions, lack of sympathy for others, disrespect for rules, unreliability, carelessness, aggression, attraction to antisocial and violent behaviors, plus cerebral neurotransmitter (metabolites of Serotonin) abnormalities triggered by childhood abuse.

Early in their lives, psychopaths are often referred for psychiatric treatment, which is found to be useless and ineffective. Occasionally, there is improvement because the disorder is sometimes associated with bipolar disorder, ADHD, addictions, or borderline or explosive personality disorders. The lack of response to psychologically-based treatments has to do with the inner defects in ego formation as well as the absence of the capacity for love or compassion. In psychoanalytic terms, they lack the ability to form a positive transference to the therapist.

In society, the career of the criminal is reflective of their socioeconomic status. On the lowest level, they become members of criminal gangs. The more erudite become con men, and some are members of subcultures, such as the Irish travelers, the Chicago gangs of the prohibition era, or the drug dealers of today's culture. Psychopaths who have come from higher socio-economic levels often are more socially adept and become white-collar embezzlers or unethical CEOs of large corporations and get involved with stock fraud. Some learn how to set up shell corporations, Ponzi schemes, and pseudocharities, or they become manipulators of the stock or commodities markets. Some become adept at politics and enter government where they become corrupt officials. When psychopathy is limited primarily to sexuality, pedophiles infiltrate religious or youth organizations to which they are attracted by the availability of victims. They wear the sheep's clothing of the cleric, scout leader, coach, camp counselor, etc. Diagnostically, all the above-cited examples calibrate below 200, a serious warning sign. Psychopaths characteristically do not admit guilt even when caught red-handed or photographed on videotape.

The dual-personality criminal is often unsuspected unless it is held in mind as a possible explanation for puzzling cases that include a subordinate psychopathic personality camouflaged by a seemingly normal, respectable persona. The two personalities may be completely split and even unknown to each other (see later). The normal personality protests its innocence because it is actually unaware of the split-off, depressed criminal personality.

From the above classifications, it can be seen that it is important to correctly diagnose the violator of the law instead of lumping all violators together, which is obviously doomed to failure, as it would be in medicine where effective treatment is completely dependent upon a correct initial diagnosis. The normal person who violates the law responds to consequences such as fines or probation, or, in more severe cases, imprisonment. The normal violator of the law also responds to education, such as a required driving re-education course or restriction of a driver's license. The normal person is also inhibited from further violations by shame, guilt, remorse, public disgrace, fear of consequences, and fear of loss of social and self-esteem.

True crime implies a more serious violation, and here again, the diagnosis is critical. The question to be answered is whether or not the basic personality is psychopathic or relatively intact. The law historically differentiates crimes of passion, crimes committed under the duress of financial crises, and passing life situations. Both the violator of the law and the normal person who commit a crime are responsive to therapeutic techniques of group or individual psychotherapy, psychiatry, philosophical re-education, counseling, faith-based programs, or reacculturation. This is an area where anger management classes, referral to 12-step programs, probation, and supervision do eventually bring about amelioration. Again, it is critically important to make a correct diagnosis because the application of consequences or therapeutic attempts is usually ineffective if the underlying personality of the perpetrator is sociopathic.

Criminality is an established recidivist lifestyle for which no effective therapeutic endeavor has thus far been found. The basic personality is unchanged, and, with experience, the perpetrator does not change the behaviors but becomes more clever in learning how to escape detection.

To a person with normal psychological makeup, a prison sentence is frightening. The culture is foreign and brings up guilt, fear, and aversion to the prior behaviors. These responses are totally lacking in the psychopathic personality to whom prison life is a very familiar culture; the individual is merely removed from the streets to another location and continues uninterruptedly. The basic tenets and lifestyle of criminality are actually the internal rules of conduct within any prison's population and are attenuated in their expression merely by the threat of the prison administration.

In the prison population, the gangs maintain control just as they did on the streets, and in order to survive, the prison inmate quickly learns how to play the game. To the psychopath, time in prison has no impact on subsequent behaviors other than a refinement of cleverness.

The calibrated level of the psychopathic personality of the typical criminal recidivist is generally between 35 and 80 on the Scale of Consciousness. So far, criminality has failed to respond to any therapeutics or course of techniques, and thus, society can only respond by maneuvers to protect itself as best it can, i.e., quarantine in prisons. Because the psychopath scorns rules and regulations, even those that would be called "common sense," the police detain citizens for what seem to be minor infractions because they know that the psychopath is irresponsible as a lifestyle. Thus, stopping cars for having a taillight out brings a high capture rate of criminals who are wanted for more serious crimes. This is the wisdom of the "three strikes and you're out" legislation that has been demonstrated to be highly effective in taking the criminals off the streets, resulting in the reduction of over fifty percent of street crime.

It is naïve to look at such laws with the sentimentalism that "it is unfair to put somebody in prison for stealing a pack of cigarettes." The facts reveal that the chronic criminal has been caught for maybe only 1/100th of the number of crimes they have committed. The typical pedophile has usually abused scores and in some cases even hundreds of victims before arrest and detection. The car thief has stolen hundreds of cars before finally getting caught. The domestic abuser has been violent dozens of times, and the chronic thief has stolen thousands of items, etc.

Due to legalities, the courts, together with defense attorneys, preclude a presentation of the defendant's past history to the jury whose capacity for balanced judgment is therefore impaired by the deliberate withholding of critically important information. The diagnosis is completely different between the recidivist and the opportunistic perpetrator of a crime under duress or temporary weakness of personality. The "one size fits all," strictly punitive approach is only effective with persons who are basically psychologically intact and have fallen into deviant behavior but are able to learn from their mistakes. For some such fortunate individuals, incarceration is the experience that brings about the critical "hitting bottom." Many such people do go through major turnarounds and become model citizens and spiritually oriented.

When it is realized that psychopathic persons are unable to help themselves and that no effective treatment is available, a compassionate view incorporates the realization that while the psychopaths are perpetrators, at the same time, they are victims of their own condition. The evolution of their consciousness is primitive and seems to be arrested at the predatory-animal level. Other than quarantine, society has no other solutions as yet.

Espionage and Political Criminality

Ethel and Julius Rosenberg	175	Los Alamos Defectors-	
Walker Family (Navy spies)	120	Manhattan Project	80
Harold Philby	120	Double Agents	130
FBI and CIA Moles	110-175	Alger Hiss	205↓160
Aldrich Ames	105	Robert Hanssen (spy)	80
The Cambridge 5	75		

This group is unique and includes the combinations of greed, pseudopolitical rationalization, character defect, defective conscience, and the capacity for psychological compartmentalization (which is also seen in some serial killers, especially those who kill sequential spouses and lead an ostensibly normal lifestyle in the interim).

Along with these defects, there is an accompanying intellectualism. The defectors who revealed the atomic bomb secrets considered themselves to be the intellectually superior elite and their actions thereby excusable as a consequence of their capacity for rationalization. Although "ethics" was an essential element of discussion of the morality of the development of nuclear fission, individuals with intellectualized grandiosity rationalized their behaviors, which were actually examples of deception as demonstrated by the calibrated levels of their consciousnesses. If their erudition were truly superior to the rest of mankind, then their consciousness calibrations would have been in the high 400s or the 500s.

"IN THE UNITED STATES DISTRICT COURT FOR THE EASTERN DISTRICT OF VIRGINIA
Alexandria Division

UNITED STATES OF AMERICA	)
	)
v.	) CRIMINAL NO. 01-188-A
	)
ROBERT PHILIP HANSSEN,	)
	)
Defendant.	)

SENTENCING MEMORANDUM

"Robert Philip Hanssen is a traitor. For all the words that have been written about him, for all the psychological analyses, the speculations about his motivation, and the assessments of his character, this is, at the end of the day, all that really warrants being said about Hanssen. He is a traitor and that singular truth is his legacy.

"He betrayed his country—and he did so at a time when we were locked in a bitter and dangerous cold war with the Soviet Union. Hanssen's brazen and reckless misconduct, its surpassing evil, is almost beyond comprehension. Using the very tools he acquired as an FBI counterintelligence expert, he covertly and clandestinely provided the Soviet Union and then the Russians information of incalculable significance, extraordinary breadth, and exceptionally grave sensitivity. He did so knowing that his disclosures could—and ultimately did—get people killed and imprisoned, and he did so knowing that they placed in jeopardy the safety and security of our entire nation.[1] That we did not lose the Cold War ought blind no one to the fact that Robert Philip Hanssen, for his own selfish and corrupt reasons, placed every American citizen in harm's way."

"[1] All one has to do is look at the descriptions of some of the documents he compromised to the Soviets. See, e.g., Count 8 ("A TOP SECRET United States intelligence analysis of the effectiveness of Soviet intelligence collection efforts against certain United States nuclear weapons capabilities...") and Count 12 ("A highly restricted TOP SECRET/SCI Analysis, dated May 1987, of the Soviet intelligence threat to a specific and named highly compartmented United States Government program to ensure the continuity of government in the event of a Soviet nuclear attack....")" (Court's Notes)

(From FindLaw.com)

So much for the posture of "moral superiority" favored by the "Far Left" as a smoke screen.

The puzzlement about Alger Hiss is clarified by the discovery that he had double compartmentalized personalities. One calibrates at 205 (public image) and the other at 160 (the conspirator). This condition is more common than suspected in espionage agents and in other cases of duplicity.

Because such individuals are of extreme danger in today's nuclear world, which is also beset by terrorist bombers, their early detection by routine consciousness calibration screening of high security risks is critical to security. High-profile defectors, as well as others, were already detected in the early 1970s by consciousness research and demonstrated on videotape (Hawkins, 1995, Video #1). At that time, moles in both the CIA and the FBI were identified by calibration as to their level of consciousness. At the time, there was no point in pursuing their exact identities, which could have been easily revealed upon investigation in a matter of minutes. They were later exposed and made the headlines (Robert Hannsen and Aldrich Ames).

While dual compartmentalized personalities are recognized in psychiatry, this relative rarity (dissociative states, multiple personality disorder) obscures their detection in the public arena. Each of the double agents (Manhattan Project, FBI, and CIA) was responsible for the deaths of very many people, despite their claims to superiority as a rationalization for their duplicitous treachery. (The whole Cold War, as well as the current nuclear arms race, arose from the loss of atomic secrets to the former U.S.S.R.)

Detection of this disorder is difficult because the covering normal personality is what is presented to the public. Typically, the deception is expertly and successfully carried off for years without eliciting suspicion. The disorder is seen in the normal family man who has a secret sex life, in pedophiliacs and serial murderers, and in fire fighters who are secretly pyromaniacs. These are real-life Jekyll-and-Hyde personalities.

Compartmentalized dual personalities often arise in the media as high-profile cases that puzzle the public, the Court, and the jury. The crime is "out of character," as they are described as "normal," if not "just wonderful people." (Character witnesses confirm that they are "wonderful.") The position of the defense is, how could such a person possibly have committed such a crime? During the trial, the respectable, seemingly normal suspect characteristically has mask-like facial control, primarily emotionless and carefully guarded. Normal people with nothing to hide would automatically show a whole panoply of emotions, facial expressions, body language, etc. The reason the denial of guilt seems real is because the presenting personality, in fact, did not commit the crime; it is the second personality that is the savage criminal. Less severe examples are seen in cases of embezzlement, kleptomania, sexual compulsion, deviant behavior, and where men live dual lives, with separate wives and identities.

Of importance is that in dissociated dual personalities, the two personalities are actually not aware of each other. Although such disorders are statistically rare in the overall population, they are relatively common in criminal cases, as the second personality is often very active and surfaces via the action of the repressed criminality.

This split of personality occurs before age three, as the infant responds to parental correction not by modifying the personality but by dissociating the personality into the "good me" and the "bad me." The "bad me" then becomes repressed, disowned and unameliorated, and begins to lead a secret life, free of restraint. The "bad me" is sometimes given a different name and only emerges periodically to commit acts of cruelty or bizarre behaviors and serial murders. These people often become famous criminals, e.g., "Jack the Ripper," and the elusive serial killers that make the headlines as serial rapists, pedophiliac child killers, cannibalistic murderers, and talisman criminals who taunt the police and public with signatures to their crimes.

The discovery that two completely different personalities can exist in the same individual came about accidentally. Some years ago, a prospective visitor was screened by consciousness calibration prior to the visit. Upon rescreening as the date for the visit approached, a widely different calibration was obtained (originally 350; the second time, 135). This was the first encounter with the phenomenon. Further questioning revealed that there was a wide disparity between the intentions of the two different persons in one body. One was benign and the other malicious, and therefore, the visit was cancelled. Several years later, an employee who had been acting somewhat strangely was also found to have a second, untrustworthy personality and had to be terminated, despite an excellent curriculum vitae.

Consciousness calibration is the only decisive method for the detection of dangerous individuals. The process, as was demonstrated on the videotape, is quite simple. One merely states, "This person is integrous." (Yes/No) "The second in command is integrous." (Yes/No) "The third level down is integrous. (Yes/No) When the level is determined, the roster, especially by identification photos, reveals in a few seconds those individuals who make the arm go weak to an investigative team that has no idea who these persons might really be. A well-trained and integrous team is only interested in the truth. They do not need or even want to know the names of the individuals. The test subject can even be a child, as was demonstrated in the video, who knows nothing of the matter.

The same procedure reveals terrorist suspects, e.g., "Heathrow Airport contains a dangerous terrorist." (Yes/No) Then determining the location is easy. Using a map, one states "In Section A." (Yes/No) "In Section B. In Section C," and so on. Then the flight number is identified. "A terrorist is trying to board Flight 222, which is scheduled to leave at 4:15 PM." (Yes/No).

This procedure can be done with the video surveillance of a crowd, such as at a football stadium or a parade. The only requirements are that the intention and purpose are integrous, the persons doing the questioning have the authority, and they have received permission to ask about a given matter prior to using the arm-response technique.

Although individuals with severe character disorders are adept at dissimilation, they can only control their personality performance and cannot disguise their low calibratable level of consciousness, which is in the "public domain" of the universal, impersonal field of consciousness that has no opinions or intellectual limitations. Like an impersonal electrostatic field that merely crackles and gives an electrostatic response to the presence or absence of electrons, it is beyond deception and has no motivation. The kinesiological test is not truth versus falsehood but merely indicates truth or its absence. An electrostatic field simply fails to respond if it is not presented with a stimulus, but it visibly "lights up" commensurate with the strength of the stimulus and thereby serves as a diagnostic function of impressive elegance.

Truth and Survival

By analysis, it is revealed that the highest fruits of our society are the automatic consequence of truth, and society's problems are the fallout from falsehood. Freedom, peace, and, as we have seen, even survival itself, are supported by the social fabric field in which truth prevails. How, then, is such truth to be identified inasmuch as man's mental apparatus precludes it by design, and seventy-eight percent of the world's population (forty-nine percent in America) lives by principles that are not integrous? In a free society, the nonintegrous are vociferous and convincing, and the media magnify their influence.

CHAPTER 12
Problematic Issues

As is apparent from an analysis of the functioning of consciousness and its various levels in the human domain, the different levels of consciousness can be identified not only by calibration but also by the characteristics of that particular field itself. In society, claims to truth are bandied about by vested interests whose subterfuge can only be detected by those who themselves are integrous, seasoned, and balanced by wisdom and experience.

Ignorance of the law is no excuse in court nor does ignorance of the truth prevent one's death by violence. This underlying reality is intuited by modern society in which the quest for truth is almost the essence of every public discussion and news report. Survival is not secured by means of political persuasion, sociological theories, highly emotional demagoguery, political elitism, or religious dogma. The capacity to recognize the truth is a potential within human consciousness, and the combined intention of the consciousness of all people in that direction intensifies the overall field. At some intuitive level, everyone knows that truth supports life and falsity brings death. In a world with nuclear capacity, the differentiation is now a literal, concrete, pragmatic necessity. The price of denial or unawareness of truth is to be blindsided by death and destruction (i.e., Pearl Harbor and 9/11).

Problematic Positionalities and Issues

Acrimonious	160	Naysayer	190
Anarchy	100	Neo-Fascism	160
Anti-/hate America	160	Neo-paganism	180
Anti-religion/God	135-180	Niggardly	190
Apologist	190	"Offended"	180
Atheism	165	"One wrong justifies	
Bearing false witness	60	another"	100
Birchism, (John)	160	"Open Society"	180
Blame	180	Paranoid	120
Capital Punishment (adults)	160	Petulant	185
Capital Punishment		"Politically Correct"	190
(adolescents)	130	Politically "Elite"	160
"Causes"	175	Protagonist	190
Conspiracy theories	180	"Protest" suicide	70
Contentious	170	Rulings, (collective) 9th	
Contrary	185	Circuit Court:	
Criticalness	120	Appeals reversed by	
"Dead White Men,"		Supreme Court	185
Concept of	130	Secularism	165
Denigration	185	Sedition	105
Depravity	80	Sedition disguised as "Art"	135
Disloyalty to country	160	"Sensitive"	180
"Entitlement"	180	Sentimentality	190
False accusation	160	Skeptic	120
Frivolous jurisprudence	190	Social myths	180
"Ghetto Lit"	90	"Stupid White Men"	130
Grudge	70	Social arrogance	155
Hatred of authority	120	"Superior" views	155
Ingrate	190	Treason	80
Insulting	160	Turner Diaries	130
Intimidation by litigation	150	Ultra-conservatism	150
"Left-wing" activism	165	Ungrateful	190
Liberationists	185	Victimhood	130
Litigiousness	140	Victimology	160
"Made uncomfortable"	175	Victim/Perpetrator	
Malicious slander	135	(Model)	130-150
"Man/Boy love"	80	Vilify legitimate authority	120
Misogeny	160	"White Lies"	190
Narcissism	140	White Supremacist	160

All the above denote a pervasive negative trend that undermines the integrity of the intellectual world and its social commentators. The underlying myth is that being critical (negative) is "cool," superior, and indicative of "intelligence" and, therefore, of superiority (calibrates as "false").

Criticalness actually calibrates low because it is more often an expression of envy, niggardly smallness, and spite out of jealousy. A "big" person accords recognition and respect for excellence, and the "prune minded" begrudges such recognition out of inner spiritual miserliness. The small-minded person hates that which is praised, like an envious schoolchild hates the recognition given to the best students.

Criticalness as an attitude is a defect, not a virtue. Mature evaluation weighs all sides of an issue but does not interject negative emotionality. It reviews rather than denigrates. Paradoxically, denigration (cal. 185) diminishes the stature of the critic rather than that of the target of ill will. The difference is due to motivation and intent. A true critic reflects appreciation of value and merit and is therefore "balanced." A spurious "critic" tries to look important via "cheap shots."

The low calibrations of the above indicate serious departure from integrous truth and the catering to narcissistic self-interests that result in perceptual distortions and socially projected misinterpretations. The common basis is the ego's protest at having to give up its egocentric, imaginary sovereignty to self-control and rationality, which the infantile ego resents and sees as obstructionist limitations to impulse gratification. All authority is resented and hated, and thus arises the dualistic victim/perpetrator paranoid distortion that is then projected onto society as an "out there" perceptual distortion, with grave consequences to society. A striking example is that of Karl Marx (cal. level 130), whose paranoid distortions became the basis for the death of many millions of people at the hands of Lenin (cal. level 70) and Stalin (cal. level 90), plus the Cold War, the KGB, American double agents, and near-nuclear war. Marx then lived on in the philosophy of Herbert Marcuse and the Frankfurt School of Philosophic Relativism (see later in this chapter). At the other extreme, the fallacious theories of fascism resulted in the massive death and destruction of World War II that was built upon fallacious propaganda of philosophical error. Truth brings peace and falsehood brings war, as also exemplified by the cultural wars that are polarizing current society.

Rejection of rationality and integrous logic (termed "misology") forms the basis for rejection of ethics and morality. This undermines support for balanced, mature codes of behavior that counterbalance social anarchy and hedonistic excess. Without structure and order, social behaviors become like an engine without a governor or a flywheel and collapse into chaos.

Historically, political extremism has been the invitational open door to revolution and takeover by the other extreme wing, which has been reinforced by protesters of the prior excesses. The Buddha warned twenty-five hundred years ago to avoid extremes and stay balanced via the "middle way."

Because the ego's perception is dualistic, it is preset to fall into paranoia, which is the substructure of all political extremes, either left or right. As noted above, the core error is that the ego's dualistic, distorted perception sees everything in terms of the perpetrator/victim model (cal. level 130). This releases hatred and the production of the "straw man" who is then subject to vilification that releases malice, hate, and attack (e.g., America as the "great Satan," or the "political Jihad" of the current "hate America" campaign). The unfortunate price of becoming the president or leader of a country is that the person then automatically becomes the target for the paranoid projections of personal disgruntlements, as well as the opposing party that bitterly awaits its revenge for imaginary, inflated "wrongs" and therefore initiates a campaign of blame, slander, and propaganda.

The lure of these problematic positionalities is enhanced by the appeal to base emotions that are justified by the ridicule of ethics, reason, and logic. This results in the popular perception of the "politically correct" or the "lunatic fringe," which is viewed as an effete affectation of narcissistic pseudo-empowerment via artificial ego inflation of being superior to others. It is anti-egalitarian, as indicated by public media posturing and attention seeking.

Collectively, people with these impaired perceptions live in an "altered reality" (Pitts, 2004), which is fast losing its initial chic and becoming passé, as it has lost its trendy cachet.

Slander calibrates very low because of the intention, i.e., to injure. (Free speech is a two-edged sword—it cuts down the slanderer as well.) In normal life, the intellect provides corrective balance. The appeal of "pop" attitudes and slogans is to appear *au courant* and be perceived as being within the "elite" celebrity class, with its implied exclusivity. Because of their instant ego inflation, "causes" are widely popular, and the public is bombarded with their endless solicitation propaganda, proselytizing, and emotionality, reinforced by selective polling, junk science, and manipulated statistics. These emanate from all kinds of Orwellian "rights" groups as well as sentimental protestors, "health police," "language police," etc.

Paradoxically, the truly elite are unknown to society and avoid publicity and celebrities. They live in very private enclaves and belong to clubs unheard of by the media. Mutual recognition is by subtlety, and pretense is quickly detected by even a single glance or intonation. Distinguishing characteristics of this social class are simplicity and completeness. Nobody "wants" anything or is seeking gain, approval, or recognition, and celebrity status is avoided. Fulfillment results in contentment, which arises from within.

Anyone can have real, genuine "class" by merely accepting who they are at any given moment or level of life. Real class means "genuine." The world loves really classy waiters, clients, actors, sports stars, cab drivers, and true celebrities (e.g., Satchmo (Louis Armstrong), Clark Gable, Spencer Tracy, Knute Rockne, Ronald Reagan, etc.). People who feel fulfilled are a "class act" and receive recognition not for rank or popularity but because of their integrity and courage to be "who they are" and thus fully human.

Sophistry

An understanding of how fallacious sophistry propagates century after century is provided by two concepts:

1. The vulnerable consciousness level of 130-195 characterizes a large percentage of the world's population in every generation, i.e., distribution of the learning curve as a consequence of the evolution of consciousness.

2. The spread or persistence of an idea via a key term, concept, or word is technically called a "meme." The essential quality of a meme is that, like a computer virus, it is self-propagating, imitative, and has a catchy-phrase attraction. By strict repetition and commonality, the idea is accorded importance or status and therefore a presumptive acceptance as though it were an axiom of successful living. Richard Dawkins coined the term "meme" in the book *The Selfish Gene* (Dawkins, 1989, 1992).

The central idea of a meme is that it tends to attract repetition and imaginative elaboration, so a story grows over time and accumulates suggestive implications. This is one factor of positive cultural change as well as the persistence of superstitions, vicious propaganda, and fallacies, such as are propagated by gossip, the media, and also the Internet, which has become the biggest library in history of fallacy and disinformation. Memes can also be germinal, constructive concepts that are shorthand for cultural values. Their study is called "memetics" and is of sociological importance (Csikszentmihelyi, 1993; Beck and Cowan, 1996).

Mankind is fortunate that Joseph Goebbels is dead for he would have flooded the Internet with Far Right propaganda so that the percentage of fallacy would exceed even the current level of sixty-five percent. (Currently, there are more than five thousand "hate" websites.) He was an expert at spreading memes and their disguised hatred. The same technique is now played by Far Left financiers of organized extremist political attacks (O'Reilly, 2005) that plant spurious stories with a network of "bloggers." Negative memes are carefully crafted distortions of reason that hide the underlying motivational forces of malice that fuel social disintegration and staged protest demonstrations that are purportedly spontaneous and genuine but are actually expertly crafted seventy-five percent of the time. They are designed to influence

the naïve and gullible public as well as the media. The Communist party learned the technique over a century ago. The same
principles of crowd manipulation are in use today for a variety
of supposed "causes." There are thousands of people who are
addicted to the thrill of protest for its own sake. The reality or
truth is actually irrelevant.

The problem of "just" and "unjust" protest or revolution is quite
complex, and adequate coverage would require the writing of a
whole test to adequately research the subject, including historical examples, moral/ethical principles, philosophical, spiritual,
and religious aspects, as well as legalities, political inference, the
circumstances and intentions of all parties involved, and their
cultures. Perception is also subject to illusion and distortion,
or even delusion (Bittner, 2004). The subject of differentiating
freedom fighter (cal. 200) from terrorist (cal. 30) is covered in
Chapter 16.

Socrates taught that all men seek only the "good" but do not
know what that good actually is (e.g., immediate and material,
ego gain [being "right"], or long-term spiritual growth). Thus, the
resolution and calibrated level of consciousness of each decision
represents a concordance of karma, intention, the proximate field
of complex influences, and factors both known and unknown.
Later criticisms are equally prone to error by virtue of comparing
the actual to the hypothetical and "Monday-morning quarterback-
ing." Even seemingly integrous intention may sometimes result
in social disaster. ("It seemed like a good idea at the time.")

While approximately ninety percent (by calibration) of public
displays of social protest is primarily motivated by romanticized
egotism, the remaining ten percent includes integrity of intention,
correct perception and interpretation of all factors, and justification based on confirmable facts and not just on emotionalized
opinion. If justification is based on propagandized fallacies, then
error is introduced. Neither is moral conviction a reliable basis
for action.

Every revolution has its rationalization and rhetoric, appealing only to segments of society. Everyone's ego likes to think it is
embarked on a "noble cause," including the barbarians, invading

hoards, religious militants, shoe bombers, suicidal terrorists, dynamiters of school children, etc.

Americans like to cite the Revolutionary War and the Declaration of Independence as well as the example of Jesus Christ to rationalize situations as latter-day examples of the Boston Tea Party. Seldom, however, does the analogy apply. Nonviolent protests have had equally successful results (e.g., Mahatma Gandhi, Nelson Mandela, etc.).

There is a quick, simple way to diagnose very complex situations by the use of "critical point analysis" (Hawkins, 1995). This identifies the core "attractor field" of an overall, total multifactoral situation, extracts the central fundamental thrust, and dispenses with argument, fallacy, emotionality, and pretense. The core of truth of multiple interacting complexities reveals itself by diagnosing the basic intention. For example, the intention of the U. S. nuclear program overall is 460. The current intention of the Iran nuclear program is 170-190 (December 2004). From the Map of Consciousness, the basic motive reveals itself. Calibration level 190 indicates pride, status, etc. ("Join the Nuclear Club"). Critical point analysis thus is like a laser beam that cuts through the camouflage and subterfuge of political rhetoric and gamesmanship.

Application of this essential diagnostic technique to international relations and prevention of war, along with its implications for survival, is explained in Chapters 15 and 16. In ordinary life, quickly revealing the essence and core of a problem has numerous obvious applications to complex social questions.

Because the strength of freedom stems from its source as integrity and truth, vigilance is its safeguard. Therefore, nonintegrous positionalities, despite popularity, cannot just be excused as harmlessly sophomoric and swept under the rug while wisdom says that "unless you're a liberal when you're young, you have no heart, but if you're still a liberal when you're older, you have no head." What the axiom fails to state is that in the interim, a lot of damage occurs and millions die. (It takes generations for the fallacies of Marxist communism, totalitarianism, fascism, or religious fanaticism to collapse.) Therefore, socio-political "isms" justify careful scrutiny.

From the previous chart, one can see that emotional rhetoric is a slippery slope from social protest down into demonstrations and crowd violence, and then into protest arson and bombings. Even Mother Theresa refused "anti-war" parades. She comprehended and represented the dictum that "anti-war" is not the same as pro-peace (e.g., anti-vanilla is not pro-chocolate).

It is better to succeed than to "win." The Parisian enclave of expatriots of the last century brought about literary and artistic social progress and truly greater freedom of expression and creativity. Society is responsive to creative innovation and the inspiration of new discoveries. It was not necessary to attack and defame the old-fashioned kitchen icebox in order to replace it with a modern refrigerator.

Problematic Philosophies

"Academic Left"	180	Pacifism	185
Afrocentrism (Racism)	180	"Peacenik" (Politicalization)	180
Anarchism	100	**Philosophical Theories:**	
Atheism	165	Baudrillard, Jean	175
Authoritarianism	180	Caputo, John	185
"Critical Theory" (Marcuse)	145	Chomsky, Noam	135-185
Deconstructionism	190	Da Lauze, Gilles	190
Demonize	80	Darrida, Jacque	170
Dialectical Materialism	135	Foucault, Michel	190
"End Justifies the Means"	120	Husserl, Edmund	195
Epistemologic Relativism	190	Irigary, Luci	155
Eugenics	105	Kristeva, Julia	150
Fascism (Secular)	80	Kuhn, Fritz	195
Fascism (Theocratic)	50	Lacan, Jacques	180
Fascism (Islamic/Militant)	50	Lyotard, Jean-Francois	185
Feminist Politics (Sexism)	185	Manchu, Rigoberta	180
Hate	70	Marcuse, Herbert	150
Hedonism	180	Marx, Karl	135
Iconoclasm	175	Popper, Carl	185
Irresponsibility	195	Sartre, Jean-Paul	200
"ism" (Suffix)	180	Singer, Peter	195
Libertarianism	180	Vidal, Gore	180
Misanthropy	180	Zinn, Howard	200
Nihilism	120		

Political:			
Far Left	135-195	Racism	110
Far Right	135-195	Rhetoric	180
Far-Right Radical	80	Ruthlessness	180
Far-Left Radical	80	Slander	75
Revolutionary	100	Social Relativism	185
Relativism	185	Sophistry	180
Reactionary	155	Syncretism	195
Pop Sociology	165-210	Theocratic Totalitarianism	50
Populism	200	Vituperation	75
Pythagoras (Ancient Greece)	190	Xenophobia	185

Blame: The Philosophy, Psychology, and Politics of Paranoia, Hate, and War

Because, as history has repeatedly demonstrated, the pen is mightier than the sword, it is crucial to determine the level of truth of prevalent philosophies, doctrines, and belief systems that often become naively parroted and popularized as being stylish and *au courant*. Their appeal is to narcissism, i.e., the ego inflation of being superior and "special." In their effect on society, the hidden errors are like a hidden malignancy that results in catastrophe (e.g., Marxism alone cost the lives of tens of millions of people). Fallacies propagate via academia, the arts, and the media by their substitution of sophistry and conceptual relativism for verifiable truth.

The intent and thrust of relativistic philosophy is to discredit the very intellectual/philosophic basis out of which the great benefits of the modern world arose, i.e., science, antibiotics, electricity, transportation, hygiene, food production, ethics, morality, law, civil rights, the Constitution, and the economy. The recent French intellectuals, who were a primary source of the philosophical decline, as a group calibrate at 180-190, which is *far* below intellectual validity, much less excellence (cal. 460).

In America, a primary source of fallacious sophistry was the influence and writings of Herbert Marcuse (cal. 145), which were based on the Marxist dialectic and dualistic error that have resulted in academia's and Hollywood's promulgation of "newspeak," political correctness, and elitism. The theories of Marcuse are termed "cultural Marxism" (Flynn, 2004).

Among the basic ideas Marcuse promoted are:

1. Free speech should be controlled (and eliminate conservative reason, logic, or ethics).

2. Freedom is totalitarianism.

3. Democracy, ethics, truth, and morality are dictatorial.

4. Fiction and fantasy are truth; reality is false.

5. Violence is nonviolence. It is okay against governments and regulations.

6. Lies are okay if they subserve ideology.

7. Critical theory (cal. 145) deconstructs reason and its totalitarian restraints.

8. Polymorphous sex is superior to working (anti-capitalism).

9. Sensual gratification should be the primary ethic.

10. Science is a repressive political process.

11. The purpose of education is indoctrination.

12. All minorities are victims.

13. Cultural Marxism is superior to reason, ethics, and morality, which are repressive.

As is obvious from the above, the central focus of this philosophy is the infantile, narcissistic ego, as it resides in Freud's primitive "Id."

The complexities of "relativistic" intellectualization end up like the centipede that, when asked "which leg comes after which," fell upside down in a ditch. At best, the relativistic rhetoric of postmodernistic deconstructionism, reconstrutionism, and similar theories is that it does not get past the observation made by a character in Lewis Carroll's *Alice in Wonderland* (cal. level 420) that "a word means just what I say it means, nothing more and nothing less." Chapter 7 in Carroll's great classic illustrates the basis for the confusion of current socio-political philosophizing that, in effect, tends to increase the problems that are meant to be solved, e.g., the now-familiar "unforeseen consequences" of faulty social and political theories (Charon, 2004)

The Mad Hatter's Tea Party
Amorality as the Morality of Non-Morality

It is currently fashionable (and profitable) to misrepresent integrity and attack it with sarcasm and vilification. The trend is strongly expressed by the extremist editorialists, writers, movie-makers, and celebrity seekers who look for status via polemics. The "Howard Sterns" of politics have a voracious appetite to be noticed and get public attention. They are willing to sacrifice truth and integrity for the payoff of narcissistic ego inflations of a false sense of importance, with its illusion of empowerment (Howard and Clark, 2004). Headlines become intoxicating and sought for at any price, even though they appear pathetic to the mainstream. The favored targets are the traditional American standards of morality, ethics, and personal responsibility. By rhetoric excess and relinquishment of logic, proof, or reason, any representation of integrity can be distorted and set up as the straw man for clever attack. Inasmuch as Divinity is the ultimate symbol of truth and integrity, God and spiritual, religious, or even scientific and historic truths are the enemy.

The political attack on integrity, which is vociferously pseu-domoralistic, is based on the most glaring falsehood of all—that morality is immoral. The "righteous indignation" of political polemics (that usually calibrate at 130-180) is inflamed by public examples of responsible integrity, and, therefore, they are under attack by attempts to discredit them. These are frequently biased by taking actions out of context and thereby subjugating them to historical distortion.

The political extremists who calibrate far below 200 have an unerring eye for integrity, and therefore, their selected targets characteristically calibrate very high. A list of the targets for hatred and vilification is like a "Who's Who" of rationality.

Political and philosophical criticism and biased judgmentalism are based solely on moralistic presumptions; therefore, negation of the reality of moral truths removes any basis for opposition to traditional values. One cannot attack morality from the morality of non-morality. Therefore, all such positionalities calibrate far below the level of truth at 200. This leaves no rationale for political hatred and exposes that such behaviors are essentially the expression of personality disorders associated with loss of reality testing. Psychiatrically, they are classified as oppositional, defiant, or narcissistic personality disorders (American Psychiatric Association's DSM IV).

The primary targets of contentious political attack calibrate well above 200 (from 355, on up to Infinity; the average is at 455). Thus, the conflict is not really political but represents the social clash of collective levels below 200 with those above 200, i.e., between the emotionality of lower mind and the logic and reason that represent higher mind (see Chapter 14). It also reflects the hostility of the less evolved mind toward erudition itself. The underlying fantasy is that by attack, the playing field can be leveled, which is transparently fallacious since the impact of truth and integrity stems from its nonlinear source, which is immune.

Falsity can be rationalized but it represents only force (persuasion, emotionality) from which truth, like gravity, is intrinsically immune. Whereas emotionalism can distract, truth itself silently survives because force necessitates agreement, whereas truth, like gravity, stands on its own and its laws are inviolate.

The fallacy of the philosophic/academic discrediting of rationality and the inherent order of logic and truth were exposed by two revealing demonstrations. The first was the famous production of a "Postmodern Essay Generator" computer program of fictitious essays, and the second was the notorious "Sokal Affair," in which a physicist wrote a pseudoscientific article made up of pure hokum but in fancy terminology, which was published in *Social Text*, a publication of Duke University (details on the Internet).

The end result of the "question authority" bumper sticker is regression to immaturity. The denigration of science is at best an intellectual pose—nobody wants a relativistic auto mechanic or a brain surgeon who operates at consciousness level 180-190.

The source of philosophic error was the failure to appreciate that "postmodernism" and other intellectualities were meaningfully valid when applied to the *arts* (Stravinsky, Picasso, Dali) or to the study of semantics, but were grossly inappropriate when misapplied to the world of the intellect, social reality, nature, or spiritual reality (e.g., see Olson, *Zen and the Art of Postmodern Philosophy*).

The inability to differentiate the Kantian categories or levels of abstraction results in the substitution of emotionalized wishful thinking for the strict dialectic requirements of higher-mind intellection and logic. When separation of the levels of abstraction versus the concrete breaks down, there is a collapse between *res interna* (mentalization) and *res externa* (the world as it is), resulting in confusion, disorder, and incapacitation (as in schizophrenia). The hallmark of higher mind and maturity is the capacity for the discernment that differentiates between reality and emotionally motivated fantasy. While all understanding of communication entails hermeneutics (i.e., interpretation), interpretation itself is based on logical premises and the rules of syllogistic logic in contrast to emotionalism.

The successful integration of reason, science, and logic with spiritual, personal, humanistic, and environmental issues is demonstrated by the success of the rapidly growing segment of the population in the United States (estimated at approximately twenty-five percent) termed "cultural creatives" (Ray and Anderson, 2000). Described as a "movement with a heart," the overall philosophy transcends traditional political positions rather than joining in the fray. It avoids chocolate *versus* vanilla, or even chocolate *or* vanilla, and instead chooses chocolate *and* vanilla. The movement, which calibrates overall at 335, incorporates integrity and optimism, with emphasis on growth and responsibility in spiritual and personal as well as social and environmental matters.

Upon examination, the basic defect of arguments put forth by even the most esteemed intellectual proponents of anarchy is the ignoring of the rudimentary postulates and rules of logic known as "non-sequitur," "post hoc ergo prompter hoc," "begging the question," and the "undistributed middle." Thus, biased views are cited as purportedly supportive evidence so that the result is like a house of cards merely supported by other cards, e.g., America is evil because its government is evil because its politicians are evil because capitalism is evil because profit is evil because . . ., etc. The resultant paradox is that in the process, anarchy itself became a totalitarian ruling force to be slavishly served. Anti-authoritarianism is the new totalitarian "authority," and inquiry degenerates into iconoclasm (cal. level 175). Success is ridiculed and victimology promoted because the victim role brings with it a false sense of empowerment and, importantly, "entitlement."

The self-defeating dilemma of circuitous intellectualism is that all of nature, including animal and human societies, is expressed as form, which represents condensed information. The "meaning" of form is a derivation of the interpretation of perceived "relationship," which, in turn, is a mentalization projected by the observer onto the observed. Intention predetermines the content of what is found (e.g., the search engine) which, even by circularity, confirms the original positionality. This is a naïve process.

By analysis, it will be discovered that the common term "relationship" is itself an illusion that originates solely within the mind of the observer. It is an arbitrary viewpoint set up by selection of what is to be compared to what (i.e., a mentalization). To select two points for mental focus and attention does not magically change what is "out there" that now have a "relationship," just as selecting stars to look at does not cause a "constellation" to be a reality in the sky. Connecting the dots is imaginative but all "constellations" are within the observer's imagination. They are not facts about astronomy nor do they have reality as *res externa*, i.e., nature. (See Hawkins, 1995, *Power vs. Force*, Chapter 19.)

All structure and perceived relationship can therefore be arbitrarily viewed from any point one selects. Perception is thus linked to projection, and life is viewed like a Rorschach inkblot. The politics of what is basically just adolescent rebellion is languaged as intellectualized rationalizations in order to make claim to respectability. From an immature viewpoint, all integrous truth and wisdom are seen as parental. If the political/social/intellectual positions that ensue from such discourse were verifiably superior, then they would calibrate as such, but they do not, and instead, they collectively reflect the segment of society that calibrates from 130 to 190, or even lower, which includes considerable reliance on another defect of reason called "teleologic" reasoning, which is the presumption that things occur and are what they are "in order to" achieve some purported goal. This is also a defect of some biological sciences. In reality, all occurs solely by virtue of potentiality's becoming actuality in order to fulfill its own intrinsic design, e.g., the rich don't get rich "in order to" oppress the poor. In evolution, some species as well as their individual members are simply more adept.

Inasmuch as spirituality historically as well as by calibration represents the highest truth available to man, integrous scripture contains proven guidelines. Thus, in Proverbs, there are repeated stern warnings against allowing wisdom to be seduced by the "pretty woman of sophistry that whispers in one's ear." The true nature of the hidden predator beneath the sheep's clothing is quite openly revealed by its expressions as hatred, vituperation, and vilification. Significantly, the philosophies of the Far Left (Popper, Chomsky, et al.) are admittedly atheistic.

All of the theories that demonize success, the big corporations, and the country of America are examples of dualistic mentation based on the perpetrator/victim fallacy of an external "cause" (demonized) of a lamented, selected condition. Therefore, the "cause" of poverty is wealth or capital, and America is the evil cause of the world's poverty stricken, etc. All such postulations ignore the historical reality that war, poverty, cruelty, and famine preexisted before the emergence of the country of America or even the concept of capitalism.

If nature is the basis of earthly life, then by what aspect does all this "injustice" arise? Life itself is the ultimate context and power whereby evolution unfolds "unfairly," for like a cork in the sea, excellence automatically rises to the top. The strongest lion dominates; the cleverest sea urchin survives. The smartest octopus gets to be the biggest, and the fastest runner wins the race. Political ranting about the real laws of life is emotional, childish and hardly constitutes justification for attempts to overthrow reality (which is immune anyway). Creation is heterogeneous and all of life is expressed in endless variation in which every quality is articulated along a continuum.

The ego is dualistic and prone to falling into the illusion of an external "cause" to explain events instead of realizing that all comes into manifestation by the actualization of potential as a consequence of the overall field, plus intention (via choice). To avoid responsibility, the ego projects a dualistic split onto the world and thereby believes it sees the perpetrator/victim as "out there." This justifies hatred and paranoia, which then spew forth as vilification, slander, and demonization. Hate needs a target and therefore sets up the straw man as the "enemy."

Although the culture of hatred hides under the sheep's clothing of the lure of simplistic idealizations, its real nature is exposed as it gathers momentum and becomes the new oppressor. It can readily be seen that an organized attempt to discredit morality, ethics, and spiritual reality then itself merely becomes a new system of "ethics," "moral demand," and oppression (Bruce, 2003), with actual *censorship* of school books and libraries based on political ideology but, simultaneously, bizarrely teaching six-year-olds the details of sexual deviations, ala Krafft-Ebing's *Psychopathia Sexualis* (1886, 1999).

Distortions of verifiable integrous truth eventuate into social absurdities that stand out like cultural displays of moral imbecility enforced by coercion and litigious threat. In the "name of the free," the word "God" is illegal (so much for the First Amendment "Freedom of Speech"). School principals forbid teaching the Declaration of Independence because it refers to the Creator (which is not even the word "God"). Other schools do not allow teaching why or to whom the Pilgrims celebrated Thanksgiving (even as historical fact). Another school has "cross-dressing" day, and the annual Christmas tree in the nation's Capitol cannot be called a "Christmas" tree (free speech?).

Public displays of symbols of all religions are permitted in other areas so long as they are not Christian. In other social areas, organizations devoted to adult male solicitation of boys for pedophilia are legal but Boy Scouts are not. Even incest is now seeking approval via the movies, and criminality and drug-dependent personalities are media icons. Sedition has also become just "free expression," as have slander and bearing false witness.

While all the above is tragi-comical, more serious is the vilification of the police and enforcement of law and order, e.g., a
suspicious truck is stopped and found to be hauling three tons of
marijuana. The arrest is later deemed illegal because the drivers
were black (therefore arbitrarily "racial profiling," which does not
arise if the police officers are black and the criminals are white).
On television, the news from this "free society" is that a soldier
in the heat of battle who shoots an enemy combatant that is playing possum is held up for criticism and possible court martial.
At the same time, the military is inviting young men to enlist to
serve their country.

From the viewpoints of theology, religion, spirituality, ethics,
reason, morality, philosophy, tradition, history, and the common
sense of maturity, the above-described social attitudes exemplify
what has classically become termed the "Luciferic inversion," in
which good and evil are transposed. Historically, this has been
the sheep's clothing for the emergence and dominance of the
"satanic," meaning violence, the subversion of Divinity, and sovereign permission for mass slaughter by terrorism and/or war. Such
progression was displayed by the fall of the greatest empire the
world had ever seen, the Holy Roman Empire. The same process
befell both prior and succeeding empires, both Byzantine and
Arabic, such as the Ottoman and that of Attila the Hun.

While the upside of liberalism is the elimination of religious
theocratic oppression, the downside is to overshoot the mark and
merely substitute secular oppression, which is equally destructive
to true freedom, as discussed in Chapter 13.

In a free society, a citizen should be free to discuss *Lady Chat-
terley's Lover* as well as God or the subject of Thanksgiving Day
and the impact of Christ, Moses, or Muhammad on history and
civilization. An inversion of truth and its decline are indicated by
a culture that legalizes child pornography but forbids the mention
of God or religion as an academic study. It is dishonest to distort
truthful history and its importance as an attempt to proselytize.
The next move could be the elimination of all paper money that
says "In God We Trust" because it makes some neurotic "uncomfortable." It is important to question whether pathological mental

states such as personality disorders should be legislated as the norm. Is psychopathology an adequate model for legislation?

One can sympathize with attempts to destigmatize human defect or misfortune by linguistic and semantic manipulation, but the downside of fallacy is distortion. In the 1960s, the sophistry of "deconstructionism" was exemplified by such efforts as psychiatrist Thomas Szaz's writings, which sought to discredit the medical condition termed "mental illness" by calling it a "myth." Semantically, a term means just what it is defined to be (i.e., *res interna*), but what was overlooked in the redefinition of deconstructionism is that a term also refers to verifiable facts (*res externa*). To pretend that mental illness is solely a semantic "myth" (cal. 160) has been disastrous.

Clinically, the supposed "myths" of schizophrenia, depression, ADD, ADHD, mania, epilepsy, or bipolar cycling disappear promptly with psychopharmacology. The symptoms recur if medications are stopped. Obviously, if clinical conditions that have existed in all cultures throughout history were just "myths," they would not be turned on and off by medications. (ADHD is related to the amount of time a child watches television prior to age three. Watching television interferes with the neuronal process of circuits, plus genetics.)

Deconstructionism is intrinsically nihilistic in that it negates both experiential reality (i.e., history, the holocaust, etc.) as well as confirmable *res externa* and thereby circuitously negates its own premises (dialectic, i.e., the error of mixing levels). Meaning is derived from structure and definition, without which society degenerates, becomes amorphous, and life becomes meaningless sensation-seeking. A society without intellectual, moral, or ethical structure and discipline becomes not free, as implied by the promises of deconstructive relativism, but instead collapses by degeneration into chaos, civil disorder, and behavioral infantilism. The whole deconstructive theory is the child's game of pretend. Its absurdity is exemplified by sophomoric attempts to apply it to a staid publication, such as *The Economist*, which satirizes such attempts in an article, "Capitalistic Sexist Pigs" (December 18, 2004).

Certain human conditions are stigmatized by the ignorant. The cure is to educate the ignorant rather than pretend the condition does not exist or is just a linguistic construct. To "pretend" means it is naïve to believe a condition will just disappear if it is no longer discerned or nominalized. The mentally ill were put out of the hospitals to wander the streets and end up in jail or commit suicide with drugs and crime. It did not "go away" when it was relabeled "alternative lifestyle." Thus, current politicized euphemisms deny reality because they arise from the distorted perceptions of projected narcissism (i.e., "sensitive"). Limitations or impairments need to be the focus of education and upliftment, which is not accomplished by fairy tales that simple neurological disorders indicate that a child is an "advanced being from the future," etc.

A Summary and Explanation of "Relativism" (Cal. 185)

Because it is critical to understand this subject, which is likely to be unfamiliar to many people, it deserves special attention. "Relativism" is a rather general philosophical term that can be applied to the intellectual (epistemological), moral, social, ethical, and political realms, or to semantics and linguistics. Its applications, as well as misapplications, have had a widespread impact on law, the judiciary, government agendas, the media, and public opinion.

The intellectual thrust of the relativistic school of philosophy primarily stems from a group of French intellectuals, none of whom calibrates over 200. From nonlinear dynamics, we know that there is a "sensitive dependence on initial conditions." Thus, even a slight error when multiplied many times over ("iteration") can have a massive negative impact. The error of relativism, repeated ideologically throughout all areas of society (politics, government, the media, literature, and sociology), can become magnified in its destructive capacity to even a whole society. Relativistic "memes" contaminate academia, with serious consequences. Unchecked, the error of "relativism by iteration" has the potential to bring down American society. This statement calibrates at 490—very true.

The potential for a disastrous downside to relativism is apparent, first, by its consciousness calibration level of 185, which is below the critical level of truth (at 200), and, second, by the basic principles of relativism itself. These are:

1. There is no independent, universal, verifiable truth as such, and therefore all supposed truths are merely arbitrary consequences of definition that are only linguistic constructs with no necessary objective, inherent reality.

2. Language is structuralized social myth, the product of repressive forces, such as logic, politics, law, science, medicine, psychiatry, religion, etc.

3. Definition is therefore only social labeling, a semantic myth, because it is not a product of nature but only of political-social bias.

4. Meaning is a consequence of conceptual framework and linguistic/semantic/cultural structure and therefore reflects prejudicial empowerment of repressive elements.

5. Because structure is seen to be the basis of the perceived repression, it can be eliminated by the process of "deconstruction."

6. Progress requires destruction and attack on the prior norm rather than creation of a new paradigm. This requires revolution, anarchy, and vilification of integrity.

7. Morality and ethics have no reality basis and are therefore invalid.

8. Because there are no universal or verifiable truths, there should be no social parameters, restrictions, or guidelines such as mores that are repressive (e.g., "the man").

9. To conform to all the above, the meanings and definitions of language and history should be changed accordingly.

10. Because there is no absolute truth, God/Divinity is nonexistent and society should therefore be secular/atheistic/populist/libertarian and basically anarchistic.

11. Social problems are due to victimization by perpetrators. Therefore, there is no personal responsibility.

12. To reconstruct society, it is necessary to demonize integrity, morality, truth, logic, success, and excellence and replace it with the sophistry of narcissistic rhetoric and propaganda. Therefore, history itself has to be revised, as do language, meaning, and values. This is accomplished by "reconstruction" so that the reconstructed interpretations are in accord with and support the tenets of relativism.

The appeal of relativism, therefore, is to imbalance and excess rather than to truth, wisdom, or caution. The young are also romantically idealistic and impressionable as well as gullible and easily propagandized by the media and cultural icons. They are like sheep that follow the herd in idolization of pop media figures. Immaturity is also status seeking and therefore vulnerable to memes such as "politically correct," "elite," etc.

To the prideful, narcissistic ("sensitive") ego, responsibility is "uncomfortable," as are certain facts of reality that impinge on social image. Thus, to protect itself, the ego welcomes the concept of "labeling" (cal. 150) to dispense with unwanted realities. The illusion is that by declaring a reality to be a "myth" and just a "label," it will disappear. The problem that evolves is that the result is obfuscation of the real issues, i.e., the military becomes more obsessed with its television image than with handling the problem at hand. Relativism appeals to ego-mind (see Chapter 14), which "thinks" but fails the criterion of reason required by higher mind.

Although the collective calibration level of America overall is very high and integrous at 421, approximately forty-nine percent of the population is still below the level of integrity and truth at 200. This represents a vulnerability that historically has been the source of mankind's great disasters. Although intellectual, philosophic, academic, and spiritual error can be excused as a lack of erudition or intelligence, its danger cannot be ignored for the consequences of fallacy and rhetoric continue to be severe. A society at 421 cannot allow itself to be injured by a vociferous element that collectively calibrates at 180-190, or even lower. Elitism is regressive, not progressive, and runs counter to the overall progression of the evolution of consciousness.

It is unlikely that a naïve or unsophisticated mind would intuitively detect the inherent fallacies of the distorted herme-neutics of problematic relativistic epistemology that underlie the rhetoric of pop socio-political trends. Proponents are attracted to the puffery of attention-getting public utterances that pose as "oh so brave and gallant."

A serious downside to the pseudo-intellectualism of relativism is that it is a trap for academia, which confused intellectualism with erudition or intelligence. Sophistry does not increase one's I. Q. for it merely mimics what it does not really comprehend. Fallacious babble is merely pretense.

By research, it was discovered that the championed extremist positionalities appeal to only five percent of the U. S. popula-tion. Seventy-five percent of Americans view them as "stupid" and attention seeking. A similar number of U. S. citizens view them as seditious and treasonous. Twenty percent are undecided or uninterested, and seventy percent consider extremists as the "lunatic fringe."

It does not escape the notice of the public that vociferous enemies of the fundamentals of America's freedom and success are themselves multimillionaires or even billionaires whose "hate America" stance appears disingenuous at best. The most common comment is that if they despise America so much, why don't they just leave the country. It would appear that vociferous critics of capitalism are personally very attached to the wealth of capital itself. In his 1953 Inaugural Address, President Dwight D. Eisenhower said, "A people that values its privileges above its principles soon loses both."

Classically, in inner spiritual work, the allure of temptation is called a "test." These tests are sometimes painful to own and face, but in the end, the results are worth it. Statistically, the philosophic/political extremists represent only five percent of the population but, like a crying baby in a theater, they disturb the entire audience. The "whines and complaints" (e.g., the famous

Time magazine cover, 8/12/91) of narcissism are given a false image of importance by the attention of media that themselves are heavily influenced and even dominated by the same elements. This propensity to "milk" a favored position is well documented and does not escape attention.

Despite its great progress and overall erudition, ours is still a naïve society that, for instance, does not fully understand the difference between religion and spirituality, which is the very crux of the U. S. Constitution itself. (For reference, "religion" is clearly defined in the tax regulations of the Internal Revenue Service.) The danger of theocracy was precluded and thereby established freedom *for* religion as well as freedom *from* it. Mere mention of the name "God" does not thereby establish a "religion" or ninety percent of the American public would qualify as being tax exempt.

The Constitution says to let the Congress not establish any religion nor prohibit the free practice thereof. It does *not* say "separation of church and state," which is a purposeful misquote in order to broaden the meaning and give justification to political attacks that violate the Constitution by trying to prohibit the "free exercise thereof." Currently, such attacks are selectively directed to the public observance of Christianity. Paradoxically, the enemies of religion draw their roots from Christian principles upon which the Constitution was founded. (The misquote, "separation of church and state," recalls the truism that the most efficacious lie is one that contains a little truth.) They also fall into the same trap as did theocracies, i.e., coercion by force. Secular coercion by judicial decree or historic papal decree is the same in form and operation. Prohibition of the historical practice of religious observance is basically the same as coercion to practice it.

The Constitution at calibration level 710 is more than just "fair and balanced"; it is pristine and in an unparalleled class by itself that hardly needs interpretation from the arguments of sophistry that calibrate at 185.

It is also important to note that secularism calibrates at 165, and that the secularism of Europe is understandable in view of the historical oppression of theocratic monarchies and centuries of ecclesiastic abuse. It was this very thing that the founders of the republic of the United States sought to preclude (calibrates as "true").

In contrast, "freethinkers" have a long and honorable history, and their rights deserve to be safeguarded (see Jacoby, 2004). It is informative to note that secularism and atheism both calibrate at 165, whereas agnosticism calibrates at 205 and "freethinkers" at 335. That is a very significant difference. Several signers of the Declaration of Independence were themselves freethinkers who supported the theists, even though they themselves were not. They saw to it that Americans could have chocolate *and* vanilla and thus, by wisdom, precluded contention and bitterness, thereby establishing "freedom and liberty for all." The integrous are the true liberators from the totalitarianism of either political extreme.

Free Speech

Central to the problem of identification of truth from falsehood is the much-daunted principle of "free speech," which has become an icon that has misfortunately displaced truth as an ideal. Free speech, in and of itself, is a two-edged sword, the usefulness of which, like dynamite, is determined by intention. It thus can lead to salvation and progress or, alternatively, to malice and destruction.

Significant Calibrations

Free Speech defined by the Bill of Rights	265	Interpret	400
		Evaluate	390
Free Speech in "Traditional America"	265	Constructive Criticism	210
		Wall Street Journal	440
Speech as Diplomacy	375	Stewardship	415
Discernment	375	Testimony of U.S. Government Officials at 9/11 hearings	255
Discussion	380		
Clarity	390		
Understand	400	Oratory	200

Contrasting Calibrations

Free Speech currently in U.S.	190	Protagonist		190
Freedom of expression		Labeling		150
in U.S.	190	Radicalism		120
Fordham Univ. journalism		Vociferous political hate		
course (2004) "How To		speeches by prominent		
Think Critically"	190	senior politicians		145
Chicago Tribune Editorial		Critics of testimony of U.S.		
Section, 4/11/04	185	Gov't. officials regarding		
Editorial sections of top 10		9/11		170
major U.S. newspapers	190	Political cartoon ridiculing		
Criticalness	120	Tillman's loyalty and		
Contentious	185	death		100
Proselytize	180	Pedantry		190
Exaggeration	160	Do-Gooderism		190
Hypothetical example	120	Social "Crybabies"		180
Obfuscation	120	Insulting Speech		165

Whereas the average American naively assumes that "free speech" is the bulwark of civil freedom, the opposite is just as true—it is also the most serious threat to liberty (e.g., Adolph Hitler proclaimed that the purpose of the Third Reich was to "make a better world." Karl Marx exhorted the populace to "lose their chains," etc.) Thus, it is not "free speech" itself that is the vaunted savior of freedom but the purpose for which it is put to use, e.g., a two-edged sword. While it can be the bastion of liberty, it can also be the arena of the slippery slope of nonintegrity and the disasters that ensue from falsehood. Note that wisdom calibrates much higher than free speech.

The naïve belief of integrous people is that public figures, celebrities, and officials in high office would not really purposely distort the truth. "Oh, sure," they say, "it is expected that they will favorably 'shade it a little' but not deliberately deceive the public." The downside of misplaced faith is that it is painful to overcome denial. It is disillusioning and therefore creates anger, which is also unpleasant to integrous people. Pride also precludes awareness that one has been duped. Whole populations choose to follow an egomaniacal madman to their own death rather than admit they were mistaken. That is the downside of blind faith.

The vulnerability of democracy to its deprecation by the non-integrous elements of society was noted by Socrates in 350 B.C. For that reason, he favored an oligarchy in which only the most sagacious and wise were the appointed rulers; otherwise, self-ish rhetoric would eventually prevail and weaken the republic, progressively leading to its downfall. In the Fourth Century B.C., the complacency and self-delusion of the affluent, free Athenians led to their downfall by Phillip II of Macedonia. Free speech was the road to freedom but also to enslavement and death.

Whereas sincerity can be convincing, it can also be in error. Passion about beliefs is not an indication of truthfulness because it is often primarily the emotionalized imbalance of a positionality. Balance is more often indicated by modesty of beliefs. Until the discovery of how to tell truth from falsehood and a science of consciousness, the average human has been at the mercy of prevailing belief systems, the influence of memes, propaganda, and the persuasiveness of "Popular Extraordinary Delusions and the Madness of Crowds" (Mackey, 1841, 1980). In the past, many people did adhere to the dictum "be vigilant for truth," as there was no means to ascertain what was the truth, much less to what degree or in what context. As is obvious in today's world, the truth has been frequently quite unwelcome.

The pervasiveness of nonintegrity in today's society is considerably a product of the impact of the media, which tend to pander to the contentious elements in society for their headline value and attraction of attention. In "traditional America," for instance, the New York Times published only "All The News That's Fit to Print" to differentiate itself from less integrous, biased "yellow journalism" and "gossip rags." Discretion was exercised by reporters and the broadcast media so that the airwaves were not inundated by provocative or salacious material. Programming for children was nonsexual because sex education was considered to be the province of parents and biology that of the schools.

With the progressive decrease in acceptable standards of decency in the name of total freedom, the media output is now a "free for all" that constantly pushes the limits of credibility and tolerance. The other extreme is censorship; thus, the problem is how to express freedom, yet maintain a responsible and responsive manner.

While the above is obvious and blatant, a more serious skew to editorial influence is the current trend of critics to favor negative comment as being *au courant* and elite and positive comment as being naïve and not "cool." Thus, positive commentary about the country or its leaders is actually unwelcome. The media are unduly negative and promulgate contention and conflict, feeding off artificially inflated controversy (e.g., the New York Times' front-page repetition of the Abu-Ghraib incident forty-five times, a columnist's fatuous editorial on how much they hate Christianity, comments on President Regan's death ("He did not do much for AIDS in Africa"), the acidic attacks on Tillman's death, President Bush's visit to the troops in combat, etc. All the above calibrate in the range of 170-180, which indicates a serious degree of bias, warp, and catering to the political fringe.

Naively, people believe that the First Amendment means no restrictions, consequences or accountability. It just states that "government" cannot interfere, but others, such as employers, etc., are not prevented from doing so. Employees get legally fired for nonjudicious or intemperate speech, as "bloggers" recently discovered when the lost their jobs (Jesdanun, 2005).

Social Narcissism (Cal. 180)

Social narcissism as a new, purportedly "progressive," standard of acceptable behavior results in social distortion, with major negative consequences to oneself and society. Inflated egotism results in "sensitivity" by which personal responsibility is projected in paranoid style to cultural discourse. The perceived "offender" is depicted as a perpetrator from whom apology is now extorted by the demand of indignant self-righteousness and declaration of victimhood. To further add to the social distortion, the hypothetical perpetrator is brainwashed into guilty self-recrimination for being the *cause* and thus ignominiously wallows in guilty obeisance. Thus, the supposed perpetrator is now actually the victim of moral blackmail as well as extortion.

"Narcissistic personality disorders" are classified as such by the American Psychiatric Association and are considered to be in need of treatment for persistent infantilism, with associated interpersonal distortion and conflicts.

As pointed out by George Will (January 2005), a narcissistic crisis can express itself as hysteria, with concomitant physiological disruption and emotional imbalance and excess, as well as impaired judgment. As Will noted, campus-based indignation is now a social industry that proselytizes imaginary bias and "operatic reactions to imagined slights." A widely reported incident was triggered by a remark made by the president of Harvard University who said that in some aspects of human capability, biology influences fate. This idea was so upsetting to a listener that she had to immediately contact the major pubic media with her lament.

While on the surface such a story is tragi-comical, the consequence to society is quite injurious when the judiciary validates the distortion of victimology as reality. In a society where anyone can frivolously be declared a guilty perpetrator on a whim, nobody is safe and everyone is at risk without protection by logic, reason, and balance of the traditional rule of law. Thus victimology becomes operationally a social racket with extorted benefits plus artificially sanctioned, inflated egotism of "pseudo-importance."

Unlike an iron filing that has no say as to where it will be pulled within a magnetic field, the human spirit is gifted with the option of choice, and by its own hand (spiritual will) determines its fate. By comprehending the nature of the evolution of consciousness itself, forgiveness and compassion arise at the witnessing of human suffering and anguish that are the consequences of ignorance and naïveté.

SECTION III
TRUTH AND THE WORLD

CHAPTER 13
Truth: The Pathway to Freedom

Introduction

In reality, we are free to the same degree that we are enlightened, both individually and as a society, but what is true freedom and how can we know what it really is? Everyone imagines that they know the answer for themselves, but do they? Is freedom a psychological/emotional way of experiencing life or merely intellectual/political idealism and just an appealing slogan?

To even try to define "freedom" turns out to be rather complex and baffling. To define the term requires, as it did in defining truth, not only content but also context, i.e., for whom and under what conditions.

Upon investigation, the problem is solved by discovering that there is a whole scale of relative degrees of freedom and that the term refers back again to calibrated levels of consciousness, along with the difference between inner subjective experience versus external conditions, both real and perceived. To truly understand freedom is to experience it and not just think or hypothesize about it. Operationally, it could be said that everyone is as free as they believe they are and able to accept it. It can be asked if that is an imaginative fantasy or confirmable reality.

Definition

The dictionary states that freedom is a "state of liberty and independence; ease; manner; privileged; self-determining; free of restraints." Constitutionally, Americans are guaranteed "life, liberty, and the pursuit of happiness," to which President Roosevelt added the four freedoms of "freedom of speech, freedom to worship, freedom from want, and freedom from fear of the world." (Address to Congress, January 6, 1941.) We see that freedom is defined in terms "of" desirable values and freedom "from" the undesired. Thus, freedom is defined in words that reflect human wants and needs versus "want nots" and deprivations.

It quickly becomes obvious that as defined, freedom is purely a subjective phenomenon that reflects the interface between desires and their degrees of fulfillment and is therefore a relative state of experiencing. It is also obvious that a person who has few wants or aversions would feel an inner freedom the majority of the time, and that persons with lots of aversions, likes, dislikes, and desires would seldom feel free at all, even when surrounded by abundance.

Thus, maturity and the level of a person's consciousness determine the quality of the experience, which is personal; therefore, to what degree is society obligated to fulfill these expectations? Is social freedom defined in terms of accomplishments or opportunities? Is it realistic to expect society to expand its perimeters so that no one feels "uncomfortable" inasmuch as that is an internal condition and not actually a social factor? Should the laws of the land be modeled after the pathology of neurotic problems and personality disorders? (Everyone is free to not feel uncomfortable if they so wish.)

To understand the relationship of the individual to society requires a reexamination of the mind itself, out of which dreams, desires, aversions, and dislikes arise. Some people are uncomfortable most of the time just because of who they are and their infantile expectations of being catered to. Clinically, and through research, it is found that the farther below consciousness level 200 a person calibrates, the less their inner experience of freedom; and at the lowest levels of consciousness, such experience is precluded. The corollary is that the higher the person's level of evolutionary development, the greater the opportunity, likelihood, and degree of freedom experienced. Above calibration level 540, freedom is a constant, inner experiential reality that is independent of the world altogether. With evolution, success, happiness, and freedom are all independent inner states that are the gift of the realization of the Source of one's own existence.

Freedom as a Product of Mind

Because experiential freedom, whether personal, social, or political, is an emotionalized mentalization, much can be learned by a practical and nontechnical understanding of mental functions, including expectations.

As a result of evolution, "mind" is not just a "thing" that everyone equally "has" for, upon observation, it is discovered that there are really two dominant energy fields of mentalization, and each is correlated with a calibratable, dominant level of consciousness that is reflective of an "attractor field" (as defined by nonlinear dynamics). Alignment with a specific, calibratable level-of-consciousness energy field is a consequence of genetic/karmic inheritance, modified by experience and intention. Mind is thus describable on two primary levels, which are, in turn, reflective of differences in brain physiology and the emergence of the etheric (energy) brain of higher mind. Lower mind is thus restricted to the capacities of a physical brain and its neurochemistry. A description of these two levels of mind is also concordant with traditional knowledge and human experience. These can be portrayed as follows:

Table 1: Function of Mind—Attitudes

Ego Mind (Cal. 155) Content (specifics)	Higher Mind (Cal. 275) Content plus field (conditions)
Concrete, literal	Abstract, imaginative
Limited, time, space	Unlimited
Personal	Impersonal
Form	Significance

Focus on specifics	Generalities
Exclusive examples	Categorize class—inclusive
Reactive	Detached
Passive/aggressive	Protective
Recall events	Contextualize significance
Plan	Create
Definition	Essence, meaning
Particularize	Generalize
Pedestrian	Transcendent
Motivation	Inspirational, intention
Morals	Ethics
Examples	Principles
Physical and emotional survival	Intellectual development
Pleasure and satisfaction	Fulfillment of potential
Accumulation	Growth
Acquire	Savor
Remember	Reflect
Maintain	Evolve
Think	Process
Denotation	Inference
Time = restriction	Time = opportunity
Focus on present/past	Focus on present/future
Ruled by emotion/wants	Ruled by reason/inspiration
Blames	Takes responsibility
Careless	Disciplined

All gradations exist between the contrasting pairs that reflect intensity, e.g., there is a difference between craving, wanting, desiring, "must have," and demanding in contrast to the options of preference, hoping for, wishing, choosing, favoring, or accepting. The difference in just this one single quality alone can spell the distinction between homicide, rage, depression, and misery versus contentment, relaxation, and being easy-going in one's expectations.

Psychology, psychiatry, and brain chemistry, as well as philosophy, pay little attention to a study of attitudes, which is surprising considering how important they are to human happiness, satisfaction, and success. "Attitude" can be defined as a habitual mindset that relates the perceived self to the perceived world and others. In our society, attitudes are studied within the so-called field of "self-improvement" for which there are workshops and voluminous literature. The common collective experience is that expectations of self and others become modified with growth and progressive maturity, along with spiritual evolution. Thus, the cultural field of growth attracts the progressive segment of society recently labeled "cultural creatives" (Ray and Anderson, 2000). As a simple exercise, merely surveying the contrasting lists, including the one that follows, has a freeing effect as it brings various options to awareness that have been overlooked.

Table 2: Function of Mind—Attitudes

Ego Mind (Cal. 155)	Higher Mind (Cal. 275)
Impatient	Tolerant
Demand	Prefer
Desire	Value
Upset, tension	Calm, deliberate
Control	Diffuse
Utilitarian use	Sees potential
Literal	Intuitive
Ego-self directed	Ego, plus other-oriented
Personal and family survival	Survival of others
Constrictive	Expansive
Exploit, use up	Preserve, enhance
Design	Art
Competition	Cooperation
Pretty, attractive	Aesthetics
Naïve, impressionable	Sophisticated, informed
Guilt	Regret
Gullible	Thoughtful
Pessimist	Optimist
Excess	Balance
Force	Power

Smart, clever	Intelligent
Exploits life	Serves life
Callous	Merciful
Insensitive	Sensitive
Particularize	Contextualize
Statement	Hypothesis
Closure	Open-ended
Terminal	Germinal
Sympathize	Empathize
Rate	Evaluate
Want	Choose
Avoid	Face and accept
Childish	Mature
Attacks	Avoids
Critical	Accepting
Condemning	Forgiving

Table 2 reveals further options and possibilities that benefit self-awareness. Limiting attitudes have been called "character defects," and groups that support spiritual growth have noticed that these defects begin to diminish as soon as they are recognized and owned.

The benefit of accepting one's defects instead of denying them is an increase in an inner sense of self-honesty, security, and higher self-esteem, accompanied by greatly diminished defensiveness. A self-honest person is not prone to having their feelings hurt by others, and therefore, honest insight has an immediate benefit in the reduction of actual as well as potential emotional pain. A person is vulnerable to emotional pain in exact relationship to the degree of self-awareness and self-acceptance. When we admit our downside, others cannot attack us there. As a consequence, we feel emotionally less vulnerable, and more safe and secure. Most domestic arguments stem from the refusal to own or take responsibility for even simple character defects, such as forgetting an errand or some triviality, which, oddly enough, constitutes the majority of interpersonal conflict. Most bickering represents the endless mutual accusations over trivialities that emotional maturity and honesty would have prevented in the first place. Battered spouses and marital homicide start out over mundane affairs and then escalate as they trigger the release of the narcissistic ego to which "being right" is astonishingly more important than even life itself.

The key to painless growth is humility, which amounts to merely dropping pridefulness and pretense and accepting fallibility as a normal human characteristic of self and others. Lower mind sees relationships as competitive; higher mind sees them as cooperative. Lower mind gets involved with others; higher mind becomes aligned with others. The simple words "I'm sorry" put out most fires painlessly. To win in life means to give up the obsession of "who's at fault." Graciousness is far more powerful than belligerence. It is better to succeed than to "win." (A little honest humility would have saved a high-profile celebrity from a jail term.)

Table 3: Function of Mind—Attitudes

Ego Mind (Cal. 155)	Higher Mind (Cal. 275)
Guarded	Friendly, charitable
Cynical, skeptical	Optimistic, hopeful
Suspicious	Trusting
Selfish	Considerate
Stingy	Generous
Calculating	Planning
Devious	Forthright
Quixotic	Stable
Fussy, choosey	Easy to please
Short of money	Adequate for needs
Insists	Requests
Excess	Balance
Rude	Polite, gracious
Extremes	Compromising
Rush, hurry	"Keep moving"
Avarice	Money isn't everything

Lust	Desire
Ungrateful	Appreciative
Downgrades	Compliments
Condemn	Disapprove
Sexist	Humanist
Stultified	Progressive
Focused on self	Concern for others and the world
Opportunistic	Fits life plan
Complacent	Self-improvement
Vulgar, gross	Restrained, subtle
Prevaricate	Honest
Envy	Appreciation, respect
Grim, heavy	Sense of humor, lighthearted

Self-respect stems from self-honesty and allows for the dropping of cantankerous, contentious defensiveness and the "chip on the shoulder" attitude of ego inflation, with its focus on unrealistic expectations. In a normal childhood, the give-and-take of teasing and kidding helps the maturation process that diminishes oversensitivity and feelings of being slighted when the ego has not been catered to. Children call each other "dumb" but learn to get over it instead of being neurotically, reactively defensive.

The secret of success is that it is quite simple to change others merely by changing oneself. Is New York City a cold, rude, callous place or friendly and polite? It all depends not on how New Yorkers are at all but on who we ourselves are. A very evolved person considers New York City a friendly, almost home-town-like place. An immature person sees it as cold and rejecting because the world mirrors the reflection of one's own projected perceptions.

Success is the automatic byproduct of constructive attitudes and simple, common-sense basics, as were described by Jack Cornfield in *The Success Principles* (2004). The process is not arduous but very enjoyable and self-rewarding. Success is the consequence of rather simple principles.

The development of higher mind is strongly supported by early-life exposure to aesthetics, especially classical music, the arts, ballet, and nature, as well as religious upbringing (even if it is rejected in later life), all of which have a positive influence on developing interconnected energy patterns and neuronal configurations in the physical brain itself.

Freedom and the Ego

The basis of war, crime, and all social conflict, including genocide, is diagnosed as originating from the core of the ego itself, specifically the infantile ego, with its impatient wants, loud protests, and unrealistic expectations. With maturation, the grandiosity of the ego ("unruly ox" of the Zen ox-herding pictures) becomes quieter, tamer, and easier to ride. The evolution of psychological consciousness occurs by several different mechanisms, as shown below.

1. **Repression:** The primitive drives are repressed, subsequently denied, and then projected onto others (social paranoia).

2. **Surrender and Sublimation:** With good parenting, narcissistic primitive drives are given up in return for a better gain, such as love, acceptance, and identification with supportive parents and authority figures.

3. **Compliance:** This is a way of avoiding maturation and represents the continuance of primitiveness because egocentricity is only suppressed, and the omnipotence/grandiosity of the inner narcissistic "king baby" attitude persists. This results in seeing all thwarting of inner wants as arbitrary, hateful authoritarianism, which results in resentment, rebellion, defiance, and persistent immaturity. This duality also leads to serious distortions of reality, such as splitting events into the perpetrator/victim model that is then projected onto society with extremely dire consequences. It is this split in the narcissistic ego that has cost the lives of over one hundred million people in the last century.

Thus, the failure of maturation leads to pathologic personality disorders, including criminality, chronic political dissidence, and the egomania of the grandiose tyrants and dictators who kill not only their countrymen but even their own family members.

Freedom Versus Infantilism

The infantile ego misinterprets freedom as indulgent libertinism and the instant gratification of hedonism, with no concern for others. In attenuated form, this person constantly pushes the envelope and seeks to overturn any and all restrictions. It also leads to the unrealistic expectation that there should be no consequences for transgressing boundaries. This is the artificially induced expectation that is now notable among teenagers who have been inculcated with the idea that they are victims and therefore not answerable for social transgressions, resulting in deleterious attitudes (as was noted by Bill Cosby who saw that the adolescents were victims of politicized "victimology" brainwashing).

Extremism eventually precipitates counter-reaction as the "shock jocks" of the public media have recently discovered. Abuse of a "good thing" and nonintegrous exploitation are self-defeating because they violate the basic requirements of social structure and survival. Exploitation of freedom leads to its loss.

Frustration of the narcissistic ego is the most frequent trigger for hatred, which, in current society, is freely expressed openly towards all authority figures and institutions. Politically, the infantile ego is atheistic and anarchist, which tends toward paranoia and the prevalent perceptual distortion that sees all situations in terms of perpetrator/victim. Over the last few decades, lack of social development has been blamed on the "me" generation of the 1960s in which it was "cool" to flaunt all social conventions. The downside was the naïveté of that position, which ignores consequences that, as was discovered, can be quite grave indeed, including even death or life imprisonment.

As was explained in the evolution of life on this planet, the earliest life forms were innately "greedy," and in the human, this persists as a constant hunger/wantingness/desire that is insatiable. The persistence of an unmitigated narcissistic ego in adulthood leads to a personality that is bitter and basically feels "deprived." The inner vanity cannot be satiated, which leads to being "sensitive" to real or imaginary slights. Thus, status seeking, jealousy, and envy in the form of malice and gossip are social attributes that characterize "back stabbers" who turn on a friend or become a "whistle blower" out of malice rather than integrity. (The situation makes the difference.) Thus, such persons are not capable of loyalty and are quick to sell out others and violate their trust. The same psychodynamics apply to those who turn against their own country, fellow colleagues, or comrades in arms.

That hostility to (parental) authority is intrinsic to current political trends is exemplified by the progressive disenfranchisement of legal parental authority and functions that are now replaced by government-sponsored school agendas, e.g., sexuality, ethics, etc. This is characteristic of all totalitarianism, in which programming of children replaces traditional parental functions (e.g., Hitler's youth, Mao's China, and Islamic militants). Children are deliberately programmed with "new think," memes, and social and political attitudes. The state replaces the parental role and then makes the rules. Because the young are vulnerable and malleable, they are routinely preyed upon by power seekers, from Islamic Mullahs to supposed "liberationists," all of whom seek control and feed off the naïveté of the young.

With maturity, social life is seen as a balance and consequence of trade-offs in which animal impulses are sublimated in return for higher gains, such as love, security, success, respect, self-esteem, and personal liberty. Whether a boundary or social/legal regulation is restrictive or protective is reflective of a point of view rather than some external reality. Society thus reflects collective ignorance but also collective wisdom, which often comes at the price of great suffering and pain. Unrestrained by society, the narcissistic ego is like an engine without a flywheel, and with maturity, one begins to understand that police, laws, ethics, rationality, and morality ensure one's true freedom by denying its illusory substitute of unaccountability and nonresponsibility.

In the intellectual realm, infantilism sees reason, logic, morality, and ethics as arbitrary authoritarian impositions and restrictions, and, therefore, that sublevel of society glorifies the criminal, the criminal culture, and the vulgar. It sees the anarchist as a hero and concordantly vilifies esthetics and beauty. The ego is clever and can rationalize its infantile motivations of hatred and violence by either getting rid of God or, paradoxically, by justifying the massacring of others in the "name of God" (Allah), i.e., Jihad.

The Dream "Freedom" of the Id

The inflated infantile ego "demands" and grandiosely feels "entitled" to and is indignant over its "rights" and expects to be allowed self-indulgence with no consequences or accountability. Therefore, social structure is seen overall as the great frustrator of impulsiveness. The core of the ego is a rebellious anarchist, atheist, and exhibitionist that expects life to be an endless Roman orgy, including intoxicated abandon and polymorphous, perverse sexuality that permits abuse of the naïve and vulnerable. Even children are exempt from restrictions, and their victimization should be approved by society and even made legal by the sophistry of declaring that such predatory behavior is excused as "free speech" (e.g., child pornography). The same mind processes seek to change the meaning of the term free "speech" to instead denote totally free and unrestricted "expression" or "behaviors." Thereby, the wolf is disguised in the sheep's clothing of a political slogan.

What identifies the core of the narcissistic ego is its inability and refusal to accept personal responsibility, and any such request is vociferously rejected as being oppressive. It feeds off the false sense of empowerment of being the "victim" and distorts reality in order to be seen as the victim. At this point, social discernment falters under a barrage of propaganda that obscures the differentiation between progress and regression. It cannot discern the difference between progressive and degenerative, despite history's example that all great empires have fallen by virtue of moral decay from within rather than by aggression from without. The reason for this is quite obvious—as the calibration level diminishes, so does the level of power; therefore, the inner strength to survive is lost, both individually and collectively.

With maturity, authority is seen not just as a "bad guy" where the criminal is pictured as a victim; on the contrary, authority as societal representatives is seen as protective. To the criminal, the police are enemies; to the law abiding, they are friends. Integrous people feel more secure if they know that public events and streets are under video surveillance, but a guilty and nonintegrous person, because of the innate paranoia that accompanies such attitudes, resents and hates public surveillance, which they feel is an invasion of their "rights." Surveillance cameras are a part and parcel of current society and exist because of the narcissistic personalities that abound in that society. Casinos and department stores are as sophisticated about surveillance as are governmental investigative agencies and frequently even better at it.

Narcissism is inherently paranoid and therefore constantly tries to hide, which is an absurdity in today's world of computers, which keep an ongoing dossier on everyone in minute detail that is available worldwide. Every detail of "personal" life is automatically revealed as a cumulative trail that tracks any purchases, inquiries to web sites, financial moves, clues to interests, politics, education, and more. Everyone lives in the public domain and protestors merely come up on the Internet databases identified as such.

The projection of distorted perception has disastrous fallout when political pressure groups misapply it to governmental agencies. The current disasters in America and elsewhere in the world affecting American embassies and military operations are the unintended consequence that followed well-intentioned but naïve and unrealistic constraints on critical agencies, thus impairing their capacity to function in protecting the lives and welfare of the citizenry. Historically, the same naïveté also blinded Secretary of War Stimson's (cal. 180) forewarnings of the Japanese movements prior to World War II, a similar event that was abetted by the lack of reality testing exhibited by Neville Chamberlain (cal. 185) who, after meeting with Hitler, returned to England with the slogan "Peace in our time." (Hitler scoffed at his "stupidity.") Appeasement of terrorism calibrates at 155. It is viewed with contempt as weakness and cowardice and invites aggression (i.e., wolf-pack animal mentality). Below calibration level 200, the strong attack the weak; above 200, they protect the weak.

Rationalized lack of responsibility is also exhibited by the positionalities of apologists who sympathize with the most decadent and dangerous persons in the world instead of their more obvious victims. Thus, lower mind becomes a tool of the narcissistic ego, the pathology of which in operation is so severe that it cannot differentiate between a messianic megalomaniac who calibrates at 60 and an integrous statesman who calibrates at 460 (i.e., between a friendly dog and a Komodo dragon). The infantile ego thus hates society in general but especially its representative institutions, such as governments, schools, industry, capitalism, successful commerce, big corporations, or true winners and successful people (Gibson, 2004).

In the psychoanalytic experience, it quickly becomes subjectively apparent that one's attitudes toward authority stem from infantile fantasies and experiences of which the father figure is perceived as either threatening (hated and feared) or protective and just (trusted). Consequently, all authority becomes imbued with the projected attitudes, and one either joins and supports structure or becomes a malcontent and a revolutionary, depending on the success or failure of the resolution of the unconscious conflict/complex. These unconscious emotional attitudes were observed in patients for more than 50 years in clinical psychiatric practice. The mind automatically projects its own images and distorted belief systems onto others. The phenomenon is subjectively very real emotionally and occurs spontaneously without any prompting or interpretation by the psychoanalyst ("transference"). The Oedipal complex itself has, of course, been demonized and Freud "demythologized" by those who have not resolved their own Oedipal complex and therefore project it onto society rather than becoming conscious of it. The primary value of understanding psychodynamics is not the theory of the Oedipal complex but the understanding of the ego's mechanisms for handling conflict.

As an aside, it is of interest to note how important the consequences to society can be from an "unresolved oedipal complex." In the significant German schools of philosophy of the early 1800s, Hegel was the most important respected teacher and authority. Although Marx was an early follower, he rejected father figure Hegel, especially Hegel's primary principle of the Absolute (which calibrates at 570). Instead, Marx competitively threw out Hegel's important comprehension and substituted a dualistic theory that calibrates at 130 and was attractive, therefore, to the inner rebellious adolescent in other revolutionaries. The confusion between progressive and revolutionary persists to this day, and it is perhaps unfortunate that there is no current, truly integrous "progressive" political party as such. (It calibrated at 360 in the Midwestern United States in the 1930s and 1940s.)

It is notable that the egoism of celebrity status itself is often the slippery slope that leads to the downfall of politicians, dictators, erstwhile gurus, and political dissidents for whom Karl Marx (cal. 130) represents the cultural hero. "If by their fruits we shall know them," then the downside fallout of the calibrated level of 180 poses perhaps the greatest danger to all societies, and even the world itself, because of its psuedoplausibility and ease of propagandizing, which preys upon the innocence of the human mind and its lack of development and maturity in large populations (seventy-eight percent worldwide and approximately fifty percent in America).

Freedom and the Brain

In the developmental process, learned behaviors influence the development of neuronal connections in the brain and cerebral cortex. This also continues on into later life. Even a specific skill, such as learning how to juggle, under experimental conditions results in the increase of neurons and the complexity of their interconnections, as well as the mass of specific areas of the brain. Disuse of the skill results in a progressive decrease in the number of neurons and the mass, which confirms the common phrase "use it or lose it." This is a principle with increasing significance to offset the decline of old age, but it also has major significance in the impairment of intellectual development of school dropouts and children who are parentally neglected.

A consequence of the failure of socialization and maturation results in the impairment of neuronal patterning, which thereby retains primitive configurations that impair reality testing and the development of the more intricate basic neuronal patterning and connections that are fundamental to the development of higher mind. The stultification of spiritual awareness and socialization of instinctual drives results in the preponderance of primitive reflexes as outlined in a previous chapter. A less-developed brain and resultant level of mind mean that the animal drives continue to dominate. The rationalized sophistries of lower mind therefore seek to change society instead of oneself. This more primitive undeveloped mind set then rebels against all true rationality and seeks to reinforce its weak position by proselytizing or intimidating by litigation.

Freedom Versus Sophistry

Sophistry began in ancient Greece, where it was taught to would-be politicians as persuasive rhetoric, with subtle disguise of hidden agendas. Training was provided in what is really propaganda in the form of the presentation of plausible and persuasive argument based on distortions that would slyly slip by detection by the less educated.

Joseph Goebbels was the world's most renowned expert of recent times and was able to persuade a whole population to give up its life for the sophistries that justified the aggression of the Third Reich. The rationale of the Nazi annexation of Austria and subsequent invasion of Europe was based upon a dualistic distortion of the reality of perpetrator/victim, but with the reversal of roles. Hitler's sophistry was that he proposed to "right the wrongs" of the Versailles Treaty. The Versailles Treaty required reparations from Germany for its savage perpetrations and destructions of World War I, which could hardly be considered as innocent conduct. The infantile ego expected no consequences for its ravagings and was indignant when any responsibility or accountability was required. Therefore, as paranoids do, it sought revenge for imaginary injustices. To the infantile, any responsibility or reparation for consequences is considered an outrage.

Thus, the extremes of political positionalities, whether they are far left or far right, calibrate extremely low and represent the egocentricity of lower mind, which, as we have noted from previous levels of calibration, have a potentially extensive audience. Cultural conflict can therefore be contextualized as primarily between the representations of lower mind versus higher mind, which have quite different paradigms of social reality and expectations. As a consequence, the far left sees tradition, ethics, morality, and intellectual integrity as fascist, and the far right sees the far left as treasonous. Perception is therefore a product of brain physiology, the presence or absence of an "etheric" brain, maturity, the calibrated level of consciousness, and spiritual evolution, all of which are collectively in accord with the overall evolution of the consciousness of mankind itself.

The Reality of Freedom and Happiness

Just as all that is destructive has a common source, so do freedom, success, health, and peace have a common source, which is that of spiritual truth and integrity.

Everyone is potentially free to be free. It is merely a matter of choice to follow the pathway to truth to the degree that one can discover it as identifiable, knowable, and confirmable. Instead of envying or hating success, the truly successful imitate it, copy it, identify with it, and develop the patterns. To take responsibility for one's own actions and their consequences is, in itself, extremely powerful and almost instantly raises one's calibrated level of consciousness to over 200.

An extremely valuable insight that is learned by all spiritually evolved persons in the course of their development is seeing one's own personal consciousness as the decisive influence that determines all that occurs in one's life.

Another operative principle, whose recognition results in greater respect for positionalities, is that the mind either consciously or unconsciously tends to manifest that which is held in mind. It is very helpful to see that, in reality, chocolate is not the enemy or the opposite of vanilla but represents only a contrasting option. It is also well to recognize that the infantile ego that secretly hides within is extremely needy, constantly hoping for praise and input, and is obsessed with being "right," as well as nursing "wrongs," "grievances," injustices, and grudges. It takes little reflection to see that the ego gets much energy and benefit from negative positionalities, and that spiritual evolution is accelerated greatly by the willingness to forego these dubious payoffs in return for real gains.

Pathway to Freedom and Happiness

The steps out of failure, unhappiness, frustration, lack, want, anger, and depression are deceptively simple. Life is a voyage comparable to being out at sea in which a shift of one degree on the ship's compass will determine by the end of the trip whether or not one is hundreds of miles off course. The strongest tool, which already exists within, is the spiritual will itself, which, when firmly set, will face and take on any obstacle. It is this spiritual will that determines the success of the venture. From subjective experience, as well as many years of clinical practice, spiritual education, and research, it is confirmed that the spiritual will is the primordial rudder that determines not only this lifetime but also the course of one's consciousness over great expanses of time, classically termed karma (cal. 1,000).

By one simple decision, the impossible becomes possible because the lead sinkers that were attached to the cork have been released and now the cork effortlessly rises because of the density and power of the field. Thus, one can let go of the egoistic illusion that spiritual progress is difficult and that one has to do it all alone. On the contrary, illusions of lack disappear and powerful energies now help to sustain one's progress, which is now accompanied by the pleasure of increased self-esteem, and the world magically begins to appear to be a friendly and helpful place. The brain's neurochemistry changes in a positive direction, and like a butterfly out of a cocoon, the etheric brain springs forth as a consequence of the onset of the flow of spiritual (i.e., kundalini) energy, and the experience of life and the self in the world begins to transform.

It will be discovered that the ego consists of interlocking building blocks and that to move even one unsettles the whole pile, which then begins to fall of its own gravity. Even a seemingly small effort can have very major effects, and one discovers that just a simple smile can totally change one's life. The many thousands of people who follow self-improvement and spiritual pathways confirm the reality of this discovery.

Following is a list of "winner" attitudes, all of which are quite simple to choose and have extremely long-term benefits. Life lived in the energy field of a calibration level over 200 is quite different from life lived from the consciousness calibration level of 180.

Spiritual Foundation – The Basics – Part I

Available	265	Firm	245
Balanced	305	Flexible	245
Benign	225	Friendly	280
Calm	250	Genuine	255
Considerate	295	Glad	335
Content	255	Happy	395
Cordial	255	Hard Work	200
Decent	295	Healthy	360
Dependable	250	Helpful	220
Diligent	210	Honest	200
Diplomatic	240	Honorable	255
Easy Going	210	Humane	260
Equitable	365	Humility	270
Ethical	305	Idealistic	295
Fair	305	Kind	220
Faithful	365		

The table above reveals qualities that are valued and supported by all successful societies throughout time that calibrate over 200. The road to spiritual awareness is supported by the fact that higher motivations are reinforced by energies that reflect power, whereas egoistic positions are weak, limiting, and exhausting. Just as negative qualities are intertwined with each other, positive qualities are as well, so that progress in one area brings surprising improvements in other areas that were not even consciously addressed. Whereas negative qualities are polarities and therefore trigger their opposites, above level 200, one is dealing with realities that have no opposites. Thus, "unfriendly" is not the opposite of "friendly" but merely the absence of friendliness.

Progression through the positive levels becomes habitual, easy, and a lifestyle in and of itself. It is discovered that each level of consciousness represents a powerful field; therefore, what one chooses to align with invisibly influences the quality of one's life. Experientially, one discovers why "the rich get richer while the poor get poorer," why "nothing breeds success like success," why "like goes to like," why "birds of a feather flock together," or why "sleeping with dogs brings fleas." Finally, one realizes that "stick with the winners" means to receive benefit from the overall field and to pick it up by osmosis. One then realizes that "beauty is as beauty does."

From consciousness research, one can quickly confirm that the adoption of an attitude immediately invites in that entire field of consciousness, which then unwittingly begins to dominate the personality and thoughts. What are considered to be "my thoughts" are merely thoughts common to that particular energy field and are not really personal at all. It is well to avoid rather than oppose negativity and resist the temptation and illusion that one can play with it and not get burned. The nonintegrous fields of consciousness contain seductive programs that are extremely cunning. They have been crafted and refined over the centuries and are thereby cloaked and disguised in seductive presentations. Jesus Christ said do not oppose that which is negative but merely avoid it. Research as well as extensive clinical experience demonstrate that one cannot really just "play" with the fire of nonintegrity; therefore, the spiritually aware learn to discern that which is a lure. Those who exploit and make great profits and gains have learned how to take advantage of the gullibility of naïveté and how to refine the glamorization of the lure, making it extremely seductive, as is currently represented by the downside of the entertainment media.

Spiritual Foundation – The Basics – Part II

Loyal	345	Rational	405
Maturity	280	Reliable	290
Modest	245	Respectable	250
Moral	200	Respectful	305
Nice	255	Responsible	290
Normal	300	"Salt of the Earth"	240
Open	240	Sane	300
Orderly	300	Sense of Humor	345
Patient	255	Sensible	240
Persistent	210	Stable	255
Pleasant	220	Supportive	245
Pleasing	275	Thoughtful	225
Polite	245	Tolerant	245
Positive	225	Warm	205
Protective	265	Wisdom	385

While the frantic person flails in the water and drowns, the more evolved person learns how to float. The ultimately buoyant sea that supports spiritual progress is the overall, powerful field of consciousness. It is the power of this field that precludes the possibility of even death itself. Man has intuited and known this since the very beginning of civilization and has been aware that life cannot be extinguished but can only change form. (That statement calibrates at 1,000.)

Choices determine consequences, which is a mechanism that is really impersonal and operates automatically because energy fields are invited in as a consequence of choice. The individual, as a consequence of choices, is like an iron filing whose position in the field is the direct consequence of its own decisions. To accept this reality is simultaneously uplifting and freeing. At the same time, it is frightening and brings about some degree of consternation. Therefore, the only true freedom in the universe is the freedom of choice, which is the gift received by mankind. One then realizes that there is no hand on the tiller but one's own and that "I myself am heaven and hell" (cal. 700+). The acceptance of this overall truth brings the strength of resolve instead of futile wishing.

What really frightens people about spiritual reality is that it confronts one with the reality that their destiny is solely within the power of their own hands. Heaven, like hell, is the result and consequence of one's own choices; therefore, the key to freedom is by the grace of the given karmic inheritance of all mankind by Divine ordinance.

Philosophers and Philosophies

Altruism	435	Greenspan Economics	400
Aristotle	498	Heritage Foundation	265
Authority	400	Hobbes, Thomas	475
Avatars, the Great		Hoffer, Eric	505
Teachers	1,000	Humanism	365
Ayers, A. J.	475	Husserl, Edmund	499
Bacon, Roger	460	Idealism	200
Behaviorism	400	Imperialism	200
Boy/Girl Scouts of America		Intellectualism	395
(Laws)	455	Kierkegaard, Sören	410
Boy/Girl Scouts of America		Laissez-faire	305
(Oath)	450	Logical Positivism	380
Burke, Edmund	410	Mach, Ernst	490
Capitalism (Philosophy)	340	Malthus, Thomas	204
Carnap, Rudolf	485	Morality	405
Chivalry	465	Naropa Institute	405
Christian Fundamentalist	205	Neoconservatism	395
Collectivism	200	"New Deal"	
Comte, Auguste	485	(Pres. Roosevelt)	340
Conservatism	405	NRA Political Position	205
Dewey, John	455	Objectivism	400
Eagle Scout	460	Ockham, William of	535
Emerson, Ralph Waldo	485	Optimism	295
Empiricism	475	Orwell, George: 1984	410
Epicureanism	305	Phenomenalism	420
Ethics	415	Pierce, Charles	465
Existentialism	375	Plato	485
Faith-based Initiative	480	Plotinus	503
Friedman, Milton,		Pragmatism	200
Economics	400	Rand, Ayn	400
Gnosis	503	Rationalism	470
"Great Society"		Russell, Bertrand	465
(Pres. L. Johnson)	280	Saints	550

Sartre, Jean-Paul	200	Survival of the Fittest	220
Schlick, Moritz	480	Theology	460
Scholasticism	460	"Traditional" American	
Scotus, Duns	490	Philosophy	440
Social Darwinism	215	Transcendentalism	445
Socrates	540	Solipsism	300
Solipsism	410	Traditional Liberal	355
Spencer, Herbert	410	Utilitarian	240
Spiritual Sages	700		

Intellectual Disciplines

Algebra	405	Mathematics	450
Arithmetic	395	Metaphysics	460
Epistemology	475	Ontology	465
Geometry	400	Science	450-460
Geometry (solid)	405	Theology	460
Great Books of the Western World (excluding Marx)	465	Trigonometry	410

Inasmuch as the mind cannot innately discern truth from falsehood, its only defense is reliance on reason and the intellect. Thus, education is of benefit on many levels. To the unevolved ego, however, the capacity to think is subverted from reason to rationalization in order to justify emotionalized positions. The distortions of truth then tend to fall into stratified levels concordant with concomitant levels of consciousness in society.

Above consciousness level 200, truth is valued for its own sake, and, therefore, education and erudition are respected. To the self-centered ego, however, the requirements of truth are resented because they would threaten personal belief systems. Thus, morality, ethics, and responsibility are seen as oppressive and are rejected. In so doing, rationalizations by lower mind replace the dialectic and requirements of honesty so that even blatant, gross falsehoods are put forth as truth or "facts," even though they have no basis in reality. (Historically, "bearing false witness" [cal. 140] is anathema, even in primitive societies.)

In the current "cultural war," politicized sociology, sophistry, and rhetoric have now significantly replaced reason and verifiable truth. Even history, language, mathematics, and science, as well as the ethics of responsibility or accountability, have been attacked and repudiated. While these relativistic positionalities could be excused or overlooked as adolescent, naïve, and regressive, another element of this decline emerges that reveals the motivation behind the regression, that of "justified hatred."

While distortions of truth characteristic of consciousness levels 130-195 may sound attractive to the uneducated, they are the sheep's clothing for anger, envy, and malice, and justification for paranoid distortion. The hate is thinly rationalized and publicly explosive. The irate orator with reddened face and distended neck veins shakes with emotion and wild gesticulation, with much finger-pointing indignation. The same inflation is seen in displays of animal behavior.

Sophistry and rhetoric were carefully analyzed and refuted by Plato, Aristotle, and Socrates around 350 B.C., when agreement and discussion were finalized. They have, therefore, been considered a closed matter for over two thousand years by more evolved integrous thinkers. Yet, in each generation a large percentage of the population calibrates below 200, and so self-interest dogma pops up again in new clothes and replaces truth at whatever cost. Thus, to subvert truth for gain has persisted strongly, and is, in fact, the primary underpinning of war and genocide. The "virus" of catchy phrases crosses over generations, as explained by the study of mimetics (browse "mimetics" on the Web).

As previously cited, in recent times the distortions of Marx have again cost the lives of millions of people and resulted in chaotic civil disasters that afford every opportunity for the waiting right-wing fascists to vulturize the consequent social debris and chaos. The infectious meme (central idea) is that of *blame*—the weak person's substitute for integrity. Blame calibrates at 180, and, like a cancer, it weakens and operationally actually denigrates the blamer and lowers the blamer's level of consciousness so that the pseudo-victim then becomes the literal, actual, real victim.

Aristotle, however, did see a value in rhetoric in that truth has to be presented properly in order for it to be accepted. In fact, he described in political/social/ philosophical terms one of the basic tenets of consciousness research—that truth is a consequence not only of content but also of context. Thus, he described the ethical use of rhetoric as a means of effectively presenting truth, i.e., inclusion of not only dialectically correct logic ("Logos") but also the integrity of the speaker ("Ethos"), and the quality of the audience ("Pathos"). While problematic philosophies and positionalities appear to emotionalize and utilize (via lower mind) the illogical cant of "pleading the case," the discipline and laws of the dialectic of science and reason are strict, demanding, and inflexible. Verifiable truth is independent of how one might "feel" about it, which is irrelevant, personal, and basically narcissistic and biased.

Calibration level 460 indicates erudition, 470 indicates true rationality, and level 499 indicates brilliance or likelihood of genius. One can see that the calibration level of rhetoric is not even up to the level of simple arithmetic. One wonders how it could be taken seriously or adopted as public policy to be used as the basis for court decisions, i.e., does the word "speech" mean "talking" and "writing," or does it mean "any and all behaviors" under any circumstances? Is the Ku Klux Klan's burning of a cross "speech"? Is public fornication "free speech"? Therefore, permissible parameters include not just content but motive, intention, and responsibility for social impact (e.g., to incite a riot).

In ancient Greece, career politicians learned the fruits of the trade of oratory from professionals who charged a fee and taught "rhetoric," or how to shade the truth and present their case in order to win elections. This was a learned skill that, in excess, is called bombast, "putting on the spin," or "just hot air." It is meant to impress the gullible, the less educated, or the educated who have a personal agenda. This violation of truth outraged Plato, Socrates, and Aristotle, who totally demolished the credibility of the protagonists. However, they did come away from the dialog with two important conclusions: (1) intelligence as philosophy depends on fulfilling the demanding requirements of the dialectic (structure) of argument, and, (2) it is important that integrous truth be presented properly to an audience in order to facilitate its comprehension and acceptance. This is in accord with consciousness research in that verifiable truth is a product of both content and context.

Leaders often fail to supply a missing piece of information that would completely recontextualize the impact of their presentation. The downside of intellectually integrous people is that they think that truth itself should be convincing to others, which ignores the fact that just the opposite occurs—the nonintegrous hate and reject truth or label it as falsehood because it is seen as a rejection of their own motives. When truth is properly contextualized, it is empowered by credibility, and then falsehood need not even be countered because it falls of its own accord.

While truth itself stands on its own merit, oddly enough, it often has to be "sold" by making it appealing or palatable. Populations with lower consciousness levels are only interested in gain. That "the truth will set you free" is a warmly accepted concept by the integrous, but to the nonintegrous, truth is a danger and an enemy that threatens their whole position.

If falsehood has legal "equal rights" with truth and, in addition, has academic approval, plus propagation by the media, then Goebbels, Hitler, Eichman, fascism, and the Holocaust were legitimate, as were Stalin, Pol Pot, and Buchenwald. It can be seen that the problem is not falsity itself but its (Luciferic) designation as truth.

The perversion of truth and integrity in our current society is already so rampant that it only recognizes the desecration of truth when it becomes bizarrely extreme, such as stating that the victims of 9/11 were really Nazi "Eichmans" who deserved to die (cal. 90). The statement was later defended by sympathizers whose own capacity for rationality was seriously impaired by fallacious reasoning by stating that "the victims deserved to die because of the Iraqi war." (Fox News, 2/04/05). The Iraqi war, factually, of course, was subsequent to the 9/11 bombing and was a consequence, not an antecedent. Thus, relativism substituted fallacy for truth to the accompaniment of "hurrahs" from the supporters who themselves were pathetic victims of academic brainwashing.

By application of the same principles that falsity is both legal and justified, then so are sedition, treason, and the treachery of espionage agents (just exercising their "rights" to free speech). The same dictum then supports the "rights" of hate and the forces of destruction because "speech" is now legally defined so as to include action. The paradox is that if anarchy is "legal," then there would no legal rights of law by which to enforce it. Law is based on truth and, therefore, without the requirement of truth, there is no law by which to protest the "rights" of the lawless.

Conclusion

Freedom is an independent inner state, whereas liberty is a consequence of collective social judgments and subject to restriction in order to serve the common good. It is a serious error to confuse the two as all actions and choices have consequences.

We eventually have to accept responsibility for our choices, decisions, and their consequences. Every act, thought, and choice adds to a permanent mosaic; our decisions ripple through the universe of consciousness to affect the lives of all. Every act or decision made that supports life supports all life, including one's own. The ripples we create return to us. What previously may have seemed to be a metaphysical statement is now established as a scientific fact.

Everything in the universe constantly gives off an identifiable energy pattern of a specific frequency that remains for all time and can be read by those who know how. Every word, deed, and intention creates a permanent record; every thought is known and recorded forever. There are no secrets, nothing is hidden, nor can it be. Everyone lives in the public domain. Our spirits stand naked in time for all to see. Everyone's life, finally, is accountable to the universe (calibrates as "true" at level 1,000).

CHAPTER 14
Countries and Politics

The evolution of consciousness, as expressed in intellectual development, proceeded over thousands of years and multiple civilizations, punctuated by periods of severe conflict, catastrophic monarchies, civil wars, and bloodshed. Out of this long, painful experience, the best intellectual insights, which were distilled as a consequence, calibrated in the mid-400s. In the establishment of America, they were combined with the genius of spiritual rather than religious inspiration and resulted in the world's foremost dominant and successful country and culture.

Theocracies and monarchies had been tried but had fallen and served as bad examples to be avoided. After the Reformation, the countries of Europe recreated themselves in a secular rationalist model but with integrous intention. Therefore, many of them calibrated in the mid- to high 300s and became democracies based on fairness and rationality.

All in all, the Western civilized world was therefore a fertile field that welcomed the discoveries of science, and their application to human problems was astoundingly successful. Science plus its ensuing technology conquered major diseases, doubled the life span, and exalted education as the keystone to progress. The most impressive of these spectacular successes emerged, however, primarily during just the last one hundred years, which, in evolutionary time, is barely the blink of an eye. From these enormous gains in such a short time, it could be reasonably expected that the future must indeed hold even greater promise for humanity, that is, with the exception of its Achilles' heel—international relations.

From an encyclopedic worldview, this critical area of failure glaringly stands out as the most serious and prominent problem remaining to be solved before any reliable condition of world peace can be achieved, much less guaranteed. Like a tectonic fault line or a dormant volcano, this gross defect lurks below the visible horizon like a hidden time bomb. The enemies of peace rattle their sabers and make solemn pledges to destroy the leading edge of the advance of civilization and especially its standard bearer, America. Its weapons are a combination of pseudoreligious propaganda, invective brainwashing techniques, and a paranoid perception of the Western world, purposely distorted so as to justify its aggressive actions and rhetoric. Jihad is a religious declaration of war that has resulted in a change of the whole style of the daily life of Western society, whose weaknesses are its denial, its traditional ineptitude, and its lack of a reliable science of diplomatic relations and function.

For lack of reliable data, international diplomacy is often astoundingly not only inept but actually obstructive to its ostensible goals. (The current United Nations calibrates at 185-195.) This is inevitable because, without verifiable data or a scientifically based body of knowledge, diplomacy has been like primitive exploration without a map, a compass, or a GPS (global positioning system).

Without reliable information, a whole gamut of stopgap measures ensues, accompanied by emotionalism, the pressure of public outcry, and political expediency. Surreptitious deal making and endless rhetoric, fruitless intellectualizations, and "one size fits all" political positions reinforce these. These appear to be unreliable techniques upon which to base the safety and security of entire countries and their societies.

From even a brief survey, it is obvious that the most pressing need of the world today is a reliable science upon which to base international diplomacy. To this end, an historical review provides orientation and information from which to construct a reality-based science of international relations and diplomacy.

Political Systems

Oligarchy	415	Feudal	145-200
Democracy/Republic	410	Tribal	200
Iroquois Nation	399	Theocracy	175
Coalition	345	Communism	160
Socialism	305	Dictatorship	135
Monarchy	200	Fascism	125

Surveying the above figures is quite interesting, and we notice how closely the political structure of the Iroquois Nation is to current democracy. In fact, many of its factors were actually incorporated into the U. S. Constitution. We also see that Monarchy at 200 depends in its application upon the calibrated level of the particular monarch in charge, but it is not intrinsically out of integrity. Tribal governments can also be quite integrous, depending on who is in charge. It also reveals why either the Far-Left or the Far-Right political ideologies tend to fall to low levels of integrity. The calibration of theocracy indicates why it was carefully rejected and defended against out of historical experience by the founding fathers of the United States.

Dictatorships, for good reason, have a bad name everywhere, from Haiti to Castro, Hitler, Mussolini, Saddam Hussein, and other current, ongoing dictatorships in the world. Therefore, the preponderance of dictators sooner or later demonstrates the characteristics of grandiose, malignant, messianic narcissism, with oppression and savagery towards their own people. The philosophic basis of democracy had a long evolution in the intellectual world, and in its development, it utilized the thinking of the best minds available throughout the centuries.

Historical Societies

Plains Indian (America)	210	Bushmen	110
Ancient Greece	255	Cannibals	95
Ancient Rome	202	Headhunters	95
Ancient Egypt	205	Incas	65
Atlantis	290	Aztecs	65

Neanderthal Man	75	Predecessors of modern
Cro-Magnon Man	80	man 60,000 years ago,
Anasazi	85	Homo sapiens idelta 70-80
Homo erectus (Java Man)	70	

Political History
Major Figures

Akhenaten	220	Magna Carta	460
Alexander the Great	290	Mary, Queen of Scots	340
Attila the Hun	90	Mongol Hordes	70
Barbarian Hordes	35-85	Montezuma	45
Bonaparte, Napoleon	450↓175	Nefertiti	205
Caesar, Julius	140	Nero	70
Caligula	30	Peter, the Great	385↓190
Charlemagne	230	Pope Gregory	475
Columbus, Christopher	320	Pope Leo	475
Conquistadors	40	Queen Victoria	230
Constantine (Emperor)	410↓385	Ramses I	205
Cortez, Hernando	85	Ramses II	210
Cromwell, Oliver	208	Rasputin	120
Disraeli, Benjamin	405	Robespierre, Maximilien	405
Frederick the Great	325	Russian Czars	55-385
Henry VIII	170	Tutankhamun	200
Ivan, the Terrible	55	Vikings, Huns, Goths	55-85
Justinian (Emperor)	435	Wallace, William	490
Khan, Genghis	140	Wellington, Duke of	420
Machiavelli	225		

Recent

Arafat, Yasser	440↓65	King Faisal (Saudi Arabia)	480
Ataturk, Mustafa Kemal	250	Lenin, Vladimir	405↓80
Churchill, Winston	510	London Blitz	40
Franco, Francisco	190	Mao, Chairman	185
Gestapo	35	Marx, Karl	130
Goebbels, Joseph	70	Mengela, Dr. Joseph	25
Gorbachev, Mikhail	500	Montgomery, Gen. Bernard	450
Goring, Herman	350↓150	Nazism	50
Himmler, Heinrich	35	Noriega, Manuel	60
Hitler, Adolf	430↓40	Duvalier, Papa Doc	25
IRA	100	Pol Pot	35
KGB	55	Stalin, Joseph	70
Khomeini, Ayatollah	75	Trotsky, Leon	205

Current

Abbas, Mahmoud	230	Khutami, Muhammad	200
al-Qaeda	65	Kim Chong II (N. Korea)	160
al-Zarqawi, Abu Musab	60	Milosevic, Slobodan	130
bin Laden, Osama	40	Musharraf, Gen. Pervez	425
Castro, Fidel	445↓180	Pinochet, Gen. Augusto	155
"Chemical Ali"	160	PLO	55
China prior to reforms	150	Putin, Vladimir	190
China after reforms	195	Sharon, Ariel	205
European Union	205	Sistani, Grand Ayatollah Ali	125
HAMAS	105	Taliban	65
Hezbollah	85	UNESCO	355
Hussein, Saddam	65	United Nations	195
Kadafi, Omar	160↑190	United Nations Security	
Karzai, Hamid (Afghanistan)	415	Council	180

Note: Two numbers with an arrow ("↓" or "↑") between them indicate early-career and then later-career calibrations. Many leaders fall in integrity due to corruption by earthly power (e.g., Arafat 440↓65.) Arafat's replacement by Abbas (cal. 230), together with Sharon at 205, renews hope for peace in that long-standing, violent conflict.

The above figures speak for themselves. One curiosity is that both Napoleon and Hitler calibrated in the mid-400s early in their careers and later apparently succumbed to megalomania because both showed a severe drop in calibration and their lives ended in disaster. They apparently started out with constructive ideas and left a legacy of benefits to their societies, but then they succumbed to the downside of secular power. Because kinesiological research is beyond time and space, we can identify almost the exact moments when these changes occurred. With Napoleon, it was at the time that he made the decision to crown himself as emperor, thus usurping the prior authority of the Church in which only popes had the power to crown an emperor.

With Adolf Hitler, it was at the time that he simultaneously became the sole leader of all branches of government as well as the army. Whereas, in history, monarchs were still answerable to the highest religious authority of the day (e.g., the Pope, the head of the Eastern Orthodox Church, or their equivalent), but each of these dictators was answerable to no one. Nero even proclaimed himself to be God. In each case, the ego was proclaiming itself to be God and thus revealed its secret ambition, which is repressed and disguised as part of the inner core of the ego.

Countries and Regions of the World (Current)

400s		300s		200s		High 100s	
Australia	410	Bolivia	300	Argentina	285	Jordan	185
Canada	415	Brazil	300	Iceland	255	Kuwait	190
Germany	400	Central America	355	Indonesia	215	Middle East	170
Hawaii	405	China:		Manchuria	200	North Korea	175
Hong Kong	400	People's Rep.	300	Nepal	205	Palestine	185
Netherlands	405	President	320	New Guinea	202	Saudi Arabia	175
Singapore	405	Govt.	150↑190	Puerto Rico	250	Sicily	175
South Korea	400	Egypt	350	Russia	200	South Africa	190
Switzerland	400	Europe	355	Taiwan	295	Syria	155
United States	421	France	305	Tibet	200	Turkmeni-	
		Greece	300	Turkey	245	stan	150
		India	355			Yemen	160
		Italy	380	**High 100s**		**Low 100s**	
		Japan	355	Balkans	185	Iraq	120
		Mexico	300	Bosnia	180	Lebanon	130
		Scandinavia	350	Burma	155	Pakistan	140
				Cuba	180	Ukraine	140
				Iran	190	Vietnam	140
				Israel	190		

Below 100

Haiti	55	Congo	70
Algeria	90	Angola	50
Libya	90	Rwanda	70
Sudan	70	Uganda	40
Nigeria	55	Oman	90

In the 2005 edition of *Freedom House*, a U. S. study group, of the 192 countries in the world, forty-six percent are classified as "free," twenty-six percent as "not free," and the balance as "partly free." Under Putin, Russia moved down to the "not free" category. In 2004, twenty-six countries showed gains and eleven showed declines. The eight most repressed were listed as Burma, Cuba, Libya, North Korea, Saudi Arabia, Sudan, Syria, and Turkmenistan. In the Middle East, only Israel was rated as "free," and twelve countries were rated as "not free" (Ingram, 2004).

From the presentation of even the crude raw data, rather profound implications are already apparent that, in practical use, require further refinement and application to the specifics of a situation, such as the disparity between populace, government, and officials, as well as its various departments and representatives. A country or society that calibrates in the 400s is already ruled by and operating under the principles of rationality, with their implied ethics, morality, accountability, and a sense of responsibility by the regime for the welfare of the populace. Such a country is also ruled by law and the principles of its founding constitution and governmental structure. Thus, such countries can be successfully approached through logic with their implied ethics and morality.

This overall approach, however, may be inappropriate and doomed to failure when applied to a country that calibrates below 200 and is thus operating under completely different principles, such as self-interest and gain, personal power, lack of obligation to the populace, and lack of ethics, morality, or even legality. Such countries operate primarily out of pride, arrogance, competition, vengeance, media image, and most seriously, the megalomania of its leaders, which expresses as paranoia, secrecy, and deception. Leaders have no compunctions at all about making completely fallacious statements to the point of absurdity. Dictatorial leaders tend toward pomposity and grandiosity, and some are actually psychotic (narcissistic, messianic egotism calibrates at 35-60), with delusions of grandeur. They seek to be actually worshipped and seen as saviors; thus, the ubiquitous display of their pictures and status. All must bow to the "Great Leader," a telltale sign. An integrous leader is satisfied by simple respect.

An understanding of the elements and psychodynamics of megalomania is important. They do not differ in essence from that of recidivist criminality (the psychopathic personality of the chronic sociopath), which entails the incapacity to feel remorse, regret, or responsibility for others or to learn from experience. The other consequence of megalomania is the failure to pay attention to warnings and foresee consequences (and thus end up having to be dug out of a "spider hole").

Historically, many messianic megalomaniacs end up in suicide rather than accepting personal responsibility. Because this degree of pathology is so far outside the reality of the average person, if it is not taken into account, there can be grave consequences to society. People who deal with such criminal personalities are not at all surprised by their flat denial of the execution of a crime that is actually documented on videotape.

Countries that calibrate below 200 are dominated by the principle of self-interest; therefore, political pretenses such as "seeking peace" are utilized as propaganda and manipulative slogans. Peace would result in the defeat of a ruling party, the loss of profits from the munitions industry, and the loss of support of the population and the power base. Such societies thrive on and are built on the foundation of war and conflict. They are adept at game playing, media manipulation, deception, and spurious diplomatic moves and pronouncements. They are also skilled at manipulating crowd hysteria and surreptitiously creating inflammatory incidents to keep the pot boiling, such as enraging the enemy by extreme maneuvers exemplified by blowing up busloads of innocent children. Each side then plays the deceptive game of an "innocent victim" versus an "evil perpetrator" in what is basically a blood sport that is totally foreign to a culture dominated by reason and the value of human life. The extremes are then "justified" by right-wing religious fundamentalism, which is addicted to the "high" of the glamour of war and the drama of the macabre and grotesque, such as slowly beheading helpless civilians with a saw on worldwide television.

The Dangerous Naïveté of America

America is repeatedly blindsided by its infatuation with the "holy grail" of democracy and waving the flag of freedom. It repeatedly fails to grasp the underpinnings of its grave blindness and instead projects blame on militant aggressors who eventually attack the vulnerable, tempting target.

Foreign cultures do not play by the Marquis of Queensbury rules, and "fairness," "honesty," and all such values are deemed childish and ridiculous. The idea of "peace" has no value at all to countries that calibrate below 200, nor are honesty, kindness, and quality even perceived as virtuous. America is envied, hated, and frankly seen as "stupid." A country that "hat in hand" begs the blatantly anti-U. S. United Nations for "help" or "approval" is seen at best as ignominious. Whereas, in America, weakness calls forth compassion, in the major countries of the world that are overtly and strongly very, very macho, weakness brings forth *disdain*, not mercy. The same applies to America's routine pathological disregard for intelligence operations necessary for survival. (Being blindsided and caught off guard calibrate at 180.)

This pattern preceded the attack on Pearl Harbor, the Bay of Pigs, the Korean War ("surprised" by a half million Chinese Communist troops!), the assassination of John F. Kennedy (open car), the 9/11 bombing, militant Islamic terrorism, uncontrolled borders and immigration (witness the consequences in Europe), trust in the United Nations, etc. This repetitive "Groundhog Day" type of pattern represents failure of responsibility as well as acumen, the inroads of relativistic political ideology, and the government's stewardship of citizen survival. The same idealistic naïveté supported Communist sympathizers as well as the American Nazi party of the 1930s and 1940s. (It is fatal to trust positions that calibrate below 200.)

The United States strains in trying to maintain a saintly media image; in fact, image has become more important than winning a battle. Naively, America thinks that if it has a saintly image, the world will love the United States. Nothing could be farther from the truth. The result has actually been an international loss of face. The world is currently being bullied by very tough challengers who are calling the shots. The call to "wake up and get real" is getting louder on a daily basis, and the price of denial is escalating.

A vignette from the author's childhood may be illustrative:

At age twelve or so, as a bespectacled, ectomorphic youth busy with reading Plato, the mesomorphic peers were into wrestling, football, and various sports and masculinities. By strict Christian upbringing, non-combativeness and "turning the other cheek" were inculcated mandatory values. Being bullied was tolerated, but noncombativeness did not solve the problem but seemed to make it worse. The consequence was bloody noses and getting beat up and ambushed on the way home from school, despite hopefully preventive, evasive maneuvers.

Finally, grandfather declared, "Enough is enough," and arranged for boxing lessons at a professional gym that thereby had to initiate a "mosquito weight" class. Learning the manful "art of self-defense" resulted in a diminution of being "picked on" by fellow choirboys, which resulted in greater self-confidence and a feeling of safety. Then one day, alone in a rougher neighborhood, a "looking for a fight" type of bully approached menacingly. He was no boxing-class trainee but instead a "dirty street fighter" who played by entirely different "win at any cost" rules. His "below the belt" kick to the groin brought home the lesson—never depend on "Marquis of Queensbury" rules when you are ensnared by a seasoned, tough street fighter or you'll end up on the pavement being jeered at by the street-smart crowd to whom gentility is a sign of weakness and an easy mark that brings contempt for what is perceived as effete.

Every member of street culture knows the above lessons, and that is why allowing oneself to be "dissed" in the "'hood" can be and often is fatal. Appeasement is viewed as cowardice, and vulnerability is viewed as invitational.

In contrast, calibrations above 200 indicate the emergence of sincerity, integrity, the capacity for honesty, and concern for the welfare of the population. They are comparably much more integrous than those below 200.

Countries that calibrate in the 300s have reached a real basis of successful survival, have mastered performance techniques, and have discovered enthusiasm, ambition, group solidarity, and the value of equitable rewards. Societies in the 300s can then be approached with appeal to rationality and the presentation of opportunities for their further development, such as support of their education, commerce, technology, science, and health needs. In the 300s, there is appreciation for the value of support itself.

To governments below 200, true democracy is obviously a threat to which they may give lip service if, in so doing, it subserves some goal, such as profit or gain of political power. Thus, pseudodemocracies appear but their performance belies their name and they continue to operate intrinsically on the same nonintegrous principles as before, but now, nonintegrous operations are disguised within the operations of the political structure itself, e.g., the government is formally a democracy but operationally, it is corrupt. Upon inspection, it would seem that America's over idealization of democracy as the purported "one size fits all" magical resolution of the inadequate infrastructure of countries is not realistic, and America's aggressive proselytization is often seen to result in resentment rather than in appreciation. As a review article states, "America seems to lack a basic conception of how its collective attitude, culture, and general ignorance of the world affect other nations." (*Philadelphia Trumpet*, 2/04)

Countries in the low 100s or below are faced with the realities of basic survival and can therefore only be realistically approached with the realization of where they are in a survival crisis. In barren lands, it is far more important to own a gun, a cow, a water pump, or a vehicle. Literacy is absent and governments are run by cronyism, payoffs, tribal warfare, and contentious fiefdoms that are still tribal and pre-feudal. In these societies, it is accepted that the strong ravage and abuse the weak. Rule is by gun power and treachery, which are accepted as the norm.

As an example, Afghanistan is the home of the poppy and thus is the primary source of the world's heroin, out of which comes money, guns, and political power. At the end of the Afghanistan conflict, the poppy fields were left standing. When one considers America's ostensible "war against drugs," this compromise curiously produced almost no public discussion although it is capable of explanation if one looks at the elements involved in the process of triage. Without an endemic source of money (from the poppy fields), the United States would have been faced with the cost of feeding the entire starving population, accompanied by attack from adverse propaganda. This had to be weighed against the cost, however, to societies of heroin addiction, which also runs into billions of dollars. Allowing poppy fields to stand (after paying al-Qaeda $40 million to destroy them) also brought cooperation from tribal chieftains.

Consciousness research data and techniques have actually been validated by specific application to a previous critical world conflict in which failure would have had grave consequences. In the specific application, all factors were calibrated, including intentions that would prevail under different conditions. By so doing with exactitude, the precise, successful moves that were necessary to prevent ballistic-missile war were revealed. In this application of the principles described, the resolution was swift and successful.

In a world that now includes the possibilities of nuclear war, the margin for error has narrowed and thus demands increasing precision, knowledge, and wisdom. It is unrealistic to expect other cultures to incorporate our values; instead, those cultures need to be approached with an understanding of what their values are.

Developing a Science of Diplomacy and International Relations

The fate of entire nations depends on diplomatic and political expertise. When it is defective or miscalculated, the cost is often devastating and is paid for by the death of millions of people. Even a single major miscalculation can throw and has thrown the whole world into war (e.g., Neville Chamberlain's miscalculation of Adolf Hitler prior to World War II), or Secretary of War Stimson's disdain for intelligence reports about the war plans of Japan prior to Pearl Harbor. Such grave error has been recurrent throughout the history of civilization in which whole empires were under the capricious control of megalomaniacs. In view of the overriding importance of international diplomacy, there is no higher priority for mankind than the development of a fact-based science upon which even the very survival of human life itself now depends in a nuclear age.

After the devastation of World War I, it was hoped that a League of Nations would be a means to resolve international conflict but, like the United Nations that replaced it, such organizations proved to be futile. Both organizations were idealistic in theory but inept in practice. (The League of Nations calibrates at 185; the UN calibrates overall at 190, and the International Criminal Court calibrates at 195.)

Although the United Nations has proven to be a successful humanitarian aid organization, it has primarily produced rhetoric (cal. 185) rather than resolution. (The United Nations' Political Affairs Committee calibrates at 180.) Its overall position is anti-American. (America pays approximately twenty-five percent of U. N. expenses, plus provides the building on the East River, a choice location in Manhattan.) Mankind cannot place its fate in the hands of an organization that calibrates at the ineffective level of 185-190. (Who would want a brain surgeon or pilot at that level of incompetence?) To survive, mankind has to put aside sentimentalism (cal. 190), rhetoric, and its mainstay of sophistry (cal. 195). Every hardheaded businessman knows that the way to most diplomatically handle an unrealistic proposition is to kill it by assigning it to a committee. The United Nations is the ultimate committee.

Map 1 - Distribution of Prevailing
Consciousness Levels-Western Hemisphere

Overall Calibration 355

From even this rudimentary, initial general survey, it is apparent that the Western hemisphere operates primarily from an overall integrous climate. Only Haiti is far below, at calibration level 55. Its recent history has seen the catastrophic rule of the Duvaliers and their notorious, oppressive police force that is famous for grotesque atrocities. The populace is also involved in the practice of voodoo (cal. 50), typified by blood sacrifice rituals. Past attempts at financial aid paradoxically worsened the poverty because of its effect in increasing the birth rate.

Also notable is that, despite rule by Fidel Castro's regime (cal. 185), Cuba's populace is at about calibration level 255. This reflects a quite common disparity between the ruler, the populace, and a government itself. In practice, for diplomatic negotiations, it is important to know the calibration level of each of the three components, i.e., the people, the government, and the ruler or leader. In recent history, Castro hosted the first real world assembly of terrorists and terrorist organizations, out of which has erupted worldwide terrorism. Tyrannical monarchs, Ivan the Terrible, Lenin, Hitler, Stalin, and the others calibrate so low that they rival even the Komodo dragon at level 40 (i.e., Pol Pot at consciousness level 30) or serial killers (levels 30-35).

The overall situation of the Eastern Hemisphere is in stark contrast to that of the Western hemisphere:

Map 2 - Distribution of Levels of Consciousness— Eastern Hemisphere

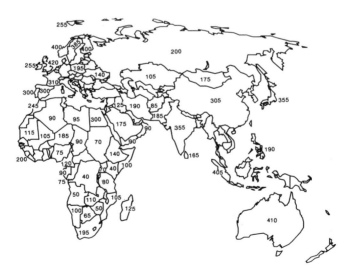

Overall Calibration 190

Here is seen the underlying hotbed of almost certain conflagration. Australia reflects the rationality of Western culture, and Northern Europe, India, and Russia now appear to be quiescent (overall) as does even China. Now it is Africa, especially North Africa, and the Middle East that look most ominous.

Map 3 – Distributions of Levels of Consciousness
Africa and the Middle East

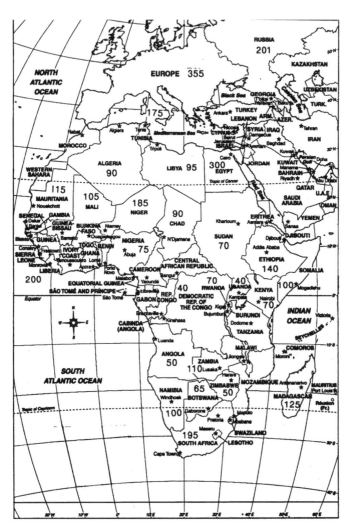

Egypt	300	Oman	90
Iran	190	Palestine	185
Iraq	120	Saudi Arabia	175
Israel	190	Syria	160
Jordan	185	Turkey	245
Kuwait	190	UAE	180
Lebanon	130	Yemen	160

Even a quick survey of Map 3 reveals the basis of current as well as recent world conflict and war. Regions that calibrate below level 100 are characteristically torn by internal problems, starvation, and ravishing by local citizens as well as by pervasive disease, malnourishment, high fertility and infant mortality rates, short life span, and illiteracy. They are so weakened by all the factions that, in and of themselves, they lack the strength or resources to be a threat to world peace.

The situation in North Africa and the Middle East, however, is quite different because at consciousness levels 180-195, the countries now have enough money and resources, plus negative and hostile attitudes, to become real threats. Rival countries that calibrate at those levels constitute an ominous match. Interfering parties need to be forewarned that well-meaning efforts may merely fan the flames of hatred, and that they likely will be perceived as enemies and vilified and attacked for their efforts (like intervening unasked in a marital battle down the street).

Practical Solutions

A very simple diagram affords a quick but decisive reading of the essence of diplomatic impasses and struggles:

Basic Diagnostic Chart of Relationships

		"Them"		"Us"
God-view	Self-view	Level	Log	Log
Loving	Benign	Love	500	500
Wise	Meaningful	Reason	400	400
Merciful	Harmonious	Acceptance	350	350
Inspiring	Hopeful	Willingness	310	310
Enabling	Satisfactory	Neutrality	250	250
Permitting	Feasible	Courage	200	200
Indifferent	Demanding	Pride	175	175
Vengeful	Antagonistic	Anger	150	150
Denying	Disappointing	Desire	125	125
Punitive	Frightening	Fear	100	100
Uncaring	Tragic	Grief	75	75
Condemning	Hopeless	Apathy, hatred	50	50
Vindictive	Evil	Guilt	30	30
Despising	Hateful	Shame	20	20

Diagnostic Chart of International Relationships

	Other Countries			America
God-view	Self-view	Level	Log	Log
Log				
Loving	Benign	Love	500	421
				Canada 415
				So. America 300-360 421
Wise	Meaningful	Reason	400	400
Merciful	Harmonious	Acceptance	350	China 300 350
Inspiring	Hopeful	Willingness	310	310
Enabling	Satisfactory	Neutrality	250	U.N. 185-190 250
Permitting	Feasible	Courage	200	Middle East 180 200
Indifferent	Demanding	Pride	175	175
Vengeful	Antagonistic	Anger	150	150
Denying	Disappointing	Desire	125	125
Punitive	Frightening	Fear	100	Central Africa 40-80 100
Uncaring	Tragic	Grief	75	75
Condemning	Hopeless	Apathy, hate	50	50
Vindictive	Evil	Guilt	30	30
Despising	Hateful	Shame	20	20

The basic Relationship Diagnostic Chart can be applied to any relationship situation in order to clarify expectations and effective modes of communication, such as advertising, community outreach programs, business, and bureaucratic affairs.

In application to international relations, it is important to realize there is often a wide disparity between a country's populace, its leaders, its actual government operations, and its diplomatic representatives. Adequate diagnosis of international situations can prevent the repetition of the catastrophes of the past that cost the lives of millions of people. This will be glaringly apparent in the next chapter in which the setup for catastrophe is starkly obvious and overwhelming in its implications.

Naïveté is the presumption that all people are pretty much the same, with similar values, motives, standards, and general morality. This is a dangerous miscalculation in diplomatic affairs and accounts for the deaths of over 100 million people in the last century.

Characteristics of Dangerous Political Leaders

Ruthless, glib, cunning	Peace is irrelevant
No regard for human life	Vain, pompous, despotic
No value to truth	No personal honor
Lies are routine and normal	Atheistic, avaricious
Facts are irrelevant	Religion is merely a tool
Win at any cost; predatory	Vengeful, jealous
No morality or ethics	Envy, malice, and hate
No spiritual values	Malevolent, vicious
No humanistic ideals	Incapable of love
No concern for others	Spouts rhetoric, is bombastic
Pride at getting better end of a deal	Fakes honesty, deceptive
Gloats at clever deception	Skilled at oratory and rhetoric
Values only conquest, win, defeat	Free of guilt, no conscience
Willing to sacrifice family, society	Scorns women and children
Manipulative, clever, ruthless	Egoistic, narcissistic
Power oriented, no limits	Vain, self-centered
Greed is valued and okay	Makes false accusations
Presumes others are lying	Assumes others same as self
No value to honesty	Attracts naïve Apologists
Ridicules weakness	Unrestrained by logic or reason
Sadistic, cruel	Capable of gross miscalculations
Enjoys suffering of others	Paranoid, alert, guarded
Thrives on conflict	Eventually overreacts and fails
Does not identify with human-kind	Unaware of consequences, backfires
	Sees military as cannon fodder
	Weak "deserve" their fate

Manipulates patriotism and integrity	No scruples, ethics, or morality
No concern for loss of life	False accusations are okay
Willing to "poison the well"	Hates honesty and integrity
Despises honesty, integrity as weaknesses	Hates enviable figures
	No compassion; violent
Assumes grandiose title (Great Leader, etc.), theatrical displays	Extols terrorism, threats
	No concept of sin, karma, accountability, integrity
Uses others with no compunction	Megalomaniac, grandiose
Willing to sell own soul for gain	Willing to destroy life
Attracts and values underlings	Irrational but deceptive
Feeds off adulation	Clever rather than intelligent
Controlling, domineering	Calculating, scheming
Faithless, no remorse	Promotes and supports depravity
Blames others for own failures	Sanctimonious, sacrilegious
Seeks wealth and trappings	Willingly bears false witness
Displays "macho" stance, boots, whip	Exploits innocence and naïveté
	Ravages the weak and vulnerable
False piety	Considers populace as idiots, dogs
Exploits, hides behind religion	
Views normal people as simpletons	Repays loyalty with elimination, death
Racial and religious prejudice	
Seductive; recruits followers	Intrinsically dishonest, defies truth
No allegiance to countrymen	
No value for human life	Refuses guilt or even a "decent regret"
No value to fairness, balance, or consideration for others	
	Considers self above the law
Unforgiving and vindictive	Devoid of insight; savage
Plays victim to justify violence	Merciless; extremist
Oblivious to suffering	Barbaric (saws off heads…slowly)
Condones brutality, death, pain, and suffering	Breeds conflict; duplicitous
	Favors severe torture
Willing to impoverish others	Compartmentalized
No constraints, extremist	"Good face" to the public
Employs criminals as henchmen	Maintains "innocence"
Despises "Marquis of Queensbury" Rules, or fairness	Uses fear and threats
	Reneges on agreements

Commentary

From the above (which collectively calibrates at consciousness level 80), it becomes obvious why the average person, as well as integrous diplomats, routinely grossly miscalculate forces that have to be dealt with in earthly life, either individually or collectively. Another important consequence to which history bears witness is that in an encounter with predators, the naïve person's integrity is turned against them as a weakness. The predators count on the "fools" paying their bills and worrying about loss of life and concern for the welfare of others. Thus, honest persons are easy marks and easily manipulated into being sympathizers and apologists who race to embrace and seek favor with clever tyrants who often pose as virtuous liberators and supposed "people's" heroes. (Hitler, Pol Pot, Hussein, Stalin, Castro, the Japanese emperor, bin Laden, et al., killed more of their own countrymen than did the "enemy.")

Victimhood and naïveté are a loser's game, and its implications for politics and diplomacy are starkly apparent. America and its press like to play the pretend game out of a pious sense of "fairness," etc. That is the game of "sitting duck."

Although integrous people may deplore all the negative qualities of the above-listed characteristics of nonintegrity, they have to be taken into account and respected as being other people's reality by which they are dominated (the principle of invincible ignorance). Americans are notoriously naïve worldwide and considered fair game. ("They can afford it," or "They deserve it.")

There are entire cultures of multimillions of people to whom "honesty" is a foreign concept and actually considered to be ludicrous, and a successful, profitable con job is laudatory. To sell an American a fake item at the price of the genuine article is considered to be praiseworthy.

Countries, leaders, or regimes that calibrate below 200 are aligned with neither truth nor freedom and are therefore intrinsically untrustworthy. Many, in fact, officially promulgate hate policies that actually advise killing and destroying the United States, its Western culture and values, as well as its populace (Freedom House Report, 2005).

Savage cutthroat empires, regimes, and rulers have come and gone, and history is replete with the catastrophic consequences of the failure to recognize and adequately deal with them. Such regimes are very active and alive today and press for world domination at any cost, just as they have in the past.

If the fallacious victim/perpetrator model is discarded, one can see that the victim is also playing a pernicious game that prompts and seduces the criminality of the perpetrator by the use of tempting vulnerability cloaked as pious innocence. That is equally nonintegrous and sly. The provocateur hides behind the cloak of purported innocence and pretends nonresponsibility by a façade of supposed goodness and egoistic moral superiority. Every child knows this game and plays it with parents and teachers. Thus, the invitational posture of the tempter is as *dangerous* as that of the overt aggressor.

This is the role now represented in the U. S. culture by the ideology of the "far left" and academia that demonizes honest assessment of high-risk factors that are as blatantly obvious as an elephant in the living room. It was these same apologists that were responsible for World War II, Pearl Harbor, and the 9/11 bombing of the World Trade Center. The sophistry of apologists is actually more dangerous than the bombast of the aggressor who paradoxically is actually more honest and blatantly forthright. Survival depends on the capacity to discern the above facts, and death is the consequence of the failure to do so. The apologist is equally the criminal. Imbecility is no defense in the world of survival. To predators, sitting ducks "deserve" what they get, like car owners who leave the keys in unlocked cars.

Integrity and true honesty are not a hearts-and-flowers, "holier than Thou" image game of pseudo-saintly television image and sanctimonious spirituality. Truth calls a spade a spade. The sword of truth is the pathway to peace and freedom. Falsity brings death, destruction, and agony. *Unless one aligns with the Sword of Truth, one ends up facing the sword of steel.*

CHAPTER 15
Truth and War

Introduction

More people have died in human history as a result of war than from any other cause, including even pestilence, starvation, or natural disasters, as immense as they may have been. Despite this fact and the stunning horrors of war, society has not as yet been able to diagnose or identify the crucial, pathological underlying factors. Thus, purported preventive measures have failed miserably over the years for the same reasons that infectious diseases were not curable until they were correctly diagnosed, and it was discovered that they were due to germs and infection, not to miasmas, astrological influences, or "bad air," etc.

When leeches and bloodletting were discarded and penicillin and other drugs were instituted, it opened up a whole new era of antibiotics and modern pharmaceuticals. Within just this lifetime, the endless victims of contagious diseases, such as polio, typhoid, malaria, plague, yellow fever, diphtheria, septicemia, otitis media, brain abscess, meningitis, tuberculosis, and syphilis, to name the most memorable, stressed the hospitals for infectious diseases. The importance of recalling these diseases is to emphasize that no cure is possible until a correct diagnosis has been made. The delay in discovering the cure was due to the lack of the necessary technology, but with the invention of the microscope and the development of bacteriology, the hidden subculture of bacteria was identified. Then, fortuitously, Sir Alexander Fleming discovered penicillin. Without the development of antibiotics and the much-criticized pharmaceutical industry, a large portion of the current population would not even be alive.

Analogously, the subculture of social disease is now discernible through the equivalent of the microscope afforded by techniques that enable us to actually calibrate consciousness or even thoughts beyond time and space. Thus, we are now able to research and discover the very roots of the sufferings of mankind.

War is the socially extreme demonstration of the action of force, and its emergence can be predicted in advance by simply calibrating the elements of a situation, including the interactive countries, their governments, leadership, and active elements.

Basic Premise

Peace is the natural state when truth prevails, and war is the consequence of falsehood. In the history of human civilization, *peace has prevailed only seven percent of the time, and war has prevailed ninety-three percent of the time!* (Calibrates as "true.") The basis of war is ignorance, which is the automatic consequence of the fact that man's mind cannot discern truth from falsehood because of his evolutionary condition. Thus, people cannot differentiate between a true leader and a megalomaniac.

Because of man's innate innocence (the structural incapacity of the human mind to differentiate truth from falsehood), the human mind is easily programmed with fallacy in response to persuasive rhetoric, sophistry, and propaganda. The costs of the failure to recognize and correctly appreciate this basic limitation are agony, death, and the horrors of mass destruction, plus ensuing debt, grief, guilt, prisoners, and hatred. Included in the price are psychic trauma, as well as long-term stress, painful memory, and anguish.

Diagnostic Calibrations

The critical elements starkly reveal themselves through blind testing techniques. While the consciousness level of approximately seventy-eight percent of the people worldwide is below the critical level of 200, fifty-one percent of the population in America calibrates over 200. The overall consciousness level in America is at 421, which is the highest of any country in the world and a fact of quite some significance.

The Great War: World War II
Calibrations

Positions Above 200		Positions Below 200	
Winston Churchill	510	Adolf Hitler	45
President Roosevelt	499	Josef Stalin	90
President Truman	495	Mussolini	50
General Eisenhower	455	Heinrich Himmler	40
General MacArthur	425	Third Reich	70
U.S. Government	395	Neville Chamberlain	185
U.S. Embassy in Japan	300	Japanese Embassy in US	55
Normandy Invasion	365	Japanese Government	130
Robert Oppenheimer (early)	435	Robert Oppenheimer (late)	70
U.S. Treatment of War Prisoners	255	Los Alamos Double Agent	70
U.S. Internment of Japanese	235	League of Nations	185
Heisenberg	465	Pacifists	145
Werner von Braun	400	Secy. of War Stimson (position)	180
U.S. Military	315	Attack on Pearl Harbor	45
German Military	205	Joseph Goebbels	60
Triage	390	Nazi Treatment of Prisoners	70
Los Alamos	400	Japanese Treatment of Prisoners	40
General Rommel	203	Nazi Invasion of Europe	40
Leni Riefenstahl	450	Concentration Camps	30
U.S. Military at Pearl Harbor	250	London Blitz	30
Kamikaze Pilots	390	Dr. Joseph Mengela	15
The Luftwaffe	345	"Cambridge Five"	95
Emperor Hirohito	200	The Rosenbergs	40
Tojo	205	Klaus Fuchs	115
Admiral Yamamoto	205	Harold Philby	110
Conscientious Objectors	210	William Joyce	100
82nd Airborne Division	465	Traitors	30

Tuskegee Air Squadron	465	Lord Haw-Haw	50
101st Airborne Division	465	"Tokyo Rose"	85
Navajo Code Talkers	375	U. S. Intelligence before	
U. S. Intelligence (late)	295	Pearl Harbor	190
von Staufenberg, Col. Klaus	440		
British Intelligence, MI-6	210		
KGB Intelligence	210		

The data is relatively self-explanatory and has few surprises. Notable is that armies and warriors, including kamikaze pilots, are often far more integrous than their leaders. They are indeed literally "cannon fodder," and nonintegrous leaders frequently actually abandon whole armies to certain death to satisfy their own inflated egos. They display lack of loyalty to their very own troops by allowing them to be needlessly slaughtered (e.g., the armies of Stalin and Hitler) and subsequently by killing off victorious generals and returning victorious troops or putting them in gulags.

It is difficult for the average person to even imagine that such moral deficiency could lie within persons of such high rank. Upon examination, megalomaniacs can be diagnosed as having a rather specific and reliably diagnosable psychosis similar to that of Nero, termed "malignant messianic narcissism." This understanding allows for some compassion, which is aided by the realization that many tyrants began their careers with integrous motives.

The megalomaniac calibrates at the same level as a serial killer and represents a form of criminality. The panorama of human life is inclusive of the maximum range for spiritual choice. Extreme lows seem to reflect atavistic regression in which the reptilian rhinencephalon still present in the back of the human brain gains dominance. This can be seen reflected in the Japanese attack on Pearl Harbor, which calibrates at 45, and the Jihad attack on the World Trade Center on 9/11, which calibrates at an even lower 35. The attack on the Oklahoma Federal Building a few years ago also calibrates in the same range.

By "Critical Factor Analysis" (Hawkins, 1995), it is possible to identify the precise point in a complex system where the least minimal effort can produce the greatest result, e.g., a giant clockworks can be stopped by applying pressure at a very specific point, just as a giant locomotive or battleship can be brought to a complete stop if the correct switch is located.

The conditions prior to a war exhibit poised, interrelated, complicated positions, tensions, and a complexity of factors that are beyond intellectual comprehension, such as timing and weighting of factions. Thus, early diagnosis can stop the locomotion of war before it gains unstoppable momentum. However, at each succeeding moment, there is again a new critical point accessible to intervention so that in a time series of events, a series of diagnosable, correlated critical-factor points of opportunity present themselves in sequence. Thus, as applied to World War II, the entire war was easily stoppable at minimal cost or risk at the point of Hitler's first invasion of the Rhineland, Sudentland, and Czechoslovakia. (His intention calibrated at level 100.)

Notable is that nations such as Russia, Germany, Japan, and even Belgium all have effective, well-developed intelligence operations at calibration level 210-215, while the U. S. intelligence was defective (cal. level 190) until it decoded the Japanese JM Code.

The only technique available that is also pragmatic and identifiable is by means of consciousness calibration research because the field of consciousness is all-inclusive, and each instant integrates all factors and influences, condensing them into a specific, identifiable numerical factor. The implications of the above analysis go beyond just this obvious and crucial exhibit. This is now a world where all stands revealed and where there are no more secrets that can be hidden in order to blindside the innocent.

As will be seen, although prior to World War II, Neville Chamberlain's intention was virtuous (cal. 500), because of denial, naïveté, and lack of "hard headed" reality testing, his capability was devastatingly poor (cal. 140). Hitler's intention calibrated at 90, his capability, unfortunately for Europe, was at 450. From this and other illustrations to follow, the patterns that spell serious damage to the world become apparent:

1. Good intention but defective capability (e.g., the present United Nations).

2. Malignant intention but poor capability (e.g., North Korea).

3. Malignant intention plus high capability (e.g., Cold-War Russia).

4. Malignant intention plus high capability, plus malignant messianic totalitarianism (e.g., Stalin, Hitler).

Similarly, the calibrated levels of the elements of World War II quickly reveal the whole story:

1. Weak position of denial by Secretary of War Stimson (refused intelligence reports). Denial calibrates at 190.

2. Weak positions of Neville Chamberlain and pacifists. (Pacifism calibrates at 195.)

3. Pathological calibrations (diagnoses) of Hitler, Mussolini, and Japanese positions and their intentions.

4. Lack of military intelligence (cal. 190) prior to Pearl Harbor despite warnings. Discontinuance of code breaking (later resumed by President Roosevelt).

5. Failure to diagnose the Third Reich, Stalin's megalomania, the caliber of Gen. Rommel, the Luftwaffe, etc.

6. Weakness and the low calibration of the League of Nations (cal. 185).

7. Failure to diagnose double agents who revealed atomic secrets to Russia and thereby precipitated the Cold War.

The threat to national security and world peace that is the consequence of faulty philosophies and political views that calibrate below 200 is starkly revealed by the impact on world history of the espionage agents who infiltrated the atomic nuclear research facilities in both the United States and Britain. Security lapses, in retrospect, are somewhat appalling but not too dissimilar from more recent events and current security lapses (as yet undetected). Note that "blindsided" and "caught off guard" calibrate at 180.

Any top security activities, of course, attract the world's best spies. Los Alamos and the Manhattan Project, as would be expected, attracted Klaus Fuchs (cal. 115), Harold Philby (cal. 110), William Joyce (cal. 100), the Rosenburgs, and Ted Hall, as well as a group made up of Martin Sobel, Harry Gold, Donald McLain (The Cambridge Five), etc.

All the members of the group were Marxists, and Stalin spoke kindly of these "martyrs." The spread of that ideology into Hollywood and intellectuals in the State Department fueled the McCarthy hearings. The major downside was the Cold War, international competition, and nuclear buildup, the fear of which supported the ideological basis for the Iraqi war. Today's nuclear jeopardy is thus the aftermath of the intellectually "elite" of their own generation. That same pathologic defect continues to weaken detection of the sources of danger to current society (calibrates as "true").

In this and other wars (including the Iraqi war), preceding events are nearly identical: a megalomaniac leader propagandizes their populace to militancy while the intended victim goes into denial with faulty intelligence (cal. 190), naïve diplomatic ineptitude, and poetic fantasies of "if we're nice to them, they'll be nice to us" illusions. Factually, grandiose "macho" dictators *despise* such weak "feminine," "cowardly" positions and are, in fact, further inflamed into aggression by the primitive predator/prey instinctual animal brain response, i.e., passivity invites aggression.

The weak masculine fears and hates women or the feminine (except for lust). This is exemplified by gangster rap that calls women whores and pumps up "kicking" pregnant, degraded women in the belly. The strong masculine does not feel threatened by women but instead honors and is protective of them. True masculinity is self-assured and has no need to strut or demean others. It honors women.

Malignant Messianic Narcissism

The world's failure to identify this pathologic syndrome accounts for the death of millions of innocent people in every generation. It is really the responsibility of governments and their leaders, as well as the populace, to become familiar with this disease that is so far removed from normalcy that the average person can scarcely even imagine it to be a social reality.

The public in general tends to be naïve about mental disorders, even when blatantly displayed. People commonly believe that other humans are basically just like they are. Nothing could be farther from the truth. There are many people who are the diametric opposite of normalcy and all that is perceived to go with that idealized state. The world is full of people who hate love, integrity, peace, and truth; in fact, it infuriates them. (See Peck, *People of the Lie*, 1983.)

While the psychopathology of criminality (Chapter 11) and malignant narcissism (Chapter 14) have been reviewed, malignant messianic narcissism warrants further attention as the ultimate, severe degree of these disorders. It is a combination of composite pathologies of an extremely low level of consciousness (cal. 30), plus the deficits of reason; an absence of conscience; the inability to identify with or value other human life; the disdain for human, moral, or ethical values; disdain for women; greed for power; infatuation and aggrandizement of the self; and ego inflation to messianic grandiosity. The disorder is often difficult to recognize because it occurs in two distinct forms: (1) early onset (childhood bully type), and (2) adult life onset after some years of normalcy subsequent to the gaining of power (i.e., "Power corrupts; absolute power corrupts absolutely").

The second form does not occur in democracies because power is split between the head of state and other heads of government (judiciary, parliament, congress, military, diplomatic, etc.). Thus, the disorder is unique to dictatorships, monarchies, and theocracies (Nero, Caesar, Hussein, Khomeini, Napoleon, Hitler, Ivan the Terrible, etc.) It also afflicts top, highly paid executives who "lose their sense of reality" and feel "entitled" to help themselves to the company's cash and assets (Chandler, 2004).

At the present time, the trials of Milosevic and Hussein afford a valuable opportunity to examine and become familiar with this gross disorder and thereby learn to recognize it. In each case, the setting was the same. Early signs were the narcissistic display of the "great leaders," philosophies, and images via billboards, statues, parades, and constant repetition via the media, as well as propagandizing in schools and "special" youth groups where militant ideology was inculcated with well-recognized brainwashing techniques. Importantly, "the leader" replaced God and was worshipped with idolatries and special arm salutes. The great leader's ego, already inflated, then became full-blown grandiosity through adulation, elaborate public military parades and mass theatrical public events and carefully staged demonstrations of public acclaim. Women wept with emotion and children were persuaded through propaganda to serve and joyously give up their lives for the "Great Leader."

Current as well as past megalomaniacs display the same contempt for fellow countrymen and even their families. Hitler stated that the German populace deserved to die because they lost the war. Hitler as well as Stalin hated their own successful generals and killed them. Hussein called his populace "dogs" and slaughtered three hundred thousand. Hitler "exterminated" six million Jews. Stalin murdered millions in the gulags, including even his own victorious returning troops.

Another symptom is the desecration of places of beauty or worship, e.g., churches (blow up the ancient, great Buddha in Afghanistan; burn down Paris, Rome, etc.) Desecration takes the form of the slaughter of women, innocents, and mere civilians. The savagery is both bizarre (beheading, evisceration, mutilation, "hung and quartered") and theatrically displayed (televised slow beheading with a saw, cutting off tongues, hands, and feet). It is really easy for normal people to understand the psychology and motives of malignant, messianic narcissists—they are simply the *exact opposite* of who you are in every detail.

Contrasting Wars—Calibrations

Korean War

South Korea	300	Communist Regime	90
U.S. Position	300	U. S. Intelligence	190
North Korea	80		

Vietnam War

U. S. Position (early)	405	Vietnam Populace	70
U. S. Position (later)	350	Viet Cong	40
U.S. Military	335	U.S. Media	185
War Protesters	201	Communists (U.S.)	130
PTSD a fact?	Yes	U. S. Intelligence	190

Cold War

U.S. Position	400	CIA	185
West Germany	310	FBI	185
President Nixon (position)	400	East Germany	165
President Kennedy		Russian Position	75
(position)	430	KGB	40
U.S. Media	215	Khrushchev	80
U.S. Intelligence		Breznev	90
Operations	195	Communists (U.S.)	130

Gulf War

President G. H. W. Bush		Saddam Hussein (position)	95
(position)	400	Kuwait	195
U.S. Military	310	U. S. Intelligence	190
Gulf War Syndrome a fact?	Yes		

World War I

President Woodrow Wilson	400	The Red Baron	
Shell Shock a Fact?	Yes	(von Richthofen)	385
Kaiser Wilhelm	165	U. S. Intelligence	190

Comparative: Napoleonic Wars – Waterloo

Duke of Wellington	420	Napoleon	75

Although each of the above deserves more extensive and detailed examination and reporting, for the sake of brevity, even a few rudimentary calibrations rather accurately summarize the overall situation. Note that U. S. intelligence operations are consistently defective (cal. 190).

As noted elsewhere, not only power but also fame itself can corrupt. Both Hitler and Napoleon calibrated in the mid-400s during the early constructive phases of their reigns but later fell to very low calibration levels, which led to their defeat due to grandiosity (ignoring the counsel of seasoned generals, etc.). Fame itself can have a similar effect as it did with Herman Goring.

Calibrations: Iraqi War (Early)

Above 200:

President Bush (position)	460	The Congress	450
Secretary of State Powell (position)	460	Tony Blair (position) British Prime Minister)	440
Secretary of Defense (position)	460	U.S. Population	431
U.S. Military (Intention)	450	U.S. Media	320
U.S. State Dept. (Intention)	450	Peace Vigils	305
		Pre-emptive War	360

Below 200:

U. N. Security Council	190	Iraqi Population (position)	140
Intention of UN Security Council regarding the United States	135	Iraqi Media (position)	140
		Syria Regime (position)	130
		Middle East	110
Ambassador Joseph Wilson's Report of Statement: "Bush Lied"	160	Saddam Hussein (early)	65
		Iraqi Military Leaders	65
		Jihad	50
Iran (position)	185	Islamic Terrorists	50
Palestine (position)	180	Taliban	65
Israel (position)	180	bin Laden	40
Peace Demonstrations	170	al-Qaeda	65
"Peace" as a Political Slogan	130	U. S. Intelligence	190
Turkey (position)	165		

Although the above results are what reasonable people would expect, protest may arise from people influenced by distorted media and emotionalities of acrimonious debate that exploit the intrinsic innocence and limitations of the human mind. Like the hardware of a computer, the mind has no choice as to its software programming. The concepts and wisdom of triage and pre-emptive war are not comprehensible to minds that calibrate below 360. Again, as in prior wars, U. S. intelligence is at an inept calibration level of 190.

Calibrations also reflect the input of elements unknown at the time by the general public, e.g., recent revelations regarding "food for oil" profits siphoned off by members of the United Nations.

Further Calibrations - The Iraqi War (Late)

U.S. Department of Defense	455	Position of Conservatives	455
The Pentagon	455	Position of Republicans	450
U.S. Attorney General	455	Position of Democrats	310
United Nations Security Council	190	Position of Far Left	180
Leadership of the United Nations	195	Private Military Companies	345
		Triage	390
Position of Great Britain	355	Halliburton	275
Position of France	210	U. S. Intelligence	190
UN Investigation Inspectors	205		

Media Coverage of the Iraqi War

Boston Globe	195	Fox News	420
CBS News	255	NBC News	255
CNN News	290	The O'Reilly Factor	460
New York Times	190		

The first chart above reveals the levels of integrity and its focus on the questions of 9/11 in which more Americans were killed than at Pearl Harbor. Not only were three thousand innocent civilians killed, but also the Pentagon itself was attacked and thus defined the attack as an act of war. (War against the United States was formally declared by bin Laden in 1998.) The plane that crashed was intended for the White House itself (calibrates as "true").

The public's comprehension of the true meaning and impact of the 9/11 attacks was impaired by the relentless repetition of the images of the burning Twin Towers. They were dramatic and thus became the focus of public interest, which detracted from the more important and significant attack on the Pentagon and the attempt to bomb the White House. (This is analogous to bombing Number 10 Downing Street in London, the House of Parliament, or even the Kremlin.)

The attack was thereby formally an "act of war" by definition, declaration, and intention. (Calibrates as "true.") Osama bin Laden formally declared war prior to the Pentagon attack, which fulfilled the warning of Jihad, a Holy War. It obviously was not just a "criminal act" anymore than was the Japanese bombing of Pearl Harbor.

Lack of clarity about the correct definition of the event resulted in the later confusion about whether detentions were to be legally classified as criminals, prisoners of war, combatants, noncombatants, saboteurs, etc. As a precedent, in World War II, a Nazi submarine delivered five saboteurs (plus bombs) to the coast of Long Island. All were caught and subsequently executed.

The disinclination of former Allies to join in the endeavor was understandable within the context of their independent cultures and social realities such as sizable Arab populations. In addition, a difference was that in World War II, the countries of Europe were themselves direct targets, whereas they were exempt from identifying with the calamity of 9/11 and, in their best judgment, concluded that a response was not their responsibility. There was also the implied but unstated perception that America had sufficient strength and resources to handle the emergency on its own. As was later revealed (Duelfer, 2004), officials at the United Nations had been bribed by Hussein and were on his payroll for many billions of dollars of "food for oil" money from which the U. N. itself was also profiting (Brooks, 2004).

The presidential decisions that followed were dictated by the preceding events, plus his sworn oath of office to defend the country against aggressors. Actions at the time were based on available intelligence sources (U. S., Russia, and Britain). The U.S. Intelligence persisted at calibration level 190.

Partisan Ambassador Joseph Wilson's 2002 purported investigative report alleged that Iraq had not sought access to Niger uranium, when, in fact, Iraq actually did do so (later confirmed by Commissioner of Inquiry Lord Robin Butler). Wilson committed other serious errors (including false reports to the Washington Post in 2003 regarding the CIA and Niger uranium).

The attacks on "Bush's famous 16 words" in his 2003 State of the Union Address ("The British government has learned that Saddam Hussein recently sought significant quantities of uranium from Africa") were based on spurious misinformation that he had misled the public. The retraction of errors was belated and relegated to the back pages. Whereas the New York Times calibrated overall in the year 2000 at 250, by 2004, its calibration level had dropped to 195, and its coverage of the Iraqi war to 190.

The unpreparedness of the government (cal. 190) represented the "culture" of the preceding decades, as well as restrictive legislation and lack of integration of the CIA, FBI, and other intelligence-gathering agencies. The overall climate of lack of preparedness and denial was very similar to the situation prior to Pearl Harbor. As events turned out, the primary threat was not specifically Iraq itself but Pan-Arabic Wahhabism as expressed by violent al-Qaeda extremists. Thus, the real enemy was not really a specific country but a militant ideology that had actually begun in Saudi Arabia and spread to Iran and across the entire Middle East. It then became politicized and favored by the Iraqi ruling party. Thus, the true identity of the aggressor became clouded. This confusion was abetted by Sadam Hussein's repudiation of the United Nations' mandate on fourteen occasions, which was the real trigger of overt war.

Over time, further information will surface, as it does after all wars. The future always affords the benefits of hindsight and thus, hopefully, wisdom rather than regret or blame. The road of the evolution of human consciousness is bumpy. The lesson is recurrently "Be vigilant for truth." Until the present time, that was not an actual possibility, but a new era has dawned that calibrates above 200, indicating that integrity may prevail.

The Iraqi War stopped the killing of fellow Iraqis by Saddam Hussein, who routinely killed more of his countrymen than did the Gulf and Iraqi wars combined (thirty thousand mass graves). Subsequent to the war, the Iraqi insurgents continued to kill other Iraqis, despite the occupation troops. All in all, more Iraqis have been killed by fellow Iraqis than by the invasion forces in their preemptive military strike, and no end is in sight.

Some of the political response that ensued thereafter is an example of a peculiarity of the human ego in which perpetrator and victim become confused and the roles are reversed. Paradoxically, those with a naïve or unevolved consciousness rushed to embrace the nonintegrous, almost criminal perpetrator and vilify that which was integrous. The posture of the United States' response calibrates at 460, the 9/11 attack itself at 35, and its perpetrators at 50-70. The inability to discriminate between severe depravity and integrity is indeed a major limitation to understanding and a source of error.

Freud first noticed this strange proclivity of the unconscious to symbolize things in terms of their opposite (Freud, 1900), e.g., the current fad of identifying victims as perpetrators and vice versa. It is a primitive mechanism of the lower elements of the ego in its struggle to control and suppress the Id—that reservoir of raw animal instincts and violence. Therefore, hating war does not bring peace anymore than hating sin brings purity or holiness. A virtue is achieved by choosing it rather than by vilifying its opposite.

Because of continued focus on the Iraqi war, more calibrations will complete the picture. We can then go on to do more basic research about the real roots of war.

Additional Calibrations at the Time of Iraqi War (Late)

Position of Liberals	205	Pacifism (political)	95
Position of War Protestors	185	Position of Saddam	
Hollywood Leftist Elite	130	Hussein (late)	45
Academy Awards (2003)		Iraqi Military	95
public outburst toward		Taliban	65
President Bush	65	al-Qaeda	65

Islamic Terrorists	50	American Treatment of Iraqi	
Treatment of Prisoners by		Prisoners (Abu Ghraib)	165
Iraq	65	Position of Women in Iraq	95
Military Intention of Iraqi's		Position of Children in Iraq	75
Ruling Party	45	Position of Dogs in Iraq	40
Iraqi Media Coverage	45	(Position of Dogs in U. S.	450)
Iraqi Treatment of		U. S. Intelligence	190
American Prisoners	155		

Calibrations Subsequent to Iraqi War

For reasons pointed out elsewhere, the dualistic nature of the ego and its perpetrator/victim projection onto world events leads to the search for the "bad guys," the "cause" of 9/11, in accord with the ego's proclivity to project blame. In actuality, phenomena are the consequence of an overall field or "climate" that indirectly and unintentionally facilitates the emergence of selectively observed phenomena, such as the 9/11 catastrophe. The "climate" prior to 9/11, as previously noted, was almost identical to the one that preceded the attack on Pearl Harbor on December 7, 1941. In psychological terms, it would be described as naïveté and denial, but that is an insufficient explanation in and of itself. The elements of the actual climate calibrate as follows:

9/11 Calibrations

U. S. National Defense		Patriot Act	375
(Bureaucratic)	190	Editorial Sections of Top 10	
Reno/Goralick Decision		U.S. Newspapers	
(The Wall)	190	(excluding *Wall Street*	
Church/Pike Committee		*Journal* and *Christian*	
Hearings	180-190	*Science Monitor*	185-190
Clinton Administration		Critics of testimony	170
Position	180-190	(In contrast, constructive	
Torricelli Principle	160	criticism calibrates at	210)

The calibrations underscore the extreme importance of the dictum that truth (cal. over 200) brings peace, and falsehood (cal. under 200) favors war. The pre-9/11 situation was almost identical to that exhibited by Secretary of War Stimson prior to the Japanese attack in 1941. He refused to heed daily intelligence briefings with the comment that "Gentlemen don't read other gentlemen's mail"—in this case, the dire forewarnings of Japanese explosive militants and Hitler's overall war strategy, all of which is like ignoring bin Laden's "declaration of war" on the United States in 1998. In contrast, North Korea's nuclear threats were not taken as lightly.

Calibrations of the 9/11 Investigative Committee Hearings
(April-July, 2004)

Testimony of Government Officials	255	Cal. Level of Investigative Panel Leaders	255
Testimony of Richard Clarke	200	Final 9/11 Commission Report (July, 2004)	255
Critics of Testimony	170	C. Duelfer Investigative Report to Senate	
Overall Cal. Level of Hearings	255	(October 6, 2004)	305

It is useful to specify "positions" to differentiate them from personalities or countries themselves. Positions are situational and subject to change due to partisan influence, stress, or social attitudes. Society is the organic, ongoing evolutionary process and subject to constantly shifting conditions. Survival often requires flexibility and adaptive maneuvers. People "rise to the occasion" and thereby discover hidden strengths. At other times, there are rueful reflection and reconstruction.

A Contextualization of the Iraqi War

As has been described earlier, it is not possible to understand *content* (i.e., the Iraqi War) unless placed in historical *context*. Since its inception, Islam has been militant. Its first Jihad was started by Muhammad who, three years after he dictated the Koran, dropped in consciousness calibration from level 700 to 135. This was apparently the consequence of temporal lobe epilepsy (see Chapter 18).

Early Islam was spread by the sword until it was stopped by Charles Martel of France and by its defeat at the battle of Granada in 1492. The second great Jihad was performed by the Ottoman Turks, which ended with defeat in Vienna in 1529.

The emergence of the Islamic sect of Wahhabis in Saudi Arabia (see Chapter 18) marked the onset of the third and still ongoing Jihad as was exemplified by the Ayatollah Khomeini in Iran and bin Laden's Taliban. As a consequence of its anti-West stance, the Wahhabis took down the pro-Western Shah of Iran and Sadat in Egypt and attacked Hussein in Jordan, Mubarak in Egypt, and Musharraf in Pakistan. The overall plan is to infiltrate and take over governments in Egypt, Turkey, Pakistan, Indonesia, the United Arab Emirates, Sudan, Tunisia, Libya, Algeria, Morocco, Yemen, Syria, Lebanon, Jordan, Malaysia, and then, with Pakistan's nuclear capacity, take down Israel. In this process, the United States would also be attacked (Word Trade Center, Twin Towers, plus others in planning stages). Growing Arabic populations would deter Europe from U. S. alliances and lead to Arabic dominance in the United Nations.

It was against this background that the U. S. strategy was to prevent militant Islamic-Arabic takeover of seventy-five percent of the world's oil supplies and its huge financial power base (L. Abraham, 2004), plus the acquisition of nuclear materials by al-Qaeda, i.e., bin Laden, via Pakistani nuclear scientists, Russian sources, etc. (Berger, 2004). A Western power base in Iraq would split the Arabian continent in two and deter Arabic takeover and coalescence. Thus, Afghanistan and Iraq were strategic targets for multiple reasons to preclude a clash of civilizations of Islamic militancy with the Western world, which could go on for centuries, as it has in the past. Only the United States had the power to prevent such an ongoing cataclysm, as the United Nations was ineffectual and its Security Council impaired by food-for-oil kickbacks of billions of dollars to various members siphoned off by bogus sales, etc. ("Food for Oil," 9/19/04). Thus, with this overall world contextualization (which calibrates at 465), the war in Iraq would therefore appear to have been a long-term strategic move to preclude a far worse multinational and perhaps centuries-long series of progressively severe cataclysms (e.g., the triage decision of a pre-emptive strike).

The context of the Iraqi war was that of a spreading, violent, militant ideology inflamed by distortions of Islam that sanctify hatred and violence and justify terrorism and the killing of innocents by labeling them as infidels. This has become a Pan-Arabic disease, and specific violent events that captivate the media are only symptoms.

The malignant messianic leaders Osama bin Laden, Ayatollah Khomeini, Saddam Hussein, et al., are only the many heads of the hydra. The disease is also implanted in other countries across the world where surreptitious recruiting of radical converts is well orchestrated and funded. The disease hides under the camouflage of religion, and mosques in the United States are funded by militant Arabic groups as recruitment centers from which the ideology is spread via academic sympathizers that allow Jihad parades under the quasi-elitist banner of "fairness," etc. The goal of Islamic terrorists is theocratic fascism (Newosh, 2004; Bridis, 2004).

Of considerable importance is the finding that Islamic converts include a dangerously high percentage of radicalized militant extremists amenable to terrorist indoctrination and training. The recruitment rates are:

United States	10%
Europe	15%
Arab Countries	35%

These figures denote the alignment of allegiance to the terrorist ideology, which defies all reason and sanctifies homicide, thereby bypassing all forms of rational restraint.

Support of this trend by apologists (cal. 185), notably academics, rights activists, etc., would seem lacking in wisdom and discernment. The same trend in earlier decades turns out to be catastrophic (American Nazi Party, American Communist Party, white supremacist religious extremists, atomic energy scientists sharing secrets with the former U.S.S.R., the resultant Cold War, etc.).

The "Hate the Leader" Syndrome

Throughout history, and quite prominently in current society, is the recurrence of the symptoms of focused negativity on leaders or personifications of secular, political, economic, or religious power. The leader becomes the straw-man target for the projections of disturbed people who, by splitting their own repressed desires, externalize them and see them as "out there." With calibration techniques, that phenomenon, which is quite shrill and overt in recent times, can be diagnosed. The pattern has been equally intense concerning past presidents (Lincoln, Roosevelt, Clinton, etc.) where its component psychodynamics were essentially identical. We can examine the contrasts between the images of the presidents and compare them with their verifiable reality. If the ruler is truly a tyrant (Hitler, Stalin, etc.), that fact reveals itself quickly upon investigation.

The "Hate Bush," "Hate Clinton," and "Hate America" factions tend to overlap. The fallacies of the "Hate America" extremists (Gibson, 2004) have already been reviewed in a previous chapter. The "Bush" pictured by Bush haters is seen as a fascist (cal. 65), like Stalin, Hitler, and Hussein (cal. 50-80), and as a greedy warmonger and evil person willing to sell out his country and its citizens for oil profits (traitor calibrates at 80), and send innocent soldiers to their needless deaths so he can get richer and be a dictator. Thus, he is depicted as a malignant, messianic narcissist (cal. 30). These assertions are further elaborated to include surreptitious intrigue and being in league with anti-American Islamic terrorists (i.e., treachery, cal. 60, or lower).

The composite depiction of the "evil" straw man calibrates at 130. The presidency of Bush is at _460_, which indicates integrity. Collectively, the heads of all the governments of all the members of the United Nations calibrate at 190 (excluding the United States). Characteristically, critics of the U. S. defer to the U. N., which itself calibrates at 185-195. The U. N. Security Council has been involved in the food-for-oil and other payoff scandals. The Administration's attitude toward the U. N. appears to be appropriate and supported by the facts, as described in the study "Inside The Asylum" (cal. 455) by Jed Babbin, former Deputy Undersecretary of Defense.

A composite of the haters of President Bush (and the U. S., as well), collectively calibrate, amazingly enough, at 135, i.e., exactly the same as their depicted evil straw man. This displays a basic defective phenomenon of human experience as well as truth about the unconscious discovered by Freud (cal. 499) and confirmed during fifty years of psychiatric practice. Hate distorts perception, and distorted perception results in hate as falsity, e.g., Bush conducted an "illegal" war. In fact, his motive was not only legal but also approved by a vote of the U. S. Congress.

Thus, the world is like a Rorschach card, and, to a disturbed person, the inkblot "U.S." or "Bush" looks like an evil demon. Those who fear and hate authority project it onto others via ethnic, religious, or political symbols. The basis of leader hatred is simply jealousy and envy of authority figures, facilitated by the projected dualistic perceptual distortion of perpetrator/victim (the classic Marxist pitfall). In addition, narcissism results in guilt and self-hatred that is then projected onto the country and the president.

By verifiable analysis, integrous people who, by virtue of self-honesty, are themselves able to perceive integrity, can confirm that the President exercised duly-appointed responsibility and endeavored to fulfill his oath-taken duties of stewardship over a great nation in turbulent times in which the majority of the countries of the world operate from markedly lower levels of integrity, much less interest in the welfare of civilization itself (calibrates as "true").

The alternative option is to passively withdraw and capitulate to Islamic terrorism, which, with control of seventy-five percent of the world's oil supply and its vast wealth, ensures success of access to Pakistan's nuclear capacities by which Israel would be eliminated.

In the future, with Europe heavily infiltrated by Muslim immigrants and its protest silenced in the United Nations, the same process would infiltrate the Balkan States and eventually Russia, with its oil fields. Thus, the third Jihad is designed to eventually capture world dominance by the undermining of the West. All non-Islamics will then eventually be eliminated and Islamic power will rule the world, i.e., Islamic messianic triumphalism (cal. 50). (Abraham, op. cit.).

Post-9/11 Hearings Developments

Subsequent to the counter-terrorism move of the Iraqi war, several significant events then surfaced:

1. The public beheadings (cal. 10) of American and other civilians.

2. The revelation of the torture of captives in military prisons.

The public was shocked and grieved when brought into close contact with the grim atrocities and realities that occur in every war, both current and past. When the lives of comrades depend on obtaining information from prisoners, brutality results from rage. That is why spies are given cyanide capsules.

Upon examination, situational sadism is based on a psychological weakness of mankind in general. The famous Milgram (1974) and Zimbardo (1973) research revealed that out of obedience to authority (the "critical factor"), the *majority* of unselected ordinary citizens would torture even a research volunteer in a university setting. In fact, over half of the experimental volunteer "prison guards" were willing to administer a lethal electric shock to the "prisoners" in a mock prison study.

The experiments explained the phenomena of Nazi death camps; Algeria; Japanese barbarism in Manchuria; and the torture camps in El Salvador, Brazil, Haiti, the Middle East, and elsewhere. The university research experiments actually had to be called to a halt because the role-playing guards literally became progressively more savage, cruel, and actually sadistic. This propensity was portrayed in the well-known story of *The Lord of the Flies* (Golding, 1954).

The latent behavioral trait is also exemplified by the phenomenon of bullying. All of these illustrate the release of the "predator-prey" scenario, which originates in the animal brain and, as Zimbardo and Milgram demonstrated conclusively, is released by role, plus environment. The studies revealed that because of this predictable response, closer supervision of prisoners is needed by authorities that are specifically educated about the Milgram-Zimbardo research findings. It was this serious omission that resulted in the Abu Ghraib events that biased media inflated even more than was necessary (45 repetitions in the New York Times).

Not much is learned from political pretense anymore than one can cure pneumonia by pretending that it is just a cold. "Jihad" literally means "Holy War," which is a serious warning because it is the most dangerous of all positionalities since it sanctions as well as encourages the most barbaric actions by citing God as the excuse and authority for them (i.e., "the will of Allah"). The source of current Islamic extremism is traceable to the violent teachings of Muhammad ibn Abdul Mahhab (cal. 20), later reinforced by the distortions of the Koran promulgated by Sayyid Qutb (cal. 20), which glorify violence and death and condemn not only ninety percent of Muslims as idolaters but also one hundred percent of all followers of other religions as well (Forsyth, 2004). (See "Islam" in Chapter 18.) Bin Laden's declaration of war against the United States was ignored, which was understandable with U. S. intelligence operating at calibration level 190.

His "fatwah" (cal. 40) was a formal declaration that it is the religious obligation and duty for *all* Muslims to kill *all infidels*, with no exceptions—meaning all civilians, including women and children; for Jihad, there are no "innocents" among infidels. It is similar to the Roman Catholic Church's pronouncement of "anathema," i.e., an abomination to God. American sympathizers fail to realize that in the eyes of an Islamic zealot, they are merely the same as any other infidels (i.e., "mushrikun").

Aggression "in the name of God" is the most dangerous of all and is immune to all the countermeasures characteristically used by the Western world. HAMAS (which was championed by Arafat), the Taliban, and al-Qaeda are similar and identical in their origins. These groups reflect the darkest potential of which humans are capable, as did Pol Pot. They calibrate at 35 to 45, which is literally below the level of the Komodo dragon, and actually lower than that of dinosaurs because of intention. Thus, the term "atavistic" is appropriate and a clinically accurate diagnosis. It represents the expression of a very primitive "attractor" field of very early life forms of mindless, voracious killers and is the same level as serial murderers.

Terrorist Organizations

Abu Sayyaf Group (Philippines)	85	Lashkar-e-Tayyiba (Pakistan)	70
Al-Aqsa Martyrs Brigade (Israel, West Bank, Gaza)	75	Lashkar I Jhangvi (Pakistan)	75
Al-Qaeda (Wahhabism) Global	65	Liberation Tigers of Tamil Eelam (Sri Lanka)	80
Asbat al-Ansar (Lebanon)	75	Moro Islamic Liberation Front (Philippines)	80
Basque Fatherland and Liberty (ETA) France, Spain	80	Moroccan Islamic Combat Group (Morocco)	85
Chachon Separatists (Russia)	85	Nat'l Liberation Army (ELN) (Colombia)	80
Fallujah Insurgents	85	Palestine Islamic Jihad (Israel, West Bank, Gaza)	75
Islamic Movement of Uzbekistan (IMU) Central Asia	75	Palestine Liberation Organization	65
Islamic Resistance Movement (HAMAS) Israel, West Bank, Gaza	75	Real IRA (Northern Ireland)	85
Hasbullah (Lebanon)	70	Rev. Armed Forces (FARC) (Colombia)	90
Hofsted Network (Netherlands)	85	Salafist Cell and Combat Group (Algeria)	80
Ivory Coast Revolutionaries	90	"Supremist Groups" (Racist, Ethnic, Religious, Political) Worldwide	40-85
Jaishe-e-Mohammed (Pakistan)	75	Tewhid we Jihad (Iraq)	70
Jamaah Islamiya (Southeast Asia)	80	Ulster Defense Association (Northern Ireland)	85
Kach Kahane Chai (Israel, West Bank)	80	United Self-defense Forces (Colombia)	90
Kurdistan Workers Party (PKK) (Turkey)	85		

Additional Groups Listed in *Patterns of Global Terrorism* United States Department of State, 2003-2004

The following all calibrate similarly and collectively at an average level of 75-80:

Abu Nidal Organization (ANO)	Mujahedin-e Khalq Organiza-
al-Tawhid	tion (MEK)
al-Zarqawl Network	Muslim Iranian Students Society
Ansar Al-Islam (AL)	National Liberation Army of
Aum Srinrikyo	Iran
Communist Party of Philippines	New People's Army (NPA)
(CPP/NPA)	Partisans of Islam
Dev Sol	Popular Front for Liberation of
Devrimci Sol (Revolutionary	Palestine (PFLP)
Left)	Revolutionary Nuclei
Egyptian Islamic Jihad	Revolutionary Organization
Euzkadi Ta Askatasuna (Basque)	17 November
Fatah Revolutionary Council	Sangillan Force
Al-Gama'a al-Islamiyya	Salafist Group for Call & Com-
Harakat ul-Mujahidin (HUM)	bat (GSPC)
Helpers of Islam	Sendero Luminoso (Shining
Islamic Movement of Uzbeki-	Path, SL)
stan (IMU)	Talaa'al-Fateh
Jaish Ansar Al-Islam	United Self-Defense Forces /
Jama'at al-Tawhid wa'al-Jihad	Group of Colombia (AUC)
Jihad Group (al-Jihad)	World Tamil Association (WTA)
Jund Al-Islam	and Movement
Monotheism and Jihad Group	

Groups Listed in Prior Editions of *Patterns of Global Terrorism*
The average calibration of the following group is 75-80:

3rd October Organization	Morazanist Patriotic Front
15 May Organization	(FPM)
Alex Boncayao Brigade (ABB)	Orange Volunteers (V)
Al-Fatah	The Orly Group (Armenia)
Algerian Terrorism	Party of Democratic Kampuchea
Al Ummah	Popular Struggle Front (PSF)
Armenian Secret Army for the	Provisional Irish Republican
Liberation of Armenia (ASALA)	Army
Army for the Liberation of	Puka Inti (Sol Rojo, Red Sun)
Rwanda	Red Army Faction (RAF)
Chukaku-Ha (Nucleus or	Red Brigades (BR)
Middle Core Faction)	Red Hand Defenders (RHD)
Federation of Associations of	Revolutionary People's Struggle
Canadian Tamils (FACT)	(ELA)
Force 17	Revolutionary United Front
Former Armed Forces (ex-FAR)	(RUF)
(Rwanda)	Sol Rojo
Interahamwe (Rwanda)	Tupac Amaru Revolutionary
Khmer Rouge	Movement (MRTA)
Lautaro Popular Rebel Forces	Tupac Katari Guerrilla Army
(FRPL)	(EGTK)
Lautaro Youth Movement (MJL)	United Popular Action
Loyalist Volunteer Force (LVF)	Movement (MAPU/L)
Manuel Rodriguez Patriotic	Zviadists
Front (FPMR)	

All terrorist groups emanate from extreme egocentricity and narcissism and are a form of triumphalism that finds approval by mob agreement. Terrorism is a form of criminality that attracts the lowest elements of society, many of whom are inherently psychopathic personalities seeking an outlet for violence and hatred.

Basically, there is an envious hatred of true power and an effort to mimic it by force, which destroys the lives of the innocent. The ego thus replaces God as the Supreme and blasphemously claims Divinity as its authority for savage violence, even to children, and it gloats over desecration and destruction.

Throughout history, the basic energy has been referred to as "satanic," and the perversion of truth used to justify it is classically termed "Luciferic" (i.e., pride and defiance of the sovereignty of God). When the twin attractor fields that characterize denial of love and truth are combined, the rabid dogs of sadistic terrorism are loosed that demonstrate the extreme downside of the ego itself. The perpetrators are thereby the victims of delusion for they cannot tell truth from falsehood and are thus easily proselytized because they are blind to their own enslavement and its karmic consequences.

Unfortunately, savagery is an addictive potential; therefore, terrorists see peace as the enemy and cleverly subvert it as being well-documented and demonstrated by the life of now-deceased Arafat, who was the primary core of terrorism worldwide for decades.

It is informative to examine the popular meme, "one man's terrorist is another man's freedom fighter" (cal. 190). This is a seductive sophistry based on relativism and ignoring context.

"Freedom fighter" calibrates at 240, "terrorist" at 40-80. There is also the confusion of *res interna* (a mental notion) and confirmable external reality. Patrick Henry calibrates at 445 and bin Ladin at 40. The difference is in intention and context, just as the Patriot Act is integrous in times of war but not so during peacetime.

All dictators start out with propaganda as "freedom fighters" and end up as tyrants that kill more of their own countrymen than the purported enemy would have done. The human mind, unaided, cannot discern the difference between perception and essence. (Neither could Little Red Riding Hood.) The Fallujah insurgents calibrate at 85, the PLO at 65, etc.

To complicate the matter further, many leaders who start out as integrous "freedom fighters" and calibrate in the 400s early in their careers, (Hitler, Arafat, Castro, Napoleon) then succumb to the seductive glamour of power and control over others. Later in their careers, they develop egomania and calibrate at less than 100. This is almost a certainty in all dictatorships, and with most sovereigns in history, such as Nero and others. Therefore, the catchy meme should be changed to "Today's freedom fighter is tomorrow's terrorist tyrant" (cal. 495).

Terrorism has been endemic to human societies throughout the ages (Curtie, 2002) and is currently a primary threat to all countries. Very deep within the depths of the ego and Freud's "Id" are the primordial desire to kill and a thirst for the sheer pleasure of killing. We see it in the "sport killing" of blowing off the heads of prairie dogs. We see this expressed overtly in the pleasure and cheers of the crowd at the Roman Coliseum (cal. 80). It reveals itself in the excitement of the gladiator's fight to the death, and again in the pleasure and excitement of the cock fight, the dog fight, in the bull ring, and in the grim satisfaction of the public at executions and the strident call for the death penalty. Public participation decreases individual guilt, as seen in the lynch mob, or spectators at the French Revolution guillotine killing of eighteen thousand people, or the National Basketball Association riot on November 26, 2004.

Witnessing a dog-pack killing frenzy (as did the author) is rather awesome and unsettling—the dogs run from one animal to another in the barnyard and rip out the throats of chickens, then the ducks, and then the pet goat. They are not hungry and do not eat the prey but are in a state of great excitement. Notably, each kill does not slow down the pack but instead intensifies the frenzy and leads to further killing (e.g., the Japanese in Nanking and Manchuria in the 1930s). The behavior seems primitively instinctual but may subserve tribal bonding. The blood-lust excitement is contagious and insatiable and, in its human expression, is cheered on by the curious excitement of the spectator crowd. In the boxing ring, the rules prohibit actual killing and instead allow only the nearest thing possible to it—unconsciousness, bleeding, torn flesh, shock, and brain concussion.

In psychotherapy or psychoanalysis, as well in deep spiritual work, the rule is that the victim cannot transcend an impulse or instinctual drive unless they drop denial, own it, and stop projecting the repressed, forbidden impulse onto others. Diagnostically, Jihad is religiously sanctioned blood lust. It takes glee in blowing up buses full of children and destroying the innocent. This primitive instinct has no intention to stop or wars would have ended centuries ago. The primitive, evolutionary origin of the ego is still very much alive. The era of the dinosaur is not over but lives on, very much alive in today's headlines. Freud termed this atavistic drive as the death instinct, or "Thanatos," which is overruled in normal people by "eros," the life instinct. Thanatos expresses as suicide, the impulse to jump from windows, or throw oneself off a cliff. (Nine did so in the Grand Canyon in just one year.) One thousand have jumped off the Golden Gate Bridge. Others have crashed their motorcycles, etc. This is exemplified in human culture by the symbol of the skull and crossbones.

The religious precedent and justification for Islamic terrorism was unfortunately provided by Muhammad himself who, at the time of the writing of the Koran, calibrated in the 700s, but then, because of temporal lobe epilepsy, by age thirty-eight, he had fallen to consciousness level 130, taken up the sword, and begun the killing of infidels, which has continued ever since. After the battle of Medina, one of the first groups that he killed was made up of Jews (the clan of Qurayzah).

Fear and oppression still characterize Islamic countries today, and by comparison, their cultures still remain seriously primitive. Unfortunately, the entire Middle East calibrates below 200, which has unpleasant connotations. It means that its travesties are unlikely to be terminated or to be responsive to reason or appeal to morality or ethics, much less political rhetoric (i.e., the behaviors are clinically "ego-syntonic").

Politically, Islam is theocratic. The word "Islam" means surrender and submission. Islam believes the Koran should be the only law and political structure and is therefore antithetical to democracy. Turkey, however, represents a workable compromise because of the influence of Ataturk.

Of serious importance is that, whereas in America, fifty-one percent of the population calibrates over 200, worldwide, that figure is only twenty-two percent, and in the Middle East and Arab countries, the figure is even lower among subpopulations. Thus, in the problematic cultures, seventy-eight percent or more of the population operates from nonintegrous motives and is unable to respond to or even recognize rationality or give it credence. The significance is that such cultures need to be dealt with at their own level, which is, very visibly, predominantly that of self-interest, and self-interest alone. The rule in psychotherapy, psychoanalysis, spiritual teaching, or in any other educational endeavor is that the process does not start from where "you" are but from where "they" are and then works upward from there.

The civilized world is ruled by reason (the 400s). The less evolved are ruled by emotionalized self-interest and need to learn that ethics, morality, concern for others, and integrity are paradoxically quite beneficial in that they bring prosperity and mutual gain. In Western civilized cultures, this is the wisdom that has been painstakingly gained after centuries of effort and self-discipline.

Of significance is that the general population of Arabic countries is relatively poor and therefore a fertile ground for proselytization by extremists. The families of suicidal terrorists are even given financial rewards. The wealth of the Arabic world stems primarily from oil reserves that produce great wealth, which is then siphoned off by the rulers who view the common people with contempt (i.e., as "dogs"). In comparison, in Norway, the economic benefits of oil production accrue for the overall population, which thereby is relatively secure economically. Paradoxically, the great financial worth of Arabic countries is the consequence of the purchase of their oil by the United States and other Western countries. Thus, the Islamic countries are primarily supported by the Western economy.

Whereas the Western world and the United States represent more advanced cultures from which the Arabic world could learn much that is beneficial, the lesson is lost because of the media image of the West (primarily that of the U. S.) as being decadent, immoral, and ungodly. To the more pristine morality of Islamic and conservative societies, the U. S. culture appears to be degenerate, grossly obscene, and decidedly unholy, especially regarding sexuality. This view of Western culture reinforces resistance to "Westernization." In particular is the prominent media exploitation of feminine seduction. Bodily display is viewed as strongly objectionable and immoral. Thus, the West and its flagship, the United States, do not represent an attractive, positive model and are thereby rejected strongly as being decadent and envied but not admired. The resolution of the world's current cultural disparities will require the collective wisdom and intention of all who have, by virtue of good fortune and ethical intention, become more advanced, conscious, and aware. It is therefore a teaching function.

The twin tails of the bombed World Trade Center towers are merely the tail feathers of the ostrich, with its head in the sand, as the United States had prior to World War II and many other catastrophes. Truth supports and defends life. Falsity and illusion bring war and death.

Of practical interest is the role now played in various wars by private military companies (cal. 345) that have major success with far lower casualty rates than ordinary troops. Thus, in Sierra Leone, for example, a few hundred soldiers of Executive Outcomes Co. (at $10 million/year) were able to accomplish what eighteen thousand UN troops were unable to at a cost of $1 billion/year, and with far less casualties. Similar results (such as MPRI in the Balkans) indicate that disciplined private military companies may be of great service to world peace when employed judiciously in preventing conflagrations from spreading and decreasing needless civilian as well as military death rates.

There are more than sixty private military companies operating worldwide (Global Security, 2004). All of them characteristically operate with greater efficiency and humanitarian concern than do military troops because they are guided by voluntary expertise rather than by hatred, political ideology, or messianic leaders who have no concern for human life, much less the means of supporting life, such as food, water, or shelter.

Private military companies reflect the influence of reason rather than passion or revenge and thus sustain as well as inflict greatly diminished losses to both civilians and military factions. They do not indulge in mass retaliatory slaughter. Their calibration (mid-300s) indicates restraint and disciplined rationality. (Insurgent combatants calibrate at 160 or lower.)

Clinical research papers customarily end with a summary of the essential findings of the study, from which practical recommendations are made. From this comprehensive analysis of the human condition over great expanses of time that utilizes the most advanced scientific investigative technique, plus calibrating the levels of truth of the data, the following summation seems appropriate:

We can ask what is the level of the knowledge of politicians (U.S. and worldwide) regarding the important areas about which they legislate and pass laws. The answers are quite revealing and help explain the plethora of unresolved contentious issues.

Subject Matter	Politicians' Knowledge
International Relations	200
Jobs, employment	190
Medical issues	180
Outsourcing	165
Pricing of oil and commodities	180
Taxes	200

From the above, it can be seen that the sources of valuable information for politicians need to come from advisory committees and experts external to the political process itself. Politicians are swayed mostly by current public opinion and propagandized positionalities rather than hard, verifiable facts or truth.

The Persistent Problem of U. S. Intelligence (cal. 190)

From historical analysis by both history and consciousness calibration, faulty U. S. intelligence indicates the persistence of an underlying defect that would indicate the need to understand its origin. The failure to correctly diagnose a situation would be like an orthopedist failing to get X-rays prior to surgery. The cost to the United States and the world is, and has been, staggering in loss of life, agony, financial burden, devastation of cities and whole populations.

The death rate from intelligence failure is enormous (2,400 dead at Pearl Harbor, 3,000 dead from 9/11, hundreds dead from assorted bombings, 1,500 servicemen dead from the Iraqi war, hundreds more U. S. soldiers and civilians killed because of "unsuspected" insurgents). Subsequent to these and many more losses, the culprit is blamed as the evil "enemy," which is like a car owner's leaving their car parked in Manhattan with the doors unlocked and the key in the ignition and then blaming "evil car thieves."

From prior chapters, we learned that seventy-eight percent of the world's population calibrates below 200 and *all* of the problematic countries listed "unfree" calibrate below 200. Thus, analogously, we habitually park the car of the United States in a world of car thieves. The old dictum "an ounce of prevention is worth a pound of cure" seems applicable.

For thousands of years, the survival of regimes and countries has been dependent on intelligence, from the great historic rulers of Asia, to Nazi Germany, to European countries of today (French intelligence currently calibrates at 295). Even corporations and professional sports teams have far more efficient information gathering systems.

History records repeatedly how intelligence or the lack of it decided the outcomes of the great battles of history. With the United States facing a protean enemy that has surreptitiously already invaded numerous countries all over the globe, its future could well increasingly depend on accurate intelligence.

In the past, the U. S. has relied on its enormous retaliatory military potential (based on its huge industrial capacity) and good intentions. In a nuclear world, defensive retaliation may well be immaterial, especially against enemies that are undeterred by death and, in fact, seek and glorify it. Cleaning up after the explosion of a dirty nuclear bomb represents the worst possible scenario, of which the latent attacking forces are acutely aware.

Because of the repeatedly serious consequences of historically faulty intelligence, the question arises as to why it persists, war after war and up to the present-day, "hair-trigger edge-of-the-precipice" potentially explosive U. S. and world situation.

Research on the underlying source of this persistent pattern of failure indicates that it is an ideology that calibrates well below the crucial level of 200, with its political expressions, including legislation. While psychological denial is a simplistic explanation, it is insufficient. The pattern represents the coalition of a number of themes:

1. Pretentious pseudo-piety: "We're above all that." (Quote from current politicians.) Is the Defense Department "above" protecting the country and its people, or is that just a ludicrous pomposity?

2. Misguided liberalism that is unable to accept responsible authority and its necessity as an operational principle in the real world.

3. Misidentifying intelligence operations as "sneaky" and "dirty pool," i.e., misapplication of Marquis of Queensbury Rules in a world of gang-mentality militant cultures and nations.

4. Concern for the "saintly" U. S. image. (How could it be worse?)

5. Inflated egotism and its lack of reality testing, i.e., an idealistic concept of "fairness" to which nobody but the U. S. subscribes. Misapplication of schoolboy ethics (suitable to Polo or playing Cricket) to savage world situations where deception and falsehood are considered the rule, normal, necessary, and a serious responsibility (KGB, MI-6 [Britain], etc.).

6. Politicians seeking personal power via questionable ideologies of the minority rather than serving the majority and the good of the country.

7. Confusing strength with aggression, i.e., missile defense is defense, not attack.

8. The "Peter Principle" expressed in civil service terms (entrenched incompetency).

9. The childish illusion that if we are seen as "good," the world will love us (like mommy and daddy or teachers would). As is obvious from simple observation, the world begrudges any such admiration (e.g., France's anti-U. S. attitude after World War II). Being seen as "superior" triggers resentment, envy, malice, and hatred, e.g., Canada's current anti-U. S. attitude. (Over fifty percent of Canadian children actually see "good" America as evil. So much for a saintly image.)

From the above, it would seem beneficial to re-examine the philosophical, ideological, political, and intellectual bases upon which the defective U. S. intelligence policy and its implementation are based. This is a world in which *all* major countries have extensive intelligence operations. Just ninety miles offshore, Cuba is the key player in worldwide terrorism intelligence. What the world respects is *strength*. Pious superiority is seen as stupid, if not even ridiculous and laughable. Honesty is strength. The world accepts memes necessary for survival. We went into Iraq for survival, not to "save Iraq for democracy" and liberate its people. That is thinly disguised propaganda that the world saw through, therefore causing the U. S. to earn the world's disrespect and actually feed into the "hate America" meme currently popular worldwide. U. S. policy experts need a couple of good psychologists instead of politicians. Every schoolboy knows the "hate the goody-two-shoes" syndrome

Recommendations

As we see from the calibrations of political systems, although democracy calibrates high at 410, it is not quite as high as oligarchy at 415. In the higher calibration range, because the numbers are logarithmic, an increase of five points on the scale actually represents an enormous jump in power. A beleaguered society needs all the horsepower it can get, and therefore, it is suggested that the countries add to their governmental structure an "oligarchic" level (free of politics) equal to or at least strongly advisory to the Cabinet level.

Oligarchy (a term from the pinnacle of ancient Greece) means the confluence of wise, seasoned, experienced, brilliant, accomplished, integrous, balanced, proven, gracious, sagacious, educated, good-will statesmen (cal. 430) rather than politicians (cal. 180). It means mentor, advisor, mature, objective, well-rounded, well-spoken, successful, top level, self-fulfilled, and beyond the desire for gain, whether personal, political, or financial. This is the level of high-calibration experts of their own domains who are beyond neediness and who serve others by simply being who they are and feeling fulfilled by offering and sharing their wisdom.

In recent times, some degree of this wisdom was demonstrated by Switzerland: orderly, low crime, few social problems, lack of political or civil disorder or unrest, trains on time, and noninvolvement in centuries of war by *all* of its neighboring countries. Notable also is that men all have to have one year of military service/training, and becoming a citizen is not an easy process. There are requirements for citizenship, as well as immigration quotas. Until the 1970s, voting was restricted to men over the age of fifty, and sagacity rather than youthful folly has been the prevailing climate in a democracy that has traditionally also been the home of international banking wealth.

In more distant times, the survival of tribes for centuries was ensured by the wisdom of the council of elders. This has also been the style of numerous trade unions and professions as well as world religions and spiritual traditions.

It has been presumed that the presidential cabinet fulfills the role of an oligarchic council, but this is not the case. Cabinet members are appointed based on not just expertise but also party affiliation rather than sagacity. The same limitation applies to political appointees who often do not have specific education or experience.

From history, one can see that civilizations survive, not because of politics, but in spite of them, nor can "public opinion" be relied on in a world where seventy-eight percent of the people calibrates below 200. Even in America, which calibrates higher than any other country on the planet, forty-nine percent of the population calibrates below 200. In addition, fifty percent of the information on the Internet is fallacious.

Of significance is that the group of "Leaders and Revolutionaries" selected by *Time* magazine (see Chapter 9), as well as the United Nations, calibrate in the 170-195 range. This is a nuclear age in which the United States is under siege from an entire foreign militant civilization (cal. 40 to 190), as well as from ideological enemies within who "hate America" and calibrate at about 135. The question arises: Would anyone want a brain surgeon who calibrates at 190 to operate on them or a pilot to be directed by the "vote" of the passengers?

From the viewpoint of morality, America has the responsibility to itself and to the world to have the most advanced intelligence system available, not one of just self-interest, but as an expression of the recognition of integrous stewardship of its great power in the world where intelligence outweighs might.

Of great interest is that very successful corporations function at higher levels than do most government agencies. Fallacious theories and incompetence are quickly dismissed and poor leaders are rapidly replaced. No company would tolerate the haphazard, uncoordinated climate and atmosphere of government agencies that resulted in not just Pearl Harbor and 9/11, but also the bombing of U. S. embassies and the U.S.S. Cole, being "surprised" by a North Korean/Chinese Communist army of five hundred thousand troops in the Korean War, being "surprised" by the resistance of Iraqi insurgents, etc.

No commercial corporation that functions at the level of incompetence that characterizes entire governmental departments could survive. It is likely that private enterprise can outperform government in about every department at a much lower cost. (This statement calibrates at 450.)

This is demonstrated by the example cited of a private military company's outperforming U. N. troops by ten-fold, i.e., at one-tenth of the cost, one-tenth of the time, one-tenth of the number of soldiers, and one-tenth of the casualties, with all the private troops being volunteers! This shows the efficacy of critical factor analysis where real experts diagnose the core of the problem and win with precision. If such private companies had been in charge of the U. S. defense, slipshod incompetence would not have continued for decades. In private industry, if you "blow it," you are out, not re-elected or reappointed.

Is this a realistic view? The facts are commonly known by all professionals, and the difference between the top, the mediocre, and the bottom is very well known. The lives of great numbers of citizens are at risk.

As a consequence of the advancement of human consciousness, it is now possible to discern truth from falsehood. Of equal
importance is that, henceforth, *there are no secrets*. Not only can
truth but also the level of truth be quickly ascertained. Also important is that the technique is limited only to integrous people
for integrous purpose. This is a built-in safeguard by which the
world can become a much safer place and the threats to its safety
can now be rapidly exposed. As an example:

Current Application of Critical Factor, Attractor Field Analysis
International Nuclear Programs (December 2004)

Country	Intention	Capability
United States	460	460
India	200	200
Iran	170-190	160
Pakistan	155	140
North Korea	140	80
Cold-War Russia	120	275
Current Russia	200	200
China	165	170
Egypt	200	140
Islamic Militants	60	60
Islamic Militants plan nuclear attack?	Yes	

Spirituality and War

From the data presented, it is apparent that war is the consequence of both the propagation of falsehood and the absence,
ignorance, or denial of truth. Historically, these conditions were
a certainty because there were no other means of discerning
truth. War brings up moral, ethical, and political debates that
present a problem of prioritization of values vis-à-vis survival
and practicality. Thus, it represents the dilemma of hard choices
of being "between a rock and a hard place." Survival depends on
choosing the lesser of two evils (i.e., triage). This requires some

compromise with idealism, which, although it sounds moral as a principle, often merely represents the hypothetical and not an actual, doable option.

Ethically and spiritually oriented people are often conflicted and confused by the grim realities of war. The most common error is to misidentify spirituality as passivity and thus aid, abet, and invite aggression. From history, as well as consciousness calibration, we see that passivity (cal. 145) encourages aggression and thus represents weakness and not moral superiority. Historically, passivity has resulted in the deaths of tens of millions of innocent citizens for which the pacifist bears moral and karmic responsibility. Thus, passivity is primarily due to ignorance, plus often a narcissistic self-aggrandizement and pseudo-spiritual pose that, unfortunately, frequently has fatal consequences.

On the upside, passivity can represent a form of resistance to negativity and thus pressure resolution (e.g., passive resistance in India via Mahatma Gandhi). Thus, intention and motive are major determinants of consequences and the calibration level of a positionality. In the end, it takes courage and strength rather than the mouthing of pious platitudes and homilies to resolve the forces at work as the specter of the actual occurrence of war arises.

While organized resistance may resolve some conflicts, the results are consequent to the overall situation, such as cultural, economic, and political factors that may or may not be favorable. This can be seen from an analysis of prior wars, where passivity not only did not work but actually triggered war (e.g., World War II).

From the viewpoint of the actual participants in a conflict situation, as contrasted to the viewpoints of the spectators, the rueful comment is that after the protests and peace parades are over, in the end, the true situation and its serious problems have to be handled by the doers, the "hard headed" but ethical, practical realists (cal. 465), who are then subjected to politicized attack, no matter what actions are required.

What is the spiritual/ethical/moral duty of a defender from a kamikaze attack, with its barrage of bullets and bombs? The essence of valor is courage, plus the best ethical behavior that is possible under given circumstances, i.e., pray while you fight and be loyal to comrades and one's duty. With limited options, the truly spiritual resolution thus appears to be a forced compromise with the wishful ideal. This resolution calibrates at 485. When the ethical, responsible position is combined with the quality of love of comrades and country, the calibration rises to 510. When the situation is chosen as a high spiritual option, the choice that can be made is to function as required and totally surrender one's will to God. A rare option then opens up that calibrates at 595 and is the doorway to Enlightenment itself at 600 or over.

While this same opportunity actually exists at every moment of life, it is rarely recognized without a calamitous confrontation. War has thus been paradoxically the very avenue to sudden major spiritual advancement and therefore a great karmic opportunity. Rarely does anyone surrender their life and seeming source of existence (the ego) to God unless confronted by a maximal situation. The stunning consequence of total surrender in the face of likely or certain death is the dramatic and seemingly magical, sudden disappearance of all fear or terror. In its place, one is enveloped in the incredible, all-encompassing omnipresence of a Peace and stillness that is profound and timeless. Thus, "man's calamity is God's opportunity" is factual. The same phenomenon occurs in any seeming disaster situation. In 2003, the Weather Channel reported that a woman who was sucked up into the air during a tornado remarked, "I was suddenly in a still and awesome state of peace while being whirled hundreds of feet into the air."

Although the concept of karma is not familiar or commonplace in the Western world, it is a confirmable reality that calibrates at 999. Karma is a shorthand term for the totality of all factors present at birth, both physical and spiritual (i.e., the calibrated level of consciousness itself). This inheritance is both individual as well as collective, and therefore, every earthling shares in the collective karma of humankind itself and its worldly expressions, of which war is a likelihood. (As previously noted, there has been war during ninety-three percent of man's history on earth. Peace has prevailed during only seven percent of the overall time of civilization.)

The most obvious spiritual opportunity presented by war is that of forgiveness and surrender of the personal will. This stems from compassion for the human condition itself, with its inevitable limitations inherent to the (karmically inherited) ego that includes almost inevitable error and blind ignorance. "They know not what they do" is a clinical and verifiable fact.

That seventy-eight percent of the world's population calibrates below 200 is why the great avatars illuminated the way. The option of spiritual salvation is a positive gift of the human (karmic) inheritance. The wise choose the gift while the foolish squander the opportunity and choose illusion instead. Thus, by heeding Socrates' time-proven dictum that "Man chooses always only what he believes to be the good," hatred is replaced by compassion and forgiveness that thereby turn the opportunity of war into a spiritual gift to oneself and all humankind, which struggles on in a pitifully blind state.

Spiritual people repeatedly ask, "What can we do about war? What should we pray for?" A good prayer would be for all people to see war as a valuable opportunity for worldwide mutual forgiveness and compassion, which is the real road to Peace.

Finalization

To better survive, the country would perhaps benefit from the following inferences from the above study:

1. Form oligarchic advisory councils, in addition to the current political system, to guide in policy and decision-making.

2. Learn how to diagnose malignant messianic narcissism and thereby identify and counter dangerous leaders before they threaten the world.

3. Identify dangerously fallacious ideological trends before they become epidemics.

4. Contract the expertise of very successful private enterprise to conduct vital operations.

5. Develop an accurate, sophisticated intelligence capability utilizing consciousness calibration techniques as outlined

previously, which, if we had had them at the time, could have prevented all the wars of the last century, as well as the deaths of many millions of people.

6. Develop international diplomacy based on precise information obtainable by the now-available technique as described and illustrated in this and previous chapters.

7. Make greater use of trade to form alliances and facilitate cooperation with other countries (e.g., the success of our relationship with China, which only a decade ago was seen as a serious potential threat).

SECTION IV
HIGHER CONSCIOUSNESS AND TRUTH

CHAPTER 16
Religion and Truth

Section 1
World Religions

Introduction

Religion has been respected as a source of truth throughout the ages in all cultures. The consciousness calibration technique documents the spiritual reality intrinsic to the various major religions. In the calibrations that follow, it is important to realize that calibration levels are not a form of judgmentalism. A higher calibration does not imply "better than" but instead reflects the influence of the levels of consciousness of cultures from which the truth of religions historically emerged as well as the level of truth that is being expressed. The value and benefit of any religion is dependent on the motivation of the devotee, and any one of them can be the springboard to advanced mystical states or enlightenment. All, however, start with faith.

History

Research into the facts surrounding religion has resulted in probably the world's most prestigious and scholarly literature. Most investigations, however, have been primarily historically rather than spiritually oriented, resulting in great attention to archeology and documentation of historic events that, although interesting, are often irrelevant as compared to the essence and foundation of truth revealed by the core teachings.

The great religions arose out of the teachings of their founders—the great masters, avatars, and spiritual geniuses of all time. Their essential truths later often became obscured by preoccupation with ethnic, geographic, and cultural observances that are extraneous to the thrust of the teachings themselves and diversionary as well. However, at the same time, they present a cultural historic context with implications as to the meanings conveyed as well as their languaging. Because much of spiritual teaching is subtle and meanings are implied by slight changes of expression or gestures, unfortunately, that kind of information has been lost and, therefore, verbatim statements are sometimes equivocal.

In early primitive and often tribal cultures, the main impact and thrust of major high religious truth was the advent of and then later the prevalence of monotheism, which replaced the multiple pantheons of pagan Roman, Greek, and German origin. Thousands of years before the development of religion in the Western world, the ancient Aryan culture of India had already spawned very advanced spiritual teachings as the foundation of Hinduism. The teachings of the enlightened sages and rishis, who were the source of the Vedas, preceded the appearance of the Buddha by several thousand years, as well as the appearance of Moses, and later, Jesus, and much later, Muhammad.

Formal religion also replaced more primitive pantheism as well as idolatry. In the Native American culture, the presence of God as the source of life was intuited without the interface of a specific avatar or prophet. The awareness of Chief Seattle, as revealed by his very famous address, was at an impressive calibration level of 700. The structure of the Iroquois Nation contributed to the construction of the Constitution of the United States. These phenomena lend credence to the concept of "the natural law," the principle that man was created with the capacity to apprehend the reality of Divinity. Out of this doctrine arose the theological discourse of "vincible" versus "invincible" ignorance.

The Downside of Religion

The limitations of religion have been analyzed by historians from a secular viewpoint and by theologians in their criticisms, as well as by the great philosophers over the centuries. The intrinsic problems arise from the canonization of interpretations of spiritual truth that are the consequence of misunderstanding by the spiritual ego of ecclesiastics. Much is lost in translation of teachings that were not written down until centuries after they were spoken.

While the above are well-known limitations (as reflected by consciousness calibration), less attention has been paid to the relationship of the follower to the religion itself. The most obvious error is the worship of the religion instead of God (an error not made by the truly enlightened mystic). While religion provides inspiration, spiritual facts, and important information, it is only a linear, time-located body of concepts and not the Reality itself. This results in the commonly observed violation of the essential truth of the religion in the name of the religion itself (e.g., Christian and Islamic crusades, the Inquisition, putting nonbelievers to death, slaughtering the innocent in the name of the religion, political piracy of religion by theocratic totalitarianism, and rationalization of nonintegrity in the "name of the faith," etc.).

In a manner of speaking, religiosity is a subtle form of idolatry that puts the Church as an institution above God. The current slaughter of the innocent in the name of Allah the All Merciful is a glaring example. A more subtle example is the exaggeration of the external trappings and ethnic peculiarities of primitive tribal customs that become the focus instead of the core of spiritual truth. Thus, distortions result in oppression and violation of basic religious premises.

The underlying defect in all the above is obviously the downside of the ego itself, which then utilizes religion to its own ends: pride, control, gain, prestige, wealth, adoration, social image, and narcissistic gain. Religion is the means, not the end; it is the map, not the territory; it is the cover, not the book. Thus, hyper-religiosity itself, which appears as piety, can and does become an error as exhibited by scrupulosity. The great teachers taught the Truth about Divinity, not religion, which came centuries later. While the veneration of religion and scriptures is understandable, it is their truth and God that are meant to be worshipped and sought.

Heavens

Research reveals that the nonphysical spiritual heavens (celestial realms) calibrate from 200 on up to Infinite and are comparable to the calibrated scale of the levels of consciousness. Spiritual evolution continues on after the soul leaves the body, and it gravitates to the optimal levels for continued evolution.

Within the celestial levels, there are also subregions for various and diverse spiritual/religious groups that share a specific identification. Thus, the claims of "exclusivity" to Heaven made by various religious groups have a relative, partial validity but are false as a general premise. No group or religion has an "exclusive" on Heaven, but is instead the pipeline to a specific region as a consequence of a shared belief system. No religion has an exclusive on truth, and the claim itself is a limiting fallacy. (This statement calibrates at 985.) That there are "multiple heavens" resolves contentious religious positionalities that have, in the past, been used to intimidate deviations from orthodoxy.

The nonphysical spiritual realms below 200 are traditionally denoted as "astral realms," which are again stratified from higher to middle to lower (the various depths of the "Hells"). The post-mortal fate of the soul, which continues on as conscious subjectivity, is in accord with the absolute justice of Divinity, solely the consequence of the exercise of the spiritual will. Thus, the spiritual fate of the soul is determined by choice and alignment. "Judgment" is therefore a continuous, automatic process. Like a cork in the sea, the soul is positioned by its own intrinsic buoyancy. Divinity is thus the very source and guarantee of freedom itself.

Central to religions is the critical concept and subject of sin and its consequences. While theological discussion about the topic is extensive, it can be pragmatically simplified in the context of consciousness research as human action, alignment, or intention that calibrates below level 200. Thus, sin is aligned with falsity:

Venial sin	190
Mortal sin	180

The level 200 demarcates that which is supportive of life, truth, integrity, and love from that which is the antithesis of these qualities. This level also demarcates the levels of Hell (below 200) and lower astral realms from the heavens and celestial realms. This also demarcates the level that differentiates good from bad in the true meaning that refers to intrinsic qualities (*res externa*) rather than opinion (*res interna/cogitans*). This differentiation can be made with some certainty by means of consciousness calibration because the Scale is in reference to an unvarying absolute that is concordant with Divinity.

All religions and spiritual teachings are in accord and agreement as to the deleterious consequences of true sin, which, by definition, is a violation of truth and therefore calibratable on the Scale of Consciousness. Sin is described as error or trespass, and culpability is related to degrees of ignorance and related capacity for moral responsibility, e.g., vincible and invincible. This is reflected by the options of condemnation or forgiveness and opportunities for repentance, undoing, confession, or compensation by good works.

The difficulty in counteracting the spiritual/karmic consequences of sin is offset by the option of salvation for those who "believe in His name" in Christianity, Hinduism, Islam, and Buddhism. In the celestial realm, the savior is one's advocate before the judgment of God in the afterworlds of nonphysicality. In a benign contextualization, mankind is viewed compassionately as being often intrinsically incapable of transcending the negative forces of the ego if unaided from the earthly/human realm. In the Hindu and Buddhist views, this results in endless cycles of rebirth and entrapment in the earthbound human dimension, with its attendant, inevitable suffering. (Karma calibrates at 999.)

On the Scale of Consciousness, the levels below 200 are inordinately linked with attitudes, emotions, motivations, beliefs, behaviors, and activities that are spiritually and karmically detrimental, which, in this lifetime as well, result in negative consequences and gravities. They are therefore indicative of spiritual pathology.

While many people attempt to handle the problem of guilt, shame, or fear with denial or atheism (which itself is paradoxically an expression of faith and unprovable), when the psychological defenses break down, the inner truth is confrontational at a level of unimagined gravity. The hells are a subjective, experiential reality of awesome and stark degree, as those who have sunk to its depths can attest. The lower levels are experienced as timeless, eternal agony, beyond hope. Redemption by relinquishment of the ego is the only option that remains open due to there being at least an iota of good karma/virtue remaining (cal. 990).

The realities of man's spiritual options have been attested to throughout history. While a serious look at spiritual realities may at first seem intimidating, with greater understanding, they guarantee release from fear as well as provide hope and faith based on reliable knowledge. Everybody has some good karma somewhere in their spirit, no matter how seemingly depraved they may be. All that is required is just a spark that, by inner consent, then bursts into the flame of salvation, redemption, and rebirth. In this experiential lifetime, as well as that of others that have been attested to, it is only necessary to call on God. "Oh, God," is the only spark needed to open the doors to the Presence of God. Thus arose the exclamation "Gloria in Excelsus Deo," with which the books by this author open and close.

Christianity
Early

First Century - "The Way"	980	Prior to Council of Nicaea	840
The Apostles	905-990	After Council of Nicaea	
Gnostics	510	(325 A.D.)	485

Catholicism

Eastern Orthodox	490	Coptic	475

Roman Catholic

Papacy	570	Clergy	490
College of Cardinals	490	Jesuit Order	440
Faith and Liturgy	535	Church (worldwide)	450

Post-Reformation

Amish	375	New Thought	405
Born-again Christians	350	Pentecostal	310
Christian Science	410	Protestantism	510
Episcopalian	510	Puritans	210
Evangelist	385	Quakers	505
Fundamentalist Christian	325	Salvation Army	405
LDS	405	Unity	505

Adherents to Christianity comprise approximately one-third of the world's population, and its basic teachings are familiar to non-Christians as well. Christ is included in Islam as a great prophet and is likewise accorded respect in both the Hindu and the Buddhist cultures. He is also respected as a great prophet in one branch of Judaism (Messianic).

The term "Christ" generically denotes the state of incarnation of Divinity or Christed consciousness. Thus, Jesus, the Christ, is the incarnation of Divinity as man through which Christianity recognizes the Trinity of God the Father, God the Son, and God the Holy Spirit (cal. 945).

Jesus Christ calibrates at 1,000, the maximum level possible in the human domain, and his apostles calibrate in the high 900s. Interestingly, the relics of St. Peter under the altar in the Basilica in Rome calibrate over 900 (similar to the relics of the Buddha currently on public tour that also calibrate in the 900s).

Notable in the calibrations is the very major drop in the level of Christianity from the First Century, where it was in the 800s and 900s, to 485 after the Council of Nicaea in 325 A.D. This was the consequence of the inclusion of the Old Testament (cal. 190) and Revelation (cal. 70) in the official Bible (See Chapter 18). While the fall of man is allegorical (the story calibrates at 60), the downside was naïve belief and consequent emphasis on guilt and sin. With research, the "fall of man" is the emergence of dualistic thinking (i.e., the tree of good and evil), which was the trap man fell into out of a seduction of curiosity. (This explanation calibrates at 975.)

The Papacy as an office, similar to the office of the Dalai Lama, calibrates at 570. However, during the lineage of successive popes over the centuries, two popes actually calibrated below 200. Thus, institutions calibrate differently than do the core teachings of the religions, which again differ from the calibrated levels of their founders.

If we ask what is the ideal calibration for the head of a world church, we get the number 570, which is the current state of affairs. Below 570 there is not enough power to inspire the masses of the world and be immune to the onslaughts of prevalent antireligionists. Calibration levels over 570 indicate the advent of mysticism and imply illumination, which preclude interest or involvement in the necessary affairs of administration.

Over the centuries, churches as institutions perhaps had to accept compromise with basic principles for the sake of survival (e.g., "the good of the faith"). Such decisions are difficult to evaluate centuries later because the context is greatly changed. Major religions are sometimes criticized for failing to respond to passing human events; however, as institutions, they exist on a different timeline upon which worldly events, no matter how serious they may seem, are just passing events. That there is wisdom in such a policy can be ascertained from examining the effect of becoming involved in passing worldly affairs, such as has befallen some American Protestant churches via politicalization that has brought public criticism, such as that by John Leo in *U.S. News & World Report* (October 2004).

In the article entitled "When Churches Head Left," it is noted that mainline Protestant church membership is shrinking due to pro-Palestine, anti-American, and anti-Israel policies, such as divesting of investments that are not in Leftist favor. Also, such organizations as the World Council of Churches and the National Council of Churches fail to address human rights violations in oppressive totalitarian regimes and focus instead exclusively on America and Israel, with no mention of the former Soviet Union,

China, North Korea, Libya, Syria, etc.

Add to the above the effect on the general public of the trendy Episcopalian appointment of a gay bishop that has divided the Episcopal Church that was just recovering from accepting women into the priesthood, and the pedophile scandal of the Catholic church. Thus, it can be seen why traditional religion is losing ground to the social trend of spirituality per se. *Publishers Weekly* reports a public hunger for religious and spiritual truth and books with academic authority (Hilliard, 2004).

Roman Catholicism
Calibrations of Current Positions

As an institution in year 1900	460
As an institution in year 2004	305
Position on contraception	180
("Contraception" itself calibrates at	205)
Theological Theory on Contraception	180
Position on Clergy Pedophilia	125
("Pedophilia" itself calibrates at	135)

The problematic issues are the consequences of seemingly outdated ecclesiastical doctrines that have contributed to the church's decline. Churches are decreasing in number and often five or six in a diocese close up and consolidate. In some areas, due to massive lawsuits, bankruptcy is being declared. The church has declined in moral stature and public opinion due to serious scandals for which the public expects more than a passing insincere "regret" for injuring the lives of many thousands of innocent children. High-profile felonious offenders, instead of being defrocked, are merely shifted to another clerical post with consequent public outrage.

Inasmuch as both poverty and environmental pollution are consequences of overpopulation, the church's overall position on contraception at calibration level 180 contributes unnecessarily to the world problem inasmuch as contraception calibrates at 205, and the spirit does not enter the embryo until the third month

338   TRUTH vs. FALSEHOOD

of gestation. Overall, the problematic rigid ecclesiastic positions result in a world full of nonpracticing ex-Catholics. (It took the church four hundred years to retract the excommunication of Galileo.)

Big institutions, including governments, over time often fall into bureaucratic paralysis and ineptitude and become nonfunctional due to sheer complexity (i.e., Sanskrit *tamas*). The major split in the Christian church resulted from disagreement over church authority, based on disagreement over interpretations of the theology of the Trinity. Consequently, the church separated into the Roman and Eastern Orthodox divisions.

Subsequently, the Church of Rome was perceived to be in error in some of its practices, which led to the onset of Protestantism, the Reformation, and the removal of the belief in the infallibility of the Papacy. The Protestant Reformation was furthered by the invention of Guttenberg's printing press, which provided the availability of the Scriptures to the masses that had been previously limited to the clergy and written only in Latin. Protestantism supported the spreading of the Gospel and its translation into the languages of all countries.

In the calibrations, the numerical differences between the various branches of Christianity do not reflect "better than" or "worse than" but instead signify the level at which truth is to be explained and therefore the accord with an attendant audience. The major denominations, which calibrate primarily in the 400s, include rationality, reason, and intellectual level of expression comprehensible by most people.

The downside of Christianity was the most extreme at the time of the Inquisition, when religiosity degenerated into hysteria and fear. The technical, legal basis for declaring a heretic was actually not the belief held but the refusal to give it up when ordered to do so by church authority (e.g., the example of Galileo). Paradoxically, some aspects of the church came to represent the opposite of the teachings of its founder, whose essence was based on seeing sin as due to ignorance, and mercy and forgiveness as overriding principles, which Jesus demonstrated under the most extreme conditions possible.

Church institutions become vulnerable to error because the human ego is vulnerable (i.e., spiritual ego). Mystics, on the other hand, do not get embroiled in worldly affairs and therefore are not seduced by vulnerable positionalities (i.e., nonduality of ego transcendence).

Religious groups such as Universalist, Nondenominational, Religious Science, and Unity tend to be liberal, easy-going, and non-dogmatic. They are upbeat in that they emphasize the pathway to God through Love, Joy, Peace, and Goodwill rather than through guilt, shame, and penance, which is the downside of older, more "Gothic" Christian religions, both Catholic and Protestant. The liberal "New Thought" religions emphasize tolerance, acceptance, forgiveness, and compassion towards self and others as well as toward other religions. Just as Protestantism was a protest against the downside of Catholicism, these church groups are a development that rejects the downside of Protestantism, which was often overbalanced on the side of "hating sin" or being obsessed with it instead of transcending it by spiritual virtue. Interestingly, Mardi Gras calibrates at 189 and Lent at only 190.

Questions sometimes arise regarding the Mormon Church of the Latter Day Saints (LDS) because of controversy regarding its origins, practices, and the supposed discoveries of documents by Mark Hoffman. The "Salamander Letters" were proven to be bogus as were other supposedly historical documents allegedly discovered by Hoffman, who apparently was a clever counterfeiter. Joseph Smith calibrates over 400 and the LDS Church itself at 405 (consistently verified). Extremist polygamous sects, however, calibrate at 135-140, and polygamy has been outlawed by the Mormon Church since the late 1800s. Despite whatever errors may be involved historically or theologically, the calibration at 405 reflects that Mormons accept Jesus Christ as Lord and Savior, which in itself raises the overall level.

Buddhism

Mahayana	960	Tantric	515
Zen	890	Tibetan	490
Hinayana	890	Won (Won Bulgyo)	405
Lotus Land	740		

The Buddha lived five hundred years before Christ on the border of Nepal in a primarily Hindu culture. As the well-known history says, he was born of royalty and raised in an artificially protected environment by his family that did not want him to be soiled or disturbed by the downside of ordinary civilization. When he escaped this artificial protection and wandered into the streets of the city, he was shocked when he witnessed the suffering of old age, poverty, sickness, and death for the first time. This activated in him an intense desire to reach the ultimate truth of life. He sought out Hindu sages and spiritual groups for study and meditation but, in the end, realized their limitations and left them. By legend, in his determination to reach the ultimate truth, he rejected the then available Hindu teachers and instead sat alone beneath the bodhi tree in intensive meditation. With one-pointedness of mind and intensity of purpose, he progressively surrendered the illusions of the ego (maya). As he drew closer to the ultimate enlightenment, he was beset by demons and went through physical agony, feeling as though his bones had been broken (analogous to Jesus' sweating blood in the Garden of Gethsemane and the physical agonies of many of history's greatest and most celebrated mystics).

At long last, the weakened ego collapsed, the mind became silent, and then the Buddha Nature of universal, nonlinear Oneness as the unmanifest, yet the Source of All Existence, was revealed in its stunning glory. This is actually a "condition" and not a state of mind because mind itself is transcended, revealing the Self, the divine Perusha, Divinity Immanent, the Presence of Divinity as the substrate, the Unmanifest (i.e., Godhead) out of which arises all Creation. Later Buddhism is represented by two main schools, Hinayana (the lesser vehicle) and Mahayana (the greater vehicle), which differ in emphasis.

The teachings of the Buddha spread into the Far East, out of which Zen Buddhism became the best known in the West. Buddhism is benign and views other religions as limitations rather than as rivals. Later, Buddhist sects arose in response to the influence of various teachers and sages. Also, analogous to Christianity, there arose the conceptualization of the Buddha as savior, intercessor, and advocate, as expressed in Lotus Land Buddhism, which is a more practical goal, considering the extreme negativity of human life on this planet during this "Kali Yuga," or rotation of the zodiac. For practical reasons, a devotee strives for sinlessness and purity; therefore, at death, the spirit enters the celestial realm of the Lotus Land, equivalent to Christian heaven, where the Christ-like Buddha intervenes. From Lotus Land, or heaven, which is beyond the extreme negativity of the earthly life, progression of the spirit to Enlightenment is a practicality. Lotus Land and Heaven are viewed as a celestial, spiritual reality earned by karmic merit.

As an offshoot, Tantric Buddhism developed, which became involved with linear conceptualizations, other energy fields, and their esotericism. Thus, it represents a reinvolvement in the linear domain and calibrates lower than pure Buddhism. Paradoxically, although the Buddha proclaimed, "Make no images of me," statues and figurines of the Buddha are a major product available worldwide. By his statement, the Buddha attempted to preclude idolatry, and indeed, the issue of icons was central to the split between Eastern Orthodox and Roman Christian churches. This preclusion of images and icons is also common to Islam as well as Judaism.

In practice, most communities are quite hospitable to Buddhist groups and commonly help them celebrate the building of a stupa, or holy shrine. The Buddhist compassion for all of life earns it respect, and Buddhist teachings are made familiar to ministerial students in schools of Divinity, such as the Unity School of Christianity. The Dalai Lama is widely respected, as is his quote: "It is not enough for religious people to only be involved with prayer; rather, they are morally obliged to contribute all they can to solving the world's problems." This quote, in just one sentence, clarifies why Mahayana Buddhism, which is concerned with the enlightenment and seduction of sentient beings, calibrates higher (960) than Hinayana Buddhism (890), which is focused primarily on just one's own enlightenment.

The mutual respect between Christianity and Buddhism is also reflected in the formation of *avant-garde* groups of monks who, tongue-in-cheek, call their groups' orientation "Zen Catholicism." Oddly, Zen, which is actually a branch of Mahayana, calibrates somewhat lower overall than Mahayana itself. The reason is still unclear except that it perhaps became an "institution." Some current American rishis also misidentify satori states, which are temporary, with enlightenment, which is permanent. Zen in the West is at 755.

Hinduism
Ancient

Senatana Dharma (Eternal Truth) of Rishis	925	Aryan	910
Dravidian	905	Vedanta	855

The Yogas

Bhakti	935	Kundalini	510
Raja	935	Kriya	410
Jhana	975	Surat Shabd (Sahaj Marg)	495
Karma	915	Hatha	390

Others

Hare Krishna	460	Sikhism	600
Subud	470	Janism	495
Tamil Siddah Vedanta	550	Radhasoami	475

Hinduism, and its expression as the classic yogas, is the most ancient religion and reached high levels of perfection probably before 5,000-7,000 B.C. The entire culture and way of life in India reflect religiosity. Funeral pyres are seen along the banks of the Ganges River, along with rites honoring Shiva, and millions of Indians bathe in the waters. The pantheon is confusing to Westerners, and Brahma, Vishnu, and Shiva reflect various aspects of God. These are further reflected in the lesser gods, such as Dirga and Ganesh, the elephant god. The inclusive mentality of India is not well understood from the traditional Western viewpoint of the Newtonian paradigm of reality with its customary, circumscribed, logical construction. In Hindu culture, Divinity is expressed more as a holographic panoply of points of observation, and the reflection is the consequence of the point of view of the observer. Thus, God is not a definable or a limited concept, as signified by the triune of Brahma, Vishna, and Shiva.

Because Divinity is the source of all that exists, it is reflected in all that exists; therefore, it can be seen in painting, art, nature, dance, the feminine, the masculine, the animal, and the changes of nature. The illusory, apparent creation and dissolution of phenomena are displayed by the well-known Dance of Shiva, which is represented worldwide in that famous statue that depicts the effect of the selection of the point of view on what is observed, i.e., whether a phenomenon is constructive or destructive is merely a reflection of whether the event is desired or not desired, and neither construction nor destruction is innate to reality (i.e., limited to *res cogitans*).

The various yogas are not general theological belief systems but generically denote the main pathways to God and the realization of the self as Divinity Immanent. This is in contrast to most Christians who believe that God is transcendent, whereas, contrastingly, the core of Hassidism reflects the awareness that Divinity is present in all that exists.

The yogas address the primary pathways to spiritual realization through the heart and devotion, or past the mind, *Advaita*, and nonduality, and through selfless service, purification, karma yoga, and meditation. These facilitate the rising of spiritual energy up through the chakra system to the crown chakra, and then on up through the purely spiritual energy bodies (Causal, Buddhic, Christ, and Atmic), which have in turn foci of energy analogous to the chakras (i.e., spiritual vision ensues from the "opening of the third eye of the Buddhic body").

The Hindu religion is so broad and all encompassing that it benignly welcomes all spiritual seekers for it has the tolerance and confidence born of the sheer ancientness of reaffirmation by a series of mystics over millennia.

Because of Hinduism's protean expressions and diversity of teachers and techniques, it has an exotic appeal to many Westerners. A downside is that the world abounds with pseudo-gurus and swamis who are not only adept but also quite expert at imitating the genuine (see next chapter).

Islam

Sufism	700	Shi'ite (Muslims)	250
Sunnite	255	Wahhabism	30

As with all religions, the calibrated level of the mystics is characteristically considerably higher than that of formal religion itself, and the Sufis reflect that level of transcendence of the linear domain. The difference between the Sunnites and the Shi'ites is reflected in current history in that area of the world where the far-right fundamentalists tend to be militant and aggressive. The declaration of "Jihad," with its projected hatred of Christianity and America as the great Satan, calibrates at 60-90, and thereby rejects the teachings of the Koran, which calibrates at 700. Thus, the term "Jihad" negates its own claim to be "holy."

The defect of the far-right position of any religion is the activation of spiritual zealotry. True spiritual integrity comes from courage in the promotion of truth. Therefore, that is reflected in the energy of the heart as devotion to one's spiritual beliefs. Spiritual hatred, however, comes out of the spleen, which then triggers the release of animal-type behaviors. This is further energized by the promises of a warrior heaven (a belief that was prevalent also in the Vikings who thought that death and battle would send them to Valhalla). The promise to naïve, uneducated, impressionable young Islamic terrorists that in death they will go to a heaven where "seventy virgins" will reward them is certainly inventive and seductive to young men, many of whom are barely teenagers. Actually, it is spiritual seduction and exploitation (calibrates as "true") by power-seeking leaders.

The fall of Islam is the subject of extensive studies (Forsyth, 2004), from its highest expressions to its decline in the 1600s into its current dark ages or downward spiral of hate and spite, rage and self-pity, poverty and oppression (Lewis, 1990).

The current state of affairs is vividly documented in the book *Inside the Kingdom* by bin Laden's former sister-in-law, Carmen bin Laden, which reveals the daily life of women in the bin-Laden-supported Islamic world of today's Iran, in which women are captives and Westerners are held in contempt (C. bin Laden, 2004).

Although early militant Islam lost influence after Kara Mustafa's defeat at Vienna in 1683, the more serious decline began 300 years ago with the emergence of the Islamic cult of Wahhabism (cal. 30), initiated by its founder Muhammad ibn Abdul Wahhab (cal. 20), out of which emerged HAMAS (cal. 40), founded by Sheik Ahmad Yassin (cal. 35), al-Qaeda (cal. 30), and the current Jihad (cal. 30) of bin Laden (cal. 40).

The severely extreme view replaces former Islamic tolerance for all "people of the book" (the sons of Abraham) with a blanket condemnation of all people on earth (except its own followers), including ninety percent of Islamic members. All deserve death as "idolaters" ("mushrikun"). The impact on political leaders can be seen, for example, by the fall in the consciousness level of Arafat from its prior level of 440 to its final level of 65.

It is important to note that the founder of HAMAS, Sheik Ahmad al-Hassin, calibrates at 35, Muhammad ibn Abdul Wahhab calibrates at an ominous 20, and that Jihad, Wahhabism, and al-Qaeda all calibrate at 30-65. Islamic martyrdom calibrates at 60; religious fanaticism is at calibration level 80; desecrators of truth are at level 35, and malignant, messianic narcissism is at calibration level 30. These are also the calibration levels of serial murderers and killer-mutilators. Thus, as bizarre as it may seem to rational people, Wahhabism declares holy war against *all* mankind except for its own members, who were spawned out of its diverse current bases of the Arabic world.

Of historical note is that King Faisal of Saudi Arabia calibrated at 480. Thus, Nixon's reneging on his promise to King Faisal to be "fair and even-handed" in dealing with Israel and Islamic countries can be seen with the wisdom of hindsight to have been an error whereby he alienated the Arabic world by giving two billion dollars to Israel for arms. This move fostered anti-Americanism and Islamic cultural bonding, with its resultant concordance of attitudes. This favored the enculturization of terrorism as a laudatory lifestyle in the predominately anti-U.S. climate. There was already enough anti-American sentiment abroad to provide fertile ground to spread the fires of Islamic-based xenophobia and hatred. It is unlikely that pacifism and denial will suffice to offset such a militant trend.

The historical precedent for a Jihad has been explained elsewhere and was set by Muhammad himself. At the time he dictated the Koran circa 610 AD, at age 35 (not at age 40, as alleged by some historians), his level of consciousness was above 700. At age 38, his consciousness level fell very dramatically to far below 200, down to 130. He took up not the spiritual sword of truth but the physical sword of militarism. Roughly thirteen hundred years later, the misinterpretation of religious truth continues, accelerated by the fanaticism of Wahhabism. Now, instead of swords, the weapons are bombs and the blowing up of thousands of noncombatant civilians and schools filled with children. It is hard to imagine how that can be held as heroic or praiseworthy in any culture. In contrast, chivalry calibrates at 465.)

In the United States, politicalization of Islam is rampant, and New York Congressman Peter King stated (February, 2004) that extremists control eighty percent of the mosques, thus casting suspicion on Islamic converts, especially if they are young males. There is a strong likelihood of radicalization of converts to "prove themselves," reinforced by an unconscious death wish energized by indoctrination that voluntary death is a glorious sacrifice that necessitates killing infidels. In the United States, the radicalization rate is ten percent, which rises to twenty percent in European countries, and to forty percent in Arabic countries (calibrates as "true"). These teachings are directly those of Wahhab and Qutb. (See Sperry, *Infiltration*, 2005.)

The political pirating of Islam that threatens today's world is consequent to the writings of its influential philosopher, Sayyid Qutb, whose role is comparable to that of Karl Marx and communism. His influential role was described in a major article in the *New York Times Magazine* (March 23, 2003), entitled "The Philosopher of Islamic Terror—Sayyid Qutb," who calibrated early at 420 but later fell to calibration level 75. He provided the philosophic basis for al-Qaeda with the interpretation of the Koran published as *In the Shade of the Qur'an* (cal. 90).

Crucial to both Wahhab and Qutb's serious misinterpretations of the Koran (problems of the Koran itself are discussed in the next chapter) is the critical and disastrous misinterpretation of the word "sword." (The same error has been made by some Christian sects over time.) In spiritual reality and language, "sword" means the Sword of Truth, not the physical sword, which results in a meaning that is completely diametrically opposed to the teachings of all the great avatars, saviors, and prophets. The barbarian world was already ruled by massacre of the innocent by the sword, so slaughter was hardly needful of encouragement by saviors and prophets of Allah. Truth, mercy, and forgiveness are the pathways to God. Paradoxically, each verse of the Koran starts with the statement "In the name of Allah, the All Merciful." The way to God is through the heart of love, not the spleen of hatred.

The major thrust of this work is that it defined suicidal terrorism as a virtue, radicalized Islamic fundamentalism, and supported its spread throughout the Arab world in a united Pan-Arabism that seeks to establish a world theocracy. Osama bin Laden and al-Qaeda are dominated by the ego inflation of messianic triumphalism based on the ideologies of Qutb, which extol the virtues of martyrdom and demonize Christianity as heretical and therefore virtuous to destroy. He also romanticizes sacrificial death and urges young followers to actually seek it. Thus, his influence has been not only divisive but has also cast a shadow over all of Islam. It is this influence that surfaced as

9/11, the Iraqi war, the killing of civilians, bomb explosions and attacks worldwide, and changed the lifestyles in all countries. Far worse events are planned and already in preparation.

The fascist right-wing politicalization of Islam is reflected in the power-dominant religio-political leaders of recent times, such as Ayatollah Khomeini (cal. 75) and now Shi'ite Grand Ayatollah Ali Husseini Sistani (cal. 125), who, when coupled with Osama bin Laden (cal. 40), the Taliban (cal. 65), and al-Qaeda (cal. 65), may be problematic to the Western World.

The dark ages of Christianity lasted hundreds of years, during which an estimated fifty to eighty thousand "heretics" were put to death by the Inquisition. (Some estimates are in the millions.) Hopefully the dark ages of Islam will pass more quickly. Perhaps such eras serve some karmic or evolutionary purpose.

Judaism

Hasidism	605	Conservative	550
Messianic	605	Reform	550
Reconstructionist	555	Orthodox	545

Judaism is universally recognized as one of the world's primary and strongest religions that have withstood countless centuries of endless attack. The hostility of Christianity toward Judaism is rather paradoxical in that the Christian Bible includes the Old Testament and considers it a source of religious authority. This unfortunate twist of fate comes from the regrettable circumstances in which the Jewish Sanhedrin (cal. 205) turned Jesus over to the Roman secular authorities. Although the technical charge was that of a heresy, another factor was that Jesus was seen as a revolutionary who threatened the authority and power of the priest class that then acted out of self-interest in a culture that was already primitively punitive.

As with other religions, the highest calibrations are those of the mystics (see Zohar at 905 in the next chapter). The high calibration of Hasidism reflects the recognition of Divinity as the Source of All Existence and its endeavor to become conscious of the presence of Divinity in the details of everyday life. The

Messianic branch also calibrates quite high because it includes recognition of the avatar status of Jesus, the Christ.

Over the centuries, anti-Semitism was based on blaming Judaism for the death of Jesus, plus the fact that they rejected Jesus Christ as the promised Messiah. Thus, anti-Semitism was not unique in that major Semitic religions viewed each other as rivals and heretical nonbelievers, amplified by cultural and political differences.

The really virulent anti-Semitism of the last century was inflamed by a quite delusional publication that emerged in the early 1900s, entitled *The Protocol of the Learned Elders of Zion* (Nilus, 1905; later trans. Marsden, 2003), which calibrates at an ominous level of 90. This fallacious document purported to expose a worldwide conspiracy by Jews to take over control of the world, the banks, the monetary system, etc.

The authoritative style of presenting spurious suppositions was convincing to many readers, and it spread anti-Semitism throughout Europe, forming the ideological background for Nazi anti-Semitism. Unfortunately, it was accepted as truth by many influential people, even in the United States, and this specific document was the basis for Henry Ford's well-known anti-Semitism. Ford circulated copies of it to other influential people who thus fell into the belief of an international conspiracy (conspiracy theories in general calibrate at 160). Although Ford changed his mind later in his life, the anti-Semitism had been picked up by hate groups in the U. S., where it still smolders despite the major worldwide revolt against anti-Semitism that resulted from the exposure of the Nazi concentration camps and their extermination of six million Jews in Europe.

Anti-Semitism has decreased very markedly in the U. S. since World War II but it is on the rise again in Europe, fueled by Muslim extremists, aided and abetted by political propaganda and social theories. White-supremacist groups are considered by the U. S. mainstream to be the "lunatic fringe."

Other Religions

Shinto	350	Taoism	500
including Sumari code	190	Baha'i	365
including Bashido code	180	Native American	500

Shinto, at 350, is integrous in concept. The downside is the glorification of the warrior archetype, which, as previously mentioned, has the disadvantage of energizing the spleen in addition to the solar plexus and the heart. This easily leads to savagery and the butchering of innocent civilians in the release of the blood lust out of the deep, unconscious, primitive Id. This can also lead to the glorification of savagery, as revealed by the Japanese military ravages of the Pacific and the Far East in the 1930s, and later during World War II, with its death marches, starvation deaths of prisoners, and the slaughter of millions of innocent Chinese civilians, including infants. All of this blood lust was supposedly for the glorification of the emperor, who was believed to be the descendent of the Shinto sun god. The kamikaze pilot (cal. 390) reflected the integrous warrior who sacrificed his life for God and country in contrast to fanaticism, which calibrates at 60.

Taoism

Other than the familiar symbol of Yin/Yang, few Americans were aware of Taoism until Fritzof Capra published *The Tao of Physics* (1976). Ideologically, to a society that lauds assertion and aggression, nonresistance seems weak, passive, and a foreign concept. It was not understood or accepted as having any functional validity until Mahatma Gandhi, whose nonviolent stance eventually defeated the British Empire and liberated India from colonialism, demonstrated its effectiveness. The effectiveness was again demonstrated by Nelson Mandela in South Africa, and in America by Martin Luther King's civil demonstrations. There is Christian precedent in the teaching of Jesus to "turn the other cheek," and in Buddha's teaching of detachment and his statement that there is no point in hating one's enemies as they will bring themselves down of their own nature. Despite localized uprising, the relative nonresistance of the Jews in Europe to their destruction by the Nazi regime thereby allowed the full karmic responsibility to fall upon the conquerors. They realized that Judaism would survive that onslaught as it had all others over the past centuries.

Aggression can be seen as a short-term response to a challenge and nonresistance as long term. The populace of occupied countries need only wait out the domination of the invaders who eventually either leave or become integrated into the culture of the occupied country, such as the Roman army at Hadrian's Wall, where they simply married the local women and settled down to domesticity.

From a consciousness/spiritual viewpoint, the strengths of Yin and Yang are identical and equal, and the Yin/Yang symbol reflects the importance of balance in which interactive forces shape and define each other. In Western culture, this was most obvious in the male/female relationship. Traditionally, the male stereotype is aggressive and the female passive. In an earlier agrarian society that rewarded aggressiveness, male dominance was seen as superior, but as civilization advanced, neither is now seen as having more value than the other. Genderization became ingrained, however, in even language itself, as in German and other languages where all nouns are male, female, or neutral. In America, there has been much social discourse over the relationship of the feminine and the masculine, their balance, and their representations, e.g., men were advised to "get in touch" with their Yin feminine side, and women with their Yang male aggressive side, etc. In Nature, however, there is nothing more aggressive than the female's protecting her young.

Bahá'í

As the calibration indicates, the central intent is integrous to represent the spiritual core of all faiths and the ecumenical ideal. Bahá'í is also attractive in that from its very founding, it was based on the equality of men and women. The capacity of the world's great religions to coexist peacefully side by side is represented by the culture of India, which serves as a laudable teaching example as was pointed out by the Dalai Lama in early 2004. Bahá'í arose out of the teachings of Bahá'u'lláh, an Iranian who declared himself to be "He whom God shall make manifest" as the forerunner of peace via unification of the world's religions and peoples.

Bahá'í has been under attack in Iran since the rule of the Ayatollah Khomeini who, in 1991, signed the government document to extinguish Bahá'ís and demolish the House of Ba'b in Shiraz, which had been a center for worldwide pilgrimage for Bahá'ís. Bahá'ís are now viewed by militant Islamics as heretics and therefore deserving of elimination even though they are fellow Iranians (*New York Times*, 9/12/04).

Native American

There is a dearth of authoritative information and research on Native American spirituality in spite of the fact that it is one of the predominant and attractive characteristics of that culture. The high calibration (500+) reflects the acknowledgment of God as the Great Spirit/Creator and source and essence of all life, which is therefore held to be sacred.

The acknowledgment of the Divine as the source of all blessings and sustenance is part and parcel of daily life. To seek to commune with Divine will via the peyote ceremony is respected as are the sweat lodge purification ceremonies of spiritual cleansing and self-honesty. The act of sacrificing an animal life for food is also sanctified by prayer, which acknowledges the oneness of all life. Family and honor are established values as are courage, truth, and bravery encouraged as character traits.

In the 1970s, the author had the privilege of being invited to the sacred Hopi Snake Dance ceremony. There had been a long drought and the corn was struggling to survive, even though the seed was planted in Hopi style six inches deep, along with a piece of fish. The ceremony took place in old Oraibi. People crowded the rooftops and then, just prior to the start by the Antelope Dancers, the elders arrived and took their seats of honor. Even though it had not rained in many months, they all carried umbrellas! The reason soon became apparent—as the Antelope Dancers began, clouds formed in the sky, which later darkened rapidly when the Snake Dancers began to circle about, holding live rattlesnakes in their mouths. They sprinkled corn meal on the ground and, one by one, let the snakes go to crawl through it and then on into the crowd of onlookers. The snakes approached very closely and then slithered away. Calm prevailed. And then, after the prolonged, relentless, scorching drought, rain began to fall—but not on the gathered celebrants, only just past the nearby cliff, precisely onto the corn fields far below. It did not rain elsewhere but only on the acres of corn plants. It was the last Snake Dance to which white people were admitted since some of them had been disrespectful in the past.

The elders had brought umbrellas because the Snake Dance had always brought rain; they were not at all surprised. Their certainty and lack of doubt intensified the group intonation and expectation, combined with faith and gratitude.

Religion and Traditional America

In traditional America, religion was a Sunday morning event, and out of respect, all bars and liquor stores were closed until noon. Sunday was the Sabbath and therefore all stores were closed, as they were on the afternoon of Good Friday. Jewish people observed Saturday as their Sabbath and their shops were closed as they were on Jewish holidays.

Protestant, Catholic, and Jewish places of worship were respected, as were their respective religious schools. Each of the three denominations was respected for its benevolent works and each funded and ran hospitals and humanitarian charities. They supported well-run charitable clinics to which the medical community donated its services. Government and politicians maintained a respectful hands-off attitude, as the charities saved local governments sizable sums of money and provided needed public services.

Charitable hospitals and their clinics were protected from litigation and the hazard of malpractice suits. Emergency rooms were strongly staffed by resident physicians that were backed up by rotating consultants. Any medical malfeasance was handled by the local medical society from which expulsion ended a doctor's career. Charitable Christian hospitals were run by nuns and regulated by the local diocese. All of the charitable institutions were heavily funded by philanthropy and bequests. Successful industrialists and companies were major benefactors. The relationships between religious parochial schools, medical institutions, philanthropy, and the public, including local government, were generally harmonious and mutually beneficial. The overall system calibrated at 415 (prior to 1959).

The concept of charity was integrous as a fundamental religious virtue and social attitude of goodwill, selfless service, and benevolence. With the rise of egotism in the 1960s, pridefulness began to see charity as "demeaning," and so the burden of the costs of public service was gradually shifted to the taxpayer.

During the 1960s and subsequent decades, the system was progressively secularized and dismantled by political and legal inroads. Overall costs skyrocketed to what are now the highest of any country in the world (fifteen percent of the GNP). The system declined from calibrated level 415 to the level of 195 for the current system. The same disparity is seen in nursing homes. Those run by church groups (e.g., Samaritan) calibrate at 410, whereas those run by business-oriented corporations calibrate at 195.

Secular regimentation of humanistic activities brings down the calibration level of intention and paradoxically increases the cost while the level of the overall system drops precipitously. In the U.S., the quality of individual medical practice is still high overall at 430-440. The expanding "cultural creative" segment of society is attracted to spiritually oriented practitioners who, as a group, calibrate at 499, or approximately seventy points higher than secular medicine. (They also have a twenty-two percent higher recovery rate in their patients despite having a greater caseload of difficult and chronic patients that are resistant to traditional, strictly medical-model treatments.)

Experientially, the author's spiritually oriented holistic practice of psychiatry became the largest in the United States and eventually required fifty employees, twenty-five offices, plus research and clinical laboratories and attracted patients from all over the world. Its research department had one of the first computers, a huge machine that required a specially air-conditioned room and a direct electrical power line. The practice also provided specialized programs for 12-step groups as well as an Attitudinal Healing program based on the model initiated by Dr. Gerald Jampolsky, author of *Love is Letting Go of Fear*. (Jampolsky, rev. 1988) These family spiritual programs were provided at no cost, and the clinic itself, which had two thousand patients and treated one thousand new patients each year, charged reduced fees on a low-to-moderate cost basis. The clinic was financially self-sustaining and received no public funding. (It calibrated at 499.) Results of the innovative holistic treatment for relatively difficult, chronic, and hopeless patients were reported in many lectures, professional papers, worldwide articles (Hawkins, 1968-1981), and in book form (Hawkins and Pauling, 1973).

Spirituality and religion also have a positive impact on family health and overall social behavior, including children's school performance, deportment, and a lower dropout rate. There are lower rates of marital conflict and violence, fewer suicides, fewer arrests, less drug use, and lower divorce and unemployment rates. There is also a lower incidence of illnesses and accidents. The overall benefit is so striking that a reviewer concluded that "religion is warranted, even if just for its social benefits" (Robb, 2003). Overall, people who attend church tend to be more conservative, as noted by public opinion polls (CNN News, December 2003).

Atheism

Atheism represents a belief system about religion and God that covers a wide spectrum. It is also commonly characteristic of a phase of life, although in some people, it may be a life-long position. An in-depth study would be too extensive to be included here, but the primary characteristics can be calibrated since the subject is actually very important. It has, of course been examined in depth by theologians, historians, psychologists, and psychoanalysts. (See Adler, M., 1976-1980; Feuerbach, 1891; Freud, 1910-1963.)

Although the integrous skeptic or agnostic who is honestly in self-doubt calibrates at 200, the majority of atheistic positions calibrates very low. These range from ignorance and indifference to anger, resentment, and hatred of God by militant atheism at calibration level 25. If we ask what is the calibration of the karma of rebuking God or the great Avatars, the calibration levels are 20 to 40, although some of these anti-God positions are merely rejections of the anthropomorphic Old Testament depictions of God as being prone to anger, jealousy, favoritism, etc.

The psychological matrix of atheism has been well described by Feuerbach and others as the rejection of the father figure, as was the case with Karl Marx. Anger at the father figure for being less than perfect is also a factor with political expressions as pointed out by Coulter (2003). Disillusionment results in narcissistic resentment towards all authority figures. The psychology of atheism is well covered by Vitz (1983-2000), a professor of psychology at New York University (excellent 10-page summary available on the Internet).

From the viewpoint of the evolution of consciousness, atheism results from the refusal or inability to let go of the illusion that the narcissistic care of the ego is sovereign and is the source of one's life and existence. This persistence of a dualistic self-image is a consequence of the ego's basic structure, as discussed previously. One reason computer games are so popular is that they reinforce the illusion of "being in control" and thus sovereign and the "captain of one's soul." (The poem *Invictus* calibrates at 170.) Atheism is also to be differentiated from freethinkers (cal. 335) or uncommitted theists, such as those who were the designers of the United States Constitution.

The relinquishment of the illusion of self-sovereignty is the essence of the "hitting bottom" experience that is transformative and to which millions of people testify. It is also the crux of a true conversion experience, as well as a major consequence of the near-death experience. Curiously, atheism is based on faith, but on faith in falsity (the ego, intellect) and cannot be overcome except by an act of the Will.

The Will (Cal. 850)

Although there are extensive writings on psychology and all aspects of mental functions, there is a relative dearth of information on the human will itself. Its importance is overlooked even in psychoanalysis and most spiritual writings, although its function is critical to the advancement of consciousness, spiritual and religious development, and the steps to Enlightenment itself. The intrinsic power of the Will is denoted by its extremely high calibration at level 850; thus, it has the power to overcome all lesser positionalities and belief systems.

The basis of the power of the Will is that it is a function of the Spirit and not the mind, intellect, or emotions. It is thus unique as a human faculty. The mind ceaselessly sifts options and choices, coming to conclusions and chosen premises, but they are merely linear constructs with limited intrinsic power (i.e., logic, reason, and intellect calibrate in the 400s).

Everyone is familiar with resolutions that quickly fail, and changes of behavior turn out to be easier to formulate than to implement. Addictions are far more prevalent than the commonly recognized ones of alcohol, drugs, etc. In fact, almost everyone has multiple intransigent "habits" that are really quite strongly ingrained, as most people ruefully discover when they try to change a mode of conduct or emotional propensity, such as resentments, fearfulness, strong desires, or habitual emotional responses, e.g., shyness or chronic anger.

Unaided, the mind is too weak and ineffective to bring about major change; even "genius" calibrates at only 499. There are many geniuses and remarkably prominent people of great accomplishment whose personal lives are disastrous, and the public cannot understand why celebrities end up as suicides ("she had everything to live for"). Thus, a self-destructive pattern, which is easily recognized by the intellect, in practice can be an insurmountable obstacle that destroys not only happiness and family or career but also physical life itself.

Hopelessness, suffering, and pain, however, may be the final straw that breaks the ego's back, and in despair, the person invokes the only possible last source of power itself by turning to God, Divinity, and the spiritual domain by whatever name it may be addressed, a "power greater than myself," and to which surrender accesses a whole new dimension that, by calibration, begins at consciousness level 500.

The ego is very strong and interested only in its own survival. It will willingly sacrifice a person's physical existence, i.e., it says, "I would rather die than surrender" (give up its sovereignty). Humility is anathema to the ego. Some people even knowingly choose to go to hell rather than surrender to God (e.g., career criminals, Mafia "hit men," serial murderers). Timothy McVeigh, on his way to execution, declared he knew he was going to hell for willfully killing the innocent. (In the office one day, a hopeless patient begged for help. When told that the only option was joining a faith-based group, he said, "I'd rather die," and so he did.)

From all the above, as attested to by human experience, the human ego cannot be overcome except by an act of the Will, which alone can choose to open the gates to Divine Power. This is because of the perfect Justice of Divinity by which everyone is the sole determinant of one's own fate, which also determines possible options.

The key element to the empowerment of the Will is consent. This act of surrender (see Tiebout, 1949) allows for the miraculous, which is a bifurcation of the life process (as described by nonlinear dynamics and the Heisenberg principle). The intention then intensifies the emergence of potentiality into experiential existential reality. This is also the mechanism described at length in the famous *A Course in Miracles* (1975). It is also the critical first step in Alcoholics Anonymous and other faith-based groups that admit, "without God's help, we were hopeless and helpless" (*Alcoholics Anonymous*, 2000).

Note that the linear, limited personal will itself is relatively weak, but it is the decisive turnkey that opens the gates to the nonlinear, infinite power of Grace. Hope and surrender initiate the transformative process, and faith comes later, based on actual experience. Such acts and their consequences are also aligned within the allowances of prior karma. Not every prayer is answered favorably in human time.

Marginal Spiritual/Religious Belief Systems (Ideology)

Atheist Movement (Ideology)	190	"Left Behind" Apocalyptic Ideology	190
Christian Identity Movement (Ideology)	110	Mayan Religion	95
Aum Shinrikyo Cult	85	New Ageism	185
Aztec Religion	85	Solar Temple (Ideology)	155
Channeling	195	Plasma Energy Orbs (Ideology)	160
Crop Circles extraterrestrial?	No	Polygamous Sects	135
Cults	50-160	Raelians (Ideology)	130
Divination	185	Right-wing Fundamentalist Christian (Ideology)	95
DNA Code Theology (Ideology)	160	Secularism	165
Easter Island Statues	70	Shroud of Turin real?	No
Extraterrestrials real?	No	Star Children (Ideology)	145
Fortune-telling	185	Star People (Ideology)	160
Full-moon Gatherings (New Age)	180	Starseed Family (Ideology)	145
Goddess Movement	190	Tantra (Modern)	95
Heaven's Gate Cult	160	UFOs real?	No
Incan Religion	85	Urantia Book (Ideology)	150
Incoming Fifth World (Ideology)	130	Wicca (Ideology)	160

Many of these represent childlike credulity and the inclusion of positionalities that are at considerable variance from verifiable truth. The "end times" apocalyptic culture and its literature calibrate low because they are based on elaborations from the New

Testament Book of Revelation, which itself calibrates at 70, and its author also calibrates at that level, as discussed elsewhere. Its product is fear and the attraction of specialness and exclusivity.

Low calibrations prevail in variants of New Ageism, which push credibility to the limits, with glamorized claims of extraterrestrials, spirit guides, guardian angels, and prophesies of earth disasters. Other sources are claims to discovery of secret codes of God hidden in various disguises such as the stones in the pyramids, the Hebrew alphabet, DNA, famous paintings, and other imaginative obscurities. New Ageism (despite its own erroneous beliefs) is not, technically speaking, "spiritual," but instead it is actually "astral" in its practices and interests.

The attraction of many of these organizations and group beliefs is due to the curiosity and romantic imagination of the inner child that is entranced with any idea of "magic," as is demonstrated by the popularity of the Oz, Harry Potter, and Tolkein books. These popular children's versions, however, all calibrate above 200 and are integrous in their intention as represented by their fairy-tale themes of the struggles of the proponents of morality and their opponents. They are integrous because they are admittedly fiction, whereas fictional belief systems that are purported to be true calibrate low as they are thereby nonintegrous and represent falsity.

The Raelians made a brief appearance in the media with their much-publicized claim to successful human cloning. Their concepts have to do with guidance from extraterrestrials. The world of pseudospiritual fantasy also produces the imaginings of "Indigo children, star children, star families, star people, fifth-dimension incoming messengers of the future," etc. Common to all of these is a sense of uniqueness; magic; romanticized, naïve, imaginative fantasy; and the attraction of "specialness" itself.

The common basis to the appeal of many purely imaginative belief systems is the propensity of the childlike human mind to be attracted to the excitingly bizarre and preposterous. It then gains momentum and becomes an exciting and special mystique that attracts followers and enthusiasts, such as "Area 51" secrets, replete with "government cover-up" conspiracy theories that attract a whole subculture. The Jim Jones' group suicide catastrophe and the Waco standoff disaster, plus numerous other bizarre consequences of exploited gullibility and credulity represent the consequences of naïveté. While society dismisses these extremes as the "lunatic fringe," the consequences of exploited credulity are quite serious and, as history reveals, often quite grave (e.g., the Hale-Bopp comet associated with cult mass suicide).

Of historical cultural interest are the extremely low calibrations of both the Aztec and the Mayan religions in which the blood sacrifice of children and infants was essential. The god image of Quatzelcoetal is at calibration level 85.

Easter Island statues represent the self-destructiveness of the former inhabitants who apparently destroyed the trees and other vegetation, ending up starving to death, but not before they had regressed to cannibalism. They rose up in wrath against the stone statue gods, turned them around, cast them down, and broke them. Idolatry, like the worshipping of the golden calf, calibrates at only 65. The avoidance of idolatry, or even icons, is represented in both Islam and Judaism in the formal structure of the places of worship. The ego is attracted to the limitation of form, whereas the essence of Divinity is beyond all form, yet innate within it. Thus, in its ultimate significance, icons and statues of divine figures serve primarily as an inspirational function to transport awareness to the ultimate reality that lies beyond all limitation, designation, or specification. Therefore, the icon or the image is not an endpoint but a springboard or a way station to the ultimate destination.

Section 2
Places of Spiritual Interest

Alhambra	720	Machu Picchu	510
Anghor Watt	550	Maharaj, Nisargadatta,	
Aranachula Mountain	500	Attic of	510
Basilica of St. Peter (Rome)	710	Mecca	205
Bethlehem (current)	175	Medina	225
Bethlehem (in Jesus' time)	415	Mosque	495
Buddha, Relics of the	905	Nativity, Church of the	450
Cathedral of Notre Dame	790	Pieta, The	590
Cathedral of St. John the		Pyramids of Egypt	520
Divine, New York City	530	Sainte Chapelle (Chapel),	
Catholic Chapel	565	Paris	735
Chartres Cathedral	790	St. Patrick's Cathedral,	
Christian Saints,		New York City	530
(Relics of)	750	St. Peter, relics of (under	
Crystal Cathedral		floor of the Basilica in	
(Los Angeles)	410	Rome)	910
Dharamsala (India)	330	Sakya Monastery (Tibet)	390
Ganges River	515	Shinto Shrine	650
Great Buddha of Afghanistan		Sphinx, The	520
(prior to being blown		Stonehenge	599
up by the Taliban)	555	Strasbourg Cathedral	715
Great Buddha of Kyoto	780	Taj Majal	750
Jewish Synagogue	495	Tibetan Buddhist Stupa	640
Jewish Temple	505	Unity Village	510
Ka'ba' (Mecca)	530	Vatican, The	570
Karnak, Great Temple at	415	Washington National	
Lhasa (Tibet)	320	Cathedral	530
Lourdes	510	Westminster Abbey	790

Most of these calibrations are self-evident and reflect not only esthetics but also the presentation of beauty as instrumental to devotion and reflective of that spiritual intention. The Heisenberg "effect" is perhaps demonstrated most visibly by the unique example of the Ganges River, which, on the physical level, is the recipient of the sewage of over one hundred villages, towns, and cities along its course. Thousands of Hindus bathe daily in this grossly contaminated water in acts of spiritual purification. Funeral pyres, located along the riverbanks, are still smoldering. By spiritual intention, the holy river calibrates at an amazing

515, reflecting the input of the energy of sanctification by the millions of Hindu devotees over many centuries. We notice the same impact of prayer on the calibrated levels of food that has been blessed, compared to that which has not.

Aranachula Mountain is unfamiliar to most Westerners. It was the home of the famous sage Ramana Marharshi (cal. 720) who never left the site upon which his followers established a famous ashram that has attracted spiritual seekers from all over the world. It still exists today.

Another example of the phenomenon of spiritual intention is demonstrated by the effect of the consciousness level of Nisarga-datta Maharaj (cal. 720) who met with visitors in the attic above his *bidi* (tobacco) shop in Bombay. They had to climb up a ladder to visit with him in cramped quarters. His infectious spontaneity and animated demeanor charmed the many visitors, and his writings became well known. There are currently numerous students of his work, as well as that of Ramana Marharshi, which constitute an important core to the teachings of Advaita (nonduality).

The demolition of the Great Buddha by the Taliban was a purposeful act of desecration (cal. 35), indicative of the severe psychopathology of the militant Islamic fundamentalism that threatens the world today by its random choices of symbolic targets. Desecration itself is a grave warning signal as represented by the painting of swastikas on synagogues, the burning of flags or crosses, or the burning down of Baptist churches in the South. The basis is a psychotic degree of messianic narcissism, which, interestingly, calibrates exactly the same (30) as the disease of rabies or the consciousness level of serial killers of children (atavistic primitivism), and the ravenous "mad dogs" (i.e., rabid) of war.

Of great importance is the clinical fact that passivity inflames the killer blood lust (e.g., the Japanese slaughter of Manchuria, the Nazi extermination concentration camps, killer-dog packs, etc.) of aggressive primitive populations that calibrate extremely low and are therefore atavistic in their capacity for savagery and extremes of cruelty. They find rationalization in some interpretations of the Koran (Wahhab, Qutb) that provide permission for barbaric practices under certain "justifiable" conditions. From the distorted viewpoint of Islamic terrorists, such "justifiable" conditions can be projected onto almost every incident or "that all infidels who tread on Arab lands" are deserving of a gruesome death.

CHAPTER 17
Spiritual Truth

Introduction

While the majority of people in the United States believe in God (90-92%, CNN News, April 2004) and therefore tend to look to established religions for the highest truth, the source of the truth upon which all religions depend stems from the even higher primary source of spiritual reality itself. Thus, religion is the institutional consequence of spiritual truth rather than its origination or primary source. However, because religion incorporates the truths revealed by its founders, the derived teachings are sufficient and satisfactory for the great majority of people for whom the information is facilitated and made available as scripture by institutional religion.

There has been a great deal of research into the historic origins of the scriptures of all religions, resulting in much discourse and debate over the centuries as to specifics, such as dates, people, and authenticity. Some finalized versions of scripture were formalized by exclusive councils and became "canons" by virtue of scholastic authority. Technically, interpretation of their meaning is the province of theology, epistemology, metaphysics, and ontology (the science of being).

All the great spiritual teachers throughout history were mystics, and the source of their awareness of spiritual truth was the result of Enlightenment and the transformational Realization of the Reality of Divinity as the subjective knowingness that ensues from advanced consciousness by virtue of being at One with the Known. Thus, the Avatar does not speak from knowing "about" but from the actual Presence within, which radiates forth and constitutes the Essence of that which replaces the mind as the source of understanding and Knowingness (the classic *Purusha*). The process whereby this transformation occurs has been described in the history of each saint, sage, and divine teacher and is often included in the scripture itself.

From a purely research viewpoint, the calibrations of levels of consciousness can be aptly applied to verify the reality of any spiritual teaching, including their traditional scriptures. Each level represents the actuality of possibilities of consciousness and the progress from the linear to the nonlinear context, which is infinite and beyond space, time, or location.

The source of the highest spiritual truth is non-mental, and the intellect has difficulty comprehending this critical fact because the mind is intrinsically dualistic and limited, expecting a "this" to come from a "that." In the advanced spiritual Reality, duality dissolves because the "this" is the "that." The seeker and the Sought become One with the transcendence of the limitation of duality, i.e., Realization of the Self, Illumination, and Enlightenment, i.e., "The Kingdom of God is within you."

Scriptures and Spiritual Writings

Abhinavagupta (Kashmir Shaivinism)	655	Doctrine and Covenants: Pearl of Great Price	455
A Course in Miracles (workbook)	600	Genesis (Lamsa Bible)	660
A Course in Miracles (textbook)	550	Gnostic Gospels	400
		Gospel of St. Luke	699
Aggadah	645	Gospel of St. Thomas	660
Apocrypha	400	Granth Sahib-Adi (Sikhs)	505
Bodhidharma Zen Teachings	795	Heart Sutra	780
Bhagavad-Gita	910	Huang-Po Teachings	960
Book of Kells	570	Kabbalah	605
Book of Morman	405	King James Bible (from the Greek)	475
Cloud of Unknowing	705	Koran	700
Dead Sea Scrolls	260	Lamsa Bible (from the Aramic)	495
Dhammapada	840		
Diamond Sutra	700		

Lamsa Bible (minus the Old Testament and Book of Revelation, but including Genesis, Psalms, and Proverbs)	880	Psalms (Lamsa Bible)	650
		Proverbs (Lamsa Bible)	350
		Ramayana	810
		Rhubyat of Omar Khayyam	590
		Rig Veda	705
Lao Tsu: Teachings	610	Talmud	595
Lotus Sutra	780	Tibetan Book of the Dead	575
Midrath	665	Torah	550
Mishneh	665	Trinity (concept)	945
New Testament (King James Version after deletion of the Book of Revelation)	790	Upanishads	970
		Vedanta	595
		Vedas	970
New Testament (King James Version from the Greek)	640	Vijnane Bhairava	635
		Yoga Sutras, Patanjali	740
Nicene Creed	895	Zohar	905

Displayed above are integrous calibrated truths available to humankind, some for over thousands of years of evolutionary history. Any single selection is, in and of itself, sufficient for a lifetime of study and spiritual endeavor. As aspirants discover, it is one thing to know about the truth but quite another to understand it or, even more importantly, to become it. Spiritual progress is simultaneously simple and yet complex, subtle and yet cataclysmic, inspired and yet intimidating. To transcend the limitations of the ego requires intention, integrity of purpose, and resolve (plus grace: the assistance of an advanced teacher and positive karma). The journey often starts seemingly accidentally or as a consequence of curiosity. It then gathers interest and finally involvement, followed by commitment and the discovery of undreamed-of rewards.

To facilitate this endeavor, scriptures and the great spiritual classics supply critical information. Commitment to the goals of spiritual progress, in and of itself, has a transformative effect on brain physiology and attracts spiritual energies that shift alignment and power of concordant attractor energy fields. These recontextualize subjective reality and optimize realization.

From the calibration levels, it becomes evident that the great sages from the early Aryan culture of ancient India represented the first major emergence of the highest spiritual awareness available to man ever recorded. The same truths emerged later in different cultures and eras, completely separate from each other, and yet, the realization of the nature of the highest truth was essentially identical in each case, with some variation of expression that reflected cultural and linguistic differences. Thus, truth as such is not exclusive but universal, or it would not be truth. Therefore, spiritual or religious claims to exclusivity indicate the interference and errors of the egos of later followers of the original sages.

Truth, by definition, has no limitation or qualification and is not discriminatory. Inasmuch as everyone already has a calibratable level of consciousness at birth, the circumstances of that event would imply that they are not accidental but consequent to patterns of spiritual evolution as they manifest in the physical world as culture, family, time, and circumstances. (Consciousness research reveals that the particulars of *every* individual's birth are absolutely, perfectly karmically just and maximally advantageous, despite appearance or personal opinion to the contrary.)

The calibrations of the world's greatest teachers are concordant with human experience and validation over great periods of time despite the major cultural changes to which they are relatively immune due to their nonlinear essence. Because truth exists independently of its discovery, like gold, its rediscovery elicits excitement and attraction to a new source.

Advanced spiritual students value all sources of truth and often study combinations of them. Thus, the study of Christian mystics clarifies the truths revealed by the Vedas, and, in turn, the Vedas clarify Buddhist teachings that then clarify the teachings of Jesus Christ.

The limitation of traditional religious practice has been that it often gets involved with the peripheral issues of times, places, personalities, and ethnic propensities (i.e., form and content). Of greater significance is the study of material that is intrinsic to the truths revealed (i.e., the field) and not the circumstances of the events, as anecdotally interesting as they might be. These trappings, which are actually extraneous, have a negative effect in that they are deceptive, diversionary, and lead to such absurdities as people killing each other over whether or not one should wear a beard or worship on certain days of the week, the designation of which did not even exist at the time of the appearance of the great avatars. In Reality, which is nontemporal, there are no "days of the week."

Religious zealots who kill "nonbelievers" for trivia, such as hats, beards, diets, and designated days of devotion, display the negative fallout of undue emphasis on cultural eccentricities. As readers of the original scriptures can see for themselves, every day is a day of devotion; every day is Sabbath. In the hands of barbarians, trivial differences are magnified and then become merely tools of war that "justify" serious sacrilege and violation of even the simplest of spiritual principles. Perhaps transmission of spiritual truth is best done by example and attraction rather than by promulgation to people who are incapable of appreciating its value, appropriate use, and intention.

True missionaries spread valid information and teach by example. Those who are incorrectly motivated become sources of oppression, which leads to revolt (e.g., the Boxer Rebellion).

Missionary zeal reaches its ultimate expression as theocracies and the establishment of state religions that utilize force and punitive government regulation. The history of Europe reflects the utilization of religion in the name of monarchies and power struggles involving the nonintegrous exploitation of church authority. Religious conflict has led to religious wars, which have traditionally been the worst of all wars over the centuries and in almost all parts of the globe, even as reflected in current events arising out of the Middle East. Spirituality unites, whereas, unfortunately, the downside of religion divides. Severe distortions of religious truths lead to their becoming the exact opposites in practice.

Questionable Scriptures and Notes on the Christian Bible

Old Testament	190
Book of Revelation	70

The construction of the Bible was the result of a long process that proceeded over several centuries. Within the first few centuries A.D., there were well over one hundred manuscripts by numerous authors, each purporting to be valid descriptions and interpretations of the teachings of Jesus Christ. These presented a dilemma over which scholars discoursed and put forth their best efforts. As a result, there was a sequence of a collection of writings that had periodic revisions. Many manuscripts were set aside, such as *The Book of Enoch*. Later some, such as *The Apocrypha*, were included by some groups but not others.

Of obvious practical value is the application of the calibration of the levels of consciousness, especially to the differences between the calibration levels of an avatar, a saint, or a sage and their alleged scriptures or canonized holy books. If there is a wide discrepancy between the teachers and the available teachings, this is indicative of error, meaning that much was lost in translation, in transmission, or in misinterpretation. This can be observed most strikingly in dissimilar quotations of Christ's words on the cross between the King James and the Lamsa versions of the Bible, i.e., it makes a world of difference whether Jesus said, "Father, why hast thou forsaken me" (King James Version) versus "My father, thou hast not forsaken me. From this I have been spared" (Lamsa Translation). Upon reflection, the incongruence of the first quotation is indicated by the fact that an incarnated, fully Enlightened Master who is united with the Oneness of Divinity would unlikely feel deserted by the very source of that Realization within.

Highly interesting data and important information are provided in the brilliantly clear exposition in the first few pages of the Introduction in the Lamsa Bible, which is a translation from the original Aramaic Peshitta manuscripts that were taken to Constantinople and that constitute the foundation of the scripture of the Eastern Orthodox Church. In the Lamsa Bible's Introduction, comparison is made to the King James Version, which came from the Greek (and calibrates lower).

If all of the Books that calibrate below the credible level of truth at 200 are removed from either the King James or Lamsa versions of the Bible, the overall calibration level increases markedly. This is even more pronounced if the Old Testament, with the exception of Genesis, Psalms, and Proverbs, is removed, along with the Book of Revelation in the New Testament.

It would take detailed historical analysis to "explain why" erroneous writings were inadvertently included in canonized scripture, but the obvious explanation is that the overall level of consciousness of the cultures of Biblical times was at 90 to 100, and the great teachers were long dead and unavailable for guidance. Also, there was no means of accurately accessing levels of truth or determining the qualifications of experts.

To recapitulate, the Old Testament calibrates overall at 190, with the exception of Genesis (660), Psalms (650), and Proverbs (350). The Lamsa Bible (from the Aramaic) calibrates twenty points higher than the King James Version (from the Greek). Understanding the sources of error in the Old Testament requires detailed knowledge of ancient Hebrew culture and its history, which involved relapses into idolatry, division of the tribal kingdoms, conflict among the priesthoods, and inclusion of local cultural myths and legends, especially anthropomorphic depictions of God with egoistic human feelings of jealousy, anger, favoritism, revenge, pride, etc. (e.g., Freud's projections from the unconscious).

Revenge, anger, and other negative human emotional traits are linear limitations that are not concordant with the nonlinear parity of Divinity. They are more depictive of other non-celestial realms.

Although the Books of the Old Testament (with the exception of Psalms, Proverbs, and Genesis) calibrate below 200, many individual verses do calibrate quite high:

Calibration of Verses of the Old Testament

60% calibrate over 200	20% calibrate at 600 or over
50% calibrate over 300	10% calibrate at 700 or over
50% also calibrate over 400	2% calibrate at 800
30% calibrate at 500 or over	10 verses calibrate at 1,000

A more detailed analysis would be an interesting project but is beyond the parameters of this chapter and space limitations.

In the New Testament, the Book of Revelation (cal. 70) by John (cal. 70) is starkly discordant. Its origin (as described previously) is from the lower astral realms into which many visionaries have been enticed over the centuries. The depictions are that of a particular lower astral level (cal. 70) and therefore not of some level of actual truth, which would thereby calibrate at least over 200. Followers of the Book of Revelation often go into fearful proselytizing about the coming "end times" and form reclusive survival groups, complete with bunkers, food storage, etc. Unfortunately, because of their prior reputation or persuasiveness, such leaders impact vulnerable followers. In extreme cases, this fearfulness has led to group suicides or paranoid delusional systems. It is important to know that such visions of lower astral origin are recurrent and described similarly in different generations, right up to the present times, with earthquakes, floods, California's falling into the ocean, and pillaging hordes. This does not originate from heavenly realms, which calibrate at high levels, but just from a specific lower astral location (cal. 70). All visitors to that realm in astral states of consciousness report experiencing its life-like pseudoreality. (One such "teacher" was well known by the author. The fall into the astral trance state was disastrous and brought down his level of consciousness from high to low. (See later in this chapter.)

At the highest level of understanding, it is obvious that no confrontation between truth and nontruth is possible inasmuch as falsity is the absence of truth and not its opposite. That which is fallacious can obscure truth by impressive persuasion because the human mind is innately unable to discern truth from falsehood and is easily programmed when further weakened by fear.

From research, it is concluded that the highest version of the Bible is the Lamsa translation, with deletion of the Book of Revelation from the New Testament, plus deletion of the Old Testament, with the exception of Genesis, Psalms, and Proverbs. The overall effect is to raise the calibration of the level of truth of the Bible from 475 to 880, which then puts it on the level represented by the great mystics of history.

It is important to recognize that Jesus Christ did not write the New Testament, but instead, it was written by followers who, by word of mouth over many generations, repeated what they thought Christ said or meant. As any spiritual teacher knows from experience, there can be a wide disparity between what was actually said and what a listener thought they heard. When one considers the historical process over the centuries by which the Books of the Bible finally became assembled, it is truly impressive that it calibrates as high as it does. This does lend credence that Divine inspiration was available to the scholars involved in its final versions.

Questionable Scriptures: Notes on the Koran

The social impact of misinterpretations of the Koran was described in the previous chapter on Islam. Like the Old Testament, the Koran also includes errors that have serious consequences to mankind. Aside from its references to "the sword," as discussed previously, there are many verses that are incongruous with "Allah the All Merciful." These verses recurrently speak of "beholding infidels" and condemn slaughtering nonbelievers. The Koran calibrates overall at 700.

Calibration of the Verses of the Koran

30% calibrate below 200
25% calibrate below 150
14% calibrate below 100

If the verses below 200 are removed, then the Koran calibrates at 940. Inasmuch as "religious homicide" calibrates at 30, it would seem that contamination by falsity is the worst enemy of genuine, pure spirituality (calibrates as "true").

Religious Mythology

To understand the limitations of scriptures, it is necessary to look into the role of religious mythology that is common to all early cultures. There are famous Greek, Roman, and Germanic mythologies, as well as that of the Viking, Native American, and all other primitive cultural and ethnic groups. In all of these, the anthropomorphic gods have human characteristics and fallibilities. The "gods" are also blamed for catastrophes of nature, such as fire, volcanic eruptions, floods, and plagues whereby an angry god "smites" the peoples of the region.

This led to the widespread prevalence of acts of sacrifice to appease the angry, human-like gods, as seen in Aztec, Incan, Canaanite, Mesopotamian, and Semitic histories. When succeeding revelations of much higher spiritual reality were revealed by the teachings of the really great avatars, often the old mythology persisted as belief systems and was incorporated in or tacked onto the newer teachings. While mythology is of historical interest, it is clearly devoid of the higher truths now available to mankind. These ancient myths and legends still have adherents for ethnic and emotional reasons, but they are also fallacious and misleading, as revealed by their low calibrations. They are also misleading distractions to the seekers of spiritual truth. The ethnic and cultural identifications of religious myths and legends also lend themselves to separatism and cultural clashes, including persecution and genocide.

In summary, it is important to differentiate religious mythology from verifiable spiritual reality; clarification is of obvious importance. Historic religious legends and fables can be classified as cultural treasures but they should not be confused with verifiable, higher Truth, which is independent of all cultures (calibrates as "true").

Religious Error and False Teachings

The downside of religious error is demonstrated by history over the centuries of religiously justified genocide, homicide, cultural wars, torture, execution, witch trials, burning at the stake, the Inquisition, current Islamic terrorism, and Jihad ("Holy" War). It is represented in Christianity by the great fall of its level of truth that occurred at the time of the Council of Nicaea, the fall of Islam by Wahhabism, and the depictions of Divinity in the Old Testament, which are merely anthropomorphic projections of the human ego as characteristics of depicted Divinity (jealous, angry, etc.).

These serious departures from spiritual truth are grave in their consequences and represent the intrusion of the two great classical sources of spiritual error: the "Luciferic" (pride, power, control, distortion of truth) and the "Satanic" (torture, pain, killing, sexual lust). The Luciferic invasion of truth historically opens the door to the Satanic. First is the false justification by rhetoric and clever distortion of reality, which is the Trojan Horse that, once inside the gates, releases the blood lust of savagery (calibrates as "true").

These distortions prey on the ignorance and naïveté that characterize the lower calibrated levels of consciousness. These negative energies have been depicted throughout history as "evil" in that the term refers to *intention* (i.e., malice, hatred, and usurping of legitimate power for malevolent purposes and self-aggrandizement). These depictions characterize levels of consciousness that all calibrate below 200 and thus reveal themselves to be the matrix out of which all the sufferings of mankind originate.

The calibrated levels are also in complete accord with the principles of spiritual destiny, accountability (karma), and the fate of the soul after physical death. A common spiritual error is made by holding God as the author of human suffering, which is actually the collective negative impact of the ego itself. This understandable error often results in atheism, which refuses to believe in a God that is the source of evil. It is a mistake that is easily transcended by simply seeing that suffering is the consequence of the ego's ignorance (falsehood) and misunderstanding of the true nature of Divinity. In other terminology, suffering is the consequence of linearity. Divinity is nonlinear and detectable as Universal Energy, the subjective essence of consciousness itself, and the primordial Source of existence.

From the above understanding, it becomes apparent why the mystics throughout history consistently calibrate higher than the religions themselves. This is because they transcend the linear domain wherein lies the source of religious error.

Spiritual Teachers

Following is a list of over 100 well-known, respected teachers from various schools. They all calibrate over 460 (Excellence), and their works have stood the test of time. The list, of course, is not complete and would include many others if space permitted.

Abhinavagupta	655	Gyalpo, Lamchen Rinpoche	460
Acharya	480	Hall, G. Manley	485
Allen, James	505	Holmes, Ernest	485
Augustine, Saint	550	Hopkins, Emma Curtis	485
Aurobindo, Sri	605	Huang, Chungliang Al	485
Balsekar, Ramesh	760	Huxley, Aldous	485
Bartaleffy, Ludwig van	485	John Paul II (Pope)	570
Besant, Annie	530	John, Saint, of the Cross	605
Black Elk, Wallace	499	Karmapa	630
Bodhidharma	795	Kasyapa	695
Bohm, Jakob	500	Khantsa, Jamyung	495
Bucke, Richard M.	505	Kline, Jean	510
Buddhananda, Swami	485	Krishna, Gopi	545
Butterworth, Eric	495	Lawrence, Brother	575
Calvin, John	580	Leadbeater, C. W.	485
Chandra, Ram	540	Linpa, Kusum	475
Confucius	590	Luther, Martin	580
Dalai Lama (Tenzin Gyatso)	570	Madhva Charya, Sri	520
de Chardin, Teilhard	500	Magdeburg, Mechthild von	640
Dilgo Khantsa Rinpoche	575	Maharaj, Nisargadatta	720
Dionysius, the Arcopagite	490	Maharshi, Ramana	720
Dogen	740	Maizumi, Hakuyu Taizan	505
Druckchen Rinpoche	495	Merton, Thomas	515
Dzogchen Rinpoche	510	Moses de Leon of Granada,	
Eckhardt, Meister	705	Rabbi	720
Erasmus	500	Mukerjee, Radhakamai	475
Fillmore, Charles	515	Muktananda	655
Fillmore, Myrtle	505	Munroe, Robert	485
Fox, Emmett	470	Nanak	495
Gadenshartsa	470	Naranjo, Claudio	465
Gandhi, Mahatma	760	Nityananda, Bhagaven	500
Gangaji	475	Origen	515
Goldsmith, Joel	480	Otto, Rudolph	485
Gupta, Mahendranath	505	Padmasambhava	595

Pak Chung-Bih, Sotaesan	510	Sannella, Lee	505
Palmo, Tanzin	510	Satchidananda, Swami	605
Paramahansa, Yogananda	540	Shankara (Sankara Charya)	710
Patanjali	715	Smith, Joseph	510
Patrick, Saint	590	Socrates	540
Phuntsok, Khampo	510	Steiner, Rudolf	475
Pio, Father	585	Suzuki, Master Roshi	565
Paul, Pope John	570	Swedenborg, Emanuel	480
Plotinus	730	Tauler, Johann	640
Po, Huang	960	Theresa, Mother	710
Poonjai-Ji	520	Theresa, Saint, of Avila	715
Powell, Robert	525	Tillich, Paul	480
Prabhavananda, Swami	550	Tzu, Chuang	595
Prejnehpad, Swami	505	Tzu, Lao	610
Pulku, Gantey Rinpoche	499	Underhill, Evelyn	460
Rabindranath, Tagore	475	Vivekananda	610
Ramakrishna	620	Watts, Alan	485
Ramdas, Swami	570	White Brotherhood	560+
Ramanuja Charya, Sri	530	White Plum Asanga	505
Rumi	550	Yuktasweh, Sri	535
Sai Baba, Shirdi (not Sathya)	485		

An interesting comparison can be made in interpreters of the ancient Vedas that demonstrates the direct spiritual purity of nonduality. Adi Sankara Charya, Eighth Century sage of "nonduality," calibrates at 710, Sri Ramanuja Charya, Tenth Century sage of "qualified nondualism" is at 530, and Sri Madhva Charya of the Twelfth Century "dualistic devotion" is at 520. Huang Po, teacher of advanced "no mind" nonduality, is at 960.

The Reality of Divinity supersedes descriptions, identifications, or nominalizations that imply exclusivity. Krishna said, "By whatever name and by whatever means I am worshipped, all who are devoted to me or call on me are equally mine and dear to me." The Ninety-first Psalm says the same thing in that all who worship the Lord shall receive his love and protection. All true religions reaffirm that salvation is a consequence of surrendering to and acknowledging God through faith, worship, good deeds, prayers, and declaration.

The Reality of the Infinite Divinity is indivisible because it is nonlinear. The actual experience and Realization of Enlightenment is beyond all designation. As the ego dissolves into the Presence as Allness, the mind falls silent in the stillness and silence; thus, no nominalization is possible. (Hawkins, 1995, 2001, 2003). This was also the teaching of the Buddha and all Enlightened Sages throughout recorded time.

The "10,000 ways to God" are operationally only one way because they are all expressions of the same intention: to relinquish the dualistic ego and its illusions to the ultimate nonlinear Reality by whatever name it is designated.

Although the writings of teachers almost always calibrate at the same consciousness level as their author, there are occasional exceptions. Plotinus calibrates at 730, his writings at 503. Huang Po is at 960, his writings at 850, and Meister Eckhart calibrates at 705 while his writings are at 600. Very advanced states of consciousness are difficult to convey in the linearity of sentences and be intelligible to the reader. The foregoing exceptions were inadvertent and not intentional (statement calibrates as "true").

Students frequently ask for a list of integrous teachers whose work has been verified on a Scale of Consciousness. The above list of verifiably integrous teachers provides a very wide array of pathways to facilitate spiritual endeavor and evolution.

Spiritual bookstores present an overwhelming variety of books, some of which are primarily spiritual fiction, notwithstanding the fame of their authors. Approximately fifty percent of the material in some spiritual libraries and bookshops is below calibration level 200. The majority below 200 is primarily fantasy, although seven percent is actually delusional. On the other hand, the top forty serious contemporary spiritual writers all calibrate in the 400s and are therefore focused on spiritual education.

Although "New Age" literature is popular and engaging, it is also the area of maximal error and fallacy. It is rife with channelings from nonintegrous sources, earth prophecies, UFOs, extraterrestrial visitors, "guides" from the future, and claims of special, unique realms and strange foretellings of invasions from other galaxies, etc. Spirituals fiction is just that, but no more than that. Naïve enthusiasts follow guides who tell them to go out in the desert where they will be transported by UFOs, etc. Even if the style of expression is psuedo-spiritually sweet and cajoling, books that calibrate below 200 can, and do, lead to serious error if they are taken seriously.

By both subjective realization and the application of a science of truth utilizing calibratable verification, some irreducible conclusions and finalizations can be stated with certainty. At this time in the evolution of consciousness, there are available to both experiential and diagnostic confirmation, identifiable and demonstrable attributes and defining characteristics of Truth itself that transcend time, place, speaker, or the limitations of dualistic mentations. They can be stated as follows:

Identification and Characteristics of
Spiritual Truth, Integrous Teachers, and Teachings

1. **Universality**: Truth is true at all times and places, independent of culture, personalities, or circumstances.

2. **Nonexclusionary**: Truth is all-inclusive, nonsecretive, and nonsectarian.

3. **Availability**: It is open to all, non-exclusive. There are no secrets to be revealed, hidden, or sold, and no magical formulas or "mysteries."

4. **Integrity of purpose**: There is nothing to gain or lose.

5. **Nonsectarian**: Truth is not the exposition of limitation.

6. **Independent of opinion**: Truth is nonlinear and not subject to the limitations of intellect or form.

7. **Devoid of Positionality**: Truth is not "anti" anything. Falsehood and ignorance are not its enemies but merely represent its absence.

8. **No requirements or demands**: There are no required memberships, dues, regulations, oaths, rules, or conditions.

9. **Noncontrolling**: Spiritual purity has no interest in the personal lives of aspirants, or in clothing, dress, style, sex lives, economics, family patterns, lifestyles, or dietary habits.

10. **Free of force or intimidation**: There is no brainwashing, adulation of leaders, training rituals, indoctrinations, or intrusions into private life.

11. **Nonbinding**: There are no regulations, laws, edicts, contracts, or pledges.

12. **Freedom**: Participants are free to come and go without persuasion, coercion, intimidation, or consequences. There is no hierarchy; instead, there is voluntary fulfillment of practical necessities and duties.

13. **Commonality**: Recognition is a consequence of what one has become rather than as a result of ascribed titles, adjectives, or trappings.

14. **Inspirational**: Truth eschews and avoids glamorization, seduction, and theatrics.

15. **Nonmaterialistic**: Truth is devoid of neediness of worldly wealth, prestige, pomp, or edifices.

16. **Self-fulfilling**: Truth is already total and complete and has no need to proselytize or gain adherents, followers, or "sign up members."

17. **Detached:** There is noninvolvement in world affairs.

18. **Benign**: Truth is identifiable along a progressive gradient. It has no "opposite" and therefore no "enemies" to castigate or oppose.

19. **Nonintentional**: Truth does not intervene or have an agenda to propose, inflict, or promulgate.

20. **Nondualistic**: All transpires by virtue of intrinsic (karmic) propensity within the field by which potentiality manifests as actuality rather than by "cause" and effect.

21. **Tranquility and Peace**: There are no "issues" or partialities. There is no desire to change others or impose on society. The effect of higher energies is innate and not dependent on propagation or effort. God does not need help anymore than gravity needs the "help" of an apple's falling off the tree.

22. **Equality**: This is expressed in reverence for all of life in all its expressions and merely avoids that which is deleterious rather than opposing it.

23. **Nontemporality**: Life is realized to be eternal and physicality to be a temporality. Life is not subject to death.

24. **Beyond proof**: That which is "provable" is linear, limited, and a product of intellectualization and mentation. Reality needs no agreement. Reality is not an acquisition but instead is a purely spontaneous, subjective realization when the positionalities of the dualistic ego are surrendered.

25. **Mystical**: The origination of truth is a spontaneous effulgence, radiance, and illumination, which is the Revelation that replaces the illusion of a separate individual self, the ego, and its mentation.

26. **Ineffable**: Not capable of definition. Radical subjectivity is experiential. It is a condition that replaces the former. With this event, context replaces content, devoid of temporality and beyond time. Reality does not exist in time, or of it, or beyond it, or outside of it, and it has no relationship to that which is an artifice of mentation. It is therefore beyond all nouns, adjectives, or verbs, transitive or intransitive.

27. **Simplistic**: One sees the intrinsic beauty and perfection of all that exists beyond appearance and form.

28. **Affirmative**: Truth is beyond opinion or provability. Confirmation is purely by its subjective awareness; however, it is identifiable by consciousness calibration techniques.

29. **Nonoperative**: Truth does not "do" anything or "cause" anything; it *is* everything.

30. **Invitational**: As contrasted with promotional or persuasive.

31. **Nonpredictive**: Because Reality is nonlinear, it cannot be localized or encoded in restriction of form, such as secret messages, codes, numbers, and inscriptions, or hidden in runes, stones, the dimensions of the pyramid, the DNA, or the nostril hairs of the camel. Truth has no secrets. The

Reality of God is omnipresent and beyond codification or exclusivity. Codes are indicative of man's imagination and not the capriciousness of Divinity.

32. **Nonsentimental**: Emotionality is based on perception. Compassion results from the discernment of truth.

33. **Nonauthoritarian**: There are no rules or dictates to be followed.

34. **Nonegoistic**: Teachers are respected but reject personal adulation or specialness.

35. **Educational**: Provides information in a variety of formats and ensures availability.

36. **Self-supporting**: Neither mercenary nor materialistic.

37. **Freestanding**: Complete without dependence on external or historical authorities.

38. **Natural**: Devoid of induced, altered status of consciousness or manipulations of energies by artificial means, (i.e., nonreliance on form).

39. Teachers dismissed for moral turpitude, open honesty.

Divinity and Avatars

Divinity—God Transcendent

God	Infinity
God the Father	Infinity
The Creator	Infinity
The Almighty	Infinity
Maker of Heaven and Earth	Infinity
Ruler of the Universe	Infinity
Maker of All Things Visible and Invisible	Infinity
Omnipotent, Omniscient, and Omnipresent	Infinity
The Supreme	Infinity
Source of All Life and Existence	Infinity
The Holy Spirit	Infinity
Allah	Infinity

AN (Dravidian – early Hindu)	Infinity
Shiva	Infinity
Krishna	Infinity
Brahma	Infinity
Vishnu	Infinity
Durga	Infinity
Isvara	Infinity
Rama	Infinity
God of Moses and Abraham	Infinity

Divinity—God Immanent

The Christ	Infinity
Christ Consciousness	Infinity
Christ as God Incarnate	Infinity
Purusha	Infinity
Self	Infinity
Atman	Infinity

Other Denotations of Spiritual Reality
(Celestial Hierarchy)

Angels	500 +	Deity	720
Archangels	50,000 +	Yahweh (Yewah)	460
Buddha Nature		Jehovah	205
(as Allness)	1000 +	Word "God" as intellectual	
Buddha Nature (as Void)	980	concept	460
Native American Great			
Spirit	850 +		

Unless mankind, including all of its greatest spiritual geniuses and saints, has been totally wrong throughout all of history, the results of the calibration of the reality of Divinity are what one would simply expect as a result of "common sense," innate intelligence, and intuition. Calibrations simultaneously confirm the pragmatic value of the consciousness calibration system in evaluating the levels of truth. "God" as a concept calibrates at only 460, as would be expected, because it is a mentation.

God is the Ultimate Reality, as confirmed by consciousness research, which also validates the existence of the Omnipresence of God as both transcendent and immanent (it could hardly be otherwise), i.e., Jesus said, "Heaven is within you."

The terms "immanent" and "transcendent" are merely mentations of dualistic thinking and obviously do not denote two different realities. In the Western world, however, God is conceived as being "up there" in some distant realm of time and space, having thrown the dice of Creation. God is thought to retire until that awesome confrontation on Judgment Day. In the meantime, he "sits up there" where he is bombarded with requests, advice, solicitations, and entreaties, as well as epithets.

The calibrations of the levels of angels and archangels indicate that the energies of Reality are analogous to a step-down-transformer type of stratification between man and God. The celestial or heavenly realms are identifiable and known to mankind. Throughout history, it is recorded that successful contact has been made by individuals with a karmically gifted talent to make conscious contact with teachers from celestial realms. Unfortunately, some individuals have used the gift to contact lower realms, and they hear an impersonator of God, as happens in a psychotic state. The terms "Jehovah" and "Yahweh" calibrate lower because of mythological connotations and origins, as explained in the section on religious legends and mythology.

Avatars and Great Spiritual Teachers

Jesus Christ	1,000	John, the Baptist	930
Buddha	1,000	Moses	910
Krishna	1,000	Abraham	850
Zoroaster	1,000	St. Paul (Saul of Tarsus)	745
The Twelve Christian		Muhammad (at the time he	
Apostles	980	dictated the Koran)	700
Name of God as "Om"	975	Muhammad (after age 38)	130

The list is not exhaustive but includes those who are best known. The term "avatar" is from Sanskrit and means "incarnation by virtue of crossing over by descent of Divinity." The result in the human race is a fully illumined being who, because of the knowledge revealed, embodies the power of that level of truth and its concordant field of consciousness and radiates it out to mankind, thereby supporting and catalyzing the evolution of consciousness.

Veneration and respect are appropriate responses because they acknowledge the value of the innate gift to mankind of such an uplifting energy. Interpretation and comprehension of the revealed truths of these great teachers fall within a spectrum that reflects not only the level of truth of the original teaching but also the consciousness level of its cultural expression and comprehension.

Other References to Divinity

Greek Gods	90	Gods of War	90
Germanic Gods	90	Pagan Gods of Rome	100
Scandinavian Gods	90		

By historical analysis, the evolution of human consciousness over great expanses of time has been documented and verifies collective experience and wisdom. It would therefore be expected that religious and spiritual error would be a natural consequence, because it would be the byproduct of the progressive levels of the advancement of consciousness.

Spiritual Reality is omnipotent and omniscient. Its reality has no opposite; there is no opposite of truth but only its absence. Consequently, in Reality, there is no war between Reality and that which has no reality. Even as perceived, heaven and hell are completely different dimensions, *paradigms*, and realms, e.g., there can be no war between whales and birds anymore than there can be a war between Divinity and its absence; they represent totally different levels of conceptualization.

The spiritual catastrophe of Muhammad has already been noted, and the consequences to civilization are ongoing in today's world. Also, not unexpectedly, the consciousness level of paganism is reflected in the invention of its historic gods of various cultures.

The meaning of "He" in reference to God is generic and not

indicative of gender. The Infinite is obviously beyond gender and therefore the designation "He" is linguistically analogous to the term "man" for mankind. The term "human" includes the same generic designation, just as the term "woman" already is inclusive of man, i.e., she is the female expression of mankind, and out of her _wo_mb is birthed _man_.

Genderization of nouns is not prevalent in English like it is in other languages, such as German, where all pronouns or nouns are identified as feminine, masculine, or neutral ("die" = feminine, "der" = masculine, and "das" = neutral). Even the designations of Yin and Yang indicate positionalities and arbitrary points of observation. Thus, positionalities obscure the reality that is beyond both.

Reverence for God is reflected in the pronouns "Thy," "Thou," and "Thee," e.g., "Thou art my salvation; in Thee do I trust for Thine is the Kingdom"; and, "Thy will be done."

Spiritual Experiences

Buddha Nature	1000 +	Ramadan	495
Christ Consciousness	1000 +	Sweat Lodge Ceremony	560
The Supreme	1000 +	Smudging	520
Near-death Experience	520 +	Christmas: Peace on Earth,	
Satori	585	Goodwill to Men	675
Enlightenment	600 +	Sound of Tibetan	
Christian Communion	700	Buddhist Horns	320
Passover	495	Nirbija Samadhi	800
Durga Puja Festival	480	"Amazing Grace" (Hymn)	575
Hanukkah	515		

The following spiritual concepts calibrate as true:

1. Chi Energy ("Shakti") energizes the acupuncture systems.

2. Kundalini (spiritual) energy activates the chakras and produces the pure-energy etheric brain and shifts brain physiology (see diagram, Chapter 7).

3. Negative interference with acupuncture energy flow precedes physical illness.

4. Etheric Body.

5. Reincarnation.

6. Karma.

7. Jesus' thirty-three miracles.

8. Jesus miraculously fed the thousands.

9. The miracles of the Christian apostles.

10. Speaking in tongues.

11. Pentecostal flame.

12. John, the Baptist, was killed for revealing the truth.

13. Jesus was killed for revealing the truth.

14. Wait three days before burial or cremation of the body after physical death.

15. The consciousness level is already set at birth.

16. The exact time of bodily "death" is karmically set at birth.

Correlation with the *gunas* (the basic dominant energies of life from the Sanskrit):

Tamas = lower resistance, inertia energies below calibration level 200.

Rajas = energy of constructive action, levels 200-400.

"High *rajas*" = calibration levels 400-499.

Satva (peace, tranquility) calibrates at 500-599.

Moksha as enlightenment is 600 and over.

The list includes a great variety of reported subjective experiences and practices. Their value is corroborated by large numbers of people. They are therefore accepted as truth in some cultures but seemingly foreign to others.

Karma

The term "karma" is specific as well as generic and refers to the evolutionary and experiential continuity of the soul, to which all religions and spiritual truth are in agreement. The fate of the

soul is a central focus of all religions. Awareness of its continuity was prominent in ancient Egypt and prehistoric cultures in
which thanatology was a prominent element of the culture. It is
to be differentiated from reincarnation, which is only one option
of numerous possible courses of evolution that can take place
on different planes of spiritual existence. Destiny is determined
by the level of consciousness and choices thereby available,
plus unknown factors, such as Grace, Salvation, Divine Mercy,
and Intercessors via faith and worship. The karma of atheism as
hatred of God, or denunciation of Divinity itself, all calibrate at
very serious levels of 40-70, thus indicating a very dire spiritual
destiny that calibrates at the lower astral level of Hells. (Calibrates
as "true.") In contrast, atheism as an intellectual/philosophical
position calibrates at 165-190, which is the level of (intellectual)
pride.

Generically, karma is represented by the totality of one's inheritance at birth, at which time everyone already has a calibratable level
of consciousness. The circumstances are optimal for the progress of
the individual's soul and include multiple specifics that are the expression of the linear mechanics of pre-existing karmic propensities.
These include parents, geography, physical build, I.Q., sex, health,
genetic traits, religion, etc. That the collective factors are optimal
has to do with not only "good karma" but also the opportunity for
the undoing of "bad karma." (Calibrates as "true.")

Other Phenomena and Belief Systems

Ghosts are real	False
Haunting	False
Prophesied End Times	False
St. Matthew's prophesied End Times	False
One can experience one's own physical death.	False
Earth prophesies, DNA, Sphinx Mayan calendar, pyramids, etc.)	False
Reincarnation as lesser species	False
Popular Spiritual Fiction	175

Mary and Jesus were married	False
Jesus' descendants became French rulers	False
da Vinci's "Last Supper" contains a secret code	False
Knights Templar held secrets about Jesus and Mary	False
Hidden Bible code	False

Comparative Experiences

Alien Abduction	70	Devil Worship	25
Ankh (the symbol)	160	Divination Game Boards	175
Black Magic	20	Inquisition, The Historic	35
Black Witchcraft	5	Occult	135-185
Cult	120	Satanism	45
Cursing (using Lord's name in vain)	45	Tarot Readings	190
		Transmediumship	190
Damning other people to hell	15	Voodoo	45

Most of these practices are avoided by people with even minimal spiritual intuition and conscious awareness. The advisability of avoiding these errors is emphasized within the Commandments themselves, e.g., to not abuse the name of God or bear false witness against one's neighbor. They are also universally recognized as having negative karmic consequences, e.g., in Christianity, the fate of the soul after physical death.

Most of the prevalent negative spiritual practices attract the spiritually naïve by their "feel good" glamour and uniqueness, e.g., get a psychic reading or Tarot card séance, have fortunes told, get "channeled" advice from a "master" on the "other side," or dabble in the occult with various forms of magic, séances, or rituals.

The Paranormal

Paranormal phenomena are confused with the supernatural and are attractive to the curious. Traditional scripture, as well as highly evolved sages and teachers, warn "not to go there" because the astral realms are not spiritual and represent other realms and dimensions for which the human mind is not equipped with protective discernment. Thus, it is perilous to invoke spirits and otherworldly entities. Occult practices have a sizeable and unseen downside, despite the popularity of various Tantric exercises, "white magic," incantations, Tarot cards, channeled masters, psychic readers, etc.

Altered states of consciousness and the paranormal phenomena are relatively complicated and are unique areas for study. They are further obscured by the glamour of specialness and are an attractive novelty to impressionable curiosity. Without a science of calibration of levels of truth, past erstwhile researchers themselves have been taken in and fooled by the appearances of unfamiliar phenomena, such as spiritualism replete with table tapping, the honking of horns, ectoplasmic apparitions of fortune tellers, séances with trance mediums, contact with the dead and "masters on the other side," card readings, throwing of stones, tea-leaf reading, divination, etc.

All the above were highly developed practices in ancient Mesopotamia, and ancient peoples consulted oracles, seers, shamen, and a variety of practitioners of magic and otherworldly secret, mystical rites and rituals, plus a great variety of psychics, channelers, trance mediums, and medicine men and women with special connections to a variety of spirits.

Various rituals were also intertwined with hypnotically induced states via repetitious chanting and body movements or ritual dances, plus altered physiological states induced by repetitious breathing exercises, body contortions, postures, and a variety of sexual practices (e.g., "Tantric" sex). In addition to a variety of "feel good" practices, there were strange diets, esoteric herbs, psychedelics, and magic mushrooms. Later came designer drugs,

Ecstasy, LSD, Psilocybin, psychomimatic alkoloids, and even animal tranquilizers, plus a variety of amphetamines and psychostimulants, as well as psychopharmacological agents.

In addition to the above artificially-induced states of consciousness, there were scientifically designed attempts in the same direction via biofeedback and alpha-wave training devices designed to induce altered brain-wave patterns. Meditators of a variety of practices (TM, Zen monks, etc.) have been studied by researchers at Duke University of the EEG frequencies in various parts of the brain to investigate parapsychology, psychic healers, distant viewing, alterations of water surface tension, and psychokinesis. The Monroe Institute researched and taught the techniques of out-of-body astral projection and altered states of consciousness induced by manipulation of sound waves. To these investigations was added the "brain mirror" device, which lit up according to the most active portion of the brain in altered states.

Interest in altered states has also been a consequence of their spontaneous occurrence throughout history. Psychiatry has studied and described dissociative and fugue states, compartmentalization of multiple-personality disorders, as well as delusional, hallucinatory, and hypnogogic conditions, along with hypnotic phenomena, including the effects of suggestion, mind control, and brainwashing techniques. In addition, psychology and psychoanalysis have investigated dreams and the various regions of the unconscious, including the influence of the Jungian archetypes.

While science has addressed many of the above issues and phenomena, it still lacks awareness of not only differing levels of calibratable consciousness but also of the possibility of other dimensions of existence, such as other spiritual or various astral realms.

Altered states of consciousness, such as oneiriform, dream, or fugue states occur spontaneously, and some families even exhibit a genetic pattern (e.g., mother-daughter psychics). The human mind is primarily experiential and the experience is then presumed to be "real," which is familiar in the dream state.

Trance/fugue states can occur in normal persons and may last for prolonged periods of minutes, hours, or even days, such as in conditions of amnesia. In an auto-trance of even short duration, there can be the subjective experience of far greater time periods—in a few minutes, visions of other dimensions may include hours or even days of seeming events. Visionary states are also common to some personalities and are frequently associated with temporal lobe seizure disorders. However, they can occur in people with normal brain physiology as well.

As can be readily surmised, the "reality" of all the foregoing conditions and states has not as yet been unraveled. They are often a challenge to even the most experienced clinician/researcher. For many years, the author was a consultant simultaneously to ministerial and meditation groups, the Episcopal and Catholic dioceses, a Zen monastery, and the residential communities of various religious orders, as well as spiritually-based recovery groups and institutions. Sometimes the differential diagnosis was difficult, e.g., "Samadhi" or catatonia, etc.

Alien abduction is another very unique phenomenon. The calibrated level of the experience (not the person) is always at about 70, the same as experiential apocalyptic visions (e.g., John, the author of Revelation). These experiences of astral fields of consciousness have been similar throughout the ages and recur repeatedly with the same negative scenarios. The experiences are very real to the subjects who are thereby convincing in their retelling of the revealing visions. Often a cult emerges and takes off to remote survival encampments. The visions characteristically are fear provoking and the entranced followers tend to form a group identity. The downside over periods of time can be very considerable as the myth propagates through fear, suggestion, and the virus of memes (e.g., the "End Times" as imminent, etc.)

The problems and true nature of these various combinations and states have been obscure and thereby produce a bewildering array of explanations and postulations as well as attempted scientific explanations. At the present time, the clinical approach of consciousness calibration research opens a new means of elucidation of the true nature of these phenomena. The calibrations at least clarify the levels of truth and consciousness involved. Research is complicated by the fact that delusions, illusions, dreams, visions, amnesias, and trance and fugue states are subjectively astrally experienced, yet "objectively" unreal, and therefore not confirmable as an actual reality. Prophecies come and go as epiphenomena of the potentiality of consciousness itself, which is the common substrate that affords an absolute constant from which greater clarification will emerge.

If we apply consciousness research to the phenomenon of the channeling of "teachers" from the "other side," the first area of inquiry is the genuineness of the operatives themselves. Indications are that fifteen percent of clairvoyants, ten percent of psychics, twenty percent of channelers, and twenty-five percent of trance mediums are legitimate and genuine. Of the channeled "masters" or entities on the "other side," fifty percent calibrate *below* 200, and only five percent above level 450. Therefore, the rule of *caveat emptor* applies. The downside, as it is in the ordinary world, is the risk of following a teacher whose motivation is control. This can be suspected when followers are given personal-life direction instead of being led to look within themselves for answers by following inner spiritual work.

Some "teachers" from the other side have messianic delusions of grandeur that are contradicted by their calibrated level of consciousness. In clinical psychiatry, these are observed as "exalted states" in which the patient has a sudden revelation that they are literally Jesus Christ. At one time, back in the 1950s, before anti-psychotic drugs became available, there would be two or three "Jesus Christ" patients in the hospital at the same time. To the patient, the experiences were experientially "real." (We also had queens and Napoleons.)

A genuine transformational spiritual experience is confirmed by its very positive and often very profound influence on a person's life, which is confirmed by those who have had near-death experiences of spiritual truth. Such calibratable benefit is also seen after genuine conversion experiences, frequently in the context of "hitting bottom." Such persons are indeed "reborn" in a genuine sense as confirmed by sometimes dramatic increases in their levels of consciousness. This has been witnessed in attendees at spiritual lectures where jumps of up to even 150 points have occurred. (The average is about ten points for the audience.)

Differentiation of genuine spiritual states from abnormal mental conditions has been described previously (Hawkins, *I: Reality and Subjectivity*, p. 104). They are as follows:

Authentic Spiritual State	Pathologic State
Samadhi	Catatonic
Religious Ecstasy	Mania (bipolar hyper-religiosity)
Illumination	Grandiosity
Enlightenment	Religious delusion
Piety	Scrupulosity (obsessive-compulsive)
Inspiration	Imagination
Visions	Hallucinations
Authentic spiritual teacher	False guru, imposter, spiritual con artist
Devotion	Zealotry, Hyper-religiosity
Committed	Obsessed, brainwashed by cult, victimized
Dark night of the soul	Pathologic depression
Detachment	Withdrawal, indifference
Nonattachment, acceptance	Passivity
Transcendent state	Mutism
Trusting	Naïve
Advanced state	Psychosis, egomania
Beatific	Euphoria
Humility	Low self-esteem
Spiritual sharing	Proselytizing
Commitment	Religiosity
Inspired	Messianic
God shock	Schizophrenic disorganization
Spiritual Ecstasy	Manic state, high on drugs
Genuine spiritual leader	Spiritual politician, cult leader
Free	Psychopathic
Teaching	Controlling

Cultism

Cults ensnare the unwary by their specialness and false promises. Members have an "insider" status and a special "lingo." The group leader is charismatic, seductive, and courts the initiate, who is flattered by the attention. The leader is very "special" and treated with adulation, which is quickly turned into control of members, including especially their money and sex lives, as well as lifestyles, diets, clothing, etc. Members must take allegiance and break off relationships with family or even spouses and often associations or groups.

The group often forms a geographic, restrictive enclave and develops a group paranoia as well as a characteristic "cult glaze" (cal. 120) as though in a hypnotic state (the effect of isolation and brainwashing). Once detected, that glaze is easily recognized (the "programmed cult look," as one observer described it). There is a flatness and automaton style to rationalizations where content is like a "party line" that is parroted from having been programmed. Cults especially target celebrities and exploit them as showpieces.

The influence of cult leaders is so strong that large groups of people will willingly kill not only others but also themselves (e.g., Heavens Gate, Jim Jones, Islamic terrorists, suicide bombers, Aum Shinrikyo subway gassers, Bolsheviks, Nazi party, al-Qaeda, the Taliban, White Supremacists, Ku Klux Klan, liberationists, etc.).

Another characteristic of cultism is proselytizing and insistence on following the party line of a pseudo-religious group belief system by which individuality is scorned or even threatened. Leaders are very power-oriented, and control plus paranoid egoism are dominant themes.

Sometimes a spiritual leader will calibrate as integrous early in their career but then will fall victim to the seduction of prestige, money, sex, or the adulation of followers. Then the original spiritual group degenerates into a cult, or a spiritual technique becomes actually trademarked and then commercialized and marketed by hired publicists. In that case, the technique calibrates above 200 but the organization itself falls below 200 and becomes primarily a marketing organization that trades on the original concept or exclusive technique. The technique is thus only taught for a price and "trainees" are forbidden to reveal the secret teachings (which are usually merely a few simple phrases or sentences with a general application to "improve health," "attract abundance," "increase love life," "be more popular," "fulfill your potential for success," "attract a mate," etc.). Some of the promoted techniques can be found in any fortune cookie, e.g. "One smile can change your life forever" (cal. 350), or "Success goes to one who is kind" (cal. 360).

The true value of such workshops is not the magic of a central concept or technique but the disciplined practice of actually applying it with regularity in daily life instead of merely quickly dismissing it as "I already know that." The value of training workshops then lies in learning of the value of steady application and actually putting a valuable tool into practice and steady focus, e.g., the "faithfulness" of *A Course in Miracles* workbook.

Another expression of cultism is the cultification of splinter groups from traditional religions, e.g., the far-right "fundamentalism" most prominent and visible in Islam, Christianity, and ethnic variations of worldwide religions.

Spiritual Practices

Aum (mantra)	210	Om Namaha Shivaya	630
Baptism	500	Prayerful hand clasp	540
Bathing in the Ganges	540	Prayer of Jabez	310
Confirmation	500	Prayer of St. Francis of Assisi	580
Devotional acts	540	Random Acts of Kindness	350
Devotional burning of		Saying the Rosary	515
incense	540	Shanti Shanti Shanti	650
Genuflection	540	Surrender (at depth)	
Golden Rule	405	one's will to God	850
Gregorian Chants	595	Surrender the World to God	535
Hajj (pilgrimage to Mecca)	390	Turning prayer wheels	540
Japa	515	Twelve Steps of Alcoholics	
Jesus Prayer	525	Anonymous	540
Kirtan (Yogic Chant)	250	Transcendental Meditation	295
Kneeling to pray	540	Visualization (healing)	485
Last Rites	500	Wailing Wall, The	540
Lord's Prayer, The	650	Walking the Labyrinth	
Om (pronounced ōm,		(Chartres Cathedral)	503
as in loan)	740	What is held in mind	
Om Mane Padme Hum	700	tends to manifest	505

All of these denote devotion and are therefore common to all genuine religions. By intention, man symbolically sanctifies and commits both self and others, as well as places of worship. Because of intention, all styles of blessing and prayer calibrate over 500, and their collective effect can immeasurably impact the overall level of collective human consciousness. This is suggested by the observation that the last two major jumps in the overall level of human consciousness occurred successively after the Harmonic Convergence in the late 1980s, when the collective consciousness level went up from 190 to 205, and then again at the time of the Harmonic Concordance in November 2003, when it jumped from 205 to the current 207. At both times, spiritually committed people all over the world prayed simultaneously. The witnessing of the transition from 205 to 207 happened fortuitously at the end of a lecture in San Francisco (which was videotaped) when a spiritually committed group of four hundred people simultane- ously prayed and sounded "Om," followed by meditation on the chanting of the Lotus Sutra in Sanskrit. This occurred between the hours of 5:15 and 5:25 PM California time. In front of the audience at 5:15 PM, the consciousness level of mankind was calibrated at 205. It was then recalibrated at 5:30 PM, following the prayer, and the level had concurrently increased to the present level of 207.

Other Teachings, Schools, and Spiritual Traditions

100th Monkey		Fundamentalism	200
Phenomenon	205	Hatha Yoga	260
Agnosticism	200	Holotropic Breathing	202
Anti-Creationism	150	Huna	260
Anti-Evolutionism	150	I Ching, The	430
"Archangel Channeler"	190	Keys of Enoch	265
Astrology	210-405	Kirlian Photography	160
Biofeedback	202	Knights Templar	400
Bodywork	205	Kung Fu	410
Codependency (concept)	190	Metaphysics	460
Creationism	200	Numerology	210
Crystals	210	Qi Gong	240
Druids	450	Rebirthing	250
Eckankar	230	Reiki	340
Enneagrams	390	Rolfing	205
Esoteric	390	Rosicrucians	405
EST (Erhard Seminars		Soul Midwifery	240
Training)	400	Superstition	200
Ethical Culture	350	Telepathy	250
Falun Gong	195	Theosophy	365
Feng Shui	185-210	Universalist Church	320
Firewalking	200	White Brotherhood	560
Free Masonry	510	White Magic	203
Freethinker	350	Wu Den	275

Calibration levels do not indicate that one level is "better" than another but only different, analogous to the selection of clubs when playing golf, which depends on whether one is going to "putt," "chip," or "drive." Therefore, efficacy is the result of intention and not just a technique in itself.

Many spiritual students have explored a variety of these approaches and report pragmatic and experiential benefit. The application of spiritual principles to many human dilemmas is widely acknowledged as efficacious, even when there is no original conscious motivation, such as the hopeless alcoholic who, after being ordered to attend AA meetings by the judge, miraculously recovers and becomes an inspiration to others by practicing the spiritual principles of "carrying the message to others," i.e., sharing rather than proselytizing.

Spiritual integrity manifests as hope, faith, charity, and inspiring others by example. Integrous spiritual organizations that have an open door grow by attraction rather than by promotion, and they are devoid of dogma. Reliance on the power of the field is indicated by the group experience that people "get it by osmosis" instead of by intellectualization.

Conclusion

Confirmation of spiritual reality by means of consciousness calibration techniques is of great value in the advancement of human knowledge in that it represents a capacity to explore realms previously inaccessible, much less verifiable, due to the limitations of the intellect. While advanced spiritual awareness and reality are "home" to the mystic, it still seems foreign to large populations and subgroups for which spirituality is less familiar than the more traditional religious or secular domains of mentation and Newtonian logic.

CHAPTER 18
Summary and Resolution

In ancient times, the sole source of higher truth was through the revelations of the great mystics, saints, and avatars, and thus, the spiritual core of religion was respected and revered. The followers of established religion did so out of faith and awe at the revelations of Divinity. Subsequently, however, the knowledge was appropriated and became primarily the property of the priestly class, which established the dictum of the orthodoxy of ecclesiastic doctrine.

Eventually, the higher truths, which are nonlinear and calibrate from 540 to 1,000, became surrounded by an aura of mystery and authoritarianism, which subsequently attracted great wealth that enabled the construction of the great temples and magnificent architecture of the great gothic cathedrals, mosques, and the magnificent Alhambra in Spain.

Reverence became codified and structured in its expressions, which were then authoritatively imposed as requirements. Thus arose coercion and fear, as well as divisiveness and militancy. Out of these qualities arose political power, with its rivalrous temptations of secular control of people, territory, and riches, plus the acquisition of impressive ranks and titles.

The faith of the followers became exploited, and aggrandizement fed the ego instead of the worship of God. Religion was corrupted by the ego inflation of zealous religiosity, which led to millennia of ceaseless wars that continue unabated to this very day. By virtue of these distortions, the holy books of the Sons of Abraham became the very justification for conflict, war, and genocide.

Despite the abuse and misappropriation of organized religion by usurpers within each faith, the essential truths were preserved and still available beneath their obfuscation and upstaging by pomp and ceremony. Thus, doctrine became the tool of oppression and fear rather than liberation by truth. Freedom was neither a value nor a practical alternative where the consequences for alleged heresy were grave indeed. Orthodoxy was therefore the only safe mode of life, and its perimeters were enforced by the fear of excommunication and the ominous consequences of sin readily enforced by the terrorization of the Inquisition and its persecution of mystics.

In the Far East, however, spiritual truth did not fall prey to the ego's greed for secular power, nor did religion take on its dark image as it did in the Middle East and Western society. Taoism, Buddhism, and the ancient Hindu teachings of the great yogas (the pathways to God) brought about a more serene climate that was foreign to militant genocide or persecutions. Although sometimes imposed in a doctrine fashioned by some rulers, the teachings themselves were that of nonviolence and nonmateriality and were thus protected by their own purity.

While Western religions required and depended on submission to ecclesiastic authority, Eastern religions taught to look within for truth rather that without. Importantly, in a parallel development, the great philosophers of ancient Greece had discovered that the intellect itself could be the sought-for road to truth. Socrates, for example, was committed to truth with such sincerity that he followed the order to drink hemlock and accept death rather than violate the tenets of truth. In that instance, he was given the choice whereby he could save himself by compliance with the prevailing authorities, but to do so, he would be violating his own teachings. Thus, with great integrity, he chose to follow the dictum "To thine own self be true."

The ancient philosophers then established the roads to truth via metaphysics, theology, epistemology, ontology, and the sciences of intellection based on the dialectics of reason and logic rather than blind faith. The Dialogues of Plato, Aristotle, and Socrates, by the power of their pristine intention, laid the groundwork and inspiration for the subsequent intellectual development of the Western world, which flowered forth as scientific discovery within the ensuing fruits of astronomy, physics, chemistry, advanced mathematics, and on to the present day of computer science, quantum mechanics, nonlinear dynamics, and M-theory.

The discoveries of Newton, Kepler, Haley, Copernicus, Galileo, and succeeding generations of scientists transformed the world and dazzled and simultaneously benefited mankind with their stunning brilliance. Understandably, mankind then revered the intellect, reason, and science as hope for earthly life, and in so doing, set religious belief aside. Religion thereby became compartmentalized and continued on in a more limited scope as personal ethics plus a belief system that applied to life after worldly death. Faith and belief were not denied but were held in abeyance and separated from the practical, everyday "real" world of survival and business.

This division of orientation seemingly worked for many centuries, during which the calibratable level of consciousness of mankind was less than 200. But, as the predominant consciousness level of mankind overall passed from 190, where it had been for centuries, over the critical line to 205, and then to its current 207, the overall ambiance of society at first went through a subtle but then very visible major change of expression. Collective society now became far less tolerant of nonintegrity, egoistic greed, and the focus solely of gain. It became progressively more humanitarian, caring, and appreciative of spiritual values. A progressive concern emerged for fairness, balance, protection of the vulnerable, and appreciation for the quality of the environment, as well as for the dignity and rights of individuals. Rather than adherence to orthodox doctrine, the new call was for freedom and equality, such as had already been defined and specified in the Constitution of the United States, which calibrates at an impressive 710.

Paradoxically, the new emphasis and thrust to spiritual values was taken over by the egos of power-seeking proponents, which was exactly the same as the church had done in the past. They sought to usurp the basic truths to establish a new form of oppression and control over others. The tool was the distortion of valid intellection as rhetoric; that was the very downside of democracy via the mechanism of free speech foretold by Socrates in 350 B.C.

While science, logic, and intellectual integrity all calibrate in the mid- to high 400s, the contentious rhetoric is the consequence of fallacies that are intrinsic to calibration levels 135 to 190. These distortions of truth masquerade as humanistic idealism but, on the contrary, are merely the reemergence of narcissism in new clothes. The motive is secular totalitarianism by legislated control of others and the substitution of romanticized positionalities that appeal to ego mind and immaturity. The expressions of these energy fields or violations of truth are revealed by the pathognomonic diagnostic sign of the emergence of hatred, which is foreign to either intellectual or spiritual truth.

The energy fields below 200 are seen to be reactionary because they are contrary in direction to the overall progression of consciousness of the world itself at its current 207, much less America, which calibrates at 421. How this conflict resolves itself will influence the character of society until its core elements are identified and resolved.

The implications of a study of the calibrated levels of consciousness of the many aspects of the evolution of mankind in its expressions reveal significant and pragmatically useful information. While blind faith was and still is a main avenue to truth for the majority of mankind, in more recent times, "modern man" has relegated and compartmentalized it. Subsequent to the age of faith, the intellect reawakened from ancient Greece, and the age of reason again prevailed and evolved as modern science, which in turn became the new repository of faith. Because of the high calibration of science in the mid-400s, its fruits have been a bonanza to modern man, who has thereby been relieved of major sources of suffering.

Modern man is now confronted with the dilemma of which way to turn for real truth, other than science and technology. Blind faith seems regressive, and returning to traditional religion reawakens old fears of theocratic oppression, sin, and guilt. As an alternative, philosophy and education, which once were erudite, have now been contaminated with excessive political positionalities and drowned in the sophistry of contentious relativistic postulations that calibrate below 200. Although they are popularized as supposed progress, they actually represent regress.

Science remains relatively unsullied, but operationally, it has been limited primarily to the Newtonian paradigm. So, the true seekers of truth rediscovered the pristine teachings that had been at the core of the peaceful societies of the Ancient East—the nondualistic pathways to the truths of Buddhism, Taoism, and Hinduism as taught by the great teachers and *rishis* of the great yogis. This led to the resurgence of interest in mysticism and its goal as Self-realization. While Western cultures traditionally had been focused on transcendent divinity, the East focused on the discovery of divinity immanent as the source of Existence itself. The rediscovery of a new paradigm of reality that transcended the limitations of the intellect or blind faith became progressively more appealing. In addition, the inner pathway was accessible to all, well documented, and nonregimented.

The core of all the ancient teachings was to transcend the limitations of the ego and its belief systems, which are the basis of the illusions that are the distortions of truth consequent to the dualistic structure of the ego. Thus Enlightenment has become the leading focus for investigation and effort as demonstrated by the great current interest in the self-improvement movement, as well as the Cultural Creatives who collectively eschew violence, contention, and controversy. They instead seek truth through inner transformation and fulfillment to the realization of the Oneness of all life.

The straightest way to Enlightenment is by transcending the limitation of the ego/mind by dedication to verified truth itself. This process is suitable for modern humankind and devoid of conflict with science or religion.

When mankind, in frustration or disillusionment, moved from faith in the unseen to faith in the linear world of science, new hope arose, reinforced by the very tangible and visible benefits of trust and faith in the linear, external world of ego perception. But then, the very same process resulted in giving priority and power to the content of consciousness rather than to the unseen power of consciousness itself, by which content could be realized and recognized. The power was in the Light and not in the details of what was illuminated. The linear is also limitation and thus prone to error by virtue of the intrinsic defect of misidentifying perception as reality.

To transcend the linear to the nonlinear is the way of the mystic—the pathway of nonduality—to realize the inner light of consciousness itself, the True Immortal Self. Everyone trusts the inner sense of reality or capacity to "know" that underlies all experiencing and witnessing, no matter what the content. The content of mind thinks, but only the nonlinear field "knows," or how else would it be possible to know what is being thought?

Because everyone actually lives in the experiential at every moment, the Source of the capacity to know or experience is close at hand and is itself pristine. Everyone experiences that they are continuously "experiencing," no matter what the ever-changing content might be.

The earliest function of the evolution of consciousness was basic survival. Then came sensation and acquisition, and then relationship and emotion. Next came an interest in learning, knowing, growing, and expanding the fields of knowledge, including knowledge of the personal self, motivation, and psychology, and then curiosity arose about how we know and what is intrinsic and the source of life. Next came the question of existence as life or its corollary, life versus existence, which brought forth knowledge of Divinity/Creator/God as transcendent (conceptual) or Divinity as experiential and Immanent. Transcendent is religion, experiential is spiritual. The way of the mystic transcends belief and confirms its underlying Reality. It eliminates all doubt as the Knower and the Known coalesce as Self.

Everyone is already a mystic and innately attracted to Enlightenment, whether they are aware of it or not. It is an extension of the qualities of learning and curiosity, which are innate to the mind. Thus, the pathway to "Devotional Nonduality" is open to everyone and has no requirement other than the capacity for inner honesty and the willingness to align with verifiable truth and follow it to its Source. The natural and straightest way to Enlightenment has been discussed in the books *The Eye of the I* and *I: Reality and Subjectivity*, and will be more specifically described in the forthcoming books, *Transcending The Levels of Consciousness: The Stairway to God*, and *Devotional Nonduality*.

Gloria in Excelsis Deo!

APPENDICES

A. Calibration of Levels of Truth of the Chapters   410

B. Map of the Scale of Consciousness   412

C. How to Calibrate the Levels of Consciousness   413

D. Calibrations of Movies   419

E. Index of Calibration Tables and Illustrations   423

F. References   427

Appendix A
Calibration of Levels of Truth of the Chapters

Explanatory Note

As would be expected, Sections I and III, which are devoted to the nature of truth itself and to spiritual truth, calibrate the highest. Section II, which deals with problematic and social issues, reflects worldly error and illusions as viewed from the impersonal nonlinearity represented by the calibration levels of 600 and over. Despite the duality section (II) with "worldly issues," the book overall is still at 935, which compares acceptably with the range of previous books (*Power vs. Force*, 850; *The Eye of the I*, 980, and *I: Reality and Subjectivity*, 999.8).

Section I What is Truth?

Chapter	1	Historical Perspective	900
Chapter	2	The Science of Truth	935
Chapter	3	Truth as Enigma: The Challenge and the Struggle	855
Chapter	4	The Evolution of Consciousness	860
Chapter	5	The Essential Structure of Truth	900
Chapter	6	Manifestation versus Causality: Creation Versus Evolution	965
Chapter	7	The Physiology of Truth	750
Chapter	8	Fact Versus Fiction: Reality and Illusion	760

Section II Practical Applications

Chapter	9	Social Structure and Functional Truth	640
Chapter	10	America	620
Chapter	11	The Downside of Society	635
Chapter	12	Problematic Issues	640

Section III Truth and the World

Chapter 13	Truth: The Pathway to Freedom	935
Chapter 14	Countries and Politics	645
Chapter 15	Truth and War	725

Section IV Higher Consciousness and Truth

Chapter 16	Religion and Truth	935
Chapter 17	Spiritual Truth	980
Chapter 18	Summary and Resolution	940

The Book *Truth vs. Falsehood* overall   935

Appendix B
Map of the Scale of Consciousness

God-view	Self-view	Level	Log	Emotion	Process
Self	Is	Enlightenment	700-1,000	Ineffable	Pure Consciousness
All-being	Perfect	Peace	600	Bliss	Illumination
One	Complete	Joy	540	Serenity	Transfiguration
Loving	Benign	Love	500	Reverence	Revelation
Wise	Meaningful	Reason	400	Understanding	Abstraction
Merciful	Harmonious	Acceptance	350	Forgiveness	Transcendence
Inspiring	Hopeful	Willingness	310	Optimism	Intention
Enabling	Satisfactory	Neutrality	250	Trust	Release
Permitting	Feasible	Courage	200	Affirmation	Empowerment
Indifferent	Demanding	Pride	175	Scorn	Inflation
Vengeful	Antagonistic	Anger	150	Hate	Aggression
Denying	Disappointing	Desire	125	Craving	Enslavement
Punitive	Frightening	Fear	100	Anxiety	Withdrawal
Uncaring	Tragic	Grief	75	Regret	Despondency
Condemning	Hopeless	Apathy, hatred	50	Despair	Abdication
Vindictive	Evil	Guilt	30	Blame	Destruction
Despising	Hateful	Shame	20	Humiliation	Elimination

Above 200: Levels of Truth
Below 200: Levels of Falsehood

Appendix C
How to Calibrate the Levels of Consciousness

General Information

The energy field of consciousness is infinite in dimension. Specific levels correlate with human consciousness, and these have been calibrated from "1" to "1,000." (See Appendix B: Map of the Scale of Consciousness.) These energy fields reflect and dominate human consciousness.

Everything in the universe radiates a specific frequency, or minute energy field, that remains in the field of consciousness permanently. Thus, every person or being whoever lived, and anything about them, including any event, thought, deed, feeling, or attitude, is recorded forever and can be retrieved at any time in the present or the future.

Technique

The kinesiologic response (muscle testing) is a simple "yes" or "not yes" (no) response to a specific stimulus. In holistic health, it is usually done by the subject's holding out an extended arm and the tester pressing down on the wrist of the extended arm, using two fingers and light pressure. Usually the subject holds a substance to be tested over their solar plexus with the other hand. The tester says to the test subject, "Resist," and if the substance being tested is beneficial to the subject, the arm will be strong. If it is not beneficial or has an adverse effect, the arm will go weak. The response is very quick and brief.

This test has been done by thousands of practitioners all over the world for many years, and the reliability and accuracy of the results have been well studied and documented. (See References.) *It is important to note that both the tester and the one being tested must calibrate over 200 in order to obtain accurate responses.*

The higher the levels of consciousness of the test team, the more accurate are the results. The best results are obtained if both team members are in the mid-400s, which represent clarity, awareness of context, and precision of definition, as well as integrity, self-honesty, and awareness. The best attitude is one of clinical detachment, posing a statement with the prefix statement, "In the name of the highest good, _____ calibrates as true. Over 100. Over 200," etc. The contextualization "in the highest good" increases accuracy because it transcends self-serving personal interest and motives.

For many years, the test was thought to be a local response of the body's acupuncture or immune system. Later research, however, has revealed that the response was not a local response to the body at all, but was instead a general response of consciousness itself to a substance or a statement. That which is true, beneficial, or pro-life gives a positive response that stems from the impersonal field of consciousness that is present in everyone living. This positive response is indicated by the body's musculature going strong. For convenience, the deltoid muscle is usually the one best used as an indicator muscle; however, any of the muscles of the body can be used, such as the gastrocnemias, which are often used by practitioners such as chiropractors.

Before a question (in the form of a statement) is presented, it is necessary to qualify "permission"; that is, state "I have permission to ask about what I am holding in mind" (Yes/No), or "This calibration serves the highest good."

If a statement is false or a substance is injurious, the muscles go weak quickly in response to the command "Resist." This indicates the stimulus is negative, untrue, anti-life, or the answer is "no." The response is fast and brief in duration. The body will then rapidly recover and return to normal muscle tension.

The test requires two people: the tester and the test subject. A quiet setting is preferred, with no background music. The test subject closes their eyes. *The tester must phrase the "question" to be asked in the form of a _statement_.* The statement can then be answered as "yes" or "not yes" (no) by the kinesiologic response. For instance, the incorrect form would be to ask, "Is this a healthy horse?" rather than make the statement, "This horse is healthy," or its corollary, "This horse is sick."

After making the statement, the tester says "Resist" to the test subject who is holding the extended arm parallel to the ground.

The tester presses down with two fingers on the wrist of the extended arm sharply, with mild force. The test subject's arm will either stay strong, indicating a "yes," or go weak, indicating a "not yes" (no). The response is short and immediate.

Calibration of Specific Levels
The critical point between positive and negative, between true and false, or between that which is constructive or destructive is at the calibrated level of 200 (see chart). Anything above 200, or true, makes the subject go strong; anything below 200, or false, allows the arm to go weak.

Anything past or present, including images or statements, historical events, or personages, can be tested. They need not be verbalized.

Numerical Calibration
Example: "Ramana Marharshi's teachings calibrate over 700." (Y/N)

Or, "Hitler calibrated over 200." (Y/N) "When he was in his 20s." (Y/N) "His 30s." (Y/N) "His 40s." (Y/N) "At the time of his death." (Y/N)

Applications
The kinesiologic test cannot be used to foretell the future; otherwise, there are no limits as to what can be asked. Consciousness has no limits in time or space; however, permission may be denied. All current or historical events are available for questioning. The answers are impersonal and do not depend on the belief systems of either the tester or the test subject. For example, protoplasm recoils to noxious stimuli and flesh bleeds. Those are the qualities of these test materials and are impersonal. Consciousness actually knows only truth because only truth has actual existence. It does not respond to falsehood because falsehood does not have existence in reality. It will also not respond accurately to nonintegrous or egoistic questions, such as should one buy a certain stock, etc.

The kinesiologic response is therefore, accurately speaking, either an "on" response or it is merely "not on." Like the electrical switch, we say the electricity is "on," and when we use the term "off," we just mean that it is not there. In reality, there is no such thing as "off-ness." This is a subtle statement but crucial to the understanding of the nature of consciousness. Consciousness is capable of recognizing only Truth. It merely fails to respond to falsehood. Similarly, a mirror reflects an image only if there is an object to reflect. If no object is present to the mirror, there is no reflected image.

To Calibrate A Level
Calibrated levels are relative to a specific reference scale. To arrive at the same figures as in the chart in Appendix B, reference must be made to that table or by a statement such as, "On a scale of human consciousness from 1 to 1,000, where 600 indicates enlightenment, this _____ calibrates over _____ (a number)." Or, "On a scale of consciousness where 200 is the level of Truth and 500 is the level of Love, this statement calibrates over _____." (State a specific number.)

General Information
People generally want to determine truth from falsehood. Therefore, the statement has to be made very specifically. Avoid using general terms such as a "good" job to apply for. "Good" in what way? Pay scale? Working conditions? Promotional opportunities? Fairness of the boss?

Expertise
Familiarity with the test brings progressive expertise. The "right" questions to ask begin to spring forth and can become almost uncannily accurate. If the same tester and test subject work together for a period of time, one or both of them will develop what can become an amazing accuracy and capability of pinpointing just what specific questions to ask, even though the subject is totally unknown by either one. For instance, the tester has lost an object and begins to say, "I left it in my office." (Answer: No.) "I left it in the car." (Answer: No.) All of a sudden, the test subject almost "sees" the object and says, "Ask, 'On the back of the bathroom

door.'" The test subject says, "The object is hanging on the back of the bathroom door." (Answer: Yes.) In this actual case, the test subject did not even know that the tester had stopped for gas and left the jacket in the restroom of a gasoline station.

Any information can be obtained about anything anywhere in current or past time or space. By crosschecking, accuracy can be easily confirmed. It is normal to be skeptical at first. To anyone who learns the technique, however, more information is available instantaneously than can be held in all the computers and libraries of the world. The possibilities are therefore obviously unlimited, and the prospects breathtaking.

Limitations

Approximately ten percent of the population is not able to use the kinesiologic testing technique for as yet unknown reasons other than that it is due to an "imbalance of their 'chi' energy." The test is accurate only if the test subjects themselves calibrate over 200 and the intention of the question is also integrous. Sometimes married couples, also for reasons as yet undiscovered, are unable to use each other as test subjects and may have to find a third person for a test partner.

A suitable test subject is a person whose arm goes strong when a love object or person is held in mind, and it goes weak if that which is negative (fear, hate, guilt, etc.) is held in mind (e.g., Winston Churchill makes one go strong and bin Laden makes one go weak).

Occasionally, a suitable test subject gives paradoxical responses. This can usually be cleared by doing the "thymic thump," as was discovered by Dr. John Diamond. (With a closed fist, thump three times over the upper breastbone, smile, and say "ha-ha-ha" with each thump and mentally picture someone or something that is loved.)

The temporary imbalance will then clear up. It can be occasioned by recently having been with negative people, listening to heavy metal rock music, watching violent television programs, playing violent video games, etc. Negative music energy has a deleterious effect on the energy system of the body for up to one-half hour after it is turned off. Television commercials or background are also a common source of negative energy.

Explanation

The kinesiologic test is independent of personal opinion or beliefs and is an impersonal response of the field of consciousness, which, like protoplasm, is impersonal in its responses. This can be demonstrated by the observation that the test responses are the same whether verbalized or held silently in mind. Thus, the test subject is not influenced by the question, as they don't even know what it is. To demonstrate this, do the following exercise:

The tester holds in mind an image unknown to the test subject and states, "The image I am holding in mind is positive." (Or true, or calibrates over 200, etc.) On direction, the test subject then resists the downward pressure on the wrist. If the tester holds a positive image in mind (e.g., Abraham Lincoln, Jesus, Mother Theresa, etc.), the test subject's arm muscle will go strong. If the tester holds a false statement or negative image in mind (e.g., bin Laden, Hitler, etc.), the arm will go weak. Inasmuch as the test subject does not know what the tester has in mind, the results are not influenced by personal beliefs.

Correct Kinesiological Technique

Just as Galileo's interest was in astronomy and not in making telescopes, the Institute for Advanced Spiritual Research is devoted to Consciousness research and not specifically to kinesiology. The video, Power Versus Force (Veritas Publishing, 1995), demonstrates the basic technique, which is also demonstrated in the more recent Calibration of Levels of Truth by Kinesiology (Veritas Publishing, 2005). More detailed information about kinesiology may be found on the Internet by searching for "kinesiology." Numerous references are provided, such as the College of Applied Kinesiology (www.icak.com), and other educational institutions.

Appendix D
Movies

2001: A Space Odyssey	440	Breakfast Club	300
A Beautiful Mind	375	Breakfast at Tiffany's	360
About Schmidt	435	Bridge on the River Kwai, The	385
A Clockwork Orange	70		
A Fish Called Wanda	230	Bringing Up Baby	255
African Queen, The	395	Butch Cassidy & the Sundance Kid	270
Aliens	145		
All About Eve	300	Bye Bye Birdie	245
All Quiet on the Western Front	150	Caddy Shack	205
		Carnal Knowledge	155
Amadeus	455	Casablanca	385
A Man for All Seasons	455	Cat in the Hat	130
American Beauty	380	Charade	305
American Graffiti	365	Chariots of Fire	425
An American in Paris	355	Charlotte's Web	335
Annie Hall	355	Chicago	385
Apartment, The	200	Chinatown	315
Apocalypse Now	65	Citizen Kane	400
Around the World in 80 Days	385	City Lights	355
		Cleopatra	365
Babe	350	Clockwork Orange	70
Barbarella	185	Close Encounters of the Third Kind	265
Barefoot in the Park	395		
Batman	210	Color Purple, The	475
Ben-Hur	475	Cool Hand Luke	255
Best Years of Our Lives	360	Crocodile Dundee	265
Beverly Hills Cop	180	Dances with Wolves	375
Big Blue	700	Deliverance	145
Birds, The	215	Deer Hunter, The	155
Birth of a Nation, The	140	Dickens' Christmas Carol	499
Blade Runner	225	Dr. Strangelove	225
Bonnie and Clyde	105	Doctor Zhivago	415
Bowling for Columbine	185	Double Indemnity	315
Braveheart	275	Driving Miss Daisy	395

Easy Rider	195	Harry Potter	215
English Patient, The	250	Hello Dolly	380
Empire of the Sun	490	High Noon	275
ET: The Extraterrestrial	375	In Cold Blood	80
Exorcist, The	140	In the Heat of the Night	165
Fail Safe	255	It Happened One Night	255
Falling Down	90	It's Alive	125
Fahrenheit 9/11	195	It's a Mad, Mad, Mad	
Fantasia	475	World	290
Fatal Attraction	140	It's a Wonderful Life	450
Field of Dreams	390	Jaws	140
Ferris Bueller's Day Off	330	Jazz Singer, The	390
Forrest Gump	475	Jerry Maguire	375
French Connection	275	Jurassic Park	330
From Here to Eternity	395	King Kong	175
Funny Girl	385	Kramer vs. Kramer	205
Gandhi	455	LA Confidential	205
Ghostbusters	235	Last Emperor, The	385
Giant	350	Last Picture Show	375
Gigi	375	Lawrence of Arabia	320
Godfather, The	155	Legally Blonde	355
Godfather, Part II, The	155	Lethal Weapon	105
Godzilla	180	Lion King, The	415
Goldfinger	215	Little Buddha	445
Gold Rush, The	260	Lord of the Flies	270
Gone with the Wind	400	Lord of the Rings	350
Good Fellas	100	Lost Horizon	485
Graduate, The	325	Love Story	310
Grapes of Wrath, The	385	Malcolm X	215
Grease	330	Mad Max	160
Great Gatsby, The	350	Maltese Falcon, The	325
Greatest Show on Earth	390	Manhattan	305
Guess Who's Coming		Marty	235
to Dinner?	305	M*A*S*H*	360
Halloween	85	Matrix, The	165
Hamlet	405	Midnight Cowboy	195

Miracle on 34th Street	390
Monty Python and the Holy Grail	215
Moonstruck	325
Mr. Smith Goes to Washington	395
Murder on the Orient Express	365
My Big Fat Greek Wedding	385
My Fair Lady	405
Network	255
North by Northwest	340
Notorious	145
Oliver!	365
Omen, The	85
One Flew Over the Cuckoo's Nest	160
On the Waterfront	295
Ordinary People	275
Out of Africa	390
Paper Moon	300
Passion of Christ	190
(Edited version)	395
Patton	345
Philadelphia Story, The	405
Place in the Sun, A	210
Platoon	180
Predator	145
Pretty Woman	375
Psycho	80
Pulp Fiction	25
Raging Bull	255
Raiders of the Lost Ark	385
Rain Man	410
Rebel Without a Cause	310

Return of the Kind	350
River's Edge	310
Rocky	265
Rocky Horror Picture Show	205
Rosemary's Baby	60
St. Elmo's Fire	105
Saturday Night Fever	395
Saving Private Ryan	195
Schindler's List	180
Searchers, The	315
Seven Days in May	340
Sex, Lies, and Videotape	140
Shakespeare in Love	395
Shane	390
Shining, The	55
Silence of the Lambs	45
Singin' in the Rain	415
Sixth Sense, The	310
Sleepless in Seattle	350
Some Like It Hot	355
Sound of Music, The	425
Spiderman	255
Stagecoach	350
Star Wars	250
Sting, The	295
Streetcar Named Desire	315
Taxi Driver	360
Terminator	125
Terms of Endearment	425
Thelma and Louise	140
There's Something about Mary	105
Third Man, The	200
Titanic, The	405
To Kill a Mockingbird	310

Tom Jones	195		Wall Street	225
Tootsie	355		Way We Were, The	350
Toy Story	400		West Side Story	405
Treasure of the Sierra			Wild Bunch, The	270
Madre	200		Winged Migration	495
Twin Towers, The	350		Wizard of Oz, The	450
Valley of the Dolls	200		Wuthering Heights	360
Vertigo	105		Yankee Doodle Dandy	400
Willie Wonka	345		Young Frankenstein	255
Wait Until Dark	110		You've Got Mail	275

Appendix E
Calibration Tables and Illustrations

Chapter 3: **Historical Perspective**
The Great Books of the Western World — 18

Chapter 4: **The Evolution of Consciousness**
Animal Kingdom — 32
Consciousness Level of Archeological Eras — 38
Evolution of Human Consciousness (graph) — 39

Chapter 5: **The Essential Structure of Truth**
Content, Field, and Context (illustration) — 45
Content, Field, and Context — 46

Chapter 7: **The Physiology of Truth**
Brain Function and Physiology (illustration) — 64

Chapter 9: **Social Structure and Functional Truth**
Distribution of World Levels of
Consciousness (illustration) — 89
Distribution of Consciousness Level of
Mankind (illustration) — 90-91
Distribution of Levels of Consciousness –
Regional Samples — 91
Places of Interest — 92
Daily Life — 94-95
Energy of Music – Modern — 97
Music – Classical — 98
Music – Spiritual — 98
Classical Music Performers — 98
Classical Music Eras — 99
Artists – Creative Works — 104
Sports and Hobbies — 106
Movies — 107-08
Television — 110
The Social Impact of Famous Persons — 110-11
Entertainers/Humorists — 111
News Broadcast Media — 113
Politics and Election: Voters by Party — 115
Diagnostic Scale—Politics and Election
2004 (illustration) — 116

News, Commentators and the Political
  Spectrum   120
News Print Media   121
Others   122
"100 Most Influential People in The World"   122
Literary Works of Authors   124
Industries (United States)   126
Television Commercials (not products)   128
Energy Fields of Famous Industrialists   129
Philanthropic Foundations   130
Corporations   131
Unions   133
Law Enforcement   134
Science – Theory   134-35
Science – Clinical   137
Science – Scientists   139
Major Universities and Schools   140

Chapter 10: **America**
America – U. S. Government   144
U. S. Politics   149
U. S. Government Departments and
  Agencies   150
U. S. Policies and Agencies   150
Judicial System   153
Public Service Organizations and Programs   154
Correlation of Levels of Consciousness
  and Societal Problems   159
Gallup Organization Survey – Canada   172

Chapter 11: **The Downside of Society**
Antisocial Calibrations of Society   181
Behavioral   183
Overt Violence   184
Drugs and Alcohol   185
Severe Behavioral/Psychiatric Disorders   186
Personality Disorders   187
Criminality   187
Criminals   188
Espionage and Political Criminality   194

USA vs. R. Hannsen: Sentencing
        Memorandum   195

Chapter 12: **Problematic Issues**
        Problematic Positionalities and Issues   202
        Problematic Philosophies   209-10
        Significant Calibrations (Free Speech)   225
        Contrasting Calibrations   226

Chapter 13: **Truth: The Pathway to Freedom**
        Function of Mind – Attitudes (Table 1)   235-36
        Function of Mind – Attitudes (Table 2)   237-38
        Function of Mind – Attitudes (Table 3)   239-40
        Spiritual Foundations – The Basics – Part I   251
        Spiritual Foundations – The Basics – Part II   253
        Philosophers and Philosophies   254-55
        Intellectual Disciplines   255

Chapter 14: **Countries and Politics**
        Political Systems   263
        Historical Societies   263-264
        Political History – Major Figures; Recent   264
            Current   265
        Countries and Regions of the World (Current)   266
        Map 1: Consciousness Levels –
            Western Hemisphere   274
        Map 2: Consciousness Levels –
            Eastern Hemisphere   275
        Map 3: Consciousness Levels –
            Africa and the Middle East   276
        Basic Diagnostic Chart of Relationships   278
        Diagnostic Chart of International
            Relationships   279
        Characteristics of Dangerous Political
            Leaders   280-81

Chapter 15: **Truth and War**
        The Great War: World War II   287-88
        Contrasting Wars: Korean, Vietnam,
            Cold, Gulf, World War I   294
        Comparative: Napoleonic Wars – Waterloo   294

Iraqi War (Early) Above and Below 200   295
Iraqi War (Late)   296
Media Coverage of the Iraqi War   296
Additional Calibrations of Iraqi War (Late) 299-300
9/11 Calibrations   300
9/11 Investigative Committee Hearings
    (April-July, 2004)   301
Terrorist Organizations   308-10
Knowledge of Politicians   316
Application of Critical Factor, Attractor
    Field Analysis-Int'l. Nuclear Programs   322

Chapter 16: **Religion and Truth**
Christianity (Early, Catholicism)   334
Christianity (Roman Catholic,
    Post-Reformation)   335
Roman Catholicism, Current Positions   337
Buddhism   340
Hinduism (Ancient, The Yogas, Others)   342
Islam   344
Judaism   348
Other Religions   350
Marginal Spiritual/Religious Belief Systems 359
Places of Spiritual Interest   362

Chapter 17: **Spiritual Truth**
Scriptures and Spiritual Writings   366-68
Verses of the Old Testament   371
Verses of the Koran   373
Spiritual Teachers   376-77
Divinity and Avatars   382-83
Avatars and Great Spiritual Teachers   384
Other References to Divinity   385
Spiritual Experiences   386
Other Phenomena and Belief Systems   388
Comparative Experiences   389
Authentic Spiritual State – Pathologic State 394-96
Spiritual Practices   397
Other Teachings, Schools, and Spiritual
    Traditions   398

Appendix F
References

Note: Although primary sources are preferred in academic research, they are generally not available to the reading public; therefore, many secondary sources are supplied as they are more available via the Internet.

"$445 Billion Deficit Forecast for 2004." 2004. *Associated Press* in *Arizona Republic*, 31 July.

Abraham, L. 2004 "The Clash of Civilizations and the Great Caliphate." http://www.insiderreport.net/clash_1-2.html, 10 May.

Abu-Nasr, D. 2004. "Saudi Religious Scholars Back Anti-U. S. War by Iraqis." *Associated Press*, 7 November.

"Academics and the Economist: Capitalist, Sexist Pigs." 2004. Editorial. *Economist*, 18 December. (Satire on Postmodern Deconstructionism ala Jacques Derrida and Michael Foucault as per "critical studies," the death of which studies is now proclaimed by Prof. Stanley Fish.)

"ACOG Red Alert Now Reaches 23 States. OB/Gyn Crisis." 2004. Editorial. *Arizona Medical News*, 3 September. (Crisis of catastrophic jury awards and cost of malpractice insurance.)

A Course in Miracles. (1975) 1996. Mill Valley, Calif.: Foundation for Inner Peace.

"A Defiant Saddam." 2004. *Arizona Republic*, 2 July.

Alcoholics Anonymous. 2000. 4th ed. New York: Alcoholics Anonymous World Services.

Allen, H. 2004. "Muslim Cleric Emerges As Serious U. S. Foe." (Knight Ridder) *Seattle Times*, 11 July.

Allison, G. 2004. *Nuclear Terrorism: The Ultimate Preventable Catastrophe*. New York: Times Books. (Nuclear attack by terrorists likely; focus on Iran and Islamics.)

—. 2004. "Nuclear Terror Strike More Likely Than Not in Next Decade." Special report. *Arizona Republic*. 7 December. (Al-Qaeda threats are likely to be carried out.)

"Al-Qaeda Training Tapes. 2004. *CNN News*, 8 August. (Terrorist instruction.)

"American Discoveries: Smithsonian's Phenomenal, Respectful New National Museum Does Native Peoples, Nation Proud." 2004. Editorial. *Arizona Republic*, 19 September.

American Film Institute. 2003. "100 Top Movies of All Time."

Amoroso, R. L. 2004. *What is Consciousness? Introducing The Cosmology of Being.* Orinda, Calif.: Noetic Sciences Institute.

Anchors, S. 2003. "When Angels Speak." *Arizona Republic*, 23 January, E1-2. (Channeling)

Anderson, C. 2004. "Major American Muslim Charity Supports Hamas." *Associated Press*, 27 July.

Anderson, E. 2003. "To The Victor Go The Spoils." *Wall Street Underground*, April/May 6:8.

—. 2002. "Acts of God?" *Philadelphia Trumpet*. Sept./Oct., 20-25.

Anderson, P. 1998. *The Origins of Postmodernity.* London: Verso.

Anderson, S., and P. Ray. 2000. *The Cultural Creatives: How 50 Million People Are Changing the World.* New York: Harmony Books.

Andresen, J., and R. Forman, Eds. 2000. *Cognitive Models and Spiritual Maps.* Charlottesville, Va.: Imprint Academic and Philosophy Documentation Center.

Angelin, R. 2004. "Fight over Parking Ticket Rages on for 12 Years." *Arizona Republic*, 29 March. (Costs over $250,000.)

Anglaw, R. 2004. "Agent Says Terrorists Will Hit Again." *Arizona Republic*, 21 November. (Ken Williams, Phoenix FBI agent, wrote 9/11 warning on Flight schools; field office ignored by headquarters.)

Ankarlo, Darrell. 2004. *What Went Wrong with America--And How to Fix It: Reclaiming The Power That Rightfully Belongs To You.* Nashville, Tenn.: Cumberland House Publishing.

Angler, N. 2003. "Is War Our Biologic Destiny?" *New York Times*, 11 November.

Applebaum, A. 2004. "The Decline and Fall of Network News." *Arizona Republic*, 23 September.

Appleby, J. 2004. "Pfizer Offers Drug Discounts to Uninsured." *USA Today*, 8 July.

Archibald, R. C. 2004. "Permit or Not, Protestors Prepare for Republicans in New York." *New York Times*, 24 May.

Arehart-Treichel, J. 2004. "Why Are We Taken in By Duplicity?" *Psychiatric News*, 19 March.

—. 2004. "Psychoanalysis Reinterprets Role of Religion, Spirituality." *Psychiatric New,* 19 March.

—. 2003. "Trauma May Alter Brain Structure." *Psychiatric News.* 17 December.

Argenopoulus, J. 1972. "Self-realization and Self-defeat." *New Horizons.* Escanoba, Mich.: Enrichment Bureau.

Aristotle. (330 B.C.) 1962. *The Nichemachean Ethics.* Trans. M. Ostwald. New York: Bobbs-Merrill.

—. 1952. "Logic," "On Sophistical Refutations." *The Great Books of the Western World.* Vol. 8:5-227. Chicago: Encyclopedia Britannica.

—. 1952. "Caragorias". Op cit., 227-259.

—. 1952. "Metaphysics." Op cit., 445-631.

Arlow, J. A., and C. Brenner. 1972. *Psychoanalytic Concepts and the Structural Theory.* New York: International Universities Press.

Armendoria, Y. 2004. "12.2 Million Say They Are Own Boss." *Arizona Republic*, 3 December. (Entrepreneurship on the rise.)

Arnold, R. 2004. (Reissue) *Ecoterror: The Violent Agenda to Save Nature: The World of the Unabomber*. Bellevue, Wash.: Free Enterprise Press.

Arntz, W., and B. Chase (Producers) and Vicente, M., et al (Directors). 2004. *What the #$*! Do We Know?* Yelm, Wash.: Lord of the Wind Films, LLC.

Arostagui, M. 2001. "Fidel Part of Terror Campaign." *Insight on the News.* 9 November. www.latinamericanstudies.org/us-cuba/terror-campaign.htm 12/2/2004.

Arum, R. 2003. *Judging School Discipline Is the Crisis of Moral Authority.* Cambridge, Mass.: Harvard University Press.

Atmanspacher, H., and R. G. John. 2003. "Problems of Reproducibility in Complex Mind-Matter Systems." *Journal of Science Exploration,* 17, 243-270.

"Attacking a Cult." 2004. *Arizona Republic* (Editorial), 4 August. (Polygamists hide behind religion.)

Ayer, A. J. 1966. *Logical Positivism.* New York: Free Press.

—. [1936] 1952. *Language, Truth, and Logic.* Reprint, New York: Dover Publications.

Babbin, J. 2004. *Inside the Asylum: Why the United Nations and Old Europe Are Worse Than You Think.* New York: Regnery.

Babula, J. 2004. "Doctors Trying to Convince Parents ADHD is Real." *Arizona Republic*, 7 April.

Bahá'u'lláh. 1993. *The Kitab-I-Aqdes: The Most Holy Book.* Wilmette, IL: Baha'i Publishing Trust.

—. 1985. *Waging Peace: Selections from the Baha'i Writings on Universal Peace.* Novato, CA: Kalimat Press.

—. 1976. *Gleanings from the Writings.* Wilmette, IL: Baha'i Publishing Trust.

Bailey, A. 1950. *Glamour: A World Problem.* New York: Lucius Book Co.

Bailie, G. 1997. *Violence Unveiled: Humanity at the Crossroads.* New York: Crossroads Publishing Co.

Baker, N. 2004. *Checkpoint: A Novel.* New York: Knopf.

Balleu, D. 2004. "New York City Teachers Union Contract: Shocking Principals' Leadership." Dept. Econ., University of Mass., Amherst. www.ManhattanInstituteorg.html/cr6.htm, 1-19.

Balsekar, R. 2003. *The Happening of A Guru: A Biography of Ramesh Balsekar.* New Delhi, India: Yogi Impressions Press. (The subjective state, experience, and reality of Enlightenment.)

Barbour, J. 2000. *The End of Time.* Oxford: Oxford University Press.

Bartlett, D., and J. Steele. 2004. "Why We Pay So Much for Drugs." *Time*, 2 February, 44-52. (A study of the pharmaceutical industry.)

Barone, M. 2004. "A Place Like No Other." *U. S. News & World Report*, 28 June.

Barr, S. 2003. *Modern Physics and Ancient Faith.* Notre Dame, Indiana: University of Notre Dame Press.

Bartholomew, A. 2003. "Life After Death: the Scientific Core for the Human Soul." *Readers Digest*, August, 122-128.

Beardsley, M. C. 1960. *The European Philosophers from Descartes to Nietzsche.* New York: Modern Library.

Beauchamp, T. 1992. *Philosophical Ethics: An Introduction to Moral Philosophy.* 2nd ed. New York: McGraw Hill.

Beck, D., and C. Cowan. 1996. *Spiral Dynamics.* Oxford: Blackwell.

Beck, U. 1992. *Risk Society: Towards A New Modernity.* London: Sage.

Begley, S. (2004). "Scans of Monks' Brains Show Meditation Alters Structure and Functioning." *Science Journal*. (Proceedings of National Academy of Science.)

Behr, A., et al. 2004. "New Developments in Chemical Engineering for Lower Cost Production of Drug Substances." *Engineering in Life Sciences*, 4 January, 15-23.

Behrens, J.C. 2004. "Let's Stop Dissing Each Other: Public Rudeness." *Elks Magazine*, March.

Behring, K. 2004. *Road to Progress*. Danville, Calif.: Wheelchair Foundation. (From poverty to wealth, then establishment of www. wheelchairfound.org. Welcome worldwide philanthropy.)

Belsey, C. 2002. *Post-Structuralism*. Oxford: Oxford University Press.

Bender, E. 2004. "Juvenile offenders languish awaiting mental health services, Congress learns." *Psychiatric News* 39:16, 20 August. (Thousands of adolescents kept in detention for lack of mental health services.)

—. 2004. "Psychiatrists Urge More Direct Focus on Patient's Spirituality." *Psychiatric News*, 18 June.

Benthuysan, B. 2002. "Tour of Buddhist Relics At Cultural Park: Maitreya Projects Heart-Shrine Relic Tour." *Sedona (Arizona) Red Rock News*, 8 May.

Berg, R. P. S. 2002. *The Essential Zohar*. New York: Bell Tower.

Berger, D. and R. Schnack. 2003. "Music Therapy as Clinical Intervention for Physiologic Function Adaptation." *Journal of Scientific Exploration*, 17:4, 687-705.

Berger, P. 2004. "Bin Laden, Holy War, Nuclear Connections: Russia, Pakistan, Afghanistan, Philippines, Yemen, and Recruitment in U.S. Islamic School." *National Geographic* Television Documentary, 2 August.

Berlinski, D. 2002. "Einstein and Goedal." *Discover*, March, 39-42. (General relativity, space, time, and gravity, and search for unified field theory.)

Berman, P. 2003. "Al-Qaeda's Philosopher of Islamic Terror (Sayyid Qutb)." *New York Times Magazine*, 23 March.

Bernstein, D. 2003. You Can't Say That!: The Growing Threat to Civil Liberties from Antidiscrimination Laws. Washington, DC: The Cato Institute. (Politically correct censorship; violations of the First Amendment.)

Berry, G. L. 1947. *Religions of The World*. New York: Barnes and Noble.

"Best Universities and Colleges." 2004. *U. S. News & World Report*, 30 August.

"Beyond Brown vs. Board: The Final Battle for Excellence in American Education." Rockefeller Foundation. 2004. *New York Magazine*. n.d.

Bhanot, A. 2004. "Creating A New Culture." www.lifepositive.com/mind/culturalcreatives.

—. 2003. "Spiritual and Religious Books Expanding at an Accelerating Rate." *Publishers Weekly*, 8 December.

Bingen, H. 1987. *Book of Divine Works*. Santa Fe, New Mexico: Bear and Co.

Birnbaum, J. 1991. "Exculpations Crybabies: Eternal Victims." *Time*, 12 August. (Hypersensitivity and special pleading are making a travesty of the virtues that used to be known as individual responsibility and common sense.)

Bittner, E., and J. Villa. 2004. "Paranoia Haunted Killer." *Arizona Republic*, 31 August.

Blakemore, S., D. Oakley, et al. 2003. "Delusions of Alien Control in the Normal Brain." *Neuropsychologia* 41, 1058-67.

Blakemore, S., C. Firth, et al. 1999. "Spatiotemporal Prediction Modulates the Perception of Self-produced Stimuli." *Journal of Cognitive Neuroscience* 11, 551-559.

Blankenship, J. 2004. "Women Change Face of Military." *VFW*, March.

Bloom, A. 1988. *The Closing of the American Mind*. New York: Simon & Schuster

Bloom, P. 2004. *Descartes' Baby: How the Science of Child Development Explains What Makes Us Human*. New York: Basic Books.

Blustein, P. 2004. "Consulting Firm Urges Offshoring: Only Way Firms Will Survive." *Arizona Republic*, 4 July.

Blyth, M. 2004. *Spin Sisters: How the Women of the Media Sell Unhappiness and Liberalism to the Women of America.* New York: St. Martin's Press.

Bohm, D. 1990. "A New Theory of the Relationship of Mind to Matter." *Philosophic Psychology* 3, 271-286.

—. 1980. *Quantum Theory.* New York: Prentice-Hall.

—. 1980. *Wholeness and the Implicate Order.* London: Routledge & Kagan Paul.

Bohm, D., and F. D. Peet. 2000. *Science, Order, and Creativity.* 2nd ed. New York: Routledge.

Bohm, D., and B. J. Hiley. 1993. *The Undivided Universe.* New York: Routledge.

Borger, G. 2004. "Why Church Matters." *U. S. News & World Report,* 14 June.

Bosh, L. 2004 "Nation with a Mission." State of the Nation Address. *Arizona Republic,* 21 January.

—. 2004. "How Your Love Life Keeps You Healthy." *Time,* 19 January.

Bowden, M. 2004. *Road Work: Among Tyrants, Beasts, Heroes, and Rogues.* New York: Atlantic Monthly Press.

—. 2004. "United in Greed." *Arizona Republic,* 19 November. (America went alone into Iraq. UN Security Council members on Hussein's $21 billion payout: France, Russia, Syria, China, and U.N. itself.)

Boyce, N. 2004. "Is There A Tonic in the Toxin?" *U. S. News & World Report,* 18 October. (Theory of Hormesis.)

—. 2004. "Pursuing the Poachers." *U. S. News & World Report,* 18 October. (Elephant ivory.)

Boyd, R. S. 2004. "Reagan's Lasting Mark on U.S. and the World." *Knight Ridder,* 6 June.

Brezosky, L. 2005. "Border Comeback?" *Arizona Republic,* 3 January.

Bridis, T. 2004. "Mosque Leaders Caught in Arms Plot Sting." *Associated Press,* 6 August. (Albany, N. Y. Imams.)

"British Charge 8 Linked to U. S. Threats." 2004. *Arizona Republic,* 18 August. (Al-Qaeda plans to bomb targets in New York, Washington, New Jersey. Pakistan connection. Terrorists handbook.)

Broder, D. 2004. "Media big losers in '04." *Washington Post Group,* 26 September.

—. 2004. "New Smile on an Old Visage." *Arizona Republic,* 11 June. (China)

Brooke, J. 2004. "Enemies in the Heart of Battle, Friends for 60 Years." http://www.nytimes.com/2004/06/20/national/20saipan/html?ex-1088776037/&ae:=1.

Brooks, D. 2004. "Saddam's Insanity Nearly Won." *New York Times*, 12 October. (Duelfer Report.)

—. 2004. "2 leaders, 2 Visions for Running the World." *New York Times*, 17 October. (Freedom, independence self-sufficiency, and individualism vs. interdependence, tolerance, social issues.)

—. 2003. "Educated Class Rift Splits Nation – Professionals vs. Business." *New York Times, Arizona Republic*, 16 June.

—. 2004. "Stem Cell Science." *Arizona Republic*, 16 June.

—. 2004. "We Must See the Reality of These Killers." *Arizona Republic*, 27 April.

Bronowski, J. 1976. *The Ascent of Man*. Boston: Little, Brown & Co.

Brook, A. 2004. "Kant, Cognitive Science and Contemporary Non-Kantism." *Journal of Consciousness Studies* 11:10-11, 1-26. (Self-perception is not fact.)

Bruce, T. 2003. *The Death of Right and Wrong*. Roseville, CA: Prime Publishers. (Forum)

Bruteau, B. 2002. *Radical Optimism: Practicality Reality in an Uncertain World*. Sentient Publications, 1st Sentie ed.

Budenholzer, F. E. 2004. "Emergence, Probability, and Reductionism." *Zygon* 39:2, June, 339-357.

Burns, J. 2004. "Reforming the CIA." *Washington Times*. 29 January. *News World Commentaries*. www.washingtontimes.com.

—. 2002. "1970s Laws Crippled FBI and CIA." *CNNNews.com*. 2 July.

Butler, A. 1985. *The Lives of The Saints*. New York: Harper and Row.

Butler, R. 2000. *The Greatest Threat: Iraqi, Weapons of Mass Destruction and the Growing Crisis of Global Security*. New York: Public Affairs Press.

Butler, C. 2002. *Post-Modernism*. Oxford: Oxford University Press.

Caerlinski, G. 2004. "Correlation of Levels of Consciousness and Distribution Curve Equivalents in Microwatts." Personal correspondence, 21 January.

Calabres, M., J. Dickerson, and D. Fonda. 2004. "The Truth of the Matter." *Time*, 5 April.

Calabresi, G. 2004. "Audience Gasps as Judge Likens Election of Bush to That of Mussolini and Hitler." *New York Sun*, 21 June.

"Canada Implements Gender Equality." 2004. *Toronto News*, 27 June.

Canfield, Jack. 2004. *The Success Principles: How to Get from Where You Are to Where You Want to Be*. New York: HarperResource. (Proven formulas and insights, practical rather than theoretical.)

Cannell, M. 2003. "I. M. Pei, Mandarin of Modernism." www.washingtonpost.com.

Cantoni, C. 2004. "Intellectual Nuance is First Victim of Left, Right's Immigration War." *Arizona Republic*, 27 June.

Caplan, J. 2004. "See You in Court, Teach." *Time*, 3 May.

Caplan, M. 2001. *Halfway Up The Mountain*. Prescott, Ariz.: Hohm Press.

Carey, B. 2004. "Payback Time: Why Revenge Tastes So Sweet." *New York Times*, 27 July. (Mental health and behavior.)

Carlisle, J. 2004. National Legal Policy Center. Interview. *Fox News*, 29 September. (Far Left utilizes billionaire financial character assassination to push its agenda.)

Carnap, R. 2003. *The Logical Structure of the World and Pseudoproblems in Philosophy*. Chicago: Open Court Publishing Co.

Carney, O. 1999. *The Victory of Surrender*. Bloomington, Indiana: First Books Library.

Carroll, J. 2004. "Values and the Boy Scouts." *American Legion*. February, 12-14.

Cavuto, N. 2004. *More than Money*. New York: Regan Books.

Chalmers, D. 2003. Review of *Journal of Consciousness Studies*. Dept. of Philosophy, University of Arizona. www.chalmars@arizona.edu.

Chandler, D. C. 1998. "Alex, The Gray Parrot That Counts, Talks, and Reads." *Boston Globe Online*. http://pubpages.unh.edu-jel/video/alex.html.

Chandler, S. 2004. "Execs Take Companies' Cash As a Privilege." *Chicago Tribune*, 19 September. (Top executives lose sense of reality and help themselves without restraint.)

Chandrasekher, S. 1987. *Truth and Beauty: Aesthetics and Motivations in Science*. Chicago: University of Chicago Press.

Chappell, K. 2003. "What Is Your Karma?" *Ebony*. September.

Charah, R., and J. Vseem. 2003. "Fortune 500 Companies 2003." *Fortune*. 14 April, F1-66.

—. 2002. "Why Companies Fail." *Fortune*, 27 May, 50-62.

Charen, M. *Do-Gooders: How Liberals Hurt Those They Claim To Help-- And The Rest Of Us*. Somerset, New Jersey: Sentinel Publishing Co.

—. 2003. *Useful Idiots: How Liberals Got It Wrong in the Cold War and Still Blame America First*. Washington, DC: Regnery Publishing.

Chantterjee, S. 2004. "9-11 Panel Rip Lack of Urgency. *Knight Ridder*, 31 July. (After 3 years, nobody in charge 9/11 Commission Report)." (No integrated counter-terrorism.)

Chomsky, N. 2004. "The World's Rent-A-Thug." http://www.thirdworldtraveler.com/chomsky/chomodon_thug.html.

—. 2003-2004. Misc. Articles. http://www.disinfopedia.org/wiki. phtml?title= Noam Chomsky.

—. 2003. "Hagemony or Survival: America's Quest for Global Dominance." New York: Metropolitan Books.

—. 2002. *On Nature and Language*. Cambridge: Cambridge University Press.

—. 2001. *9-11*. New York: Seven Stories Press.

—. 1998. *Profit Over People: Neoliberalism & Global Order.* New York: Seven Stories Press.

Churchill, W. [1957]. 2002. *History of the English Speaking People: New World, 1485-1688*. (Vol. 1-5). Reprint. New York: Dodd Mead.

Clancy, M. 2004. "Tucson Catholic Diocese Faces Liquidation." *Arizona Republic*, 7 November. (Bankrupted by clergy pedophilia.)

—. 2004. "Diocese Files for Bankruptcy." *Arizona Republic*. 25 September.

—. 2004. "Passion Tests Faithfuls' Emotions: Inspiration, Joy and Exhaustion." *Arizona Republic*, 24 February.

Clark, R. A. 2004. *Against All Enemies: Inside America's War on Terror*. New York: Free Press.

Cleckley, H. 1982. *The Mask of Sanity: An Attempt to Clarify Some Issues About the So- Called Psychopathic Personality.* New York: Plume Books (Penguin Group USA).

Cohen, R. 2004. "As Children Blow up Children, the U.N. Looks the Other Way." *Arizona Republic*, 3 March.

Collins, J. 2003. "The View from Abroad." *Time*. 4 August.

—. 2003. "The 10 Greatest CEO's of All Time." *Fortune*, 148:2, July, 55-68.

Colmes, A. 2003. *Red, White, and Liberal*. New York: Regan Books.

Colson, C. 2004. "The Atheist's God: the Real Madalyn Murray O'Hare." http://www.darrenweeks.net/doubters//ohare.htm.

Conniff, R. 2004. "Black Eye for the BBC: Battle of the Beeb." *Smithsonian*, April, 74-83. (Airing unfounded allegations.)

Cordova, R. 2004. "Valley Talk Radio Yields to Left." *Arizona Republic*, 23 September. (Air America)

Corliss, R. 2004. "The World According to Michael. *Time*, 12 July. " [Moore.]

—. 2003. "Omnibus of Short Films . . . Skeptical of American Power." *Time*, 4 August.

"Cosby Show: A Message Worth Listening To." *Economist*, 10 June.

Costicello, U., Y. Poulignon, et al. 1991. "Temporal Dissociation Of Motor Response and Subjective Awareness." *Brain* 116, 2639-55.

Coulter, A. 2003. *Treason*. New York: Random House/Crown Forum Publishers.

"Court Report." 2004. *Payson (Arizona) Round-up*. 16 July. (Justice magistrate courts.)

Coyle, J. H. 1997. *Pearls of Wisdom*. (Private Printing rev. 1998.) Aspen, North Carolina.

Coyne, G. 2004. (Rev.), Director Vatican Observatory. Quoted by Saylor. "God could create an evolutionary world just as He could a static one." In *Science and Theology News*, July/August, 5.

"Cracking the Cult." 2004. *Arizona Republic*, 26 August. (Fundamentalist church of Jesus Christ of Latter-Day Saints cited by authorities for child abuse, sexual abuse of children, domestic violence, child labor-law violations, income tax evasion, welfare fraud, civil rights violation, victimization, cultism.)

Crawford, A. J., and B. Hart. 2003. "Inmate Overcrowding Hits Dangerous Level: Outpaces Population Growth of 90% by 600%." *Arizona Republic*. 17 October, B-11.

Creehan, S. 2002. "Soldiers of Fortune Sue Internet." *Harvard Internet Review*, Winter. (Mercenaries.)

Cronkite, W. 2004. "What Do Democrats Stand For?" *Arizona King Features Syndicate*, 5 July.

Cross, S. 1996. *The Elements of Hinduism*. Rockport, Maine: Element Books.

Crowley, K. 2003. "11-Year-Old Nabbed for Attempted Robbery." *Payson (Arizona) Roundup*, 14:85, 24 October.

—. 2003. "When Domestic Violence Turns Deadly." *Payson (Arizona) Roundup* 14:85, 26 October.

Csikszentmihelyi, M. 1993. *The Evolving Self*. New York: Harper Collins.

"Cultural Cleansing." 2004. *New York Times*, 12 September. (Bahá'ís of the U. S.; Islamic Iran destroying Baha'i religion, its history, and foundation.)

Curtie, S. 2002. *A History of Terrorism*. San Diego: Greenhaven Press.

Czarrecki, A. 2002. "Theory of the Muon Anomalous Magnetic Moment." Seventh International Workshop on Tau Lepton Physics. Santa Cruz, Calif.

Dahlby, T. 2005. *Allah's Torch : A Report from Behind the Scenes in Asia's War on Terror*. New York: William Morrow. (Islamic terrorists and guerilla warfare.)

Dalai Lama (see Gyatso, T.).

Damkins, R. 1989. *The Selfish Gene*. London: Oxford University Press.

Damusio, A. R. 1994. *Descartes' Error in Emotion, Reason, and the Human Brain*. New York: Crosset/Putnam.

Daniels, C. 2004. "Up Against the Wal-Mart." *Fortune*, 17 May, 112-120.

Daraini, A. 2004. "Iran group recruiting suicide bomb volunteers." *Associated Press*, 29 November. (Headquarters for commemorating martyrs of the Global Islamic Movement stated on November 12 that 4,000 members signed up. Suicide campaign has unofficial government support.)

Davidson, F. (Ed.) 1953. *The New Bible Commentary*. Grand Rapids, Mich.: W. B. Eardman's Publishing Co.

Daveini, A. 2004. "Iran's plans to process uranium." *Associated Press*, 3 September.

Davis, C. 2003. "The Culture Clubs' Good Karma: Davis Advisors' Judge Compares by Their Value Systems." *Fortune*. 13 October, 2.

Deng, Fl. 2004. "History of The Sudan." *Global View*. History Channel, 30 December. (Origin of slavery.)

"Denmark Aims To Level Out Male-Female Ratio at Work." 2004. AP Wire in *Arizona Republic*, June, n.d.

DeToqueville, A. [1835] 1988. *Democracy in America*. Reprint, New York: Perennial.

Devji, M. S. 2004. "10 Qualities That Define Us As Americans." *Arizona Republic*, 3 July.

——. 2002. *The Mad Messiah: Osama bin Laden and the Seeds of Terror*. Scottsdale, Ariz.: Inkwell Productions.

Diamond, J. 1979. *Behavioral Kinesiology*. New York: Harper & Rowe.

——. 1979. *Your Body Doesn't Lie*. New York: Warner Books.

Diaz, E. 2004. "Flag Amendment Slows Bill on Cross Burning." *Arizona Republic*, May 6.

DiGiovanni, J. 2004. "Reaching for Power…Shiites of Iraq." *National Geographic*, June, 2-33.

Dinmore, L., and M. Turner. 2005. "Bush Nominates Long-Term Critic of U. N. as Next U. S. Ambassador." *Financial Times*, 8 March. (Tough-minded John Bulton assigned to help reform U. N.)

Dionne, E. J. 2004. "Moderates Defeated Kerry." *Washington Writers Group*, 10 November. (45% of electorate moderates, 34% conservatives, 21% liberals.)

Diouf, N. 2004. "Outsourcing Brings Jobs to Africa." *Arizona Republic*, 12 July.

Dossey, L. 2004-2005. "Unsolved Mystery of Distance Healing." *Shift*, December-February.

Dowd, M. 2004. "Hey, Frosty! Get Your Sorry Face over Here!" *New York Times*, 8 December. (Hatred of Christmas and ill will to all.)

——. 2004. "Kerry Slipping on All That Gore." *Arizona Republic*, 28 May. (Gore outburst on 5/22.)

Dracos, T. 2003. *Ungodly: The Passions, Torments, and Murder of Atheist Madalyn Murray O'Hair*. New York: Free Press.

Dreazen, Y. 2004. "Iraq Vote Poses Harsh Reality." *Wall Street Journal*, 17 December. (Arabics do not want Western-style democracy—Farqad Qazwini philosophy.)

Dube, F. 2004. "The Dog That Stopped a Mass Murderer." Toronto *National Post*, 25 June.

Duffy, B., et al. 2004. "Defining America." *U. S. News & World Report*, 28 June.

Dunn, J. 20204. "Trucker Shortage Hurts Freight Lines." *Denver Post*, 23 August. (Due to nationwide increase in business and economy.)

Dunnewind, S. 2004. "Pop Culture Assaults." (Children's exposure to obscenity.) *Seattle Times*, 10 July.

Dyer, W. 2004. *The Power of Intention*. Carlsbad, CA: Hay House.

—. 2001. *There's A Spiritual Solution to Every Problem*. New York: Harper Collins Publishers.

Dyson, M. E. 2004. *Mercy, Mercy Me: The Art, Loves, and Demons of Marvin Gaye*. New York: Basic Civitas Books.

Eccles, J. C. 1994. *How the Self Controls Its Brain*. New York: Springer-Verlag Telos.

—. 1989. *Evolution of the Brain: Creation of the Self*. Edinburgh: Routledge.

—. 1986. *Mind and Brain: The Many Faceted Problems*. New York: Paragon House.

Eccles, J. C., and D. N. Robinson, 1984. *The Wonder of Being Human: Our Brain and Our Mind*. New York: Free Press.

Eckhart, M. 1981. *Essential Sermons, Commentaries, Treatises, and Defense*. Newark, New Jersey: Paulist Press.

Edamaruku, S. 2000. "Now It Is Sai Baba's Turn!" *Rationalist International*, Bulletin 53, 29 October. (www.Rationalistinternational.net.)

Edelson, E. 2003. "Stroke Linked to Poverty." *Arizona Republic*, 24 June.

Ehrenreich, B. 2004. "Let's Match Gay Mom With Single Moms." *New York Times* and *Arizona Republic*, 14 July.

Eisenberg, E. 2003. "Religion Is Not The Issue." *American Republic*, 21 July.

Eisenhower, D. D. 1953. *First Inaugural Address*. 20 January. http://www.presidency.ucsb.edu/site/docs/pppus.php?admin=034&year=1953&id=1.

Elias, M. 2004. "Sociability, Support Aid Health." *USA Today*, 22 March.

—. 2004. "Wal-Mart Again Tops Fortune 500 List." *Associated Press*, 22 March. (Despite lowest profit margins.)

Ellens, J. H. 2004. "Tracking Violence to Its Religious Roots." *Science and Theology News*, July/August.

Elliott, M. 2003. "Sharon's Game." *Time*, 23 June, 33-35.

Enard, W., M. Prseworski, et al. 2002. "Molecular Evolution of the FOXP2 Gene of Speech and Language." *Nature* 418, 869-872.

Enstrom, J., and Kabat, G. C. 2003. "Study Refutes Dangers of Secondhand Smoke." *British Medical Journal* in *Los Angeles Times* and *Arizona Republic*, 16 May.

Eth, S., Ed. 2001. *PTSD in Children and Adolescents*. 2nd ed. Washington, DC: American Psychiatric Publishing Co.

Evans, H. 2004. *They Made America: Two Centuries of Innovators from the Steam Engine to the Search Engine*. New York: Little Brown. (Creative genius source of America's Wealth.)

—. 2004. "The Spark of Genius." *U. S. News & World Report*. 11 October, 44-54. (Thomas Edison)

Ewen, D. 2003. "Sacred Places." *Arizona Republic,* 10 August, T1-2.

—. "America's Best Colleges." 2003. Special Report. *U. S. News &World Report*. 1 September, 60-116.

—. 1955. *Encyclopedia of the Opera*. New York: Hill and Wang.

"Far Left, Far Right Showing Insecurities." 2004. *Arizona Republic*, 21 July, Letter to Editor.

Farrar, M. (Ed.) 2002. *The Varieties of Religious Expression: Centenary Essay*. Charlottesville, Va.: Imprint Academic and Philosophy Documentation Center.

Farrer, C., C. Firth. 2002. "Experiencing Oneself vs. Another Person As Being the Cause of an Action: Neural Correlates of the Experience of Agency." *Neuroimage* 15 (3), 596-603.

Fascanalli, N. 2004. "Five Reasons To Go Traditional." *Arizona Republic*, 18 May. (Schools.)

Faurisson, R. 1980. *Mémoire en défense* (French). Paris: La Vieille Taupe.

Faw, B. 2003. "Cognitive Neuroscience of Consciousness." *Journal of Consciousness Studies*. 11:2, 69-72.

Fawcett, J. 2004. "Clinical Ethics and the Culture of Expediency." *Psychiatric Annals*. February, 80.

Federschak, V. J. 1999. *The Shadow on The Path: Clearing Psychological Blocks to Spiritual Development*. Prescott, Arizona: Hohm Press.

Felt, S. 2004. "Mind Control." *Arizona Republic*, 20 July.

—. 2004. "NPR Legend Too Busy to Pout…Murrow Would Be Dismayed by Today's News." *Arizona Republic,* 2 June.

Fernandez, R. 2003. "Historical Assessment of Terrorist Activity and Narcotic Trafficking by the Republic of Cuba." http://www.latinamericanstudies.org/support.htm, 22 January. (Authoritative documentation of Castro's control coordinating role in international terrorist and training.)

Feuerstein, G. 1990. *Encyclopedic Dictionary of Yoga*. New York: Paragon House.

Fields, S. 2004. "Are Those Elites Fluent In French?" *Los Angeles Times Syndicate*, 8 November. (Streisand, Baldwin, Moore, Springsteen, Midler, Stewart, Dan Rather, Washington Post, New York Times, mass Supreme Court, etc.)

—. 2004. "The Phony Flimflam of Michael Moore." *Arizona Republic*, 1 June.

—. 2000. "Great Books Collect Readers, Not Dust." *Arizona Republic*, 28 January.

Fisher, A. 2004. "Think Globally, Save Your Job Locally." *Fortune*, 23 February.

Flam, F. 2004. "Civilians Flood NASA with Mars 'Discoveries'" *Arizona Republic*, 8 March. (15,000 emails a month.)

Flannery, P. 2003. "Lawsuits Battering Local Governments." *Arizona Republic*, 30 November.

Flatt, J. 2004. "Do We Want Leviticus as Basis for Our Laws?" *Arizona Republic*, 30 May.

Flurry, G. 2004. "The Shocking Story about WMDs Found in Jordan." *Philadelphia Trumpet*, June (Al-Qaeda cell has 20 tons of chemicals via Syria.)

Flynn, D. J. 2004. *Intellectual Morons*. New York: Crown Forum Publishers.

—. 2002. *Why The Left Hates America*. New York: Prima Lifestyles/ Random House.

—. 1981. *The Rig-Veda*. London: Penguin Books.

Flynn, S. 2004. *America the Vulnerable: How Our Government is Failing to Protect Us from Terrorism*. New York: Harper Collins.

"Food for Oil: Blood Money." 2004. *Breaking Point,* Fox News, 19 September. (UN Security Council Scandal)

Ford, M. 2004. "Religion Update: From the Pulpit to the Bedroom." *Publishers Weekly*, 24 May.

Forman, R. 2004. *Grassroots Spirituality*. Exeter, UK: Imprint Academic.

—. 2004. "Switzerland's ABB Ltd. Increases Chinese Work Force by 5,000 Workers." *Arizona Republic*, 26 October. (Outsourcing not just an American phenomenon.)

Forsyth, F. 2004. "Blame Not The Victim." *Arizona Republic*, 21 March.

Fossler, D. 2003. "Adolescent Brain Development Argues Against Teen Executions." *Psychiatric News*, 18 May. (Report to Nevada Assembly.)

Frank, L. 2005. "Prof Accused of Plagiarism." *Rocky Mountain News*. 12 March. (Ward Churchill Controversy.)

Franks, T. 2004. *American Soldier*. New York: Regan Books.

Fraser, R. 2004. "Land of the Free, Home of the Hated." *Philadelphia Trumpet*, November. (Analyses of internet and national anti-U.S. attitudes.)

—. 2004. "Return of the Religious War." *Philadelphia Trumpet*, May.

—. 2004. "The Other America." *Philadelphia Trumpet*, February.

—. 2004. "Home Depot Seeks Seniors As Workers: 35,000 New Job Openings This Year." *Associated Press* in *Arizona Republic*. 7 February. ("Business News.")

—. 2003. "Rhetoric." http://wikipedia.org/wiki/rhetoric.

—. 2003. "Sophist(ry)." http://wikipedia.org/wiki/sophist.

Freeman, A. 2004. "Are There Neutral Correlates to Consciousness?" *Journal of Consciousness Studies*, II:1.

—. (Ed.) 2001. *The Emergence of Consciousness*. Charlottesville, Va.: Imprint Academic.

French, L. 2004. "9/11 Testimony: FBI Had a Deficiency in Analytical Capabilities." http://cnn.allpolitics.printthis.clickability.com/pt/cpt?action+cpt&title=cnn.com+…

Freud, A. [1936] 1971 (Rev.) *The Ego and the Mechanisms of Defense*. Guilford, Conn.: International Universities Press.

Freud, S. [1976] 2000. *The Standard Edition of the Complete Psychological Works of Sigmund Freud*. J. Strachey, A. Freud, trans. Reprint, New York: W. W. Norton & Co.

—. 1994 *The Interpretation of Dreams*. Reprint. New York: Modern Library.

—. 1953. "Civilization, War, and Death." *Psychoanalytic Epitomes*, No. 4. London: Hogarth Press.

—. 1938. "Splitting of the Ego in the Defensive Process." *International Journal of Psychoanalysis* 22:65-69.

—. [1927] 1961. *The Future of an Illusion*. Reprint. New York: W. W. Norton & Co.

Freud, S., and S. Katz. 1947. *Freud on War, Sex, and Neurosis.* New York: Arts and Science Press.

Friedman, L. R. 1981. "Movies to Murder By." *Journal of Forensic Psychiatry*, March.

Friedman, T. 2005. "Muslins Need to Find New Focus." *New York Times*, 19 January. (Americans risk their lives to save Muslims in Bosnia, Kuwait, Somalia, Afghanistan, Iraq, Indonesia, and are still considered as "anti-Muslim." Muslims need to respect themselves and not the U.S.)

—. 2004. "Something's Happening Here." *New York Times, 19 December.* (Report from Dubai on progress of the U. N. Arab Human Development Reports on lack of education and economic development.)

—. 2003. "Sea Change Nips at Mid-East." *Arizona Republic*, 22 October. (Arab Human Development Report, *New York Times*.)

Fritzsch, H. 2002. *Curvature of Spacetime: Newton, Einstein, and Gravitation.* New York: Columbia University Press.

Frum, D., and R. Perle. 2003. *An End to Evil: How to Wind the War on Terror.* New York: Random House.

Feuerstein, G. 1990. *Encyclopedic Dictionary of Yoga.* New York: Paragon House Publishers.

Gallagher, S. 2004. "Hermeneutics and the Cognitive Sciences." *Journal of Consciousness Studies* 11:10-11, 162-175. (Meaning, interpretation of cognitive process.)

Gambhirananda, Swami, trans. 1972. *Eight Upanishads.* With commentary by Sankaracarya. Calcutta: Advaita Ashrama, and Almora, Himalayas: Mayarati.

Ganora, P. 2003. "Cognitive Therapy's Faulty Scheme." *Psychiatric Times*, October, 34-39.

Gantner, L. 1999. "Psst—It's the Sun." *Edmonton Journal*, 15 August. (Solar source of earth warming, not greenhouse gases.)

Gardner, H. 2004. *Changing Minds: The Art and Science of Changing Our Own and Other People's Minds.* Cambridge, Mass.: Harvard Business School Press.

Gardner, J. 2003. *Biocosm: The New Scientific Theory of Evolution: Intelligent Life Is the Architect of the Universe.* Maui, Hawaii: Inner Ocean Publishing.

Garhart, M., and A. M. Russell. 2004. "Metaphor and Thinking in Science and Religion." *Zygon* 39:1, March, 13-39.l

Garner, J. F. 1994. *Politically Correct Buddha Stories*. New York: Mac-Millan Publishing Co.

Gertz, B. 2004. "Saddam Paid off French Leaders." *Washington Times*, 7 October.

Gathja, C., ed. 2003. *2004 Movie Guide*. New York: Zagat Survey.

Geewax, M. 2004. "GAO: Few US Jobs Lost to Offshoring." *Cox News*, 23 September.

Geppert, C. 2004. "Attending to Uncertainty." *Psychiatric News*, July. (Tolerance for ambiguity a sign of psychological maturity.)

Gertz, B. 2004. *Treachery : How America's Friends and Foes Are Secretly Arming Our Enemies*. New York: Crown Forum Publishers.

Gibbs, N. 2004 "The Faith Factor." *Time*, 21 June. (Religion and the Presidency.)

Giberson, K. 2004. "Shroud of Turin." *Science and Theology News*, July/August. ("Harry Potter.")

Gibson, J. 2004. "Hating America" on "*Breaking Point*." *Fox News*, 21 November.

—. 2004. *Hating America: The New World Sport*. New York: Regan Books.

Gingrich, N. 2004. "Smear Tactics Indicate Moral Decline; No Rules Anymore." *The O'Reilly Factor, Fox News*, 13 July.

Glyn-Jones, A. 2004. *Holding up a Mirror: How Civilizations Decline*. Exeter, U. K.: Imprint Academic.

Goffman, J. M., et al. 2002. *The Mathematics of Marriage: Nonlinear Models*. Cambridge, Mass: MIT Press.

Goguen, J. A. 2004. "Musica Qualia: Context, Time, and Emotion." *Journal of Consciousness Studies* 11:3/4, 117-147.

Goines, D. 2000. *Never Die Alone*. Los Angeles: Holloway House Publishing Co.

Gold, D. 2004. *Tower of Babble : How the United Nations Has Fueled Global Chaos*. New York: Crown Forum Publishers.

Goldberg, B. 2003. *Arrogance: Rescuing America From the Media Elite*. New York: Warner Books.

Goldberg, J. 2004. "Courts in Kentucky Rule 70% Medical Liability Lawsuits Frivolous." *Medicine This Week* in *AzMed*, 23 April.

—. 2004. "The Funhouse Logic of John Kerry." http://www.jonahscolumn@aol.com, 22 April.

—. 2004 "Clinton and/or the 9/11 Blame Game." *Arizona Republic*, 20 April.

—. 2004. "Learning to Love Wal-Mart." *Economist*, 17 April.

—. 2004. "Deficits Are Dull Subjects—I'll Prove It." *Arizona Republic*. 8 March.

Golden, F. 2003. "When Sparks Flew." *Time*, 7 July, 55.

Goldman, A. 2004. "Epistemology: Evidential Status of Introspective Reports." *Journal of Consciousness Studies* 11, July/August, 1-17.

Goodykoontz. 2004. "CBS Crowing for Good Reason." *Arizona Republic*, 20 July. (Television Critics Assn.)

—. 2004. "Tune In or Tune Out?" *Arizona Republic*, 25 May. (Analysis of "American Idol.")

Goodwin, P. 2003. "China's Borders Back Private Property." *Work Post Foreign Service*. 23 December, A-1.

Great Books of the Western World, The. 1952. R. Hutching and M. Alden, Eds. Chicago: Encyclopedia Britannica.

Green, R. F. 1999. *A Crisis in Truth: Literature and Law in Ricardrin, England*. Philadelphia: University of Philadelphia.

Greenburg, H. R. "Road Kill." *Psychiatric Times*, May 2004. (Aileen Wuronos: The Throwaway Underclass.)

Greenburg, P. 2004. "9/11 Report Clearly Links Saddam to al-Qaeda." *Los Angeles Times Syndicate*. 17 August.

Greene, B. 2003. (*The Elegant Universe: Superstrings, Hidden Dimensions, and the Quest for the Ultimate Theory*. Reprint. New York: W. W. Norton & Company.

—. 2004. *The Fabric of the Cosmos: Space, Time, and the Texture of Reality*. New York: Knopf/Penguin/ Allen Lane.

Greenhouse, L. 2004. "Atheist Presents Case for Taking God from Pledge." (Michael Newdow). *New York Times*, 25 March.

Greenspan, A. 2004. "Congress Has Lost the Ability to Manage Crucial Long-Term Budget Issues." *Arizona Republic*, 22 July. (Federal Reserve Chairman.)

Grisham, J. 2003. *The King of Torts*. New York: Doubleday.

Gross, P. R., and N. Levitt, Eds. 1997. *The Flight from Science and Reason*. New York: New York Academy of Sciences.

—. 1994. *Higher Superstition: The Academic Left and Its Quarrels with Science*. New York: Johns Hopkins University Press.

Grossman, C. 2003. "Search and Destiny." *Time*, Dec. 22, 46-50.

Guigliamo, R. J. 2004. "Systematic Neglect of New York's Young Adults with Mental Illness." *Psychiatric Services*, 55:4, April, 451-454.

Guglielmo, W. 2003. "A Legal Crusader's Solution." *Medical Economics*. March, 10-12.

—. 2002. "Psychopaths Are Becoming More Violent." *Weapons of Tactics*. 6:1, 1-5.

Guillen, M. 2004. *Can A Smart Person Believe in God?* Santa Cruz, Calif.: Nelson Books.

Gunther, M. "Money and Morals at GE." *Fortune*, 15 November. (Immalt emphasizes virtue, ethics, integrity.)

Guthrie, M. 2004. "Lust in Translation: TV floozies reflect era of brainlessness." *New York Daily News*, 9 November. (Blatant, provocative sexuality pervades media because "sex sells.")

Gyatso, Tenzin (The Dalai Lama). 1998. *The Four Noble Truths.* London: Thorsons.

Haggard, P., and H. Johnson. 2003. "Experiences of Voluntary Action." *Journal of Consciousness Studies* 10, 72-84.

Hamar, D. 2004. *The God Game: How Faith is Hardwired into Our Genes.* New York: Doubleday. (Religion supports survival.)

Hameroff, S., A. Kasniak, and A. Scott. 1996-1999. *Toward A Science of Consciousness.* Cambridge: MIT Press: Bradford Books. (Tucson discussion and debates: First, 1996; Second, 1998; and Third, 1999.)

—. 2003. "Researching Philanthropy." *Foundation News Digest.* The Foundation Center, 27 October database. (Top 100 U.S. Foundations.)

—. 2003. "Foundation Giving Trends." *Foundation Today Series.* 2003 Ed. http://www.fdncenter.org.

Hanson, J. 2004. "Historical Roots of War with al-Qaeda." http://www.havanet.com, 14 June.

Hardy, D. T., and J. Clarke. 2004. *Michael Moore Is a Big Fat Stupid White Man.* New York. Regan.

Harpending, H., and A. Rogers. 2000. "Genetic Perspectives on Human Origins and Differentiation." *Annual Review Genomics Human Genetics* 1:361-385.

Harper, T. 2004. "History or Hyperbola?" *Toronto Star*, 27 June.

Harrington, A., and P. Bartosiewicz. 2004 "America's 50 Most Powerful Women in Business." *Fortune*, 150:8.

Hart, B. 2003. "Back Behind Bars: 9 of 12 Ex-cons Return to Prison." *Arizona Republic*, 29 June.

Harvey, A., and Matousek, M. 1994. *Dialogues with a Modern Mystic.* Wheaton, Ill.: Quest Books.

Harvey, D. 1990. *The Condition of Postmodernity: Enquiry into the Origins of Cultural Change.* Oxford, U.K.: Blackwell

Hauth, E. 2004. "Art and Reductionism." *Journal of Consciousness Studies* 11:3/4,111-116

Hawkins, David R. 2004. "The Science of Peace." *Awakened World, J. A. G. N. T.*, 6:3.

—. 2004. "Nonduality: Consciousness Research and the Truth of the Buddha." Rourkee, India: Indian Institute of Technology.

—. 2004. "The Impact of Spontaneous Spiritual Experiences in the Life of 'Ordinary' Persons." *Watkins Review*, 7.

—. 2004. "Transcending the Mind" Lecture Series. Sedona, Ariz.: Veritas Publishing. (Six 5-hour video, audiocassettes.) *Thought and Ideation* (Feb.); *Emotions and Sensations* (April); *Perception and Positionality* (June); *Identification and Illusion* (August); *Witnessing and Observing* (Oct.); and, *The Ego and the Self* (Dec.).

—. 2004. *The Highest Level of Enlightenment.* Chicago: Nightingale-Conant Corp. (CD, Audiocassettes).

—. 2003. "Devotional Nonduality" Lecture Series. Sedona, Ariz.: Veritas Publishing. (Six 5-hour video, audio cassettes.) *Integration of Spirituality and Personal Life* (Feb.); *Spirituality and the World* (April); *Spiritual Community* (June); *Enlightenment* (August); *Realization of the Self as the "I"* (Nov.); and, *Dialogue, Questions and Answers* (Dec.).

—. 2002. "The Way to God" Lecture Series. Sedona, Ariz.: Veritas Publishing. (Twelve 5-hour video, audiocassettes) 1. *Causality: The Ego's Foundation;* 2. *Radical Subjectivity: The I of Self;* 3. *Levels of Consciousness: Subjective and Social Consequences;* 4. *Positionality and Duality: Transcending the Opposites;* 5. *Perception and Illusion: the Distortions of Reality;* 6. *Realizing the Root of Consciousness: Meditative and Contemplative Techniques;* 7. *The Nature of Divinity: Undoing Religious Fallacies;* 8. *Advaita: The Way to God Through Mind;* 9. *Devotion: The Way to God Through the Heart;* 10. *Karma and the Afterlife;* 11. *God Transcendent and Immanent;* and, 12. *Realization of the Self: The Final Moments.*

—. 2002. *Power versus Force: An Anatomy of Consciousness*. (Rev.). Carlsbad, Calif., Brighton-le-Sands, Australia: Hay House.

—. 2001. *The Eye of the I: From Which Nothing Is Hidden*. Sedona, Ariz.: Veritas Publishing.

—. 2000. *Consciousness Workshop*. Prescott, Ariz. Sedona, Ariz.: Veritas Publishing. (Videocassette)

—. 2000. *Consciousness and A Course in Miracles*. California. Sedona, Ariz.: Veritas Publishing. (Videocassette)

—. 2000. *Consciousness and Spiritual Inquiry: Address to the Tao Fellowship*. Sedona, Ariz.: Veritas Publishing. (Videocassette)

—. 1997. *Research on the Nature of Consciousness*. Sedona, Ariz.: Veritas Publishing. (The Landsberg 1997 Lecture. University of California School of Medicine, San Francisco, Calif.)

—. 1996. "Realization of the Presence of God." *Concepts*. July, 17-18.

—. 1995. *Power vs. Force: An Anatomy of Consciousness*. Sedona, Ariz.: Veritas Publishing.

—. 1995. *Quantitative and Qualitative Analysis and Calibration of the Levels of Human Consciousness*. Ann Arbor, Mich.: VMI, Bell and Howell Col.; republished 1999 by Veritas Publishing, Sedona, Ariz.

—. 1995. *Power Versus Force; Consciousness and Addiction; Advanced States of Consciousness: The Realization of the Presence of God; Consciousness: How to Tell the Truth About Anything. Undoing the Barriers to Spiritual Progress*. Sedona, Ariz.: Veritas Publishing. (Videocassettes.)

—. 1987. Sedona Lecture Series: *Drug Addiction and Alcoholism; A Map of Consciousness; Cancer (audio only); AIDS; and Death and Dying*. Sedona, Ariz.: Veritas Publishing. (Audio, videocassettes.)

—. 1986. Office Series: *Stress; Health; Spiritual First Aid; Sexuality; The Aging Process; Handling Major Crisis; Worry, Fear and Anxiety; Pain and Suffering; Losing Weight; Depression; Illness and Self-Healing; and Alcoholism*. Sedona, Ariz.: Veritas Publishing. (Audio, videocassettes.)

—. 1985. "Consciousness and Addiction" in *Beyond Addictions, Beyond Boundaries*. S. Burton and L. Kiley. San Mateo, Calif.: Brookridge Institute.

Hawkins, J., and S. Blakeslee. (2004) *On Intelligence*. New York: Times Books.

Hayakawa, S. 1971. *Our Language and Our World; Selections from Etc.: A Review of General Semantics, 1953-1958*. New York: Harper Collins.

Hayakawa, S., and R. Marshall, 1991. *Language in Thought and Action: Fifth Edition*. New York: Harcourt, Brace, and World.

Hayes, C. L. 2003 "Scholars Bone Up on Wal-Mart." *Arizona Republic*, 4 August.

Hayworth, J. D. 2003. "Mouthy Professor Should Be Fired." *Arizona Republic*. 14 April, A6.

—. 2001. "Religious Anxiety Can Mar Health." (New York Times) *Arizona Republic*. 13 August, A6.

"Hearing Hip-Hop's Pathetic Message." 2003. *Chicago Tribune*. 14 September, 9.

Hefley, J.C. 1991. *Truth in Crisis*. New York: Hannibal Books.

Heisenberg, W. 1958. *Physics and Philosophy*. New York: Harper.

Hendershott, A. 2002. *The Policies of Deviance*. San Francisco: Encounter Books.

Henderson, N. 2004. "U. S. urged to cut deficit." *Washington Post*, 20 November. (A. Greenspan, Fed. Res. Chmn., wants to trade gap deficit of $550-650 billion, which has been financed by foreign investors. Recommends less spending and more saving by U. S.)

Hermann, A. 2004. *To Think Like God: Pythagoras and Parmenides: The Origin of Philosophy*. Las Vegas, Nev.: Parmenides Publishing.

"High Court Keeps 'One Nation Under God.'" 2004. *USA Today* in *Arizona Republic*, 15 June.

Higuera, J. J. 2004. "Census Bureau Reports 1.3 Million Americans (12.5%) in Poverty; U. S. Household Median Income $43,318." *Arizona Republic*, 27 August.

Hilliard, J. C. 2004. "The Peril and The Promise." *Publishers Weekly*, 15 November.

—. 2004. "Business Ethics Brings Religious Principles into the Workplace." *Publishers Weekly*, 24 May.

Hilliker, J. 2003. "The War Over Marriage." *Philadelphia Trumpet*, Sept-Oct., 3-11.

"History of God, The." 2004. *History Channel*, 25 December.

Hjelt, P. 2003. "The 500 Largest Corporations in the World." *Fortune*. 147:7, 14 April.

Hoaver, H. 1977. *Lives of the Saints*. New York: Catholic Book Publishing Co.

Hollander, P. 2004. "Bold Hatred." University of Massachusetts, Amherst. *Arizona Republic*, 1 August. (Hatred of own country by Americans is unique to the U. S. Other countries hate U. S. but not themselves.)

"Holy Land Islamic Foundation Raises $12.5 Million for Terrorists." 2004. *Fox News*, 6 August.

Hopkins, E. C. 2003. *Edinburgh Military Tattoo*. BBC Television/Royal Bank of Scotland, EPM Production. Http://www.edintatoo.co.uk. (Video.)

——. 1974. *High Mysticism*. Marina del Rey, Calif.: DeVorss & Co.

Hora, T. 1996. *Beyond the Dream: Awakening to Reality*. New York: Crossroads Publishing Co.

House, B. 2004. "We Will Prevail." *Arizona Republic Washington Bureau*, 3 September. (President Bush's Speech at Republican National Convention.)

——. 1995. *Death of Common Sense: How Law is Suffocating America*. New York: Random House.

House, B., and M. Sauerzopf. 2004. "Polarized American in Eyes of Beholder." *Arizona Republic*, 17 October. (U. S. no more divided than it has been.)

Howard, P. K. 2001. *The Collapse of the Common Good: How America's Lawsuit Culture Undermines Our Freedom*. New York: Ballentine Books.

Howe, L. 2004. "Is Dark Matter the 'Heavy Shadow' of Visible Matter?" www.earthfiles.com/newsefmID=629.

Hudson, D. W. 2003. *An American Conversion: One Man's Discovery of Beauty and Truth in Times of Crisis*. New York: Crossroad Publishing Co.

Hughes, K. 2004. *Ten Minutes from Normal*. New York: Viking Press.

"Hunting Bountiful." 2004. *Economist*, 10 June. (Polygamy in Canada fundamentalist sect in defiance of LDS ban on polygamy in 1890.)

Ibrahim, S. E. 2004. "The Sick Men of the World." *Washington Post*. 28 March.

Ingram, J. 2004. "Group Lowers Russia Status to "Not Free." *Associated Press*, 21 December. (Reports by Freedom House of degrees of freedom in various countries of the world.)

"Inside the New China." *Fortune* 150:7, 4 October. (12 authors cover comprehensive special edition.)

Irins, M. 2004. "4 More Years of W Wired to Our Necks." *Creators Syndicate*, 8 November.

Isaacson, W. 2003. "Ben Franklin: Revolutionary Ideals and 7 Great Virtues." *Time*. 7 July, 40.

"Islamic Militants Bomb 5 Christian Churches Across Iraq." 2004. *Wire Service*, 2 August.

"It's A Mad, Mad World." 2005. *Economist*, 8 January. (Madison County, IL, a haven for tort awards, scandal.)

Jackall, G., and J. M. Hirota. 2000. *Image Makers*. Chicago: University of Chicago Press.

Jacoby, J. 2004. "The Bottom Line for Teachers Unions." http://alabamaconferenceofeducators.org/teachersunion.htm, 1-29.

—. 2001. "Why No Talk of Radical Islamism?" *Boston Globe* via Jacoby@globe.com.

Jacoby, S. 2004. *Freethinkers: A History of American Secularism*. New York: Metropolitan Books.

Jaffe, G. 2004. "Twisted words and phrases." *U. S. News & World Report*, 25 October. (Arab humiliation fallacious propaganda – advertisement.)

Jaffe, G. 2004. "Twisted words and phrases." U. S. News & World Report, 25 October. (Arab humiliation fallacious propaganda – advertisement.)

Jafrey, S. 2004. "Kinesiologic test teams test accurate if they themselves calibrate at 461-484." scott@creativecrayon.com. December. (Personal communication.)

James, W. [1902] 1987. *The Varieties of Religious Experience: A Study in Human Nature*. Reprint. Cambridge, Mass.: Harvard University Press

Janz, B. B. 2003. "Who's Who in the History of Western Mysticism." http://www.clas.ufl.edu/users/gthursby/mys/whoswho.htm, 13 October.

Jaoudi, M. 1998. *Christian Mysticism, East and West: What the Masters Teach Us*. Manwah, New Jersey: Paulist Press.

Jasser, M. Z. 2004. "A disgrace upon Islam." *Arizona Republic*, 26 September. (Fascists pirate the religion and give it a bad name.)

—. 2003. "Paved With Good Intentions: Unintended Consequences of Federal Regulations." *AzMed*, July-August, 10-14.

Jesdanun, A. 2005. "Web Blogs Get Workers in Trouble." *Associated Press*, 14 March. (Bloggers' imprudence gets them fired; First Amendment free speech restricts only government control, not that of employers.)

—. 2004. "Internet at 35: Scientists working to make it better." *Associated Press*, 30 August.

John, E. R. 2003. "A Field Theory of Consciousness." *Consciousness and Cognition* 10, 184-213.

John, G., and B. Dunne. 1997. "Science of the Subjective." *Sound Scientific Exploration, II*, 201-224.

Johnson, G. 2003. "Green River Killer of 48 Women." *Arizona Republic,* 3 November.

—. 2003. "U. S. Tort System More Expensive than Any in World." *National Center for Policy Analysis.* 15 December.

Johnson, H. 2004. "Two Jailed in Teen Sex Case." *Arizona Republic*, 2 July. (HIV-Positive adults via Internet contact infect 30 boys.)

Johnson, R. A. 1998. *Balancing Heaven and Earth*. San Francisco: Harper Collins

Johnson, W., ed. 1973. *The Cloud of Unknowing.* New York: Doubleday.

Jung, C. 1951, 1959. "Matter of Heart." BBC Video Interviews. New York: King Video.

Kahn, D. 2004. *The Reader of Gentlemen's Mail: Herbert O. Yardley and the Birth of American Code Breaking.* New Haven, Conn.: Yale University Press.

Kallenbach, R. 2003. History of Europe. (Personal Communications.)

Kant, I. 1959. *Foundation of the Metaphysics of Morals.* L. W. Beck, trans. New York: MacMillan.

—. 1929. *Critique of Pure Reason.* London: MacMillan.

Kaplan, A. 2004. "Youth Violence Conference Explores Prevention, Risk Factor, Interventions." *Psychiatric Times* XXI:14, December.

Kaplan, D. E. 2004. "Mission Impossible." *U. S. News & World Report*, 2 August. (Failed spy organizer.)

Keller, J. 2004. "Biology Links Religious Attendance and Survival." *Science/Theology News*, December. (Religious attendance lowered levels of stress hormone Interleukin-6 [IL-6] and increased longevity.)

Kelling, G, and C. Colas. 1996. *Fixing Broken Windows*. New York: Free Press

Kelly, C. M. 1988. *The Destructive Achiever: Power and Ethics in the American Corporation*. New York: Perseus Publishing

Kelly, U. 1997. *Schooling Desire-Literacy, Cultural Politics, and Pedagogy*. New York: Routledge.

Kenfer, J. 2002. "America's Dumbest Intellectual Equals Anarchist Noam Chomsky." *City Journal*, Summer.

Kennedy, R. S. 2004. "Multimedia Reviews: Weblogs, Social Software, and the New Interactivity on the Web." *Psychiatric Services*. 55:3, March, 240-247.

Kenny, R. 2004. "The Science of Collective Consciousness." *Enlightenment*, 25: May/June.

Kernberg, O. 2002. "Aggressiveness and Transference on Severe Personality Disorder." *Psychiatric Times* XXI: 2.

Khamenei, A. 2004. ("Supreme Leader") "Islamic Revolution Stamped Expiration Date on Forehead of the Imperialistic Nihilistic Government: The Great Satan" (The U.S.) http://www.wilayah.net.

—. 2004. "List of Countries with Nuclear Weapons." http://www.wikipedia.org. 5 December. (Nuclear powers)

—. 2004. "Nuclear status, Nuclear numbers." *Proliferation News-Resources*, 5 December. (Carnegie Endowment for Internet, Peace)

Kinney, D. 2002. "Forrester Lashes Out at Torricelli over Spy Policy." *Capital Report. N. J. Capital Public Affairs*: http://www.cpenj.com/Capitalreport/pages/campaigncorner; July 2002/forrester.

Kirn, W. 2004. "Thomas Jefferson: Life, Liberty, and the Pursuit of Happiness. *Time*, 5 July, 46-82. (Special issue.)

"Kiss Privacy Goodbye." 2005. *Fortune*, 10 January. (From biometric scanners to brainwave surveillance, technological mass surveillance is a fact of modern life , as is a giant "universal data base" on everyone.)

Kittrie, O. 2004. "Iran and the Bomb: Nuclear Islam Poses Extreme Threat to U.S." *Arizona Republic*, 5 December. Special Report. (Nuclear terror strike very likely in next decade.)

Klages, M. 2003. "Postmodernism." University of Colorado: www. colorado.edu/English/engl2012klages/ pomo.htm/. 21 April.

—. 2003. "Structuralism." http://www.en.wikipedic.org/wiki/structuralism. 14 December.

Kluger, J. 2004. "Is God in Our Genes?" *Time*, 25 October.

Kniozkov, M. 2005. "Cowboy Boots Carry 'Made in China' Label." *Arizona Republic*, 3 January. (Tony Lama outsourcing.)

Knott, S. F. 2004. "Congressional Oversight and the Crippling of the CIA." University of VA. http://han.us/articles/380.html.

Koch, C. 2004. *The Quest for Consciousness: A Neurobiological Approach*. Englewood, Colo.: Roberts & Co.

Kohn, B. 2003. *Journalistic Fraud: How the N. Y. Times Distorts the News*. Nashville, Tenn.: WNB Books.

Kongtrul, D. 2004. "Realizing Guiltlessness." *Tricycle: Buddhist Review* 54, Winter. (Guilt is egoistic, regret and selflessness lead to transcendence.)

Koppin, A. "The Sad Results of Appeasement." *Sedona (Arizona) Red Rock News*, 14 July, Letters to Editor. (Denial results in defect.)

Kotkin, J. 2004. "Where the Dems Went Wrong." New America Foundation. *Arizona Republic*, 7 November.

Krauthammer, C. 2004. "Arafat's Only Legacy Was Poison." *Washington Post Writers Group*. 20 November. (Architect of terrorism, airplane hijacking, violence, mass murder, killing children, hatred as a political tool; enemy of peace.)

—. 2004. "Wake-up Call of 9/11 Beginning to Fade." *Washington Post Writers Group*, 14 July. (Denial setting in.)

—. 2004. "Sexual Link of Prison Abuse Hits Arab Fears." *Arizona Republic*, 10 May. (Jihadists fear equity of women.)

Krishna, G. 1971. *Kundalini's Evolutionary Energy in Man*. Bombay: Shambala.

Krugman, P. 2004. "Mr. Bush, These Job Figures Just Won't Spin." *New York Times*, 11 August. (Job growth interpretation.)

Kuhn, T. 1970. *The Structure of Scientific Revolutions*. 2nd ed. Chicago: University of Chicago Press.

Kunz, M. K., K. F. Yates, et al. 2004. "Course of Patriots with History of Aggression and Claims after Discharge from A Cognitive-Behavioral Program." *Psychiatric Services*, June, 654-659.

Kurtz, H. 2004. "Rather Regrets False CBS Reports." *Washington Post*, 21 September. ("60 Minutes" exposé based on bogus information of Bill Burkett, chronic Bush hater.)

Kurtz, P., B. Karr, R Sandhu. 2003. *Science and Religion: Are They Compatible?* Amherst, NY: Prometheus Books.

Kushner, H. 2004. *Holy War on the Home Front: The Secret Islamic Terror Network in the United States.* Somerset, New Jersey: Sentinel Publishing Co.

——. 2002. *Encyclopedia of Terrorism.* London: Sage Publications.

Kusik, K. S. 2003. "The Evolution of the Human Brain." *Psychiatric Times.* October.

"Labor Dept. Probes Teacher's Union Spending." 2004. Associated Press in *U. S. News & World Report.* 4 March, 1-4.

Lacayo, R. 2003. "The View from Abroad." *Time*, 4 August.

Lacayo, R., and J. Stein. 2004. "Winners and Losers." *Time,* 10 November. (Political outside players: winners Ann Coulter, John O'Neill, Richard Land, Matt Daniels; losers George Soros, Michel Moore, Al Franken, "More-oh" Wes Boyd, and Joan Blades.)

Lacqueur, W. 2004. "World of Terror." *National Geographic*, November, 72-84. (Who and where they are.)

——. 2001. *History of Terrorism.* Somerset, NJ: Transaction Publishers.

LaFare, K. 2004. "A Classic Opportunity—Will the Next Mozart Please Stand Up?" *Arizona Republic*, 5 December. (Classical music style periods.)

Lambert, S. C. 2004. "Pop Tart Exhibits Crudeness." *Arizona Republic*, 20 July.

Landay, J. S., and J. Huhnhenn. 2004. "Committee Slams CIA for 'Group Think' Intel." *Seattle Times*, 10 July.

Lane, T. 2004. "The Democrats Are Out to Get You." *Fortune.* 9 February, 30. (Populism.)

——. 1996. "Noam Chomsky on Anarchism." http://www.zmag.org/chomsky/interviews/ 9612-anarchism.html.

Landsbaum, M. 2004. "Darwinism Fails True Tests." *Arizona Republic*, 21 December. ("Intelligent Design" more scientific. No supportive evidence such as "missing links" for Darwin's theory).

Larson, E. J. 2004. *Evolution: Remarkable History of Scientific Theory.* New York: Modern Library.

Larson, J. 2004. "Valley Firm Takes on Wal-Mart." *Arizona Republic*, 25 November. (Khimetrics, Inc. provides price/sales analysis software.)

—. 2004. "Offshoring Accelerating." *Arizona Republic*, 18 May.

—. 2004. "Germany's Unemployment Rate at 10.3%." *Arizona Republic*, 5 May.

Lasch, C. 1991. *The Culture of Narcissism: American Life in an Age of Diminishing Expectations*. New York: W. W. Norton and Company.

Lash, S., and J. Friedman, Eds. 1992. *Modernity and Identity*. Oxford, U.K.: Blackwell.

Lavington, C. 1998 *You've Got Only Three Seconds*. New York: Main Street Books.

Lavoie, D. 2003 "Catholic Scandal Statistics Released." *Arizona Republic*. 24 July. (Massachusetts Atty. General Report.)

Lawrence, Brother. [1666.] 1999 *The Practice of the Presence of God: Conversations and Letters of Brother Lawrence*. Reissue. Oxford: Oneworld Publications.

Leary, M. 2004. "Get Over Yourself." *Psychology Today*, July/August.

LeDoux, J. 1998. *The Emotional Brain*. New York: Simon & Schuster.

Leep, S. 2004. "Porn." *Philadelphia Trumpet*, November. (10,000 porn movies per year; Hollywood produces only 400 movies per year. Negative effects include psychological, social, and moral on marriage and children.)

Lehmann, C. 2004. "American Psychiatric Assn. Opposes Execution of Juveniles." *Psychiatric News* 39:16, 20 August. (Cites 8th Amendment ban; adolescents lack maturity.)

—. 2004. "Young Brains Don't Distinguish Real from Televised Violence." *Psychiatric News*, 8 August.

Lehr, H. A. 1994. "Vitamin C Halts Damage from Cigarette Smoke." *Science*. Vol. 265:871, 12 August.

Lehr, J., and R. Bennett. 2003. "It's the Sun." *Environment and Climate News*, 6:4, May. (Earth warming not environmental but correlated with solar surface magnetic energy cycles.)

Leicester, J. 2004. "'We Want the Truth,' Madrid Crowd Chants." *Arizona Republic*. 14 March.

Leland, J. 2004. *Hip: The History*. New York: Ecco Press.

Lemonick, M. 2004. "The Hobbits of the South Pacific." *Time*, 1 November. (Discovery of Homo floresiensis, diminutive-sized race near Bali.)

Lemonick, M., and A. Dorfman. 2003. "The 160,000 Year-old Man." *Time*, 23 June, 56.

Lemonick, M., and J. Nash. 2004. "Cosmic Conundrum." *Time*, 29 November. (Theories of origin of the universe.)

Leo, J. 2004. "The Loudmouth Emmys." *U. S. News & World Report*, 6 December. (Celebrity malevolence and grossness.)

—. 2004. "What Now, Democrats?" *U. S. News & World Report*, 15 November. (Secularist, anti-religious Far-Left agenda a loser agenda.)

—. 2004. "When Churches Head Left" *U. S. News & World Report*, 18 October.

Leonard, D. 2004. "Nightmare on Madison Avenue." *Fortune*, 28 June.

Leopold, E. 2004. "Saddam Bought Off Countries and People with Oil." *Reuters*, 7 October. (CIA report: $11 billion paid to European leaders and U. N. Security Council members.)

Levering, R., and M. Moskowitz. 2004. "The 100 Best Companies to Work for." *Fortune*. 12 January, 56-80.

Levinson, P. 2004. "Teach How to Think Critically." Interview. *O'Reilly Factor*. Fox News, 12 April.

Lewis, J. R. 2001. *Odd Gods: New Religions and the Cult Controversy*. Amherst, New York: Prometheus Books.

Lienhard, J. H. 2003. *Inventing Modern*. New York: Oxford University Press.

Limbacher, C. 2002. "Torricelli Principles." http://www.*Newsmax.com*.

Livingstone, I. 2005 "Stress and the Brain." *Physician's Health Update*, January-February. (Stress impairs cognition, memory, and hippocampus through "allustatic" load.)

Lodmell, D., and B. Lodmell. 2004. *The Lawsuit Lottery: The Hijacking of Justice in America*. Phoenix, Ariz.: World Connection Publishing.

Long, G. 2004. *Relativism and the Foundations of Liberalism*. Exeter, U.K.: Imprint Academic.

Lopez, G. 2004. *Why You Crying?* New York: Touchstone Books.

Lyle, J. 2003. "Some Post-structural Assumptions." Dept. of English, Brock University www.brocku.ca/english/courses/4F76/poststruct.htm.

—. 2003. "Characteristics of Modernism, Postmodernism, Structuralism, and Poststructuralism." www.labweb.education.wisc.edu/en1916/modtable.htm.

Lynch, A. 1999. *Thought Contagion: How Belief Spreads Through Society*. New York: Basic Books.

Lyotard, J. 1984. *The Postmodern Condition: A Report on Knowledge*. Manchester, U.K.: Manchester University Press.

MacDonald, B. 2004. "Launch into Power." *Philadelphia Trumpet*. January, 5-7. (China.)

MacDonald, H. 2004. *The Burden of Bad Ideas: How Modern Intellectuals Misshape Our Society*. New York: Ivan R. Dee Press (Manhattan Institute City Journal).

MacDonald, J. 2004. "Today's Culture Less Frills, Tastes Lousy...Morality in Short Supply." *Arizona Republic*, 14 June.

MacEachern, D. 2004. "Media continue waltz on one foot." *Arizona Republic*, 19 December. (Eighteen of 20 major media rated biased to the Left by university study.)

—. 2004. "Don't Know Nothin' 'Bout Birthin' No Stereotypes." *Arizona Republic*, 21 November. (Leftist professor attacks Condolezza Rice and Colin Powell with racial stereotypes.)

—. 2004. "Anyone Have a Spare Conspiracy Theory?" *Arizona Republic*, 26 September. (Trilateral Commission, etc.)

—. 2004. "Knocking Discipline into a Cocked Hat." *Arizona Republic*. 21 March.

MacKay, C. [1841] 2003. *Extraordinary Popular Delusions and the Madness of Crowds*. Reprint. New York: Harriman House.

Mackey, C. 2004. "Tree of Self-Defeat and Tree of Self-Actualization." http://www.geocities.com/Athens/ Acropolis/4508/growth_actual.html.

Mackey, G., and G. Miller. 2004. *The Interrogators: Inside the Secret War Against al-Qaeda*. New York: Little, Brown.

—. "The Tree of Self-Understanding." http://www.earthrenewal.org/tree.htm. (Adapted from Mother Teresa's *A Simple Path*.)

Mackin, P., and A. H. Young. 2004. "The Role of Cortisol and Depression." *Psychiatric Times*, May.

MacPachorn, D. 2004. "Election Paranoia on the Left." *Arizona Republic*, 11 July. (Bush won votes legally.)

Madigen, C. M., ed. 2004. "Perspectives in Instant History: The Week." *Chicago Tribune*, 11 April.

Maehan, T. R. 2004. *The Liberty Option*. Exeter, U.K.: Imprint Academic.

Malkin, M. 2004. "Philippines Message Clear-We Lied." *Creators Syndicate*, 15 July. (Appeasement of Islamic terrorists.)

Malone, R. 2004. "Superpower Under Siege." *Philadelphia Trumpet*. February, 5-10.

Manji, I. 2004. *The Trouble with Islam*. New York: St. Martin's Press

Marcuse, H.1972. *Counterrevolution and Revolt*. Boston: Beacon Press. (Political/social Marxism.)

—. 1969. "Repressive Tolerance" in *A Critique of Pure Tolerance*, Wolff, R., et al. Boston: Beacon Press.

—. 1967. *One Dimensional Man: Studies in The Ideology of Advanced Industrial Society*. Boston: Beacon Press.

—.1966. *Eros and Civilization: A Philosophical Inquiry into Freud*. Boston: Beacon Press. (Politicized version of Freud.)

Margasak, L. 2004. "Pentagon Pays $100 Million for Unused Airline Tickets." *Arizona Republic*, 9 June.

Martin, J., and A. Neal. 2002. "Defending Civilization: How Our Universities Are Failing America." Report of American Council of Trustees and Alumni, Washington, DC.

Marx, K., and F. Engles. 1957. "Contributions to Hegel's Philosophy of Right." In *K. Marx and F. Engels on Religion*. Moscow: Foreign Languages Publishing House.

Maszak, M. S. 2004. "Health: Driven to Distraction." *Time*, 26 April, 52-62.

Mathew, R. J. 2001. *The True Path: Western Science and the Quest for Yoga*. New York: Perseus Publishing. (Neuroscience demonstrates positive effect on brain physiology to nondominant hemisphere of region, music, art, nature, and altruism.)

Matt, D. C. 1995. *The Essential Kabbalah: The Heart of Jewish Mysticism*. New York: HarperCollins Publishers Inc.

May, A. 2004. "Juggling Makes the Brain Bigger." *Medical News Today*. 1 February. www.medicalnewstoday.com/indexphp2newsid=5615.

McCain, J. 2004. *Why Courage Matters: The Way to a Braver Heart*. New York: Random House.

McCraty, R. 2004-2005. "The Resonant Heart." *Shift*, December-February. (Heart electromagnetic fields associated with emotions; influence brain function.)

McGeary, J. 2004. "Iraq's Shadow Ruler." *Time*, 25 October. (Sistani.)

—. 2004. "What Saddam Was Really Thinking." *Time*, 18 October.

—. 2004. "Inside HAMAS." *Time*, 5 April. (Charles Dualfar Report.)

—. 2004. "Who's the Enemy Now?" *Time*, 29 March. (Jihad, Inc.: Al-Qaeda has spawned a greater movement.)

McGirk, T. 2003. "Sending A Message to The Ayatollahs." *Time*, n.d.

McLemone, C. 2003. *Street Smart Ethics: Succeeding in Business Without Having to Sell Your Soul*. Louisville: John Knox Press.

"Medicine This Week." 2004 *AzMed* 6:46, 19 November. (Costs of medical care primarily administrative, bureaucratic, and legal.)

Medley, K. W. 2004. "On Clipped Wings…Tuskegee Airmen." *Smithsonian*, May.

Medred, M. 1992. *Hollywood vs. America*. New York: Harper.

Mehlman, J. D. 1997. "Uncertainties in Projections of Human-Caused Climate Warming." *Science* 278, 21 November, 1416-1417.

Mehrens, N. P. 2004. "Unions Forget Half of the First Amendment." www.opinioneditorials.com/ freedomwriters/mehrens200403.html.

Melliott, J. 2004. "Modeling for the Future – Report by K. Kelliarokos on Young People in the Media." *Publishers Weekly*. 10 May.

"Mercenary/Private Military Companies." 2004. Global Security. http://www.globalsecurity.org./military/world/para/pme-list/htm. (Lists over 60 private military companies worldwide.)

Merton, T. 1961-67. *Mystics and Zen Masters*. New York: Farrar, Straus, and Giroux.

Mesugi, K. 2002. "Last Days of the Pseudo-Intellectuals." *Philanthropy Roundtable*. March/April.

Metzinger, T., ed. 1995. *Conscious Experience*. Lawrence, KS: Imprint Academic, Allen Press.

Meyssen, T. 2002. *9/11: The Big Lie*. Los Angeles: Continental Sales. (Gross distortion and fallacy-based anti-Americanism.)

Michael, R. F., and J. L. Gibbons. 1963. "Interelationships Between the Endocrine System and Neuropsychiatry." *Review of Neurobiology*, 243-302.

Midgley, M. 1993. *The Myths We Live By*. New York: Routledge.

Milcke, M. 2005. Recordings (CDs) of all lectures (2002-2004) on "Devotional Nonduality" by David R. Hawkins. Sedona, Ariz.: Veritas Publishing.

Milgram, S. 2004. "The Perils of Obedience." http://home.swbill. not/ravseat/perilsofobedience.html.

—. 1974. *Obedience to Authority*. New York: Harper Collins.

Mill, J. S. 1957. *Utilitarianism*. O. Piest, ed. New York: Bobbs-Merrill.

Miniter, R. 2004. *Shadow War: The Untold Story of How Bush Is Winning the War on Terror*. New York: Regnery.

Mitchell, M. 2004. "GI Guilty of Attempted Treason." *Associated Press*, 3 September.

Mnookin, S. 2004. *Hard News: The Scandals at The New York Times and Their Meaning for American Media*. New York: Random House. (U. N. chicanery.)

Monroe, R. 1992. *Journeys Out of the Body*. Revised. New York: Main Street Books.

Moore, M. 2001. *Stupid White Men*. New York: Harper Collins.

Moran, M. 2004. "Stalkers Inhabit a Reality All Their Own." *Psychiatric News*, 5 November.

—. 2004. "… Secrets of the Social Brain." *Psychiatric News*, July. (Oxytocin regulates maternal and social behaviors and the amygdale.)

Morgante, M. 2004. "DNA Co-Discoverer Dies." *Arizona Republic*, 30 July. (Scientific importance of Francis Crick.)

Morris, B. 2005. "How Corporate America is Betraying Women." *Fortune*, 10 January.

Mosley, I., ed. 2004. *Dumbing Down: Culture, Politics, and the Mass Media*. Exeter, U.K.: Imprint Academic.

"Movie Economics: Family Film Business." 2005. *Fortune*, 10 January. (Gross income from G-rated films [3% of Hollywood output] exceeds that of the 69% output of R-rated films.)

Muktananda, S. *Kundalini: The Secret of Life*. Fallberg, NY: SYDA Foundation.

Muller, B. 2004. "Pied Piper or Bully? Moore Ruffles Critics…Wraps Self in First Amendment." *Arizona Republic*, 20 June, On Film.

—. 2004. "New Website Allows Search of Government Research Sites: 47 Million Pages." AzMed., 18 June. (Medicine This Week)

—. 2004. "Film's Message Lost in Bloodiness." *Arizona Republic*, 24 February. (*Passion of Christ.*)

Mullings, J., J. Marquest, et al. 2004. *The Victimization of Children*. Binghamton, NY: Haworth Press.

Murphy, D. 2003. "Village in Jam Tells Story of Militant Islamic Growth." *Christian Science Monitor*, 23 January.

Murphy, T. 2004. "Researching Behavioral Neuroscience: Neurobiology of Religious Terrorism." http://www.innerworlds.50megs.com/terrorism.htm.

Murray, A. 2003. "The Atheist: Madalyn Murray O'Hare." Book Review. *Humanist*, Nov./Dec.

Muskin, P. 2004. "Spiritual Leader to Guide Psychiatrists from the Head to the Heart." *Psychiatric News*, 19 March.

Nadean, R., and M. Kafatos. 2003. *The Nonlocal Universe: The New Physics and Matters of the Mind.* London: Oxford University Press.

Nahmias, E., S. Morris, et al. 2004. "The Phenomenology of Free Will." *Journal of Consciousness Studies* 11, July/August, 162-180.

Nash, R. H. 1992. *Word of God and the Mind of Man: Crisis of Revealed Truth in Contemporary Theology.* Phillipsburg, N. J.: P and R Publishing.

Neubauer, R. 2004. "Evolution of Personality Fits with Biology and Theology." *Science and Theology News*. January, 20-21

—. 2002. *Voyages into Transcendence*. Austin, Tex.: Bay of Rainbows Press.

Newark, K. 2004. "Muslim-American Organization." *O'Reilly Factor*, Fox News, 5 August. (U. S. mosques funded as sympathetic to spread of al-Qaeda type of theocratic fascism. Terrorism not removed by Imams here or abroad.)

Newberg, A. 2004. "Searching for God Amid the Ganglia." *Science and Theology News*, July/August. (Neurotheology.)

Newton, P. 2004. Personal communications about Canada.

Newman, R. J. 2004. "Corporate Kleptocracy." *U. S. News & World Report*, 13 September. (Extraordinary, lavish corporate-head greed.)

—. 2004. "Al-Qaeda's Poppy Profits." *Time*, 30 August. (Hussein's main financial resource for al-Qaeda despite $40 million U. S. grant to Taliban to reduce opium production.)

Nichols, P. M. 2004. *New York Times Guide to the Best 1000 Movies Ever Made.* New York: St. Martins Griffin.

"Niger Uranium . . . Bush, Blair Right about Niger Uranium." *Arizona Republic*, 22 July.

Nilus, S. [1905, 1911] 2003. *The Protocol of the Learned Elders of Zion.* Trans. V. E. Marsden,. Athena University Press. (See also http://www.adl.org.)

"No Fan of Michael Moore's Films." 2004. *Arizona Republic*, 27 May. Letters to Editor. (Moral depravity.)

"Novel Attempt at Fighting Crime on Mexico City's Metro." 2004. *Arizona Republic*, 24 January.

"Nutty Professor: Ward Churchill." Freedom House (2005) Report in *Investors Business Daily*, 2 February.

Obeidi, M., and K. Pitzer. 2004. *The Bomb in My Garden: The Secrets of Saddam's Nuclear Mastermind.* New York: John Wiley & Sons.

O'Connell, J. 1979. *The Lawsuit Lottery: Only the Lawyers Win.* New York: Free Press, Macmillan.

O'Donnell, C. Ed. 2003. *Culture, Peers, and Delinquency.* Binghamton, NY: Haworth Press.

"Offensive Billboard Simply Truthful." 2004. *Arizona Republic*, 27 April. Letter to the Editor.

"Old Evils, New Faces." *Arizona Republic*, 7 December. Editorial. (America's pattern of being blindsided.)

Olson, C. 2000. *Zen and the Art of Postmodern Philosophy: Two Paths of Liberation from the Representational Mode of Thinking.* Albany, New York: State University of New York Press.

O'Murchu, D. 1997. *Quantum Theology: Spiritual Implications of the New Physics.* New York: Crossroads Publishing Co.

Orecklin, M. 2004. "Study Links TV, Kids' Attention Woes." *Arizona Republic*, 5 April.

—. 2003. "Can You Sing Om?" *Time*, 6 October, 62.

—. "Walk-ins for Evolution." *WE Magazine*, 39, 3rd Quarter, 2003.

O'Reilly, B. 2004. "Slander Is Profitable and Dishonest Defamation Commercialized." *O'Reilly Factor,* Fox News, 12 July.

—. 2004. "Judicial Meltdown – 9th Circuit Court of Appeals." *O'Reilly Factor*, Fox News, 14 June.

Orloff, J. 2004. *Positive Energy*. New York: Harmony Books (Random House).

Ornstein, R. E. 1972. *The Psychology of Consciousness*. San Francisco: W. H. Freeman & Co.

Orwell, G. 1983. *1984*. New York: Harcourt.

Pagatchnik, S. 2004. "Stephen Hawking Changes Mind about Black Holes." *Associated Press*, 22 July. (17th Intl. Conference on General Relativity and Gravitation, Dublin.)

Page, C. 2004. "Cosby Has the Message Right." *Arizona Republic*, 2 June.

—. 2004. "Poor Blacks Must Raise Their Game." *Arizona Republic*, 25 May.

Painton, P. 2004. "Target America." *New York Times*, 8 August. (Al-Qaeda selecting New York targets.)

Pancrazio, A. C. 2004. "Rosie's Still Riveting." *Arizona Republic*, 28 May. (Women of WWII.)

Paris, J. 2003. *Personality Disorders Over Time: Precursors, Course, and Outcome*. Arlington, Va.: American Psychiatric Publishing, Inc.

Parker, K. 2004. "Can't Afford a Safari? Log on with This Sick-O." *Tribune Media Service*, 20 December. (Live shot cam– Fortuna's worst tech game of the year, "Grand Theft Auto," etc.).

—. 2004. "Cynicism Is Terrorist Trump Card." *Tribune Media*, 5 August. (President attacked no matter what he does.)

—. 2004. "Did Bush Have A Choice on Iraq?" *Tribune Media*, 15 July. (He didn't.)

—. 2003. "Good Goddess, What's Going On?" *Arizona Republic*, 6 August.

—. 2003. "Just How Weird Can We Get?" *Arizona Republic*, 2 July.

Pauchant, T., ed. 2002. *Ethics and Spirituality at Work: Hopes and Pitfalls of the Search for Meaning in Organizations*. Newport, CT: Quorum Books.

Payne, A. 2004. "Gangster Rap Definitely Encourages Crime and Imitation of Suggestive Career." TV interview. *O'Reilly Factor*, Fox News, 7 July. (Declaration by ex-20-year-member of "The Bloods" street gang.)

Pear, R. 2005. "Life Expectancy Changes Debated." *Arizona Republic*, 1 January. (Longer lives mean greater cost to Medicare and Social Security.)

"Pearl Harbor: It Might Have Been Avoided." *Alameda (California) Times-Star*. http://www.prisonplanet.com/071203pearlharboravoided.html.

Pearson, M. 2004. "Don't Play the Blame Game." *Globe* and *Mail* (Canada), 25 June.

Peck, M. S. 1983. *People of the Lie*. New York: Simon and Schuster.

Penrose, R. 1994. *Shadows of the Mind*. New York: Oxford Press.

Pepperberg, I. M. 1995. "Studies to Determine Intelligence in African Gray Parrots." University of Arizona Proceedings Internet Aviculturasists Society. 1/11/95.

Peters, T., and M. Hewlett. 2003. *Evolution from Creation to Now; Creation: Conflict, Conversation, and Convergence*. Nashville, Tenn.: Abingdon Press.

Peterson, J. 2003. *Scam : How the Black Leadership Exploits Black America*. New York: Nelson Current.

Pfeffer, C. R. 2004. "Trauma, Violence, and Victimization." *Psychiatric Times*, April, 57-74.

—. 2004, "Deadly Silences: 9/11 Probe Reveals Wall of Bureaucracy Puts U.S. at Risk." *Arizona Republic*, 4 June. (Gorelick/Reno).

Pine, R. (trans.) *The Zen Teaching of Bodhidharma*. New York: Farrar, Straus, and Giroux (North Point Press).

Pinkerton, J. 2004. "Freedom Is A Messy Thing." *Los Angeles Times Syndicate*, 6 July. (Howard Stern is anti-Bush.)

Pitts, L. 2004. "Facts? We Don't Need No Stinking Facts!" *Tribune Media Services*, 29 December. (Social tendency to merely express politicized positions that completely ignore the facts, thus living in an "alternate" reality.)

—. 2004. "Gutless Hypocrisy at NBC and CBS." *Tribune Media Services*, 5 December.

—. 2003. "Why Are the Religious So Often Poor Advertisements for Religion?" *Arizona Republic*, 29 September.

Plato. 1952. "Protagorus." *The Great Books of the Western World*. Vol. 7:38-65. Chicago: Encyclopedia Britannica.

—. 1952. "Georgia's." Op cit. pp. 252-295.

—. 1952. "Phoeduus." Op cit. pp. 115-142.

—. 1952. "Sophist." Op cit. pp. 551-580.

Pockett, S. 2004. "Does Consciousness Cause Behavior?" *Journal of Consciousness Studies*, 11:2, 23-40.

Poerksen, B. 2004. *The Certainty of Uncertainty: Constructivism.* Exeter, U. K.: Imprint Academic.

Political Compass Team. 2004. "Authoritarian/Libertarian . . .About the Political Compass." www.digitalronin.f25.com/politicalcompass/analysis2.html. 6 January.

"Politics of Values, The." 2004. *Economist*, 9 October.

Polkinghorne, J. 2005. "The Continuing Interaction of Science and Religion." *Zygon* 40:1, March, 43-51.

Polshy, N. W. 2003. *How Congress Evolves: Social Bases of Institutional Change.* Oxford: Oxford University Press.

Portes, E. 2004. "Jobless Data Tied to Health Costs." *New York Times*, September, n.d. (Business can't afford full-time employees because of high escalating cost of health benefits.)

Powe, L. 2001. *The Warren Court and American Politics.* Cambridge, Mass.: Belknap Press.

Powell B. 2004. "The Struggle for the Soul of Islam." *Time*, 13 September, 46-71.

—. 2004. "Al-Qaeda in America: The Terror Plot." *Time*, 16 August.

"Powers, J. M. *Freedom in the World 2005: Civic Power and Electoral Politics.* New York: Freedom House. (Study of freedom and partial freedom and partial freedom in the world's 192 countries.)

—. 2004. "The Dumbing Down of Medicine." *AzMed*, November-December.

Prager, D. 2004. "Moore's Leftists in Love with Hating America." *Arizona Republic*, 11 July. (Leftists' adolescent hatred of Christianity and Judaism, America and Israel.)

Prechter, R. R. 1999, 2002. *The Wave Principle of Human Social Behavior and The New Science of Socioeconomics.* Gainesville, Georgia: New Classics Library.

Preston, I. 1994. *The Tangled Web They Weave: Truth, Falsity, and Advertisers.* Madison, Wisc.: University of Wisconsin Press.

"Prevalence of Personality Disorders in U. S." 2004. *AzMed*, 6 August. (15% of Americans [31 million] have diagnosable personality disorders.)

"Private Military Companies." 2004. Fort Liberty: http://www.fortliberty.org./privatemilitarycompanies.shtml. (Major military companies worldwide.)

Puhakka, K. 1999. "Form and Formless in Spiritual Practice." Esalen Center Conference 11/28-12/02.

Pullen, R. 2004. "Passing Prop. 200 sends clear message." *Arizona Republic*, 26 October. (Calls for laws to be enforced.)

Purnick, J. 2004. "Politics Takes Back Seat to Illogic." *New York Times*, 24 May.

Pusey, A. 2004. "Justices Say Web Porn Law Still Not Legal." *Arizona Republic*, 30 June. (Child access.)

Radin, D. 2004. "Entangled Minds." *Shift*, December 2004-February 2005.

Rado, S. 1933. "Psychoanalysis of Pharmacothymia." *Psychoanalytic Quarterly* 2:1-23.

Ragavan, C., and M. Guttman. 2004. "Terror on the Streets." *U. S. News and World Report*, 13 December. (Extreme violent M-13 gang now major in the U. S.; originated in El Salvador, Guatamala, and Honduras.)

—. 2004. "A Fine Legal Mess in Motown." *U. S. News & World Report*, 13 September. (Feds incompetence in prosecuting terrorist suspects.)

Ralston, H. 2005. "Inevitable Humans: Simon Conway Morris's Evolutionary Paleontology." *Zygon* 40:1, March, 221-231.

Randal, J. 2004. *Osama: The Making of a Terrorist*. New York: Knopf Publishing.

Rao, K. R. 2002. *Consciousness Studies: Cross Culture Perspectives*. Jefferson, N.C.: McFarland and Co.

Raspberry, W. 2004. "Please Don't Take Al Franken Seriously." *Arizona Republic*, 14 April.

—. 2002. "View from Grand Jury Changes Light on Justice." *Arizona Republic*. 15 July.

Rauchi, G. A. 1971. *Contemporary Philosophical Alternatives and the Crisis of Truth: A Critical Study of Positivism, Existentialism, and Marxism*. New York: Nijhoff Publishers.

Ravitch, J. 2003. *The Language Police*. New York: Knopf Publishers.

—. 2000. "Textbook Bias Cops Ban Ideas." *Arizona Republic*. 18 May. (Review of *The Language Police*.)

Reaves, J. A. 2004. "Troubles Dogging Polygamy Prophet." *Arizona Republic*, 1 August. (Fundamentalist Church Sect of L. D. S., Warren Jeff's accusation of series of felonies.)

—. 2004. "Poke at Polygamist's Haven." *Arizona Republic*, n.d.

Regen, M. 2004. "Corporate Tsunami Aid in Millions." *Associated Press*, 31 December.

Reich, D. E., and Goldstein, D. B. 1998. "Genetic Evidence of Paleolithic Human Population in Africa." *Proceedings of the National Academy of Science, USA 95* (14) 8119-8123.

Reid, J. 2004. "Time and Three Questions That Matter." *Sedona (Arizona) Red Rock News*, 12 November. (What is going on, what does it mean, what should I do? Need for meaning, value, and rise of spirituality.)

—. 2004. "Finding Balance in an Unbalanced World." *Sedona (Arizona) Red Rock News*, 28 May. (Media and violent personality disorders.)

Revel, J. 2003. *Anti-Americanism*. San Francisco: Encounter Books.

Richter, P. 2004. "U. S. Struggles in War of Ideas, Panel Says." *Los Angeles Times*, 25 July.

Richtofen, M. 2004. *The Red Baron*. Wikipedia, 17 August. http://en.wikipedia.org/wiki/The_Red_Baron.

Rice, B. 2003. "Could a Mega Verdict Wipe You Out?" *Medical Economics*. July, 29-31.

Richards, V. 2002. "The Future of the Faith-Based Initiative." *Philanthropy Roundtable*. March/April.

Ridley, M. 2003. "What Makes You Who You Are." *Time*, 2 June, 55-63.

Riklan, D. 2004. *Self-Improvement: The Top 101 Experts*. Marlboro, NJ: Self-Improvement Online, Inc.

Rimbach, D. 2004. "Doctors Recognize Faith's Role in Recovery." *Science and Theology News*, July/August.

Robb, R. "Conservatism on the Firing Line." *Arizona Republic*, 10 December. (William Buckley's contribution to politics.)

—. 2003. "A Practical View of Religion and Faith." *Arizona Republic*, 5 December.

Roberts, D. 2004. "Secrets of the Maya." *Smithsonian*, July. (Pre-Columbian Deciphering Code.)

Rodger, T. A. 2004. "Jobsharing Threat to Union Growth." *Arizona Republic*, 13 June.

Rodgers, L. 2004. "Divine Misguidance: Ludecris Says Drugs, Sex, Rap Come from Above." *Arizona Republic*, 18 March.

Rohn, J. 2004. "Maintaining Honesty and Integrity." *AdvantEdge*, 64-65. Niles, Ill.: Nightingale-Conant.

Rohr, M. 2004. "UFO Cult, Higher Source Group Commits Suicide to Meet Hale-Bopp Comet." http://anw.com/halebopp/heaven.htm.

—. 2003. "Outside Montreal, Raelians Have Their Base: UFOland." http://www.miami.com/mid/miamiherald/4856259.htm?template=contentmodules/

Romero, C. 2004. "Only 1 in 15 Hired: Wal-Mart gets 8,000 Applicants for 500 Jobs." *Arizona Republic*, 14 April.

Rosack, J. 2004. "ADHD Meds Help Teenagers Drive Safely." *Psychiatric News*, 7 May.

Rubik, B. 2002. "The Biofield Hypothesis: Basis as Role in Medicine." *Journal of Alternative and Complementary Medicine* 8:6, 703-717.

Ruelas, R. 2004. "Is the End Really Near? Left-Behind Series of Books Inspired by Revelations." *Arizona Republic*, 7 April.

Russ, E. 2004. *The Missing Peace: The Inside Story of the Fight for Middle East Peace*. New York: Farrar, Straus, and Giroux.

Russell, B. 1913. "On The Notion of Cause." Proceedings, *Aristotelian Society* 13, 1-26.

Ryan, J. 2004. "Tolerance of Primitive Cultures Goes Too Far." *Arizona Republic*, 29 August. (Oppression of women in Islamic countries; no women sent to Olympics.)

Sadler, R. 2004. Research by Dr. Peter Fenwick reported to British Assn. for Advancement of Science News. www.Scotsmen.com. 11 September 2003. Quote in "Up Front." *Shift*, Spring.

Sadlier, S. 2000. *Looking for God: A Seeker's Guide to Religious and Spiritual Groups of the World*. New York: Berkeley Publishing Group, Penguin/Putnam.

Safire, W. 2004. "Bush Spoke the Truth in 16 Words." *New York Times*, 20 July. (British intelligence statement confirmed.)

—. 2004. "As Rip-Offs Go, Oil for Food (UN) Rubs." *Arizona Republic*, 20 April.

—. 2004. "100 Most Influential People in the World." *Time*, 26 April.

"Sales Report: Religious books Up 96% in October, up 41% for year." 2003. *Publishers Weekly*. 8 December.

Sanger, D., and W. Brand. 2004. "South Korea Admits Enriching Uranium." *New York Times*, 3 September.

Sanguineti, V. R. 2003. *A Rosetta Stone for the Human Mind: The Alphabets to Decipher*. New York: Psychosocial Press.

—. 1999. *Landscape in My Mind: The Origins and Structure of the Subjective Experience*. New York: Psychosocial Press.

Sannella, L. 1992. *The Kundalini Experience*. Lower Lake, Calif.: Integral Press.

"Saudi House of Hate." 2005. Freedom House (2005) Report in *Investors Business Daily*, 2 February. (Saudi government funds and spreads Wahhabist terror ideology in U.S. *officially* via its embassy in the U.S., which is the "hateful" enemy and deserves death.)

Saylor, F. 2004. "Conference Seeks Public Definition of Truth in Science." *Science and Theology News*, October.

—. 2004. "Italian Scientists Rally Behind Evolution." *Science and Theology News*, July/August.

—. 2004. "Radical Religious Movement Breeds Violence and Hate." *Science and Theology News*, January. (Christian identity movement.)

Savage, M. 2003. *The Enemy Within*. New York: WND Books.

Saylor, F. 2004. "Purpose-Driven Bestseller." *Publishers Weekly*, November. (Review of Rick Warren's *The Purpose-Driven Life*.)

Schama, S. 2004. "History of Britain." BBC via History Channel, 28 December.

Schauer, M. 2004. *Imperial Hubris: Why the West is Losing the War on Terror*. Dulles, Va.: Brassey's, Inc.

Schoff, S. 2003. "Making France Our Best Friend." *Time*, 7 July, 70-73.

Schwartz, J., and M. L. Wald. 2003. "Shuttle Loss Laid to NASA's Habits and Broken Safety Culture." *International Herald Tribune*, 27 August.

Schwartz, S. 2002. *The Two Faces of Islam*. New York: Doubleday.

Scott, A. 2004. "Reductionism Revisited." *Journal of Consciousness Studies*, 11:2, 51-68. (Nonlinear Science)

"Searchers Blast CIA for False Info Re Iraqi Threat." 2004. *Los Angeles Times* and *Arizona Republic*, 10 July.

Searle, J. R. 2004. *Mind, A Brief Introduction.* Oxford: Oxford University Press.

"Security is Bush's Job One: Dean's Paranoia Yelpings Aside, President Must Respond to Threats." 2004. *Arizona Republic*, 3 August. (Editorial)

Segal, T. D. 2004. "The French-Muslim Connection." www.gopusa. com/commentary/ tsegel/ 2004/ts_0503.shtml.

Selye, H. 1978. *Stress of Life.* New York: McGraw-Hill.

Sepulsky, R. M., K. C. Krey, and B. S. McEwen. 1986. "Neuroendocrinology of Stress: the Glucocorticoid Cascade. *Endocrinology Review,* 7:3, 284-301.

Serwer, A. 2004. "The Waltons: America' Richest Family." *Fortune*, 15 November. (Worth $90 billion and modest: Family Philanthropies.)

Shapiro, B. 2004. *Brainwashed: How Universities Indoctrinate America's Youth.* Nashville, Tenn.: WND Books.

—. 2004. "Universities Giving Students Hard Shake to the Left." *Arizona Republic*, 14 June.

Shaw, R., and S. Wood. 2004. "Nation of Brats: Why Kids Are Behaving Badly Today." *Arizona Republic*, 8 February.

—. 2003. *The Epidemic: The Rot of American Culture, Absentee and Permissive Parenting, and the Resultant Plague of Joyless, Selfish Children.* New York: Regan Books

Shearer, D. 1998. "Outsourcing War." *Foreign Policy*, Fall.

Sheldrake, R. 2004. "Morphic Fields." *Shift*, December 2004-February 2005.

—. 1981. *A New Science of Life.* London: Victoria Works.

—. 1981. Essay in *New Scientist*, 18 June, 749, 766-768.

—. 1981. "Formative Causation." *Brain/Mind Bulletin.* No. 6, 13 August.

Sheldrake, R. and A. Morgana. 2003. "Testing A Parrot for Telepathy." *Journal of Scientific Exploration,* 17:4, 601-617.

Shepherd, T. 2003. "I've Always Wondered About UNESCO and The Association of Unity Churches' Warnings on Sathya Sai Baba." *Vanity*, Sept.-Oct., 25.

—. 2003. "HMOs Given 'No Confidence' Vote by U. S. Public." AzMed, 15 August, 2.

Sherman, M. 2004. "House Votes To Break Up 9th Circuit Court of Appeals into 3 Courts." *Associated Press*, 6 October.

Shore, S. 2004. "Qwest Retirees Sue…$6 Billion Loss Pension Fund." *Associated Press*, 15 July.

Shorter, E. 1997. *A History of Psychiatry: From the End of the Asylum to Prozac*. New York: John Wiley & Sons.

Siblani, O. 2004. "Arab-American News." Fox News, 12 May. Interview. (Beheading of Berg a criminal act rather than a political statement.)

Siegel, B. S. 2003. *365 Prescriptions for the Soul – Inspiration, Hope, and Love*. New York: New World Library.

—. 1986. *Love, Medicine, and Miracles*. New York: Harper Collins.

Singer, J. L. 2004. "Public Smoking Ban Simply Tyranny." *Arizona Republic*, 24 November. (CDC falsified data that actually showed a negligible risk.)

Singer, P. 2000. *Marx*. Oxford: Oxford University Press.

Slivka, J. 2003. "Wars Challenge World's Thinkers." *Arizona Republic*, 22 July.

Smart, J. J. C. 2004. "Consciousness and Awareness." *Journal of Consciousness* Studies. 11:2, 41-50.

Smoley, R. 2002. *Inner Christianity: A Guide to the Esoteric Tradition*. Boston: Shambhala.

Smith, W. 2004. *Official Handbook of the Vast Right-Wing Conspiracy*. Washington, D. C.: Regnery

Snyder, N. 2004. "Religious Media Boom." *The Nashville Tennessean*, 20 November. (Spiritual books now mainstream.)

Sohn, S. W. 2004. Quoted in Strope, L., "Rich Get Richer." *Arizona Republic*, 17 August. (Internet, economy, and technology have eliminated many jobs by global competition, not politics.)

"Sokol Affair and Postmodernism, Reference to." 2004. http://en.wikipedia.org/wiki/postmodernism; http://en.wikipedia.org/wiki/Sokal_Affair.

Solomon, P. J. 2004. "A Lesson from Wal-Mart." *Washington Post*, 28 March.

Soros, G. 2003. *The Bubble of American Supremacy: Correcting the Misuse of American Power*. New York: Public Affairs.

Sowell, T. 2004. *Affirmative Action Around the World: An Empirical Study*. New Haven, Conn.: Yale University Press.

—. 2004. "Sharing the Lawsuit Wealth." http://www.townhall.com/ columnists/thomassowell/ printts20040803.shtml. (Fallacy of class action lawsuits—claimants get nothing.)

—. 2004. "Bill Cosby Needs No Lecture from Silly Columnist." *Creators Syndicate* in *Arizona Republic*, 14 July. (Blacks weakened by blame and excuses.)

—. 2004. "Wanted: More Doers, Fewer Talking." *Arizona Republic*, 14 June.

—. 2004. "There's Nothing Academic About a Lion's Threat to Kids." *Arizona Republic*, 26 May.

—. 2004. "Fahrenheit 9-11 Awarded Prize as Best Film at Cannes." *New York Times*, 23 May.

—. 2003. "Milton Friedman Put Common Sense into the Economic World." *Arizona Republic,* n.d.

—. 2003. "When Did We Start Penalizing Our Achievers?" *Arizona Republic*, 17 October, B-11.

Sperry, L. 2004. "Ethical Dilemmas: Assessment of Outcome." *Psychiatric Annals*. February, 107-113.

Sperry, P. 2005. *Infiltration: How Muslim Spies and Subversives have Penetrated Washington*. New York: Nelson Current. (Spread of Islamic terrorism plus infiltration of U. S. intelligence agencies.)

Sraves, L. 2004. "New Ways to Know God." *Science and Theology News*, July/August. Letter to Editor. ("The science of consciousness probably only field to link science and religion.")

Stapp, H. 2005. The Mindful Universe [Book in Prep March 12, 2005] http://www-physics.lbl.gov/~stapp/ (stappfiles.html - 15 March).

—. 1999. "Attention, Intention, and Will in Quantum Physics." *Journal of Consciousness Studies* 6 (8-9), 143-164.

Stapp, H., and D. Bourget. 2004. "Quantum Leaps in Philosophy of Mind." *Journal of Consciousness Studies* 11:12, December. (Critiques and replies.)

Steckner, S. 2004. "Kids See Doctor for Free." *Arizona Republic*, 21 July. Letter to Editor. (Medical care for indigents provided by Salvation Army and St. Joseph's Hospital.)

—. 2004. "Abuse to Chickens Revealed." *Arizona Republic*, 21 July.

Stein, A. 2002. *Inside Out: A Memoir of Entering and Breaking Out of a Minneapolis Political Cult.* St. Cloud, Minnesota: North Star Press of St. Cloud, Inc.

Stein, J. 2003. "Just Say 'Om.'" *Time*, 4 August. (Meditation.)

Stimson, H. "Biographical Sketches: Henry Stimson." Truman Library. http://www.trumanlibrary.org/ hoover/stimson.htm.

—. "1929-1933: Secretary of State Henry Stimson." 2004. Bureau of Public Affairs, U. S. Dept. of State.

Stearns, J. 2005. "The New Science of Happiness." *Time*, 17 January, A1-8.

Stone, A. A. 2004. "Sweet Sixteen: Realism, Not Escapism the Mission of Films." *Psychiatric Times*, April. (Cashiers du Cinema)

Stossel, J. 2004. *Give Me A Break: How I Exposed Hucksters.* New York: Harper Collins Co.

Stossel, S., and B. Moyers. 2004. *Sarge: The Life and Times of Sargent Shriver.* Washington, DC: Smithsonian Institution Press.

Strong, R. 2004. "A History Of Spiritualist Fraud In The 19th And 20th Centuries." http://www.skepticreport/psychics/spiritualized fraud.htm. 1 July.

Suplae, C. 2004. "A Stormy Star." *National Geographic*, July. (Sun's magnetic fields, fusion, sunspots, and earth climate effects.")

Sutel, S. 2004. "Consumer Attitude High." *Associated Press* in *Arizona Republic*, 27 July. (Rise in jobs, stock market, home sales, and economy over last 2 years.)

—. 2004. "Al Franken Firing Up Liberals on Airwaves." *Associated* Press in *Arizona Republic*, 1 April.

Suzuki, D. T. 2004. "Immigrant Physicians Account for 27% of Medical Residents." *AzMed*, 2 July.

—. 1960. *Manual of Zen Buddhism.* New York: Grove/Atlantic.

Szasz, T. 1974. *The Myth of Mental Illness: Foundations of a Theory of Personal Conduct.* New York: Harper & Rowe.

—. 1973. "Mental Illness As a Metaphor." *Nature.* 30 March, 305-307.

Talbott, J. A. 2004. "Care of the Chronically Mentally Ill—Still a National Disgrace." *Psychiatric Services* 55:10, October.

—. 1985. "The Shame of the Cities." *Hospital and Community Psychiatry*, September.

Taleb, N. N. 2001. *Fooled by Randomness: The Hidden Role of Chance in The Markets and in Life.* New York: Thomson Texere Publishing.

Talton, J. 2003. "For a Time in '90s, Terror Was Nobody's Business." *Arizona Republic*, April, n.d.

—. 2003. "Instinct to Trust Could Be Brain-Hormone Related." *Arizona Republic*, 3 December.

Tanner, R. 2004. "US Radiologists Outsource Work." *Arizona Republic*, 7 December.

—. 2004. "Education Chief Calls National Education Association a Terrorist Organization." *Arizona Republic*. 24 February.

Targ, R., and J. Katve. 2003. "Close to Grace: The Physics of Silent Transmission." *Spirituality and Health*. July-August.

"Tax Cutbacks and Bush." 2004. *Arizona Republic*, 14 August. (Top 20% of incomes pays 63.5% total taxes, middle class pays 19.5%.)

Taylor, M. 2004. *Buried in the Sand.* (DVD). Canoga Park, Calif. Westlake Entertainment.

Telernter, D. 2003. "Don't Quit As We Did in Vietnam—Stay the Course, America." *Los Angeles Times*, 9 November.

"Ten Questions for Bill Gates." 2004. *Time*, 8 March. (Interview.)

Theresa, Mother. 1995. *A Simple Path.* New York: Ballentine Books.

Thomas, C. 2005. "Bush dumb? Yeah, like a fox." 2 February. *Los Angeles Times Syndicate.*

—. 2004. "A Few Reasons They Detest Bush." *Los Angeles Times Syndicate*, 31 August.

—. 2004. "Feeling 'Free' But With Defenses Up." *Los Angeles Times Syndicate*, 6 August. (Balance of personal liberty vs. safety.)

—. 2004. "Congress Must Share the Blame." *Los Angeles Times*, 13 July. ("It is Congress, not the President, that determines the intelligence apparatus.")

—. 2004. "Let States Do The Teaching." *Los Angeles Times Syndicate*, 6 July. (Higher federal funding/costs produces works results.)

—. 2003. "Defining Liberty for Muslims." *Arizona Republic*, 12 November, B-11.

Thomm, S. 2003. "GOP or Dem? Depends on If You Go to Church." *Arizona Republic*, 30 November.

Thompson, O. 1989. *International Cyclopedia of Music and Musicians*. New York: Dodd, Mead, & Co.

Thoreau, H. D. 1849. *On the Duty of Civil Disobedience* (orig. *Resistance to Civil Government*). www.transcendentalists.com/thoreau_works.htm.

Thottam, J. 2004. "Who Stretches the Truth?" *Time*, 11 October. (Refutation of political statements and exaggerations.)

—. 2004. "Is Your Job Going Abroad?" *Time*, 1 March.

Tiebout, H. 1999. *Collected Papers*. Michigan: Hazeldon Foundation.

—. 1953. "Surrender vs. Compliance in Theory." *Quarterly Journal of Studies on Alcohol,* 14:58-68.

—. 1949. "The Act of Surrender in the Therapeutic Process." *Quarterly Journal of Studies on Alcohol,* 10:48-58.

Timmerman, K. 2004. *The French Betrayal of America*. New York: Crown Forum Publishers.

—. 2003. *Preachers of Hate: Islam and the War on America*. New York: Crown Forum Publishers

—. 2000. *Selling Out America*. Princeton, NJ: Xlibris Corp.

Toben, B. 1975. *Space, Time, and Beyond*. New York: E. P. Dutton.

Tolson, J. 2004. "Mixing Pragmatism and Principles." *U. S. News & World Report*, 22 September.

—. 2004. "Religiosity, the Faith of Our Fathers." *U. S. News & World Report*, 28 June.

Toppo, G. 2003. "Violent Deaths Surge in Schools Across the U. S." *Arizona Republic*, 21 October.

Torray, E. 1999. *The Roots of Treason: Ezra Pound and the Secret of St. Elizabeth*. New York: Lucas Books.

Treynot, I. 2003. "The Privatization of War." *Guardian*, 10 December.

Tumulty, L. 2004. "10 Questions for George Soros." *Time*, 1 March. (Spent $4 billion on causes.)

Twelve Steps and Twelve Traditions. 1996. New York: Alcoholics Anonymous World Services.

"Twilight of the Yobs." 2005. *Economist*, 8 January. (Classical music quells youth and delinquency.)

Tyler, A. 1787. "The Fall of the Athenian Republic." Quoted in *Swindoll's Ultimate Book of Illustrations & Quotes* (2003). New York: Thomas Nelson, Publisher.

Tutu, D. 2004. *God Has A Dream: A Vision of Hope for Our Time.* New York: Doubleday.

Tzu, Sun. 1963. *The Art of War.* (Griffith Trans.) Oxford: Oxford University Press. (Originally written in approximately 500 B.C.)

Underhill, E. 1986. *Practical Mysticism.* Columbus, Ohio: Ariel Press.

—. 1925. *Mystics of the Church.* Harrisburg, Penn.: Morehouse Publishing.

U. S. Department of State. 2004. *Patterns of Global Terrorism.* U. S. Navy Website, 17 June.

Useem, J. 2004. "Should We Admire Wal-Mart?" *Fortune.* 8 March, 118-120.

—. 2004. "Meme." http://en.wikipedia.org/wiki/meme. N.D.

"US Stellar Years for Jobs and GDP." 2004. *Associated Press,* 7 July. (Fastest growth in 20 years.)

Valley, C. 2004. "Reach, Renew, and Release Taught at Nazarene Church." *Payson (Arizona) Roundup,* 21 December. (Everyone has a personal ministry to renew and instill hope and faith in others.).

Van Biema, D. 2002. "The Legacy of Abraham." *Time.* 30 September, 64-75.

Van Lewick-Goodall, J. 1971. *In the Shadow of Man.* Boston: Houghton Mifflin Co.

Van Till, H. J., D. A. Young, and C. Menninger. 1988. *Science Held Hostage: What's Wrong with Creation, Science, AND Evolutionism?* Downers Grove, Ill.: Intervarsity Press. (Review by H. H. Bauer, *Journal of Scientific Exploration* 17:2, 2004.)

Verela, F., Shear, J. 2002. *The View from Within: First Person Approaches to the Study of Consciousness.* Bowling Green State University, Ohio: Imprint Academic.

Vergano, D. 2004. "Collie Borders On Brilliant…Learns As Quick As a Child." *USA Today,* 11 June.

Vernon, W. 2001. "Sen. Torricelli Played Key Role in Closing Down CIA Ops." http://www.Newsmax.com.

Vertabadisn, R., and C. Hanley. 2004. "Nuclear Lab's Cowboy Culture." *Los Angeles Times,* 25 July. (Los Alamos dysfunctional.)

Vitz, P. 1995. "The Psychology of Atheism."
http://www.catholiceducation.org/articles/religion/re0384.html.

Viviano, F. 2003. "Kingdom on the Edge: Saudi Arabia." *National Geographic*, October.

von Krafft-Ebing, R., ed. [1886] 1965. *Psychopathic Sexualis*. London: Mayflower-Dell. (Reprint, 1999, Bloat).

Vseem, J. 2003. "The 25 Most Powerful People in Business." *Fortune*, 148:3, 56-84.

Wagster, D., and K. Blend. 2004. "Child Porn Raises Fears of AIDS." *Arizona Republic,* 3 July.

Walsh, J. 2004. "Prosecutors: Crime Shows Blur Reality." *Arizona Republic*, 19 August. (TV ["CSI Effect"] affecting juries' judgment regarding evidence).

Walsh, K. T. 2004. "The Politics of Terror." *U. S. News & World Report*, 13 September.

Walsh, T. 2004. "Let Maureen Dowd Preach to New Yorkers." *Arizona Republic*, 15 December. Letter to Editor. (Protest at columnist's negativity.)

Walt, V. 2004. "Marked Women." *Time*, 26 July. (Islamic "honor" killing of women.)

Walton, S. and J. Huey. 1992. *Sam Walton: Made in America*. New York: Doubleday.

Warren, Rick. 2002. *The Purpose Driven Life*. Grand Rapids, Mich.: Zondervan Publishing Co.

Watt, D. F. 2004. "Consciousness, Emotional Self-Regulation, and the Brain." *Journal of Consciousness Studies* 11:9, 77-82.

Waxman, S. 2004. "Christmas Jeer from Hollywood." *New York Times*, 17 December.

Weaver, J. 2004. "Puppy Love…Feel-Good Hormones." (University of Missouri). http://msnbc.msn.com/ id/4625213.

Weise, E. 2004. "Cheap Fish Sold As Premium 77% of the Time." *USA Today*, 15 July.

Weiss, C. 2004. "Until Militant Islam Is Destroyed, There Can Be No Democracy or Peace in Iraq." *Arizona Republic*, 3 July.

Weiss, R. 2004. "Man's Mind Moves Computer Cursor." *Washington Post*, 15 December. (Techno-telepathic capability: brain-computer report by Wolpaw and McFarland, Proc. National Academy of Science.)

Welch, J. 2003. *Jack: Straight from the Gut*. New York: Warner Books.

Wellek, M., and C. Kamin. 2004. "A Nation of Compassion Doesn't Execute Juveniles." *Arizona Republic*, 1 August. (Brain undeveloped, most executed in Texas.)

Wellis, C. 2004. "What Makes Teens Tick—the Brain." *Time*, 10 May, 56-65.

Wente, M. 2004. "Inside the House of bin Laden." *Globe and Mail (Toronto)*, 22 July. Review of book by Carmen bin Ladin, Osama's former sister-in-law. (Most Saudis back bin Laden's extremism. Severe suppression of women.)

Wertheim, M. 2004. "Francis Crick: Scientist at Work Unraveling the Mysteries of the State of Being." *New York Times*, 13 April.

Whitelaw, K., and D. Kaplan. 2004. "Don't Ask, Don't Tell." *U. S. News & World Report*, 13 September. (Congress incapable of overseeing intelligence agencies due to partisanship.)

Wilber, K. 2004. "The Perennial Philosophy." *Unity Magazine*, July/August.

—. 1989. *The Essential Ken Wilber*. Boston: Shambhala Publishers.

Will, G. 2005. "Pardon the Man for Thinking." *Washington Post Writers Group*, 27 January. (Narcissistic hysteria and the academic indignation industry.)

—. 2004. "Ground Zero with Nuclear Signature." *Washington Post Writers Group*, 30 August.

Williams, A. 1998. "The Holographic Paradigm." www publication via Mountain Man Graphics, Australia. (Harmital, alt-sci physics-New Theories.)

Williams, D. 2004. "Feminism Hurts Family, Vatican Says." *Washington Post*, 1 August.

Wilson, B. *The Language of the Heart*. New York: AA Grapevine Publishing.

Wilson, D. 1997. "Apocalyptic Visions Tied to Comet's Past." http://www.cnn.com?TECH/9703/27/cometconspiracy10/1/2004. (Mass suicide).

Wilson, L. 2004. "In Depth: Opening the Gate to Bird Intelligence." http://www.wingsoverus.org/brainybirds/articles/welcome.htm.

Wilson, W. 1939. *Alcoholics Anonymous*. New York: AA World Services.

Windschuttle, K. 1996. *The Killing of History: How a Discipline is Being Murdered by Literary Critics and Social Theorists*. 2nd ed. New York: Macleay.

Winik, L. W. 2004. "America's Best Hospitals." *U. S. News & World Report*, 12 July. (Special Report)

—. 2004. "The Toll of Video Violence." *Parade* 11 July, Intelligence Report. (Children watch TV 28 hrs./wk, see 8,000 murders by age 11. Killers escape 75% of time.)

Winston, K. 2004. "Religion and Politics Hot Topic Across All Faiths." *Publishers Weekly*, May 24.

Wolf, R. 2001. "CIA Powers at the 1975 Church Committee." www.labournet.net/world.

Woods, J. 2004. "Violence and Hate Websites on the Rise, from 2,700 in Year 2000 to Current 11,000 Hate Websites." *Science and Theology News*, July/August.

Woodson, B. 2004. "Center for Neighborhood Enterprise: School, Culture, Teachers, Children, Victimhood, Therefore No Responsibility." *Factoid,* Fox News, 26 February.

Woodward, B. 2004. *Plan of Attack*. New York: Simon and Schuster.

World Factbook, 2003. Washington, DC: *Central Intelligence Agency*.

"World Tells Iran To Halt Nuke Work." 2004. *Arizona Republic*, 19 September. (35 nations in UN atomic watchdog agency demand freeze on uranium enrichment.)

"World's Oldest Companies, The." 2004 *Economist*, December 18. (Companies hundreds of years old: Kikkoman since 1630, etc.)

Yee, D. 2004. "Math Error Led CDC to Overstate Obesity Problem: Agency Admits Bungling Study." *Associated Press*, 24 November.

Yohe, G. E. 2004. "Media Letting Liberals Run Wild." *Arizona Republic*, 1 July.

Yost, B. "Doctors See Positive Effect of Humor on Health." *Arizona Republic*, 27 April.

Yzaguirre, R. 2004. "Rhetoric Blurs Reality of Immigration Debate." *Arizona Republic*, 23 June.

Zimbardo, P. G. 2004. "A Psychologist's Experience with Deviance." http://www.criminology.fsu.edu/crimtheory/zimbardo.htm. (Criticism and Theory.)

—. 2004. "After Abu Ghraib, Psychologist Asks, 'Is It Our Nature to Torture?'" *Science and Theology News*, July/August.

—. 2004. "The Stockholm Syndrome." http://www.yahoodi.com/peace/stockholm.html.

—. 1977. *Influencing Attitudes and Changing Behavior: An Introduction to Method, Theory, and Applications of Social Control and Personal Power.* (2nd Ed.) New York: McGraw-Hill College Division.

Zimmer, C. 2004. *This Is My Reality.* MME Productions. Fox News, 28 May. (Influence of Gangster Rap on Inner City Youth. Seduction of Glamorized Violence.)

—. 2003. "Cognition: How the Mind Reads Other Minds." *Science* 300:5622, 1079-1080.

Zimmerman, A., and A. Schoenfeld. (2004) "Single Germans looking for spouses at Wal-Marts." *Wall Street Journal*, 14 November.

Zackerman, M. 2004. "An Election All about Values." *U. S. News & World Report*, 25 October. (Democrats moved from the little guy to the elite.)

Zuckerman, B. 2004. "A Closer Look at America." *U. S. News & World Report*, 13 December. (Politics are the culture wars.)

—. 2004. "Truth Must Be Ultimate Weapon for Sierra Club." *Arizona Republic*, 22 March. (Population increase threat to environment.)

About the Author

Biographical and Autobiographical Notes

Dr. Hawkins is an internationally known spiritual teacher, author, and speaker on the subject of advanced spiritual states, consciousness research, and the Realization of the Presence of God as Self.

His published works, as well as recorded lectures, have been widely recognized as unique in that a very advanced state of spiritual awareness occurred in an individual with a scientific and clinical background who was later able to verbalize and explain the unusual phenomenon in a manner that is clear and comprehensible.

The transition from the normal ego state of mind to its elimination by the Presence is described in the trilogy *Power versus Force* (1995) which won praise even from Mother Theresa, *The Eye of the I* (2001), and *I: Reality and Subjectivity* (2003), which have been translated and are available worldwide in foreign editions. Reviews (such as those on the Internet at amazon.com) have awarded the works with five stars.

The trilogy was preceded by research on the Nature of Consciousness and published as the doctoral dissertation, *Qualitative and Quantitative Analysis and Calibration of the Levels of Consciousness* (1995), which correlated the seemingly disparate domains of science and spirituality. This was accomplished by the major discovery of a technique that, for the first time in human history, demonstrated a means to discern truth from falsehood.

The importance of the initial work was given recognition by its very favorable and extensive review in *Brain/Mind Bulletin* and at later presentations such as the International Conference on Science and Consciousness. Many presentations were given to a variety of organizations, spiritual conferences, church groups, nuns, and monks, both nationally and in foreign countries, including the Oxford Forum. In the Far East, Dr. Hawkins is a recognized "Teacher of the Way to Enlightenment" (Tae Ryoung Sun Kak Dosa).

In response to his observation that much spiritual truth has been misunderstood over the ages due to lack of explanation, Dr. Hawkins presented monthly seminars that provided detailed explanations that are too lengthy to describe in book format. Recordings are available, along with questions and answers that provide additional clarification.

The overall design of this lifetime work is to recontextualize the human experience in terms of the evolution of consciousness and to integrate a comprehension of both mind and spirit as expressions of the innate Divinity that is the substrate and ongoing source of life and Existence. This dedication is signified by the statement "Gloria in Excelsis Deo!" with which his published works begin and end.

Biographic Summary

Dr. Hawkins has practiced psychiatry since 1952 and is a life member of the American Psychiatric Association and numerous other professional organizations. His national television appearance schedule has included *The McNeil/Leher News Hour, The Barbara Walters Show, The Today Show*, science documentaries, and many others.

He is the author of numerous scientific and spiritual publications, books, videotapes, and lecture series. Nobelist Linus Pauling coauthored his landmark book, *Orthomolecular Psychiatry*. Dr. Hawkins's diverse background as researcher and teacher is noted in his biographical listings in *Who's Who in America* and *Who's Who in the World*. He was a consultant for many years to Episcopal and Catholic Dioceses, The Monastery, monastic orders, and the Zen Monastery.

Dr. Hawkins has lectured widely, with appearances at Westminster Abbey, the Universities of Argentina, Notre Dame, and Michigan, Fordham and Harvard Universities, and the Oxford Forum. He gave the annual Landsberg Lecture at the University of California Medical School at San Francisco. He is also a consultant to foreign governments on international diplomacy and has been instrumental in resolving long-standing conflicts that were major threats to world peace.

In recognition of his contributions to humanity, Dr. Hawkins became a knight of the Sovereign Order of the Hospitaliers of St. John of Jerusalem, which was founded in 1077. This ceremony was officiated by Prince Waldemar of Denmark at the San Anselmo Theological Seminary in 1995.

Autobiographic Note

While the truths reported in this book were scientifically derived and objectively organized, like all truths, they were first experienced personally. A lifelong sequence of intense states of awareness beginning at a young age first inspired and then gave direction to the process of subjective realization that has finally taken form in this book.

At age three, there occurred a sudden full consciousness of existence, a nonverbal but complete understanding of the meaning of "I Am," followed immediately by the frightening realization that "I" might not have come into existence at all. This was an instant awakening from oblivion into a conscious awareness, and in that moment, the personal self was born and the duality of "Is" and "Is Not" entered my subjective awareness.

Throughout childhood and early adolescence, the paradox of existence and the question of the reality of the self remained a repeated concern. The personal self would sometimes begin slipping back into a greater impersonal Self, and the initial fear of non-existence, the fundamental fear of nothingness, would recur.

In 1939, as a paperboy with a seventeen-mile bicycle route in rural Wisconsin, on a dark winter's night I was caught miles from home in a twenty-below-zero blizzard. The bicycle fell over on the ice and the fierce wind ripped the newspapers out of the handlebar basket, blowing them across the ice-covered, snowy field. There were tears of frustration and exhaustion and my clothes were frozen stiff. To get out of the wind, I broke through the icy crust of a high snow bank, dug out a space, and crawled into it. Soon the shivering stopped and there was a delicious warmth, and then a state of peace beyond all description. This was accompanied by a suffusion of light and a presence of infinite love that had no beginning and no end and was undifferentiated from my own essence. The physical body and surroundings faded as my awareness was fused with this all-present, illuminated state. The mind grew silent; all thought stopped. An infinite Presence was all that was or could be, beyond all time or description.

After that timelessness, there was suddenly an awareness of someone shaking my knee; then my father's anxious face appeared. There was great reluctance to return to the body and all that that entailed, but because of my father's love and anguish, the Spirit nurtured and reactivated the body. There was compassion for his fear of death, although, at the same time, the concept of death seemed absurd.

This subjective experience was not discussed with anyone since there was no context available from which to describe it. It was not common to hear of spiritual experiences other than those reported in the lives of the saints. But after this experience, the accepted reality of the world began to seem only provisional; traditional religious teachings lost significance and, paradoxically, I became an agnostic. Compared to the light of Divinity that had illuminated all existence, the god of traditional religion shone dully indeed; thus spirituality replaced religion.

During World War II, hazardous duty on a minesweeper often brought close brushes with death but there was no fear of it. It was as though death had lost its authenticity. After the war, fascinated by the complexities of the mind and wanting to study psychiatry, I worked my way through medical school. My training psychoanalyst, a professor at Columbia University, was also an agnostic; we both took a dim view of religion. The analysis went well, as did my career, and success followed.

I did not, however, settle quietly into professional life. I fell ill with a progressive, fatal illness that did not respond to any treatments available. By age thirty-eight, I was *in extremis* and knew I was about to die. I didn't care about the body but my spirit was in a state of extreme anguish and despair. As the final moment approached, the thought flashed through my mind, "What if there is a God?" So I called out in prayer, "If there is a God, I ask him to help me now." I surrendered to whatever God there might be and went into oblivion. When I awoke, a transformation of such enormity had taken place that I was struck dumb with awe.

The person I had been no longer existed. There was no personal self or ego, only an Infinite Presence of such unlimited power that it was all that was. This Presence had replaced what had been "me," and the body and its actions were controlled solely by the Infinite Will of the Presence. The world was illuminated by the clarity of an Infinite Oneness that expressed itself as all things revealed in their infinite beauty and perfection.

As life went on, this stillness persisted. There was no personal will; the physical body went about its business under the direction of the infinitely powerful but exquisitely gentle Will of the Presence. In that state, there was no need to think about anything. All truth was self-evident and no conceptualization was necessary or even possible. At the same time, the physical nervous system felt extremely overtaxed, as though it were carrying far more energy than its circuits had been designed for.

It was not possible to function effectively in the world. All ordinary motivations had disappeared along with all fear and anxiety. There was nothing to seek, as all was perfect. Fame, success, and money were meaningless. Friends urged the pragmatic return to clinical practice, but there was no ordinary motivation to do so.

There was now the ability to perceive the reality that underlay personalities: the origin of emotional sickness lay in people's belief that they *were* their personalities. And so, as though of its own, a clinical practice resumed and eventually became huge.

People came from all over the United States. The practice had two thousand outpatients, which required more than fifty therapists and other employees, a suite of twenty-five offices, and research and electroencephalic laboratories. There were a thousand new patients a year. In addition, there were appearances on radio and network television shows, as previously mentioned. In

1973 the clinical research was documented in a traditional format in the book, *Orthomolecular Psychiatry*. This work was ten years ahead of its time and created something of a stir.

The overall condition of the nervous system improved slowly, and then another phenomenon commenced. There was a sweet, delicious band of energy continuously flowing up the spine and into the brain where it created an intense sensation of continuous pleasure. Everything in life happened by synchronicity, evolving in perfect harmony; the miraculous was commonplace. The origin of what the world would call miracles was the Presence, not the personal self. What remained of the personal "me" was only a witness to these phenomena. The greater "I," deeper than my former self or thoughts, determined all that happened.

The states that were present had been reported by others throughout history and led to the investigation of spiritual teachings, including those of the Buddha, enlightened sages, Huang Po, and more recent teachers such as Ramana Maharshi and Nisargadatta Maharaj. It was thus confirmed that these experiences were not unique. The Bhagavad-Gita now made complete sense. At times the same spiritual ecstasy reported by Sri Rama Krishna and the Christian saints occurred.

Everything and everyone in the world was luminous and exquisitely beautiful. All living beings became Radiant and expressed this Radiance in stillness and splendor. It was apparent that all mankind is actually motivated by inner love but has simply become unaware; most lives are lived as though by sleepers unawakened to the awareness of who they really are. People around me looked as though they were asleep and were incredibly beautiful. It was like being in love with everyone.

It was necessary to stop the habitual practice of meditating for an hour in the morning and then again before dinner because it would intensify the bliss to such an extent that it was not possible to function. An experience similar to the one that had occurred in the snow bank as a boy would recur, and it became increasingly difficult to leave that state and return to the world. The incredible beauty of all things shone forth in all their perfection, and where the world saw ugliness, there was only timeless beauty. This spiritual love suffused all perception and all boundaries between here and there, then and now, or separation disappeared.

During the years spent in inner silence, the strength of the Presence grew. Life was no longer personal; a personal will no longer existed. The personal "I" had become an instrument of the Infinite Presence and went about and did as it was willed. People felt an extraordinary peace in the aura of that Presence. Seekers sought answers, but as there was no longer any such individual as David, they were actually finessing answers from their own Self, which was not different from mine. From each person the same Self shone forth from their eyes.

The miraculous happened, beyond ordinary comprehension. Many chronic maladies from which the body had suffered for years disappeared; eyesight spontaneously normalized and there was no longer a need for the lifetime bifocals.

Occasionally, an exquisitely blissful energy, an Infinite Love, would suddenly begin to radiate from the heart toward the scene of some calamity. Once, while driving on a highway, this exquisite energy began to beam out of the chest. As the car rounded a bend, there was an auto accident; the wheels of the overturned car were still spinning. The energy passed with great intensity into the occupants of the car and then stopped of its own accord. Another time, while I was walking on the streets of a strange city, the energy started to flow down the block ahead and arrived at the scene of an incipient gang fight. The combatants fell back and began to laugh, and again, the energy stopped.

Profound changes of perception came without warning in improbable circumstances. While dining alone at Rothman's on Long Island, the Presence suddenly intensified until every thing and every person, which had appeared as separate in ordinary perception, melted into a timeless universality and oneness. In the motionless Silence, it became obvious that there are no "events" or "things" and that nothing actually "happens" because past, present, and future are merely artifacts of perception, as is the illusion of a separate "I" being subject to birth and death. As the limited, false self dissolved into the universal Self of its true origin, there was an ineffable sense of having returned home to a state of absolute peace and relief from all suffering. It is only the illusion of individuality that is the origin of all suffering. When realizes that one *is* the universe, complete and at one with All That Is, forever without end, then no further suffering is possible.

Patients came from every country in the world, and some were the most hopeless of the hopeless. Grotesque, writhing, wrapped in wet sheets for transport from far-away hospitals they came, hoping for treatment for advanced psychoses and grave, incurable mental disorders. Some were catatonic; many had been mute for years. But in each patient, beneath the crippled appearance, was the shining essence of love and beauty, perhaps so obscured to ordinary vision that he or she had become totally unloved in this world.

One day a mute catatonic was brought into the hospital in a straitjacket. She had a severe neurological disorder and was unable to stand. Squirming on the floor, she went into spasms and her eyes rolled back in her head. Her hair was matted; she had torn all her clothes and uttered guttural sounds. Her family was fairly wealthy; as a result, over the years she had been seen by innumerable physicians and famous specialists from all over the world. Every treatment had been tried on her and she had been given up as hopeless by the medical profession.

A short, nonverbal question arose: "What do you want done with her, God?" Then came the realization that she just needed to be loved, that was all. Her inner self shone through her eyes and the Self connected with that loving essence. In that second, she was healed by her own recognition of who she really was; what happened to her mind or body didn't matter to her any longer.

This, in essence, occurred with countless patients. Some recovered in the eyes of the world and some did not, but whether a clinical recovery ensued didn't matter any longer to the patients. Their inner agony was over. As they felt loved and at peace within, their pain stopped. This phenomenon can only be explained by saying that the Compassion of the Presence recontextualized each patient's reality so that he or she experienced healing on a level that transcended the world and its appearances. The inner peace of the Self encompassed us beyond time and identity.

It was clear that all pain and suffering arises solely from the ego and not from God. This truth was silently communicated to the minds of the patients. This was the mental block in another mute catatonic who had not spoken in many years. The Self said to him through mind, "You're blaming God for what your ego has done to you." He jumped off the floor and began to speak, much to the shock of the nurse who witnessed the incident.

The work became increasingly taxing and eventually overwhelming. Patients were backed up, waiting for beds to open although the hospital had built an extra ward to house them. There was an enormous frustration in that the human suffering could be countered in only one patient at a time. It was like bailing out the sea. It seemed that there must be some other way to address the causes of the common malaise, the endless stream of spiritual distress and human suffering.

This led to the study of kinesiology, which revealed an amazing discovery. It was the 'wormhole' between two universes—the physical world and the world of the mind and spirit, an interface between dimensions. In a world full of sleepers lost from their source, here was a tool to recover—and demonstrate for all to see—that lost connection with the higher reality. This led to the testing of every substance, thought, and concept that could be brought to mind. The endeavor was aided by my students and research assistants. Then a major discovery was made: whereas all subjects went weak from negative stimuli, such as fluorescent lights, pesticides, and artificial sweeteners, students of spiritual disciplines who had advanced their levels of awareness did not go weak as did ordinary people. Something important and decisive had shifted in their consciousness. It apparently occurred as they realized they were not at the mercy of the world but rather affected only by what their minds believed. Perhaps the very process of progress toward enlightenment could be shown to increase man's ability to resist the vicissitudes of existence, including illness.

The Self had the capacity to change things in the world by merely envisioning them; Love changed the world each time it replaced non-love. The entire scheme of civilization could be profoundly altered by focusing this power of love at a very specific point. Whenever this happened, history bifurcated down new roads.

It now appeared that these crucial insights could not only be communicated with the world but visibly and irrefutably demonstrated. It seemed that the great tragedy of human life had always been that the psyche is so easily deceived; discord and strife have been the inevitable consequence of mankind's inability to distinguish the false from the true. But here was an answer to this fundamental dilemma, a way to recontextualize the nature of consciousness itself and make explicable that which otherwise could only be inferred.

It was time to leave life in New York, with its city apartment and home on Long Island, for something more important. It was necessary to perfect myself as an instrument. This necessitated leaving that world and everything in it, replacing it with a reclusive life in a small town where the next seven years were spent in meditation and study.

Overpowering states of bliss returned unsought and eventually there was the need to learn how to be in the Divine Presence and still function in the world. The mind had lost track of what was happening in the world at large. In order to do research and writing, it was necessary to stop all spiritual practice and focus on the world of form. Reading the newspaper and watching television helped to catch up on the story of who was who, the major events, and the nature of the current social dialogue.

Exceptional subjective experiences of truth, which are the province of the mystic who affects all mankind by sending forth spiritual energy into the collective consciousness, are not understandable by the majority of mankind and are therefore of limited meaning except to other spiritual seekers. This led to an effort to be ordinary, because just being ordinary in itself is an expression of divinity; the truth of one's real self can be discovered through the pathway of everyday life. To live with care and kindness is all that is necessary. The rest reveals itself in due time. The commonplace and God are not distinct.

And so, after a long circular journey of the spirit, there was a return to the most important work, which was to try to bring the Presence at least a little closer to the grasp of as many fellow beings as possible.

*

The Presence is silent and coveys a state of peace that is the space in which and by which all is and has its existence and experience. It is infinitely gentle and yet like a rock. With it, all fear disappears. Spiritual joy occurs on a quiet level of inexplicable ecstasy. Because the experience of time stops, there is no apprehension or regret, no pain, no anticipation; the source of joy is unending and ever present. With no beginning or ending, there is no loss or grief or desire. Nothing needs to be done; everything is already perfect and complete.

When time stops, all problems disappear; they are merely artifacts of a point of perception. As the Presence prevails, there is no further identification with the body or mind. When the mind grows silent, the thought "I Am" also disappears and Pure Awareness shines forth to illuminate what one is, was, and always will be, beyond all worlds and all universes, beyond time, and therefore without beginning or end.

People wonder, "How does one reach this state of awareness," but few follow the steps because they are so simple. First, the desire to reach that state was intense. Then began the discipline to act with constant and universal forgiveness and gentleness, without exception. One has to be compassionate towards everything, including one's own self and thoughts. Next came a willingness to hold desires in abeyance and surrender personal will at every moment. As each thought, feeling, desire, or deed was surrendered to God, the mind became increasingly silent. At first, it released whole stories and paragraphs, then ideas and concepts. As one lets go of wanting to own these thoughts, they no longer reach such elaboration and begin to fragment while only half formed. Finally, it was possible to turn over the energy behind thought itself before it even became thought.

The task of constant and unrelenting fixity of focus, allowing not even a moment of distraction from meditation, continued while doing ordinary activities. At first, this seemed very difficult, but as time went on, it became habitual, automatic, requiring less and less effort, and finally it was effortless. The process is like a rocket leaving the earth. At first, it requires enormous power, then less and less as it leaves the earth's gravitational field, and finally, it moves through space under its own momentum.

Suddenly, without warning, a shift in awareness occurred and the Presence was there, unmistakable and all encompassing. There were a few moments of apprehension as the self died, and then the absoluteness of the Presence inspired a flash of awe. This breakthrough was spectacular, more intense than anything before. It has no counterpart in ordinary experience. The profound shock was cushioned by the love that is with the Presence. Without the support and protection of that love, one would be annihilated.

There followed a moment of terror as the ego clung to its existence, fearing it would become nothingness. Instead, as it died, it was replaced by the Self as Everything-ness, the All in which everything is known and obvious in its perfect expression of its own essence. With nonlocality came the awareness that one is all that ever was or can be. One is total and complete, beyond all identities, beyond all gender, beyond even humanness itself. One need never again fear suffering and death.

What happens to the body from this point is immaterial. At certain levels of spiritual awareness, ailments of the body heal or spontaneously disappear. But in the absolute state, such considerations are irrelevant. The body will run its predicted course and then return from whence it came. It is a matter of no importance; one is unaffected. The body appears as an "it" rather than as a "me" as another object, like the furniture in a room. It may seem comical that people still address the body as though it were the individual "you," but there is no way to explain this state of awareness to the unaware. It is best to just go on about one's business and allow Providence to handle the social adjustment. However, as one reaches bliss, it is very difficult to conceal that state of intense ecstasy. The world may be dazzled and people may come from far and wide to be in the accompanying aura. Spiritual seekers and the spiritually curious may be attracted, as may be the very ill who are seeking miracles; one may become a magnet and a source of joy to them. Commonly, there is a desire at this point to share this state with others and to use it for the benefit of all.

The ecstasy that accompanies this condition is not absolutely stable; there are also moments of great agony. The most intense occur when the state fluctuates and suddenly ceases for no apparent reason. These times bring on periods of intense despair and a fear that one has been forsaken by the Presence. These falls make the path arduous and to surmount these reversals requires great will. It finally becomes obvious that one must transcend this level or constantly suffer excruciating "descents from grace." The glory of ecstasy, then, has to be relinquished as one enters upon the arduous task of transcending duality until one is beyond all oppositions and their conflicting pulls. But while it is one thing to happily give up the iron chains of ego, it is quite another to abandon the golden chains of ecstatic joy. It feels as though one is giving up God, and a new level of fear arises, never before anticipated. This is the final terror of absolute aloneness.

To the ego, the fear of nonexistence was formidable, and it drew back from it repeatedly as it seemed to approach. The purpose of the agonies and the dark nights of the soul then became apparent. They are so intolerable that their exquisite pain spurs one on to the extreme effort required to surmount them. When vacillation between heaven and hell becomes unendurable, the desire for existence itself has to be surrendered. Only once this is done may one finally move beyond the duality of Allness versus nothingness, beyond existence or nonexistence. This culmination of the inner work is the most difficult phase, the ultimate watershed, where one is starkly aware that the illusion of existence one here transcends is irrevocable. There is no returning from this step, and this specter of irreversibility makes this last barrier appear to be the most formidable choice of all.

But, in fact, in this final apocalypse of the self, the dissolution of the sole remaining duality of existence and nonexistence— identity itself—dissolves in Universal Divinity, and no individual consciousness is left to choose. The last step, then, is taken by God.

—*David R. Hawkins*

For a list of available audio and video cassettes
and other publications on consciousness
and spirituality by Dr. Hawkins,
please contact:

Veritas Publishing
P. O. Box 3516
West Sedona, AZ
86340 U. S. A.
Phone: 928-282-8722
Fax: 928-282-4789
www.veritaspub.com